D0221678

Criminal Justice Theory

SOME RECENT TITLES FROM THE
CRIMINOLOGY AND JUSTICE SERIES:

Series Editor: Shaun L. Gabbidon

Community Policing in America
Jeremy M. Wilson

Surveillance and Society
Torin Monahan

Race, Crime, and American Society
Gloria Browne-Marshall

Criminal Justice Theory: Explaining the Nature and Behavior of Criminal Justice
David E. Duffee and Edward R. Maguire

FORTHCOMING TITLES IN THE
CRIMINOLOGY AND JUSTICE STUDIES SERIES:

Criminological Perspectives on Race and Crime
Shaun L. Gabbidon

White Collar Crime
Michael Benson

Criminal Justice Theory

Explaining the Nature and Behavior of Criminal Justice

David E. Duffee
Edward R. Maguire

Editors

Routledge
Taylor & Francis Group
New York   London

BAKER COLLEGE OF
CLINTON TWP. LIBRARY

Routledge
Taylor & Francis Group
270 Madison Avenue
New York, NY 10016

Routledge
Taylor & Francis Group
2 Park Square
Milton Park, Abingdon
Oxon OX14 4RN

© 2007 by Taylor & Francis Group, LLC
Routledge is an imprint of Taylor & Francis Group, an Informa business

Printed in the United States of America on acid-free paper
10 9 8 7 6 5 4 3 2 1

International Standard Book Number-10: 0-415-95480-0 (Softcover) 0-415-95479-7 (Hardcover)
International Standard Book Number-13: 978-0-415-95480-8 (Softcover) 978-0-415-95479-2 (Hardcover)

No part of this book may be reprinted, reproduced, transmitted, or utilized in any form by any electronic, mechanical, or other means, now known or hereafter invented, including photocopying, microfilming, and recording, or in any information storage or retrieval system, without written permission from the publishers.

Trademark Notice: Product or corporate names may be trademarks or registered trademarks, and are used only for identification and explanation without intent to infringe.

Library of Congress Cataloging-in-Publication Data

Criminal justice theory : explaining the nature and behavior of criminal justice /
   edited by David E. Duffee and Edward R. Maguire.
      p. cm.
      Includes bibliographical references (p.) and index.
   ISBN 0-415-95479-7 (hb) -- ISBN 0-415-95480-0 (pb)
      1. Criminal justice, Administration of--Philosophy. I. Duffee, David. II. Maguire,
Edward R.

HV7419.C753 2007
364.01--dc22   2006028335

Visit the Taylor & Francis Web site at
http://www.taylorandfrancis.com

and the Routledge Web site at
http://www.routledge-ny.com

CONTENTS

PART I
THE NATURE, METHOD, AND BOUNDARIES
OF CRIMINAL JUSTICE THEORY

LIST OF ILLUSTRATIONS

LIST OF TABLES

PREFACE

This volume began when Professor Robert Langworthy served as the program chair for the 1996 meeting of the Academy of Criminal Justice Sciences in Boston under President Ed Latessa. Bob Langworthy and Ed Latessa asked David E. Duffee if he would give the plenary address at the meeting on the topic of theory in criminal justice education. Duffee accepted and took an empirical approach to the issue, surveying all criminal justice doctoral programs with the assistance of Ed Maguire and Jeff Snipes. What they discovered was alarming to them. While the doctoral programs all had courses on criminological theory — often required — these programs basically ignored theory building and testing and types of theories about criminal justice. When asked to submit a syllabus for the most relevant theory course, many programs submitted a criminology syllabus, which usually provided no theories that explained criminal justice behavior and covered only explanations of crime. Theory was synonymous with criminological theory.

The discoveries resulting from that survey were the motivation for this work. Criminal justice phenomena can be studied scientifically, just as crime can. But explicit attention to theory is necessary if this important step is to take place: there is no science and no knowledge building without theory. To the average undergraduate college student, the title of this book, *Criminal Justice Theory*, is an interesting clash of themes. For most students, the first two words of the title, *Criminal Justice*, constitute an interesting and exciting topic. Criminal justice programs in colleges and universities are growing, often at the expense of enrollments in other disciplines. Studying "bad guys" and the system that processes them seems much more interesting to many students than pursuing traditional academic disciplines. But the third word in the title, *Theory*, often evokes the opposite reaction among students. Theories are frequently contrasted with "reality," as if theory is somehow the opposite, or the antithesis, of what happens in the real world.

The idea that these two themes — criminal justice and theory — might for some people represent such divergent perspectives is why we chose to assemble this volume. Theory is a fundamental element of the social scientist's toolkit. Theories are used in all social sciences, from economics and political science, to sociology and psychology. Yet, criminal justice, as a discipline, seems to struggle with the move toward establishing a theoretical foundation. It often seems that the field is so applied, and so tightly intertwined with an audience of practitioners who work, or have worked, in "the real world," that there is less tolerance for theory. Yet, theory can inform practice. It can help us understand how the social world works. It can help us understand why some interventions work, why some fail, and why some might produce unintended, or perhaps even negative, consequences. Underlying all social policies and programs is some implicit theory of human behavior, whether as individuals or groups. For instance, most research shows that hiring more police officers is not the antidote for crime that the public and most police think it is. The assumptions about police behavior and crime that underlie this popular remedy are based on inadequate theories. Criminology, a sister discipline to criminal justice, is full of examples of how well-intentioned programs meant to reduce crime sometimes not only fail to work, but occasionally increase crime. This does not happen because of stupidity, individual human error, or laziness: it occurs because the underlying theories about the causes of crime on which the programs are based are incorrect. Kurt Lewin once wrote, "There is nothing so practical as a good theory."[1] We agree, and that is why we chose to develop this volume.

Criminal justice theory is defined by Duffee and Allan in chapter 1 of this work as "explanations of the variations in responses to crime. … Criminal justice theory seeks to explain and examine variations in, and the causes of, aspects of government social control systems, which select the criminal sanction over other forms of social control and share the nature of the criminal sanction to be employed." In chapter 2, Snipes and Maguire define criminal justice theory as "the study of the official response to behavior that may be labeled criminal." Both sets of authors make it clear that criminal justice theory would include the basic decisions about whether and when to use the criminal sanction. Consequently, criminal justice theory includes the basic decision about whether to use punishment as a control and whether to consider people blameworthy for harmful acts.

This book is intended to advance the study of criminal justice by focusing on the role of theory in enhancing the discipline. It is meant for advanced undergraduate students as well as graduate students in criminal justice. The book presupposes that the student has had a basic course in research methods and is familiar with terms such as *independent variable*, *dependent variable*, and *cause and effect*. We have urged our authors to write using a language and tone that is appropriate for this audience. For those students who struggle with the challenging terminology and concepts used in this volume, we have included a series of discussion questions and exercises at the end of each section introduction. These can be used by instructors in the classroom as learning aids, assigned by instructors for homework, or used by individual students at home.

We also introduce each section (usually a pair of chapters) with brief overviews that introduce key points in each chapter and connect the chapters to each other and to the different phases of the theory building and testing process. These introductions should help readers identify the various aspects of the theory development process that are represented in each part of the book. In general, each section serves two basic purposes. First, each section illustrates and examines a critical aspect of the theory development process. This collection of original papers progresses from defining theory, the domain of criminal justice theory, and the basic elements of theoretical thinking (chapters 1, 2, 3, and 4) through theory building (chapters 5 and 6), to the critical assessment of theoretical knowledge (chapters 7 and 8), to theory testing and revision (chapters 9 and 10). Second, each of these sections focuses on a set of substantive theories about some aspect of criminal justice behavior. Part I deals with criminal justice in general. Part II examines police. Part III examines court-related theories. Part IV examines corrections. In addition, parts III and IV provide coverage of two distinctly different levels of criminal justice analysis — the individual actor on the one hand (chapters 7 and 9) and some kind of "macrounit" on the other (chapters 8 and 10). In the section on policing, both chapters deal with the organizational level of analysis.

Several reviewers asked for coverage of other important aspects of criminal justice behavior. We recognize that not every important dependent variable is represented in this collection, but we doubt that any single collection could do so. Our authors did, we think, a reasonable job of covering micro- and macrobehaviors in police, court, corrections, and system-wide contexts while simultaneously tackling a specific task in the process of theory development.

This volume is more than a textbook because in it we advocate a new method for thinking about scholarship in criminal justice. We urge our colleagues in colleges and universities around the world to present to their students more than simple descriptions or philosophical debates about criminal justice. We encourage them to think more and more about the *science* of criminal justice. What are its central questions? In what areas does research contribute to knowledge about criminal justice? In what areas are there major research gaps? In what ways might theories of criminal justice play a role in filling these gaps and enhancing practice? Using this volume in upper level undergraduate courses and graduate courses in the administration of criminal justice will enable instructors to expose the science of criminal justice to their students.

This volume, like others, was not born in a vacuum. Theoretical perspectives on criminal justice have played a central role for many years at the School of Criminal Justice, University at Albany. While still a graduate student at Albany, Edward Maguire had the benefit of learning these perspectives from a number of scholars including David Bayley, David Duffee, Graeme Newman, and Rob and Alissa Worden. As a longtime faculty member as well as a former graduate student and dean at the school, Duffee was particularly influenced by some of the founding faculty of the school, Vincent O'Leary, Hans Toch, and the late Donald Newman and Leslie Wilkins. While each was quite different in his or her interests and approaches to criminal justice, all four were equally devoted to the scientific study of criminal justice.

We thank all of those who paved the intellectual path on which this volume rests. We owe a special thanks to the School of Criminal Justice at the University at Albany for its longstanding intellectual devotion to the ideas espoused in this volume.

We also want to thank the chapter authors who contributed to the volume. They run the gamut from newly minted PhDs to leaders in their field of study. Several worked on short notice to prepare or revise drafts of their chapters. We thank all of them for their fine contributions. Alissa Worden also used the rough draft of the text in her graduate course on theory and criminal justice. Her reactions and her students' reactions were very helpful to the rather long and convoluted path to completion of the work. We also are indebted to Bob Langworthy whose 1996 request initiated our work. Both editors are deeply indebted to Stephanie Ainsworth, Megan Gantley, and Julie Willis, research assistants at George Mason University, for their help in preparing the manuscript.

We look forward to the readers' reactions.

David E. Duffee

Edward R. Maguire

NOTE

1. Lewin, K. *Field Theory in Social Science; Selected Theoretical Papers,* ed. D. Cartwright. (New York: Harper & Row, 1951).

ACKNOWLEDGMENTS

Bernard, T.J. and Ritti, R.R. (l990). The role of theory in scientific research. In K.L. Kempf (ed.), *Measurement issues in criminology*, pp. 1-20. New York: Springer-Verlag. With kind permission of Springer Science and Business Media.

Berns, S. (1999). *To speak as a judge: Difference, voice, and power.* © 1999 London: Ashgate Publishing.

Christie, N. (1994). *Crime control as industry: Toward gulags.* New York: Routledge.

Eisenstein, J., & Jacob, H. (1991). *Felony Justice: An organizational analysis of criminal courts.* Lanham: University Press of America. (Originally published by Boston: Little, Brown and Company, 1977).

Feeley, Malcolm M. *The Process is the Punishment: Handling Cases in a Lower Criminal Court.* New York: Russell Sage Foundation, 112 East 64th Street, New York, NY 10021. Reprinted with permission.

Fields, C.B. and Moore, R.H. (1996). Preface. In C.B. Fields & R.H. Moore (eds.), *Comparative criminal justice: Traditional and nontraditional systems of law and control*, pp. xi-xiii. Prospect Heights, IL: Waveland Press.

Hawkins, D. (1981). From Causal attribution and punishment for crime. *Deviant Behavior, 1,* 191-215. Reproduced by permission of Taylor & Francis Group, LLC., http://www.taylorandfrancis.com.

Hulin, C., Roznowski, M., and Hachiya, D. (1985). Alternative opportunities and withdrawal decisions: Empirical and theoretical discrepancies and an integration, *Psychological Bulletin, 97,* 233-250. American Psychological Association. Reprinted with permission.

Langworthy, R.H. (1986). *The Structure of Police Organizations.* Westport, CT: Praeger Publishers. Reproduced with permission of Greenwood Publishing Group, Inc.

Lincoln, J. and Kalleberg, A. (1990). *Culture, control and commitment: A study of work organization and work attitudes in the United States and Japan.* Cambridge: Cambridge University Press.

Mattessich, P. and Monsey, B. (1997). Community building: What makes it work, a review of factors influencing successful community building. Saint Paul, MN: Amherst H. Wilder Foundation (now Fieldstone Alliance, Inc.).

Mowday, R., Porter, L., and Steers, R. (1982). *Employee–Organization linkages: The psychology of commitment, absenteeism, and turnover.* New York: Academic Press. Reprinted with permission from Elsevier.

Scott, W.R. (1992). *Organizations: Rational, natural, and open systems* (3rd ed). Upper Saddle River, NJ: Pearson Education, Inc.

Slovak, Jeffry S. (1986). *Styles of urban policing: Organization, environment, and police styles in selected American cities,* p. 5. New York: New York University Press.

Tomasson, R.F. (1978). Introduction. *Comparative Studies in Sociology, 1,* 1-15. Reprinted with permission from Elsevier.

1

CRIMINAL JUSTICE, CRIMINOLOGY, AND CRIMINAL JUSTICE THEORY

David E. Duffee and Edward Allan

INTRODUCTION

This collection of original essays examines scientific theory about criminal justice. It investigates the place of scientific theory in the enterprise of building knowledge about the field of criminal justice. The authors of its various chapters:

- define scientific theory
- define criminal justice
- define criminal justice theory
- identify specific types of criminal justice theories
- review the strengths and weaknesses of different theoretical traditions
- illustrate the building or construction of theory
- illustrate the testing and revision of specific theories
- provide examples of theory integration.

In summary, collectively, the authors provide an introduction to social science theory and its application to criminal justice phenomena, provide examples of the different phases in the knowledge building process, and critically describe a variety of (although by no means all) criminal justice theories.

Scientific researchers investigating criminal justice topics have and will continue to use theory to guide and assess their research and to build their knowledge about how and why criminal justice behaves as it does. As we discuss in this chapter and Snipes and Maguire examine in chapter 2, researchers could not get very far without using theory. Consequently, there is a reasonable amount of high quality, theoretically driven research on criminal justice, and an impressive pool of theoretic knowledge, compared to even forty years ago in the mid-1960s.

Despite the practice of theory by criminal justice researchers, *explicit attention* to theory and theorizing in the field of criminal justice is infrequent and unreflective, relative to the attention that theory receives in other scientific fields. For example, a review of graduate curricula in criminal justice in 1995 discovered that it was rare to find graduate criminal justice courses on criminal justice theory, although it was common to find criminological theory required (Duffee 1995). At the undergraduate level, Henderson and Boostrom (1989) and Willis (1983) found that most introductory criminal justice texts devote little of their content to theory. In contrast, many introductory criminology texts organize much of their content around presentations of the various theories of crime causation.

The contributors to this volume are among a growing number of scholars in criminal justice who believe this situation should change. We should invest much more time and effort into the theoretical side of scientific investigation in criminal justice.

In this chapter, we define criminal justice theory and distinguish it from criminological theory. We recognize that this distinction between criminal justice and criminology may be controversial, but we argue that making it would help to achieve a number of goals. We elaborate on that distinction and on its implications for studying criminal justice rather than criminology. We also discuss how theory in these closely related fields would be connected, if their proposed definitions and boundaries were followed. Finally, we ask why the scientific knowledge building process, or theorizing, has been more difficult and more halting in criminal justice than in the related discipline of criminology. We argue that one difficulty with criminal justice theory is the preoccupation with criminal justice effectiveness. This preoccupation might help us learn something about what does or does not cause crime but it does little to help us understand what causes criminal justice. We propose that understanding criminal justice be given equal footing in scientific investigation.

DEFINING CRIMINAL JUSTICE AS A FIELD OF STUDY

In the first section of this chapter, we define criminal justice as a field of social science study. We begin this task by critiquing some commonly held notions about criminal justice study. First, we look at the idea that criminal justice is applied criminology, rather than a distinct field of its own. Second, we look at the idea that criminal justice is applied science, rather than basic science. Third, we examine the position that *criminology* and *criminal justice science* are both broad and ambiguous terms that actually encompass the same concepts. Finally, after briefly defining theory, we define the theoretical domain of criminal justice science and describe some of the problems implicit within that domain.

Criminal Justice as Applied Criminology

There is some debate about whether criminal justice is a basic area of knowledge. In a *New York Times* article on the proliferation of criminal justice programs in colleges and universities across the nation, Professor Lawrence Sherman stated that criminal justice is "applied criminology," a subset of criminology that focuses specifically on studying criminal justice agencies (Butterfield 1998, B9). The article argued that criminology is an older and more expansive field that examines the causes of crime and criminal behavior. This view of criminal justice as a narrow, applied slice of criminology is reflected in the contents of older, introductory criminology textbooks, which often devoted most of their space to describing and explaining crime but typically ended with a brief section about how offenders were processed (e.g., Sutherland 1947).

This "applied criminology" view, which is still shared by many scholars, suggests that crime and criminals are the primary, dominant concepts for study and that criminal justice is of interest only in relationship to that primary concern with crime. This idea of "applied criminology" narrows the definition of criminal justice to the application of knowledge about crime and criminals by criminal justice actors. If we took this idea to its extreme, but logical, conclusion, all basic scientific knowledge (and therefore all theory) that is related to crime is about crime itself. Under this view, criminal justice is limited to the application of the knowledge of crime reduction attempts by criminal justice officials.

Some of the problems with this narrow, but frequently espoused, description of criminal justice are apparent. There are many intriguing and important aspects of criminal justice that have little or nothing to do with applications of knowledge about crime and criminal behavior.

The notion of criminal justice as applied criminology fails to recognize the content of many criminal justice studies. Criminal justice researchers are often not engaged in explaining crime or criminal behavior at all. They may be concerned about how criminal justice systems or agencies are structured, about how the agents in these systems make decisions, or about what the agents feel and believe. In other words, the object of their theory and research is often the fluctuation in some characteristic of social control that is not related to the fluctuation in crime.

Unless the term *criminology* is used very broadly and sloppily to refer to the study of anything remotely related to crime, we do not think it is accurate to call criminal justice a branch of criminology. We will return to this broad and fuzzy version below. But first, we should comment on the idea of criminal justice as "applied" social science.

Criminal Justice as Applied Rather than Basic Science

In addition to our objection to calling criminal justice science criminology, we also take exception to the notion that criminal justice science is merely an applied science. There will always be differences of opinion about where basic science ends and where applied science begins. One of the foremost theoreticians and researchers in criminal justice, Leslie T. Wilkins, simply ignored the distinction. He recognized that the label "basic" was often used to confer higher status on some research projects and topics than on those topics that were considered "applied." But he also argued that the intent to confer differential status was the only true distinction. In other words, he saw these terms as part of the politics of science, not as part of doing science. He observed wryly that basic research ended with the discovery of mass destruction, after which all research must be judged not only in terms of the knowledge gained, but also in terms of the uses to which the knowledge was applied (Wilkins 1965, 2001). Therefore, basic research is not free from ethical judgments about the value of the research.

He also argued vigorously that applied research would never be very useful unless researchers were "free" to go wherever their theory guided them! He was fond of pointing out that the decision making research applications to parole and sentencing guidelines would never have occurred if the federal parole board had insisted on a particular application when the research began (Wilkins 1981). What he meant is that good scientific tools, such as those that limit the distribution of value on the basis of ascribed characteristics such as race and class, cannot be invented if policy or political considerations, rather than scientific theory, guide the investigation. Very often policy makers ask the wrong question. If they insist on an answer to their improper conception of the problem, either bad science or no science is possible. Consequently, no useful applications issue from the endeavor.

An example is the problem that the parole board posed to Wilkins and Donald Gottfredson: devise a system that will tell us whether inmates should be released. As Wilkins points out, there was no scientific application for that problem. In fact, it was not a problem at all. The issue was not whether to release but when to release. The researchers were led to this conclusion by building and testing theories about decision making. Only when they followed the tenets of theory development did the researchers come up with a different application. The parole board did not need a tool that would tell them when an inmate was "ready" for release. What they did need was a tool that would enable them to manage public risk while being equitable. Wilkins praised the board for its flexibility, for being a research partner rather than dictating the research question (1981).

Wilkins reminds us that all research must be judged by both its scientific and its human, ethical value. He also reminds us that scientific applications are not likely to be effective or useful tools if the policy makers who support and encourage them stifle scientific research — that is, theoretically driven research — in their hurry for a tool to address a problem or in their commitment to a particular view of the problem.

From another research pioneer, Kurt Lewin, we learn a related lesson: research applied to the most mundane problems may yield important basic insights! Lewin and his research teams contributed what are now considered basic psychological and organizational discoveries in the course of changing family menus during World War II and of deciding on proficiency standards in a pajama factory (Lewin 1947). This research provided enduring insights into the relationship between human participation in framing a problem and human commitment to implementing a course of action. These basic discoveries have been applied in a variety of other fields, including education, management, and prison reform (Chin and Benne 1969; French and Bell 1995; Toch and Grant 1982).

We do not object to the notion that criminal justice science is or should be applied to solving human problems. Walker's study of the extent to which discretion in criminal justice decision making has been controlled during a forty-year span is but one illustration of well-known, socially significant applications (Walker 1993). The applications of criminal justice science to changing criminal justice behaviors can be important, even when, as is true in the above case, the tools do not concern themselves with crime.

We would object strenuously, however, to the implication that criminal justice research may not contribute to basic knowledge. This objection is especially important in relation to (but not limited to) the way in which people regard and understand the linkage of criminal justice to criminology. Although we have already critiqued the idea that criminology is the basic science and that criminal justice is merely its application, we think it is important to briefly extend that argument.

Many scholars, and certainly many students, jump to the conclusion that crime is more basic than the response to crime. If crime did not exist, then there would be no responses, and no field of criminal justice. This view assumes that crime — a harmful event — occurs prior in time to the response and therefore is more "basic" in some sense. The problem with this view is apparent in the cursory examination of any common definition of crime. "A reasonable definition of delinquency and crime is the commission of behaviors that violate criminal law and that place the individual at some risk of arrest if the behavior were known to the police" (Thornberry and Krohn 2000, 50). In other words, crimes can be defined only through some criminal justice action, such as the prohibition of a behavior. In agreement with Thornberry and Krohn, Wilkins (1991, 13) concludes: "We may therefore consider 'punishability' as the central factor. It is the use of punishment which must be studied in its own right: it is not explained away by reference to 'crime'." Or, as Graeme Newman (1978) argues, it is the punishment response that is basic to human nature. Crime and the response to crime cannot be separated. One is not more basic than the other. If societies did not respond to some events as blameworthy or punishable, those events would not be considered crimes. Indeed, there are societies that do not rely on punishment and do not conceive of some deviant behaviors as crimes. Societal processes that lead to formal criminal justice controls, as opposed to other, informal, controls on troublesome behavior, would therefore appear to be a basic topic for social research. Looking for the causes of criminal justice actions is a scientific undertaking that examines behavior fundamental to the human condition. Criminal justice research can be as basic as any other research. This basic research may also lead to applications, as is true in criminological research.

Criminal Justice as Synonymous with Criminology

Scholars who talk about criminal justice as an applied science may not intend to limit criminal justice to the domain implied by "applied criminology." It is possible that many people simply use the terms *criminology* and *criminal justice* very loosely, and perhaps synonymously, to refer to the study of anything and everything that is related to crime (or criminal justice) in some way. This view is evident in the titles of academic programs of study in this field. Some university programs are called "criminology," some are called "criminal justice," some are called "criminology and criminal justice." In any case, students can generally find opportunities to study both crime topics and criminal justice topics in all these programs, regardless of their titles (Duffee 1995).

This approach results in a much more expansive and ambiguous meaning of criminal justice than the "applied criminology" approach. If we adopt this view, it really does not matter whether we use the term *criminology* or the term *criminal justice*. They both refer to the same areas of study. The term used by a particular scholar might depend more on historical tradition (and perhaps historical accident) than anything else. For example, two researchers might work side by side for many years studying prison guards. One might refer to herself as a "criminologist" simply because that was the name of the program she studied in and the title of her doctoral degree. Her research partner, whose career has been equally consumed by the same research, might say he studies "criminal justice" (the term *criminal justician*, while proposed, never really caught on) for the same kinds of reasons. Does it matter? Are there conceptual barriers between these obviously related, if not identical, fields?

DEFINING CRIMINAL JUSTICE

We disagree with the common perspectives described above for two reasons. First, we think that criminal justice is a definable area of human behavior for scientific investigation that is just as basic as, but distinct from, the study of crime and criminal behavior. Criminal justice is not a subfield of criminology, and it is not applied criminology. Second, we believe that the term used to describe a discipline does indeed matter. It is important to define objects of scientific study with care. If *criminal justice* and *criminology* are to be useful terms, they must refer to different phenomena, no matter how closely related they are. Indeed, we will be more productive in connecting the two if we carefully give them separate definitions. We recognize at the outset that the definitions of criminal justice and criminology that we will argue for below, and that form the foundation of this book, are not necessarily more correct than the two definitions that we are rejecting. We acknowledge that the choice among these definitions probably cannot be made based purely on logic or empirical study. The conflict among these approaches and the selection of definitions implied in them is partly, if not totally, ideological. However, every area of scientific inquiry begins with some basic set of ideological assumptions, and we believe that it is helpful to distinguish theories of crime from theories of criminal justice (or more generally, theories of social control). In our view, using the term *criminology* to refer to both theories of crime and theories of social control has done little to advance theories of social control.

In this book, we will limit the term *criminology* to mean the scientific study of crime and criminal behavior. In contrast, *criminal justice science* is the study of governmental social control premised on punishment or blameworthiness. It would include the study of the agencies typically associated with the "criminal justice system" — the police, court, and correctional agents and agencies that process suspects, defendants, and offenders. But the domain of criminal justice study would be broader than that. *Very importantly, it would include the study of societal selection of social controls.* Research questions would include: Why do some societies punish while others do not? What objectionable or harmful behavior is defined as criminal (punishable)? How severe should criminal sanctions be? What characteristics should the punishment system have? Many of these critical criminal justice behaviors occur in legislatures, executive offices, appellate courts, and popular and political culture, rather than in criminal justice agencies. The object of each of these questions is variation in the nature and amount of social control.

Under this definition, criminal justice goes beyond studying *what* the criminal justice system is doing about crime and antisocial behavior; it includes *how* and *why* a particular response is employed. The study of criminal justice would include investigations of the propriety and fairness of social control as perceived by criminal justice officials, political forces, and the general public. In short, criminal justice as an academic discipline is the study of the domains of *lawmaking* and *law enforcing*, leaving the study of *lawbreaking* to the discipline of criminology.

It is true that all three areas have traditionally been combined under the auspices of criminology (Sutherland 1947). However, with a few notable exceptions (e.g., Ross 1914), the criminology tradition was established prior to serious scientific study of social control. It is common for fields to branch off from each other as greater knowledge is gained and as specialties become more distinct. (In our view, if criminal justice is a subfield, it is a branch of the study of social control, not of the study of crime. However, social control is also a fragmented field, with portions studied in sociology and portions in political science, and so on. We would not think it wise to associate criminal justice science with only one discipline.)

Our definition of criminal justice implies that lawmaking and law enforcing are "in" but the impact of these on lawbreaking is "out." It classifies the study of the effects of criminal justice on crime as belonging appropriately in criminology, along with the study of any and all other factors that explain crime. Our approach classifies the study of the impact of crime on criminal justice as "in," along with the study of any other forces which affect the shape, scope, and functioning of criminal justice. For example, Chiricos's study of drug enforcement policy as the result of a "moral panic" about drug abuse is clearly a criminal justice study. Change in drug enforcement policy, not drug abuse, is what is being explained (Chiricos 1998).

This approach to criminal justice assumes that knowledge about criminal justice, or the response to crime, is equally as important as, but different from, criminology, or the study of the nature and causes of crime. Below we examine the domains of criminal justice theory and of criminological theory and how they are related.

CRIMINAL JUSTICE THEORY

To discuss the domain of criminal justice theory, it is first necessary to define theory. Bernard and Ritti (1990, 5) define theory as "a set of concepts bound together by explicit relationships and causal priorities." Vogt defines theory as "a statement or group of statements about how some part of the world works" (1993, 232) or "a set of related propositions" (1993, 181). Following Dubin (1978), Snipes and Maguire (chapter 2) suggest that theory has two basic elements: *what is the explanation, how cause and effect are related, and why that relationship exists.* While Dubin says these are the minimal elements for a theory, he also says that theories often suggest their own limits by indicating for *whom (or in what groups) the explanations apply, where the relationships hold, and when (or in what time periods) the relationships occur.* What, how, and why combine to provide the theoretical propositions, while *who, where,* and *when* specify the operational context, or the limits, of the theory. The *domain* of a theory is conventionally designated by the dependent variable — by the "what" that is being explained. If we use this convention, then the domain of criminological theory is crime, while the domain of criminal justice theory is the variation in the provision of social control.

Criminal justice theorists may disagree about the edges of the domain of criminal justice. Snipes and Maguire (chapter 2) state that the responses of interest in criminal justice study are *only* those by criminal justice officials. This view is consistent with Black's (1976) notion that law is governmental social control and, therefore, the behavior to be explained is official government behavior. But further examination of when to invoke criminal justice controls suggests that the boundary between "official" and "unofficial" or informal may be ambiguous, and may, in fact, be disappearing. For example, in studying decisions to invoke the law as a response to a harm, Gottfredson and Hindelang (1979a) discover that victim choices about social control are fundamental criminal justice decisions. Other scholars argue that interest groups and politicians are critical criminal justice actors (Miller, Ohlin, and Coates 1977; Scheingold 1984; Walker 1993). Additionally, the boundaries between informal and formal controls are becoming fuzzy. When the police collaborate with residents of a neighborhood to develop a set of neighborhood priorities and problem solutions, it can be difficult to separate government and nongovernment social control. This implication of the idea of "coproduction" of social order is of interest in community-based strategies, such as community policing (Duffee, Fluellen, and Renauer 1999; Skogan and Hartnett 1997). Indeed, in his now classic article, Hunter (1985) argued that the critical social control questions were not the separate actions of public, parochial, and private control systems, but how they come together. In fact, the boundaries in criminal justice are changing so rapidly, that, in its new millennium series, the National Institute of Justice commissioned an entire volume on *Boundary Changes in Criminal Justice Organizations* (Friel, Keilitz, Wellford, Riveland, and Jacobs 2000).

Certainly there will be disagreements about the boundaries of criminal justice, and therefore, the domain edges in criminal justice theory. But this ambiguity is likely to be true of any field of scientific inquiry, and can be interesting rather than worrisome if there is agreement about the core. Although the domain of criminal justice may be fuzzy at its periphery, there is general agreement that it is centered on explaining variations in the central agencies and actors of the criminal justice system (Duffee 1995; Wilkins 1991; and chapter 2).

The Fragmentation of Criminal Justice Theory

The structure of that system provides criminal justice theory with another set of challenges. Other than the sequence for processing an individual accused of criminal behavior, there is often little to tie the "loosely coupled" criminal justice institutions together (Hagan 1989b). Because of the fragmented nature of the system, theory development in criminal justice has often focused on individual institutions and their agents, rather than the system as a whole. Indeed, it was not until after the American Bar Foundation survey of the administration of justice in the 1950s and the President's Commission on Law Enforcement and Administration of Justice in 1967, along with its now famous "system diagram," that the police-court-corrections connections were approached as a "system" of social control (Duffee 1990; Ohlin 1993; Walker 1993).

Prior to those seminal reports, the criminal justice agencies were often studied separately by different academic disciplines and for different reasons. The interconnections among agencies, such as the effects of one agency's decisions on those of other agencies in the criminal process, were often not of primary concern. Although sociologists occasionally studied the police, they were more frequently attracted to penal institutions and processes. Political scientists often studied courts, but rarely looked at prisons or the police. Psychologists were attracted to specific aspects of each criminal justice institution — such as the personality of police officers, decision making by juries, and the attitudes and perceptions of prisoners. But these researchers were rarely connecting with each other and were often not even aware of each other's work. In addition, we had still other conceptions of criminal justice by lawyers (Packer 1968) and physicians (Dession 1938; Menninger 1969).

The separate theoretical traditions of these different disciplines and professions are still with us today. While the American Bar Foundation, the President's Commission, and the subsequent federalization of much criminal justice research have succeeded in bringing many disciplines together, there are vast and important literatures on the police, the courts, and corrections considered as separate entities. Does criminal justice theory have to address the "system"? Or can criminal justice theory focus on only the police, only the courts, or only corrections? Can it focus on individuals rather than agencies?

Just as we do not require criminological theories to explain all kinds of crime, it is inappropriate to expect all criminal justice theories to deal with the "criminal justice system." Indeed, important arguments have been made that the "system" as conceived in the President's Commission — the decision points along which some offenders pass — may not be the most important or the only system connections to be investigated (DeLeon-Granados 1999; Duffee 1990; Sullivan 1994).

To say that explaining one agency or actor or action at a time is often theoretically adequate is not to say that small theories alone are sufficient. We should constantly be vigilant for opportunities to examine commonalities across agencies or actors (Bernard and Engel 2001); and, as Robert Sullivan (1994) warns, we should be vigilant lest the scope of criminal justice theory becomes too narrow. If our theories deal only with individual actors rather than with agencies or with whole systems, or only with goals and values espoused or claimed by agents rather than with goals that we infer from behavior, we are very likely missing some critical kinds of criminal justice variation. We will explore some of the common limitations of criminal justice theory in the next two sections of this chapter.

CRIMINAL JUSTICE EFFECTIVENESS AND CRIMINAL JUSTICE THEORY

If we accept the idea that the domain of a theory is identified by the nature of its dependent variables (e.g., the variation that we seek to explain), then it is likely that criminal justice theory is underdeveloped relative to criminology.[1] A number of authors have commented on this lack of development. In 1983, Willis noted that, if introductory textbooks are a measure of knowledge in a field, then theory has been accorded a weak role in criminal justice. His survey of criminal justice texts found that, on average, authors devoted only 5.25 percent of their space to theory, but theory is far more prominent in criminology texts.

Sullivan (1994), based on observations of doctoral student study, and Duffee (1995), based on a survey of doctoral curricula and dissertation topics, describe doctoral training in the United States as unbalanced in two respects. First, both found that where theoretic inquiry among criminal justice students is available, it focuses on individual decisions, behaviors, and attitudes rather than on behavior of organizations or of systems. Second, Duffee found that theory and theorizing about crime are explicitly recognized and taught, but ignored or hidden when they are about criminal justice. A survey of academics in criminology and criminal justice by Greene et al. (1985) indicated that, when compared to criminologists, criminal justice academics are far less concerned about the establishment and teaching of theory and more concerned with either describing practice or assisting agencies in implementation and evaluation. In general, these research studies of criminal justice education contain two major criticisms of criminal justice theory. First, the range or scope of criminal justice theory is often seen as narrowly focused on behavior of individual programs and, even more often, on the behavior of individual agents. In Sullivan's view (1994), criminal justice theory too infrequently recognizes the larger connections between sanctioning systems and political systems and too frequently focuses on differences among individual decision makers. Second, criminal justice theory is, in general, underdeveloped. As Duffee (1995) reported, both students and faculty in criminology and criminal justice programs automatically think of the criminological domain when "theory" is mentioned. For example, a number of doctoral programs use the term *theory* to denote their comprehensive examination in criminology.

The research on criminal justice education offers an admixture of empirical findings and speculation to explain these theoretical deficits. The point of such speculation is not self-flagellation by the misunderstood criminal justice academic. The goal in examining theoretical weaknesses is to gain an understanding of how to make criminal justice study more scientific by recognizing both the steps necessary for theory to progress and to appreciate the wealth of opportunities available for criminal justice theory development.

One of the significant difficulties both in the conception of criminal justice theory and in policies about criminal justice research funding is the dominance of criminal justice effectiveness as an area of inquiry. Much of what is currently called "criminal justice research" is concerned with the effectiveness of criminal justice programs in reducing crime. Using the definitions proposed in this chapter, criminal justice effectiveness is a form of criminological research. The dependent variable — the thing to be explained in effectiveness research — is not criminal justice but some aspect of crime or criminal behavior. A large segment of National Institute of Justice research, for example, focuses on this narrow slice of criminological inquiry: does the criminal justice intervention du jour have an impact on crime?

In effectiveness or evaluation research, the behaviors of criminal justice agents and agencies are treated as independent variables, which are expected to have an effect on crime. We are not questioning the policy value or intellectual interest in criminal justice effectiveness research. However, we do wish to call attention to the incompleteness in the knowledge of criminal justice that arises from the concentration on only a few of its effects (especially crime, disorder, and fear) without equal attention to its causes. Two scenarios, one from community policing within a city and one from community prosecution nationally will serve as examples.

First, imagine a relatively large city in which community policing is first implemented in one troubled neighborhood. Presume that, after a year of working with residents in that neighborhood, the police department announces that community policing reduces crime (nationally, the research findings on this relationship are very mixed). Perhaps there is much excitement in this city about this discovery and much pressure to replicate this result in other neighborhoods. But despite good faith efforts by the police department, the replication does not seem to have the same effects in other parts of the city. In many areas, crime is unaffected by the efforts, while in a few neighborhoods crime actually goes up. Residents and the police department feel a great deal of frustration.

While many different scenarios could produce these results, a very likely one is that the department had good measures of crime, which is what the department and the residents were concerned about, but very poor measures of community policing (Duffee, Fluellen, and Renauer 1999). After the first successful experience, no one in the department or in the neighborhoods was quite sure of the elements of community policing that needed to be replicated. Moreover, even when they agreed about the characteristics of the program that they wished to reproduce, they were not really sure how to do it again. What was it about the first neighborhood application that made it click?

This is not an uncommon experience in criminal justice. It is, in our view, closely related to the emphasis on crime outcomes (Bennett 1998). Criminal justice policy replications often do not work because we have little knowledge of how the criminal justice intervention was produced. In fact, we often do not even really know if it was produced at all (Rosenbaum 1988). In other words, we often place much of our efforts in measuring the dependent variable but are often very careless in measuring the independent variable — the intervention. Very often, the intervention is described in some narrative form, but not measured. For example, in perhaps the most careful evaluation of community policing, the study of community policing in Chicago, great attention went into measures of whether specific problems were solved or not, but the steps taken to change the relationship between the police and the communities are illustrated in qualitative, case study terms (Skogan and Hartnett 1997). It is not possible to tell what kinds of police interactions with each community produced or failed to produce the problem solving successes and failures.

The second scenario involves a broader scene: a discussion about what aspects of community prosecution should receive attention from the National Institute of Justice (NIJ). Since 2003, the U.S. Department of Justice has invested significant sums in supporting community prosecution in operating agencies around the country. The practitioners and researchers at an NIJ focus group on community prosecution were asked to identify worthwhile areas of research on community prosecution. Earlier in the seminar, the group had heard a presentation on how different prosecutorial motives might affect the nature of the program that was produced. Some prosecutors would be attracted by political benefits, such as reelection, while other prosecutors might be attracted to improving communities. The focus group participants returned to this presentation during the discussion of what research NIJ should be interested in supporting. Should there be research on motives, such as these, or on other causes of community prosecution adoption? Or should the research focus on outcomes, such as case processing, citizen satisfaction, and community capacity?

There was considerable agreement in the room that impacts should be studied, and that NIJ should be interested in a range of impacts other than crime rates and convictions. But there was less interest in studying the reasons why one office might adopt such a program while another might not, or why one prosecutor might adopt program rhetoric without changing office structure and practice, while another prosecutor made significant alterations in decision making, resource allocation, assistant prosecutor behavior and employee evaluation. The groups did recognize significant differences from office to office in what was being called community prosecution by practitioners; but they were not convinced that it was important to develop theory to explain these differences and then engage in research to examine the theory.

It may well be true that, within a single jurisdiction, learning about why other prosecutors elsewhere may or may not adopt similar strategies may be of little or no immediate interest. To these practicing prosecutors, studying the causes of program adoption might appear only of passing academic interest (and they criticized researchers for not engaging in simple and useful research). But, knowledge of the causes of program adoption could matter a great deal to an agency such as NIJ, with a mission to serve criminal justice nationwide through research about criminal justice. If NIJ had knowledge of what attracted different prosecutors' offices to different levels or kinds of implementation, it might be able to concentrate program assistance funding on local offices that are more likely to adopt a particular kind of program. Or, if it were unable to withhold funds from locales that are likely to implement poorly or superficially, NIJ could still recommend the kinds of technical assistance that might overcome resistances. However, if there is no sound research that distinguishes one criminal justice setting from another in terms of its amenability to reform or to innovation, then it is harder to allocate resources on a rational basis.

Back down on the local level, prosecutors should also be interested in causal connections of another order. How is a successful community prosecution program to be implemented in different communities within one jurisdiction? This problem is quite similar to the problem above in the city disappointed with the lack of replicability of community policing. Again, being serious about the implementation side of program evaluation requires thinking seriously about the independent variable in the intervention. Thinking seriously about how to "manipulate that independent variable" (which is usually a very complex criminal justice program) would mean that we take seriously the criminal justice variables as dependent variables! We are trying to cause them to change. This requires knowledge of how and why criminal justice behaves as it does, rather than knowledge of what criminal justice affects. It would require the building and testing of criminal justice theory.

Consequently, it would seem that even if primary political interest was in outcomes for communities (including but not limited to crime levels), knowledge of criminal justice variables as dependent, rather than as independent variables is important. If we do not know how to replicate a successful intervention, it is of limited value elsewhere. We may also want to know how to avoid a damaging intervention. For example, what should we know in order to reduce the likelihood that police officers and citizens alienate each other and grow cynical about community programs (Grinc 1998)? If we know what causes crime outcomes but do not expend equal efforts to know what causes criminal justice outcomes, we may not have deployable knowledge.

PROBLEMS AND PROSPECTS OF CRIMINAL JUSTICE THEORY

Instead of focusing on crime as a dependent variable, a criminal justice theory would focus on the variation in the responses of criminal justice to crime as the outcome. Responses include decisions, attitudes, and styles of behavior by criminal justice officials; structural and procedural changes of criminal justice institutions; and the development of and changes in the substantive criminal law by the legislature (see chapter 2 for a more elaborate list).

When inquiry about such topics was posed to a colleague of one of the authors, he complained that studying criminal justice without attention to its impact on crime was "empty." Presumably, this complaint implies that the criminological domain is "full." In *Punishment, Crime, and Market Forces*, Leslie Wilkins (1991) recognizes the same criticism of criminal justice theory. He complains that while many scholars and governments find variations in crime rates of great interest, these same actors find variations in punishment rates trivial, despite the fact that the punishment rates often vary more than the crime rates.

Academic study in criminal justice policy has paid scant attention to problems of the comparative use of prison, perhaps because no explanations were seen to be necessary...[I]f the "right person" makes the decision then, by that token, it is a "right" decision. (Wilkins 1991, 6)

Both Wilkins and Sullivan (1994) suggest that governments make the decisions about crime policy, as well as most of the funding decisions about criminal justice research. Both suggest that studies of criminal justice effectiveness are done to justify the investment in criminal justice programs and policies. When, as is often the case, the evaluations suggest little positive effect on crime, there may be disappointment, but no political threat. The government response to failed policy is to craft another policy with the same espoused intent of reducing crime. The system that needs both crime and responses to crime is sustained or stable, so long as questions do not arise about the system that generates the responses, such as the selection of a behavior as a moral or criminal justice matter rather than a public health matter (Chiricos 1998). In Wilkins's terms, the primary function of blame allocation (such as in finding the guilty party or discovering the faulty program) is that it increases satisfaction with the existing social system (1991, 69).

During the War on Poverty, Roland Warren (1971) commented on this tendency in government social policy in what he called the "latent functions" of social policy. He argued that institutionalized approaches to social problems, such as public welfare or criminal justice, are so ingrained that even evidence of program failures usually is interpreted by the government in a way that strengthens the policy system, even if policy content changes. Program failures are generally interpreted as a need for more program resources (Lipsky 1980 makes virtually the same point).

Perhaps there is no better example of this than the "nothing works" discovery in correctional treatment research (Martinson 1974). The result of this finding of failure was record increases in correctional clients and correctional resources. While the "nothing works" claim, as inaccurate as it might have been, led to reduction in resources for correctional treatment, it was a banner day for punishment. Investment in criminal justice was strengthened (Garland 2001). The new policy (tougher punishment) was even less tested than rehabilitation as a means of achieving publicly stated goals. But the causes of the new policy were not questioned. Political focus remained on the claimed object of the policy change: reductions in crime. Few people questioned the disjunction between what correctional systems were actually doing and the goals that were espoused (Feeley and Simon 1992).

If these arguments have any merit, they would suggest that explanations of crime, including criminal justice effectiveness studies, are more likely to be supported by governments than explanations of government responses. Theories and studies that examine the relative favor accorded to the criminal sanction in relation to other government policies will rarely be encouraged. Theories of criminal justice, by definition, raise questions about why the government is doing what it is doing. The only causal reasoning about that issue that the government is likely to support is that the government wishes to achieve the goals it has espoused. Theory that seeks to examine why those goals were chosen over others is not received well.

One common reaction to criminal justice research questions is puzzlement, as in "everyone knows why we respond to crime; it does not need study." These reactions appear to view theories for explaining variations in criminal justice as trivial or empty. Societal or social processes that lead to criminal justice responses do not need explanation. The government (and popular) assumptions about why criminal justice does what it does are well-established, unquestioned assumptions. In the terminology of institutional theorists, criminal justice is culturally embedded (Garland 2001; Scheingold 1984; Wilkins 1991). The other common reaction to criminal justice research questions is perceptions of threat or defensiveness, although these are less visible. When researchers propose to look for explanations for criminal justice policies, their search may be seen as questioning the espoused goals of the government. Evidence that criminal justice policy is influenced by social forces beyond crime might be used by interest groups that are critical of the group (or even of the system) in power (Bernard and Engel 2001).

The cultural commitments to criminal justice as a way of addressing social issues reinforces a political system that explains social problems by allocating blame, rather than by making economic or political changes (Wilkins 1991, 57–72). Focusing on individual deviance is an aspect of the political institutionalization of criminal justice. Criminal justice theory and research would raise questions about both cultural and political forces that are often taken for granted. Studies of program results are far less threatening to ingrained values and stakeholder positions than are studies of program ideologies (Nokes 1960; Warren et al. 1974).

One problematic impact on criminal justice theory of government preference for evaluation studies is an unfortunate misperception by critical or radical audiences of scientific methods as supportive of government positions. They complain that scientists do not question the legitimacy of official goals for programs, but merely assist government by determining how well or to what extent those goals are achieved (Tifft and Sullivan 1980).

One example of the symbiosis between criminal justice research and policy making is evident in Gottfredson and Gottfredson's rational goal model of criminal justice (1988). The model proposes that rational criminal justice activity would involve the specification of measurable goals, the availability of choice among options to achieve those goals, and valid, reliable information about the extent to which the options meet goal expectations. Goldstein's proposal for a problem-solving approach to policing (1990) is a similar, if less generic, model.

There is much to recommend these approaches for the advancement of both criminal justice policy and criminal justice science. Nevertheless, there is cause for concern about the latent functions of official goals and rational models. For example, DeLeon-Granados (1999) and Lyons (1999) propose that problem-oriented policing and community policing are both concepts and practices that are used as rhetorical and political devices to build uncritical support for the police and to harden a state-driven, nonreciprocal approach to social control.

Criminal justice science must be open enough to generate and test causal propositions, regardless of their alignment with official policy (Bernard and Engel 2001; Wilkins 1991). The scientific process itself is neutral, despite some leftist propositions to the contrary (e.g., DiCristina 1997). However, the financial support of science is not neutral. Although not empirically tested, there probably exists a correlation between positivistic science and acceptance of official goals at face value. One explanation for this presumed correlation is that criminal justice data are hard to come by without government cooperation and the resources for positivistic science are hard to mobilize without government support (Wilkins 1991).

As a result, criminal justice science has increasingly become a part of the criminal justice policy system. It gains research resources in exchange for limiting theory to models that cannot threaten the legitimacy — or the presumed rationality — of the policy-making system (Wilkins 1991). It can critique results (such as impact on crime), but not policy choices (such as why drug abuse is treated as a crime rather than as a health problem). The positivist approach does gain considerable knowledge of organizational and individual behaviors and has incremental effects within specific policy paradigms (Bernard and Engel 2001).

In contrast, critical, radical, and interpretive approaches to criminal justice largely operate outside this criminal justice policy/research enterprise (Sullivan 1994). They attempt to demystify policy changes. For example, Simon (1993) claims that California's reintegration parole

policy stopped well short of any demonstrable interest in effecting reintegration. Instead, it provided a rationale for managing parolees in the
absence of jobs. Simon also claims that this interpretivist version of correctional policy is only possible in retrospect. If so, it is not an approach
acceptable to normal science. While they appear to make sense, these
understandings are always challengeable as post hoc rationalizations, at
least no less so than the official policy that Simon claims to demystify.
As Blalock says (1969), historical analysis is vulnerable to confounding
probabilities with inevitabilities.

Contrary to Simon's view, and despite being largely ignored by positivist criminal justice (Sullivan 1994), it is possible to test critical theory
using the scientific process. Wilkins (1984, 1991) calls some (but not all)
of these critical theories a "consumerist approach" to criminal justice
because it would focus research on the control of consumer demand
(for punishment) rather than on the effects claimed by official policy
(reduction in crime). He demonstrates a number of theoretical directions and empirical tests for such theories, as does Scheingold (1984).
Similarly, Hagan (1989b, 117) suggests that a scientific approach to criminal justice would focus on "the structural relationships that emerge
from a joining of organizational and political forces in the direction of
criminal justice operations." In other words, a theory of criminal justice would examine which political and bureaucratic forces combined
to influence the tightness of agency connections and the severity and
sweep of the criminal sanction.

Both Hagan and Wilkins would have us employ the normal scientific method of theory and research to generate knowledge about
the demands placed on the system and the effects these have for the
enunciation of policy positions. While criminal justice theory is likely
to be more controversial than crime theory, we can find nothing in the
nature of scientific theory itself that favors one set of political assumptions and beliefs over others. Clearly, the field of criminal justice theory
will be more vibrant if it can incorporate propositions that threaten, as
well as those that might be supportive of, the legitimacy of policy and
practice (Bernard and Engel 2001).

SUMMARY

Criminal justice theory has been defined as explanations of the variations in responses to crime. That is, the dependent variables in criminal
justice theory concern the response to crime, including what should
be defined as crime. Criminological theory has been defined as explanations of the variations in crime. Variation in crime responses, or

criminal justice, often differs more than variations in crime. The response to crime is just as basic an area of knowledge as is crime. It is just as intriguing and important to know what causes the responses as it is to know what causes crime. However, theory building in criminal justice is an understudied enterprise, despite the fact that the accumulation of knowledge requires theory development, testing, and modification. Certainly there are a number of reasons for this lack of theory development that go well beyond those we have discussed. We proposed two related reasons for criminal justice theory retardation. One is that many people assume that the reasons for criminal justice responses are already known or not problematic. The other is the emphasis on criminological over criminal justice domains in theory building. Evidence to support these views is implied by the pressure for criminal justice research to be evaluative in nature, which is another way of saying we accept positioning criminal justice variables as independent, but not dependent, variables in the causal chains which claim most of our research attention.

In other words, much of what is known now as "criminal justice research" is really applied criminology. The variables that are being influenced are crime variables. The behavior expected to have these influences (e.g., the independent variables) are criminal justice agents, policies, or programs. Much more rarely is government sponsored research truly criminal justice research, in which investigators seek to explain some variation in how the criminal justice policy, program, or agents have been influenced by something else (including crime).

As a result, criminal justice theory has not advanced very far and criminal justice as a discipline is often thought of as a component of the discipline of criminology. To rectify this situation, it would be helpful if both researchers and policy makers would break the habit of emphasizing the effectiveness of criminal justice responses to crime, while virtually ignoring the variation in those responses. It is time to examine critically and explicitly the nature of criminal justice theoretical concepts, the kinds of explanations that are used to connect them, and the extent of evidence supporting one kind of explanation rather than another. Developing a language of theories allows researchers to classify and connect research problems quickly and effectively so that knowledge may advance more efficiently (Bernard and Engel 2001).

Criminal justice theory seeks to explain and examine the variations in, and the causes of, aspects of government social control systems, which select the criminal sanction over other forms of social control and shape the nature of the criminal sanction to be employed. Criminal justice theory may seek to explain whole systems, typically by comparing cultures, nations, or states. It may also be concerned with the sanction selection and implementation behavior of an agency or of single individuals, such as official decision makers. The intellectual and practical need for criminal justice theory has become increasingly recognized since the mid-1990s. The time is ripe for developing theoretical knowledge in the discipline of criminal justice.

NOTE

1. For readers who want more explanation of independent and dependent variables and their role in theory, see the discussion questions at the end of the part I introduction, and additional discussion in chapter 2. It might also help to refer to the material on hypothesis testing in part IV. Alternatively, any standard methods text may be of assistance.

Part I

The Nature, Method, and Boundaries of Criminal Justice Theory

The three chapters in part I follow up on the introductory chapter by Duffee and Allan in several ways: they help readers decide what is, and what is not, criminal justice theory; they explore its breadth and its boundaries; and they explore its relevance to the central theme of justice.

Chapter 2 furthers the discussion of criminal justice theory by defining scientific theory in more detail and distinguishing scientific theory from both nontheory and nonscientific theory. In this chapter, Snipes and Maguire observe that much of the literature that is labeled "theoretical" in criminal justice is not scientific theory because it cannot be empirically investigated. The most typical example of this is the concept of "punishment theory." Writings about punishment theory are generally philosophical tracts concerning why punishment ought to be done in certain ways and not others. As Snipes and Maguire point out, these tracts are certainly important in criminal justice policy, but they are not scientific theory. Following their clarification of scientific theory, Snipes and Maguire review different approaches to scientific criminal justice theory. They discuss different aspects of this theory by referring to seven dimensions on which theory differs. After their examination of the nature of criminal justice theory, they describe the phases of scientific knowledge building, from theory development to theory revision, and preview the types of theories and phases of knowledge building covered in later chapters.

In chapter 3, Howard and Freilich make the case for a truly comparative criminal justice theory that accounts for variations in the justice system not only close to home, but also throughout the world. They make a strong case for the position that cross-national comparison is not a specific theoretical subject matter itself but a method that can be applied with good results to virtually any theory of criminal justice. They identify five distinct advantages of comparative study for social science, including criminal justice and criminology, and they discuss in broad terms how a social scientist would approach cross-national comparisons systematically in the attempt to build and test a theory of criminal justice. They also make the argument that much of the extant research that uses cross-national comparisons is not theoretical but descriptive. Studies examine how criminal justice is done and how it is structured in different nations, legal systems, and cultures, but very few comparative studies are theoretically driven. They do not entail conceptualizations and expected linkages among concepts that are then tested using cross-national data. One of the reasons for this deficiency is the lack of data. It often takes all a researcher's effort simply to unearth the data about a system in a nation; there is often little opportunity or energy left to determine if the same patterns can be found in data about the same criminal justice behaviors in different countries. Howard and Freilich make the point that comparison is at the heart of all theoretical research, not just comparative research, and that the comparative method would be a rich means to employ in the investigation of many criminal justice theories.

In chapter 4, Thomas Castellano and Jon B. Gould ask why there is so little justice in criminal justice theory. Castellano and Gould tackle a very difficult but important topic in criminal justice theoretical research: what is the relationship of values to social science research? They point out, quite correctly, that while criminal justice scientists are not promoting value positions they are studying value positions. The fundamental criminal justice act is the decision that a harm should be recognized as blameworthy and its perpetrator punished. That is, the fundamental criminal justice action is to conceive of some problem as a crime. This is not a "natural" occurrence (unless all human decisions are considered natural occurrences) but a judgment by some people about how to respond to that occurrence. Criminal justice affixes value (this is a bad act and it was done by a bad actor) and allocates value (the actor shall receive a specific level of sanction for that action). Criminal justice also entails adhering to other value positions in determining how those decisions about actions and actors and punishments shall be implemented. It is a system concerned about actions that have been negatively valued as crimes but it is also a system concerned about the values upheld by the officials who implement the decisions. Castellano and Gould argue that too often criminal justice study focuses on crimes as harmful events rather than decisions about those harmful events. If we forget that we are studying a struggle about values, these authors propose, we are often not in position to construct criminal justice theories. More attention to theories of how justice is defined and carried out might improve the scope and power of criminal justice theory.

All three of the chapters in part I probe the boundaries of criminal justice theory, in some cases arguing that those boundaries are too loose (such as when theories of crime are mistakenly identified as criminal justice theories), and in other cases arguing that they do not extend far enough (to include international comparison as well as more focus on justice). Readers should come away from part I with their own ideas about what criminal justice theory is, what it ought to be, and where it is going.

DISCUSSION QUESTIONS

1. Two important concepts in theorizing and theory testing are "units of analysis" and "dependent variables." Units of analysis are what or who is being studied, while dependent variables are something that varies across those units that the theory is meant to "explain." Criminal justice theories are meant to explain variation in attitudes, behaviors, or other phenomena at multiple levels, including individuals (such as police officers), working groups, agencies, neighborhoods, cities, states, and nations. Each of these levels represents a potential unit of analysis for theorizing or theory testing. Select any three units of analysis and describe some dependent variable on which those units might vary. For instance, you might select U.S. states as a unit of analysis. One way that states might vary from one another is in the rate with which people are executed.

2. In answering question 1, you practiced selecting a unit of analysis and specific dependent variables. Now select any one of the units of analysis that you listed in your response. Propose your own theory about the factors that influence the dependent variable. What forces might make that variable fluctuate? These factors that influence the variation in the dependent variable are called *independent variables*. This term connotes that we are interested in the effects or consequences of these variables, rather than their causes, in our particular investigation. Fol-

lowing up on the example in question 1, one might argue that the rate of executions in a state might be a function of four things: state laws regarding capital punishment, local legal culture, the proportion of voters who are politically conservative, and the volume of violent criminal activity within the state. Remember that in posing independent variables, it is important not only to identify factors that occur prior in time to the dependent variable, but also that the proposed causal connection is plausible and measurable.

3. If you have answered the first two questions, you have selected a unit of analysis and one characteristic or aspect of that unit, which is the dependent variable, and one or more independent variables. You are on your way to constructing a theory. Now, thinking about your emerging theory in the context of the three chapters in this section, answer the following three questions:

   • Does your theory meet the definition of criminal justice theory as outlined by Snipes and Maguire in chapter 2? Why or why not? If not, can you change the theory so that it does?
   • Could your theory be examined using the comparative approach, as outlined by Howard and Freilich in chapter 3? If not, could it be modified so that it could be examined in that way? If, instead, you feel this theory applies in only one nation, culture, or political system, why do you think so?
   • Does your theory concern any aspects of "justice" as discussed by Castellano and Gould in chapter 4? If not, is there a related dependent variable that would have a stronger connection to the explanation of levels or qualities of justice? Is it necessary for criminal justice theories to deal with justice, even if they do not deal with crime?

2

FOUNDATIONS OF CRIMINAL JUSTICE THEORY

Jeffrey B. Snipes and Edward R. Maguire

INTRODUCTION

Criminal justice has been developing as an academic field since the appearance of several influential studies and the inception of its first doctoral program in the 1960s (at the University at Albany). There are now about three dozen programs in the United States and Canada. As the field continues to grow, there is a need to track its evolution, identifying those shortcomings and inconsistencies which may affect its future growth. We will argue that criminal justice as a discipline suffers a serious flaw: There is no common understanding or teaching of theory. Instead, programs consist of scattergun approaches to study, with little effort toward unity and coherence beyond very basic organizational divisions such as police, courts, and corrections. Other social sciences do not suffer from such a fundamental flaw. For example, sociology programs teach doctrinal theory, typically in a two-semester sequence. Criminology, as an interdisciplinary field, offers nicely bounded areas of theory with a common enterprise (to explain criminal behavior). Anthropological theory is well established and heavily integrated into graduate curricula. By contrast, scholars in criminal justice, even some who are quite prominent, still lack a coherent vision of what theory entails. Some even confuse domains, not accurately differentiating criminal justice from criminology. If insiders are disoriented, outsiders are even more at a loss: When pressed, few noncriminal justice scholars can identify what the field stands for or attempts to study. Part of this can be attributed to its newness; however, part can also be explained by our failure to carve out clear boundaries and to develop a focused theoretical foundation. This chapter begins to do this, thereby opening the avenue for scholarly discourse on criminal justice theory.

THE STATE OF CRIMINAL JUSTICE THEORY

Criminal justice theory is underdeveloped for several reasons. Chapter 1 has already isolated some of these reasons, so we will only discuss them briefly. First, criminal justice has often been confused with criminology, where some view criminal justice as applied criminology and others see it as subsumed within criminology (Pelfrey 1980, 52).[1] Criminology studies *criminal behavior*, whereas criminal justice, at its most basic level, is meant to study official *response* to such behavior. While theoretical criminology consists of research based on similar goals and driven by a strong framework (such as strain, culture, or control theories), criminal justice lacks any such shared orientation. Second, and related to the first, since criminal justice is often viewed as an *applied* field whose mission is to educate criminal justice practitioners (in so-called "cop shops"), the role of theory has been downplayed.[2] Third, criminal justice is taught in departments as diverse as criminology, sociology, political science, public affairs, law, psychology, philosophy, and various other hybrid programs. Thus, the very structure of the field, including its location within universities, its reward structures, its preferred publication outlets, and its diverse disciplinary background, all interfere with its ability to develop a coherent "league of its own."

Perhaps the biggest question is whether criminal justice represents enough of a unitary, cohesive, or coordinated domain to deserve its own field of study. One helpful way of exploring an answer to that question is to trace the development of the "contemporary criminal justice paradigm" as described by Samuel Walker (1992). In the late 1950s and early 1960s, based on the pioneering work of the American Bar Foundation, scholars began to look at criminal justice in two new ways. First, based on intensive field research, they discovered the important role of discretion in the criminal justice process (e.g., J. Goldstein 1960; Lafave 1965). Second, and not independent of the first, they began to conceive of criminal justice for the first time as a "system" (Blumberg 1967). Before this, in what Walker (1992) calls the "progressive era paradigm," criminal justice was viewed as a more legalistic, formalized process consisting of a series of independent institutions, including police, courts, and corrections. The work of these institutions was in some ways related, but essentially separate. The new "systems perspective" recognized that these institutions are interdependent upon each other in a variety of fashions. At the simplest level, police outputs become court inputs, and court outputs become correctional inputs. This conception of criminal justice as a series of outputs and inputs became particularly popular following the report of the President's Commission on Law Enforcement and Administration of Justice in 1967 (President's Commission 1967a; and see Duffee 1990). This systemic approach, which focuses on the importance of discretion and the interplay between the various facets of the system, is what Walker (1992) calls the "contemporary criminal justice paradigm."

However, not all scholars agree with this systemic approach. Many have argued that criminal justice is not a system, but a loosely integrated and coordinated set of institutions with separate but related duties and goals. Duffee (1990) rejects portions of the systemic approach to criminal justice for several reasons. He challenges the assumptions that criminal justice systems are uniform across localities, that criminal justice agencies within a locality are well integrated, and that there is any integrated control mechanism available at a system level. He further argues that many criminal justice analysts "gloss over" the differences between systems in order to stress their commonalities. Others argue that criminal justice does not function as a system since each component is governed by "perverse incentives" (Wilson 1983),[3] that components serve functions that are unrelated to criminal justice (police officers deal with vehicle accidents, and courts attend to torts and contract disputes), or that the criminal justice process is not *structured* as a formal system.[4]

Therefore, the debate over the domain of criminal justice is enmeshed in another debate about whether the criminal justice system is actually a system. We argue that criminal justice might best be described as a loosely coupled system, with features like the separation of powers and checks and balances built in for various reasons. For example, police and prisons in most developed countries are based in the executive branch, and the courts in the judicial branch. Some argue that criminal justice institutions should remain separate so that they maintain an equitable distribution of power. In the United States, for example, the Fourth Amendment generally prevents the police from searching citizens' homes without prior judicial approval. In developing countries without these types of checks on police power, police may be used as agents of oppression by the ruling classes (e.g., Arthur 1988; Clinard and Abbott 1973).[5] Thus, Wright (1981) argues that goal conflict, rather than hindering the effectiveness of the criminal justice system, serves a variety of beneficial roles, such as maintaining system stability and ensuring an even distribution of power among component institutions.

Furthermore, critics of the systemic perspective who focus on the differences between criminal justice institutions may not realize the importance of the *informal* linkages which occur between actors and networks in these institutions. These informal linkages are a central theme in exchange theory, described generally by Blau (1964) and applied to criminal justice by Cole (1970). Exchange theorists argue that much of what occurs between organizations can be attributed to informal exchanges between actors from different organizations. Thus, for example, although the formal linkages between courts and police departments may be tenuous, there exists a much more powerful set of informal linkages between police officers, prosecutors, and judges. These linkages are forged on a daily basis, as the actors from each organization find themselves in repeated contact with one another (e.g., Feeley 1991).[6] One example of such linkages is Eisenstein and Jacob's (1977) "courtroom workgroup." Although the actors brought together in the courtroom — judges, defense attorneys, prosecutors, and police officers — are from different institutions, have different goals, and are formally arranged in an adversarial relationship, they often bind together in mutually convenient, *informal* networks. This perspective is important because it helps us to understand the complex relationships between the component institutions of the criminal justice process.

It is precisely that these linkages across institutions exist that gives criminal justice its own domain. Aside from one's stance on the systems debate, criminal justice involves relationships between several different institutional areas, all of which participate in formal social reaction to crime. Although the study of criminal justice relies heavily on the application of theories from other academic disciplines (such as sociology, organization theory, anthropology, and political science), the domain of criminal justice is large and complex enough to justify the existence of a separate academic field. Having now explored the foundations and current understanding of what *criminal justice* is, we now move into a discussion of what criminal justice *theory* is. We first discuss the two most common misrepresentations of criminal justice theory.

WHAT CRIMINAL JUSTICE THEORY IS *NOT*

Many scholarly efforts at criminal justice theory either abuse the traditional scientific notion of "theory" or address substantive areas that are not in the scope of "criminal justice." It is surprising to find that scholars misuse the term "theory" so frequently. Theory has been the building block of scholarly inquiry since the birth of the scientific method. Theory is to scholars as clay is to sculptors and lumber to carpenters: It is the raw material of science. Plenty of definitions of "theory" have been offered throughout the history of science. One of the most respected authorities of theory development in modern social sciences is Dubin (1978), who delineates four elements which must be present for a theory to be complete: what, how, why, and who, where, when (see Whetten 1989, for a review).

What refers to the factors that explain some phenomenon, the set of independent variables. Scientists strive to make "what" comprehensive (including all relevant factors) and parsimonious (excluding trivial factors). How refers to the causal relationship between the set of independent variables and the outcome variable: What is the direction of the relationship, is it linear? Why involves the process by which the independent variables influence the phenomenon being studied. Such processes may be social, psychological, economic, historic, and so on, but must help us understand why an independent variable (often denoted as X) influences a dependent variable (Y).

The what, how, and why elements are sufficient for establishing the basic structure of a theory, but to make the theory more complete it is necessary to qualify it with who, where, and when limitations. To what extent will the theoretical propositions hold up with different types of people, different locations, and different time periods? In other words, to what extent is the theory generalizable?

Bacharach (1989, 498) importantly differentiates the elements of a theory (as in Dubin) from the boundaries of a theory:

> Values are the implicit assumptions by which a theory is bounded. Theories cannot be compared on the basis of their underlying values, because these tend to be the idiosyncratic product of the theorist's creative imagination and ideological orientation or life experience. This may explain why perpetual debates such as those between Marxists and Structural Functionalists have made so little progress over the years.

Confusing the boundaries of theories, such as ideologies, with theories themselves, is the largest problem suffered by past criminal justice "theories."

Let us take as an example Braithwaite and Pettit's (1990) republican theory. The gut of the theory is that "while there are many goods or values engaged in social and political life, a single goal for the criminal justice system can be the basis of a sophisticated policy.... The goal in question we describe as republican or civic freedom; in a word, 'dominion'" (Braithwaite and Pettit 1994, 765). The theory also consists of theorems, such as, "The criminal justice system should implement a presumption in favor of parsimony ... " and, "The system should be designed, not primarily to punish offenders but, rather, out of community-based dialogue, to bring home to them the disapproval of others ..." (Braithwaite and Pettit, 1994, 767).[7]*

Republican theory is not scientific theory, it is an ideological perspective. Theorists may adopt this perspective, and include these values as the bounds by which they develop criminal justice theories. Some of Braithwaite and Pettit's theorems may qualify as theories — or at least as theoretically grounded hypotheses, because they explore the effect of different policies on dominion — but in whole, "republican theory," like "retribution theory," is a philosophical perspective, not a scientific theory. Normative theory is crucial to the field, but should be kept separate from traditional scientific theory, which addresses why something in the world may cause or influence something else, and the reasons or processes underlying the chain of effects.

A second problem suffered by many "criminal justice theories" is that they are not theories of criminal justice. Criminal justice, as the reader will recall, is the study of the official response to crime. In *Theories of Criminal Justice: A Critical Reappraisal*, Ellis and Ellis (1989, ix) set out to "critically re-examine several of the most prominent approaches to the *philosophy* of criminal justice" (emphasis added). Their discussion focuses on the "three main types of theories of criminal justice" (1989, xxxi): deterrence, rehabilitation, and retribution. Deterrence and rehabilitation do not focus on the official response to crime; instead they focus on the effect of different types of criminal justice interventions on crime. Crime is the dependent variable, and criminal justice response to crime is an independent variable. As Akers (1992) points out, the study of something means that the "something" is a dependent variable. Thus, in a study of criminal justice, we would expect the dependent variable to be criminal justice, not crime.

The first step in furthering criminal justice theory is to eliminate these sorts of labeling errors, such that what we call criminal justice theory is truly criminal justice theory. In advancing this effort, we begin by discussing some ambiguous areas in the definition of criminal

---

* Pg. 756–757 from "Not Just Deserts: A Republican Theory of Criminal Justice" by Braithwaite, J. and Pettit, P. (1990). By permission of Oxford University Press, Inc.

justice theory, proposing several tests for distinguishing satisfactory from unsatisfactory theoretical endeavors.

WHAT CRIMINAL JUSTICE THEORY *IS*

Criminal justice theory *is the study of the official response to behavior that may be labeled criminal.* We suggest that a series of four tests must be passed before an endeavor may be classified as criminal justice theory.

Dependent Variable Test

As pointed out repeatedly in this chapter, criminal justice theory must explain response to a behavior, not attempting to explain crime itself in any way. The phenomenon being studied must take place after some behavior has occurred, and must be a reaction to that behavior.

One might ask whether a study of official response to potentially criminal behavior must involve actual behavior (i.e., decisions, actions) exhibited on the part of the criminal justice system or its actors, or whether nonbehavioral concepts such as attitudes, ideologies, and philosophical orientations should be considered as dependent variables worthy of study? We think it is necessary to maintain a generous definition of response when setting parameters on what constitutes criminal justice theory. Responses do not necessarily have to be behavioral. Most response concepts that are not behavioral can be theoretically linked to behavioral responses. For example, a theory that explains judicial attitudes toward white-collar criminals may employ such attitudes as an intermediate variable, where the theorist ultimately wishes to explain severity of punishment of street criminals. Even if a theorist does not link a nonbehavioral response variable to an ultimate behavioral response, the theory can still be classified as legitimate criminal justice theory.

Reasonableness Test

The problem with defining criminal justice as the official response to crime is that it is the official response itself that transforms behavior into "crime." If an incident occurs in which the criminal justice system responds to a certain behavior by *not* labeling it as a crime, this may be just as theoretically relevant as if the system had labeled it criminal. Hence, criminal justice includes our response to deviance, as long as one believes that the form of deviance being studied has a reasonable chance of being labeled criminal. By broadening the definition of criminal justice in this fashion, we incorporate into its domain studies

BAKER COLLEGE OF
CLINTON TWP. LIBRARY

that, for example, seek to understand why legislatures criminalize some behaviors and not others.

Parts-of-a-System Test

We have already mentioned the debate about whether criminal justice is a system. In light of the uncertainty as to whether it is a system, it would be inappropriate to require criminal justice theory to study only systemic responses. Studies of the police, judicial, and correctional response to potentially criminal behavior may all be considered criminal justice theory. In fact, the dependent variable may be any type of response, as long as the possibility of the invocation of the formal criminal justice system is relevant to the theory. Thus, legislative, media, victim, and public responses to potentially criminal behavior may all be classified as legitimate dependent variables.

The Valid Theory Test

In an earlier section we laid out the basic properties of scientific theories. Valid criminal justice theories must conform to these standards, as they cannot be exempt from the requirements of social science theories in general.

Table 2.1 summarizes the definition and tests of criminal justice theory. A proposed theory must pass all four tests to be considered legitimate criminal justice theory. Research failing on any dimension

Table 2.1 Criminal Justice Theory: Definition and Tests

X	Criminal justice theory is the study of official response to behavior that may be labeled criminal.
X	The Dependent Variable Test indicates that response to potentially criminal behavior must be the dependent variable studied; in no way can the potentially criminal behavior itself be the dependent variable.
X	The Reasonableness Test indicates that the behavior to which the response applies must have a reasonable chance of being labeled criminal, such that the formal criminal justice system is invoked.
X	The Parts-of-a-System Test indicates that as long as the entity responding to the behavior is integrally tied to the criminal justice system, the "official" part of the definition is met.
X	The Valid Theory Test indicates that the theory conforms with traditionally accepted social science standards of theories, as delineated by such scholars as Dubin (1978).

might of course still be quite valuable, but probably either belongs in nontheoretical criminal justice areas[8] or perhaps another field altogether. Criminal justice institutions may be used as arenas in which theories that do not employ criminal justice as a dependent variable are tested, but one must remember that this does not make them criminal justice theories. Studies that examine the policy implications of criminological theories (such as deterrence) should probably be considered applied criminology rather than criminal justice theory. Our aim is not to debase work that fails these tests in any way, but to suggest that the range of *legitimate criminal justice theory* should be narrowed in scope to exclude these works.

EXAMPLES OF CRIMINAL JUSTICE THEORY

Having discussed what criminal justice theory is and is not, we now review some work that we do consider to be criminal justice theory. We are careful to avoid condensing criminal justice theory into too simple a typology that presents a narrow perspective of the field. On the other hand, our aim is not to present an encyclopedic accounting of every possible type of criminal justice theory. Thus, following the principle of parsimony, we pose seven dimensions along which criminal justice theories may lie and provide examples within each dimension: (1) historical vs. nonhistorical; (2) organizational perspective; (3) sociopolitical perspective; (4) objective vs. subjective; (5) type of response; (6) level of explanation; and (7) institutional arena.

There are certainly other dimensions along which theory could be measured, but we think these dimensions capture substantial variation in criminal justice theory. They are not mutually exclusive dimensions, and any given theory can be classified somewhere on the continuum (or in some cases, in one of the categories) in each dimension. Another reason for using these dimensions as a method of reviewing some criminal justice theory is that several of our suggestions for future directions in criminal justice theory involve integrating approaches within these dimensions.

Historical vs. Nonhistorical

Theories may "freeze time" when explaining criminal justice phenomena, or they may attempt to explain either the source (origination) or development of criminal justice responses over time. This dimension applies to virtually any area of theoretical enterprise. To the extent that a theory inherently or explicitly relies on our understanding of a phenomenon in different historical periods (or over time), it is historical theory.

One example of a historical theory of criminal justice is Robinson and Scaglion's (1987) theory of the police. Their dependent variable is the origin of the police institution. Whereas most theories of the police may ask how the police respond to behavior that is potentially criminal, their theory asks why the police even exist to respond to such behavior. Their primary independent variable is the extent to which a society is class-dominated. As a society moves from kinship-based to class-dominated, it is more likely to develop a formal police institution to deal with forms of threatening behavior. Robinson and Scaglion support their theory with anthropological examples of societies in different historical eras, at different places along the kinship–class dominated continuum, and with different types of police functions.

Nonhistorical theories are plentiful. One such example is Klinger's (1994) notion that a nasty demeanor exhibited by a suspect toward police influences the likelihood of arrest, not because of the demeanor itself, but because it is frequently viewed as an illegal act (resistance) by the police officer. Although this notion could easily be expanded into a historical theory (for example, by arguing that police over time are becoming more likely to label resistance as crime), as it stands now, it is an ahistorical theory of police behavior.

Organizational Perspective

Although criminal justice theory has adopted frameworks from many disciplines, two of the most influential have been organizational and sociopolitical perspectives. Although organization theory is massive, it is arguable that three organizational approaches have had (or will have) the most dramatic impact on criminal justice theory: the rational-goal model, the functional systems model, and more recently, the institutional model.

Feeley (1973) has provided an eloquent description of the first two organizational perspectives, as adapted from Etzioni (1960). Feeley merges Etzioni's goal model with Weber's rational-legal model, forming a rational-goal model of the criminal justice system. This perspective is preoccupied with formal goals and rules, and the assumption is that it is possible to approach goals (such as organizational effectiveness) with rational organization and procedures, as characterized by Weber's vision of the formal bureaucracy. As applied to criminal justice, this model "[implies] an elaborate apparatus which processes arrests according to highly defined rules and procedures undertaken by 'experts' who perform the functions ascribed to them by highly defined formal roles, under a rigorous division of labor, and who are subject to scrutiny in a systematic and hierarchical pattern" (Feeley 1973, 410).

Theories within the rational-goal perspective might employ criminal justice effectiveness or efficiency as the dependent variable, and the rationality of procedures and decisions as the independent variable. One example of such a theory may be the effect of judicial compliance with *In re Gault* on the effectiveness of the criminal justice system (Lefstein, Stapleton, and Teitelbaum 1969). The problem with most theories employing the rational-goal model is that they *assume* effectiveness (an ambiguous term in these theories) is influenced by such factors as judicial compliance, and the theorists spend their efforts simply assessing the extent to which compliance exists and inferring the extent to which the system is effective. These theories are tautological, because they define effectiveness by such factors as compliance, and then measure compliance to determine effectiveness. Some theories stemming from the rational-goal perspective may squeak by our proposed tests of criminal justice theory, but they are generally not well-constructed theories.

According to Feeley (1973, 413–14), whereas the rational-goal model deals with "the *rational organization* pursuing its single set of goals," the functional-systems perspective has to do with "*rational individuals* who comprise the system … prosecutor, defense counsel, police, defendant, clerks … pursuing their various individual goals." This perspective results in much more complex theories than those stemming from the rational-goal model, because individuals often have different, and frequently conflicting, goals from organizations. Unlike the rational-goal model, the functional-systems model pays special attention to nongoal functions, such as the activities and means by which workers carry out their jobs. This approach recognizes that organizations have other needs besides furthering their goals, in ensuring their survival.

Probably the best example of a theoretical area within the functional-systems perspective is exchange theory (Blau 1964), which has to do with the effect on organizational outcomes of informal linkages between actors within and between organizations, and between organizations themselves. An excellent example of exchange theory applied to criminal justice is Eisenstein and Jacob's (1977) *Felony Justice*, which examined court outcomes — particularly rates of plea bargaining — finding the strongest influence on these outcomes to be characteristics of the courtroom workgroup, which is comprised of actors with different interests (defense attorneys, prosecutors, judges) but who recognize the need for smooth maintenance of the system. The stronger these linkages (the more familiar and stable the workgroup is), the more rationalized the court processes are, with greater plea bargaining rates and fewer trials.

The functional-systems perspective has probably had more impact on criminal justice theory development than any other organizational model. It allows one to study a criminal justice actor, with his or her own interests, in the context of an organization, with its own interests and goals, and attempt to explain what is produced by the interaction between the individual and organization.

Whereas the functional-systems perspective explores the relationship between individuals and organizations, the institutional approach is interested primarily in how organizations interact with their social, political, and economic environments in producing outcomes. The introduction of modern institutional theory (Meyer and Rowan 1978) into the organizational theory literature has prompted significant research in the area of criminal justice, but only in very recent times (Crank and Langworthy 1992; Crank 1994; Mastrofski and Ritti 2000). According to institutional theory, organizations face environmental pressures to which they must succumb in order to survive; however, at its core the organization lacks commitment to these changes, and responds by engaging in such practices as the adoption of ceremonial structures. Police departments can be viewed as institutionalized organizations, and the development of community policing within a department may be a ceremonial response to (1) the public's demand for better (or different) policing and (2) the department's economic survival (Crank 1994). Removal of police chiefs after negative incidents (such as the Rodney King beating) may also be viewed as a ceremonial or institutional response (Crank and Langworthy 1992).

Sociopolitical Perspective

Many of the sociopolitical perspectives that have been adopted when forming criminal justice theories stem from conflict and consensus (Hagan 1989b). Conflict and consensus are two contrasting perspectives of the nature of society, and more specifically, the role of government in society. According to the consensus perspective, government's role is to reconcile the interests of different groups of people, and in normal society the government is able to do so. Society forms a broad consensus about what sorts of behaviors are pathological, and defines them as criminal, punishing those who commit the behaviors. This perspective is influenced strongly by Durkheim, and adopts the view that crime is functional for society: Since it is deviant and abnormal it brings the common public together in attempting to extinguish it.

On the other hand, the conflict model sees society as divided into interest groups between which there will always be conflict, as they compete for power, prestige, and material goods. The government is unable to reconcile all their differences, so it represents the interests of the most powerful groups, which attempt to continually preserve their position by oppressing the less powerful. Conflict theory is strongly influenced by Marx, who believed that at the very basis of society is class struggle between the "haves" and "have nots." From the conflict perspective, the criminal justice system is used to define and carry out laws in such a way that, as one book title says, "The rich get richer and the poor get prison" (Reiman 1984).[9]

An example of a consensus theory of criminal justice is Gottfredson and Hindelang's (1979a) examination of the effect a behavior's "seriousness" — as measured by the degree of harm to the victim — has on whether the victim reports the crime to criminal justice officials. From their perspective there is a widely held consensus that behavior past a certain threshold of seriousness belongs on the turf of the criminal justice system. Their article was written in response to Black's (1976) *The Behavior of Law*, which did not claim to be in the conflict vein, but made many assertions which are clearly compatible with conflict theory.

Conflict theory has been generated at all points of the criminal justice process: generating laws, reporting crimes, arresting, prosecuting, and sentencing offenders, and holding parole hearings. Myers and Talarico's (1986) study of sentencing in Georgia is an excellent example of a conflict theory that goes beyond asking the standard question: "Are minorities discriminated against in the criminal justice system?" Myers and Talarico (1986) examined the influence the interaction of a county's racial political representation and an offender's race within that county has on the offender's sentence. In counties where blacks had political control, whites were actually more likely to get prison sentences than were blacks. In counties where whites had political control, blacks were more severely sentenced than were whites.

Although conflict theory has perhaps been more commonly explored in terms of criminal justice discrimination once a behavior has been labeled criminal, the most broad-based conflict theories examine the beginning of the criminal justice process — namely, the formulation of laws. McGarrell and Castellano (1991), drawing from three theories (Chambliss and Seidman 1982; Galliher and Cross 1983; Scheingold 1984), have formed a trilevel, integrated conflict theory of the criminal law formulation process. At the first level, highly differentiated social structures lead to more conflict, and thus an increased number of behaviors being defined as criminal. Intertwined with high social differentiation are cultural attitudes reinforcing myths of crime. Factors at the first level produce actual crime, and hence victimization, fear, and concern, and result in a punitive response by the criminal justice system. Because fear of crime, along with media attention, results in increased enforcement of laws defining behavior as criminal, it actually brings about more crime. Triggering events are the third level of influences on legislative policy. In this "unstable and volatile public policy arena ... [a] slight dislocation, a random event, a vocal political opportunist, or a disgruntled governmental bureaucrat, can trigger events which mobilize the political arena to consider and enact crime legislation and policy" (McGarrell and Castellano 1991, 188). Once new law is passed, making even more behaviors illegal, the amount of crime and criminal justice is increased, and the feedback cycle continues.

Even though some scholars (such as Hagan 1989b) believe that conflict and consensus theories can only take us so far in exploring criminal justice phenomena, there is little evidence of abatement in their use by criminal justice scholars. Because research in the conflict vein has focused very little on the exact processes by which discrimination occurs, there is still much room for theoretical development and elaboration in conflict approaches to justice.

Objective vs. Subjective Perspective

Whereas the conflict and consensus perspectives relate to fundamental views of our political and social system, another dimension on which theory may be classified relates to our fundamental views of reality. Although it has been discussed by ancient philosophers, the question of whether objective realities exist or reality is socially constructed by observers has only been influencing social science theory for the past three decades.[10] A highly influential work by Burrell and Morgan (1979) divides the entire field of organization theory into four paradigms, organized along two dimensions. One of these dimensions ranges from objective to subjective (the other ranges from radical change to regulation). To Burrell and Morgan (1979), and many modern organizational theorists, a scholar's view on whether reality is objective or subjective substantially drives his or her theoretical work in social organization.

According to Burrell and Morgan, if a theorist who is examining the world without trying to change it adopts an objective approach, he or she is operating within the functionalist paradigm. A theorist who adopts a subjective stance is operating within the interpretivist paradigm. Much criminal justice theory has been driven by both of these paradigms. From a functionalist standpoint, the world is treated "as if it were a hard, external, objective reality" (1979, 3). A theorist approaching criminal justice as such would consider crime to be a social fact. In contrast, theorists working in the interpretivist paradigm view the world as comprised of "the subjective experience[s] of individuals in the creation of the social world…" (1979, 3). To subjectivists, facts are rarely facts; instead, they are part of a constructed reality. The same behavior is seen as "crime" to some but not to others. Some argue that behavior is observable, but can be construed in multiple ways; others argue that the very nature of subjective perception implies that any "objective" behavior is itself unobservable.

Versions of conflict theory that argue that behavior is more likely to be labeled criminal under certain power conditions and crime is more likely to be seen as serious under certain power conditions do fall into the interpretivist paradigm because they imply different realities depending upon one's position of power. On the other hand, a broader approach to crime within the interpretivist paradigm is constructionism. The constructionist view suggests that different realities may exist for different people, but it is possible to manipulate the commonly accepted reality through a variety of techniques. Unlike conflict theory, from the broader constructionist standpoint crime may be constructed for reasons other than power and prestige incentives. Rafter (1990) cites Gusfield's (1963) treatment of Prohibition and Erikson's (1966) work on the Puritans' behavior toward deviance as classic examples of moral incentives to construct realities. More recently, Gusfield (1981) has shown how moral crusaders (Mothers against Drunk Driving) have been able to bring such behavior as drunk driving more into the realm of the criminal justice system, by defining it as criminal behavior rather than as traffic negligence.

The objective-to-subjective continuum can be used to classify many more types of theories than those addressed above. For example, crime rates have been viewed not as measures of real crime, but as an output of organizational outcomes, or varying organizational realities, such that the Uniform Crime Report rate may reflect more about the criminal justice agencies that collect data rather than about crime itself (McCleary, Nienstedt, and Erven 1982).

Type of Response

Although we have already mentioned some of the different types of responses that serve as subjects for criminal justice theory, there is enough variation in this area that it deserves some elaboration. Criminal justice theorists have studied lawmaking, decisions, attitudes, ideologies, structures, styles of behavior, and routines — all as outcome concepts.[11]

Development of Laws

McGarrell and Castellano's (1991) theory (described earlier in this chapter) is aimed toward explaining the formulation of laws, which determine what sorts of behavior are criminal in our society. Most of the theoretical literature on lawmaking is guided by consensus, conflict, or constructionist perspectives.

Decisions

Probably the most studied dependent variable in criminal justice theory pertains to the gap between what laws have been formulated and what enforcement actually occurs. Only since the mid-1970s have scholars recognized and begun to study discretion (Walker 1992). The most commonly studied forms of discretion are the decision to arrest, the decision to prosecute, and the sentencing decision. Gottfredson and Gottfredson (1988) have provided what is probably the most comprehensive overview of research on discretionary decision making in the criminal justice system. Theories about the decision to report a crime also fall into our scope of criminal justice theory because the outcome is (or might be) the invocation of the formal criminal justice system.

Attitudes

Attitudes are usually studied as intermediate variables, with the assumption that they eventually influence behavioral response. Of course, there has always been debate in social psychology on the extent to which this assumption is true (Ajzen 1982, 1987; Schuman and Johnson 1976). The study of attitudes is often done in conjunction with the study of culture. For example, Church (1985), in testing a theory that court participants form legal cultures to cope with organizational demands, measured the similarity of attitudes of the various courtroom actors toward such concepts as disposition time and negotiation. He explicitly stated that in doing so he was assuming that attitudes translated into behavioral patterns. Nardulli, Flemming, and Eisenstein (1985), on the other hand, studied the same outcome, but looked at behavioral patterns instead of attitudes. Both have their shortcomings: Church (1985) had to infer that behavior resulted from process (the process was established with cultural attitudes); Nardulli and his colleagues (1985) had to assume process (a model of legal culture) from behavioral outcome patterns.

Ideologies

Whereas attitudes usually contain rather specific (or at least easily identifiable) targets, ideologies are more general philosophical orientations. In the realm of criminal justice, examples of popular ideologies are retribution (believing criminals should get what they deserve) and rehabilitation (believing we should try to help reform criminals). Some have summarized the primary ideological dimension in criminal justice as simply liberal ("soft" on crime) versus conservative ("tough" on crime) (Walker 1985). One example of a criminal justice theory studying ideologies is Duffee's (1990) *Explaining Criminal Justice*. Duffee holds that the extent to which a local criminal justice system is Moralist (promoting retribution) or Welfare-oriented (promoting rehabilitation) depends on the community's independence from nonlocal sources and the degree of cooperation within subsystems in the community. Much theory is also generated at explaining ideological orientations of individual actors in the criminal justice system.

Structures

We have already noted that structures are another type of response, or at least are intermediate variables preceding behavioral response, in criminal justice theory. Examples of theories of structure in criminal justice are Langworthy's (1986) and Maguire's (2003) studies of police organizational structure, DiIulio's (1987) examination of correctional organization structure, and Eisenstein and Jacob's (1977) work on court structure.

Styles of Behavior

Other than making law or decisions about what will be done with people engaging in potentially criminal behavior, criminal justice actors also exhibit a variety of overt behaviors in their work. Scholars have explored differences in the behavioral styles exhibited by criminal justice actors in their day-to-day work. For example, Muir (1977) has looked at police officer styles in dealing with suspects among others (see Snipes and Mastrofski [1990], for a review of other work in this area). He forms a typology of four styles of officers (Avoiders, Enforcers, Reciprocators, and Professionals). The behavioral styles officers adopt are developed from their capacity to project themselves into the circumstances of others, and from their ability to integrate the use of coercion into their moral framework. Carter (1974) has developed a similar typology for prosecutors, forming four types: Teachers, Analysts, Competitors, and Crime Fighters. The style of behavior a prosecutor develops depends on his or her commitment to due process and crime control.

Routines

In addition to discrete decision making, criminal justice theorists frequently study the formation of routines — methods formed by justice system actors to deal with the processing of cases. In this research, the process by which a case is handled is an outcome variable in itself, regardless of the final disposition. Prominent examples of this type of theoretical research include Waegel's (1981) study of how police detectives respond to organizational pressures in developing routines for slotting, selecting, and investigating cases, and Sudnow's (1965) analogous study of methods public defenders develop to classify cases. These studies typically involve examining the organizational influences on the routinization of response to potentially criminal behavior.

Level of Explanation

One could classify criminal justice theories as micro or macro, but this distinction is rather arbitrary (Alexander, Giesen, Munch, and Smelser 1987); levels of explanation range from small units, such as individuals, to large structures, such as societies. It is safe to say that the predominant level of explanation employed in the "progressive era paradigm" described earlier in this chapter (Walker 1992) is the individual. The dependent variable is frequently the behavior or attitudes of individual actors within the criminal justice system. The set of independent variables includes individual attributes, and may also include variables at higher levels of explanation, such as characteristics of the city or region in which they reside. Other examples of higher levels of explanation include situations, groups, or subcultures (such as police subcultures or courtroom work groups), local organizations (such as police departments), communities, local governments, state governments, and criminal justice agencies, and so on.

Most theories use the same level of explanation for both independent and dependent variables. It is rare for a higher level of explanation to be explained by lower level concepts. For example, we would not typically explain variations in state incarceration rates using the characteristics of individuals. More commonly, lower-level phenomena are explained by concepts at that level and higher levels. For example, R. Worden's (1994) explanation of police use of force draws upon concepts at the individual, situational, and organizational levels, to predict use of force at the individual level. In other words, when a police officer decides to use force against a suspect, the decision is motivated by characteristics of the individual officer and suspect (such as age, sex, temperament, etc.), characteristics of the situation (such as whether the suspect is resisting arrest), and characteristics of the police organization (such as the departmental policies on use of force). Theories like this, in which one or more of the independent variables are from a higher level of explanation than the dependent variable, are known as "contextual" theories. There is now a great deal of innovation emerging in the statistical modeling techniques used to test such theories (e.g., Bryk and Raudenbush 1992).

Institutional Arena

Theories of criminal justice may study areas directly located in the criminal justice system (as we think of it), or collectivities more indirectly related to criminal justice. In the first category are police, courts, and corrections. In the second category are legislatures, interest groups, executive decision-making bodies, media, victims, potential victims, community groups, and citizens-en-masse, among others. Some criminal justice theories are entirely contained within one institutional arena. Others examine responses to potentially criminal behavior that cross arenas in some fashion. Earlier in the chapter we discussed the exchange perspective, in which these different arenas and their environments are intrinsically connected. This seems to be the direction in which much criminal justice theory is moving, and as we will discuss in the conclusion, it is a movement from which we expect valuable contributions.

Another type of systemic theory does not so much address linkages between institutional arenas as it tries to explain criminal justice in such a broad fashion that it applies to any arena. Donald Black's (1976) *The Behavior of Law* is one such theory. His concept of law as a dependent variable is meant to apply to many aspects of the criminal justice system, including public perceptions of the seriousness of crime, victim reporting of crime, police use of arrest, prosecutorial decision to charge, judicial sentencing severity, and parole board decisions. In each of these cases, there will be more or less law, and Black believes five types of variables will explain the variation in law.[12]

FUTURE DIRECTIONS

Stephen Fuchs (1993)[13] presents a theory of scientific change, in which he argues that competition (present in almost any academic discipline) leads to scientific change, but the type of change depends on task uncertainty and mutual dependence. Task uncertainty refers to the degree of ambiguity there exists in how scientists perceive their mission. Mutual dependence pertains to the extent to which individuals in the particular field are socially integrated. The field of criminal justice is characterized by high task uncertainty and low mutual dependence:

high uncertainty because there is little consensus on such basic ideas as what constitutes criminal justice theory, and low dependence because instead of a core group of scholars focusing on criminal justice, research is done by scientists and practitioners working in a number of different domains, often ignorant of each other's work. This combination, Fuchs (1993, 946) argues, produces a fragmented scientific field:

> Such fields lack the strong and dense networks necessary to pro-duce facts, and so they engage in informal conversation instead.... There is not a great deal of confidence in the possibility to become scientific and objective, and so the self-understanding of weak fields is skeptical and critically reflexive.... Lacking unified research fronts that could define the overall direction of the discipline, weak fields do not really believe in the continuous progress of knowledge, and so there is a strong tendency to look back to the classics instead.[13] *

Fuchs's description of a fragmented scientific field describes the current state of criminal justice as an academic discipline. Fuchs also proposes that high task uncertainty and high mutual dependence result in the potential for "permanent discoveries," similar to Kuhn's (1970) notion of revolutionary change. In order to advance to the point where dramatic shifts in paradigm can occur, such that the state of theory can more fully develop, criminal justice as a field would need to become more integrated. Interested scholars would have to begin to guide the field, forming some consensus on where theory should go, such that theoretical research could proceed in a more organized and less frag-mented fashion.

In this chapter, we have shown that scholars in criminal justice cannot even agree upon what criminal justice is and what constitutes criminal justice theory. We have tried to present an initial framework for under-standing criminal justice theory, one which will certainly be met with criticism, but which at least might spur the field to some meaningful discussion. Because criminal justice theory is so fragmented (as should be recognized from our brief review), it seems to us that integration will be important in the development of a more cohesive theoretical enterprise. Several of the dimensions along which we have classified criminal justice theory are ripe for integration.

Sociopolitical perspectives that are seemingly bipolar may actu-ally be compatible if brought together in the right theoretical context.

---

* From *Social Forces*, Volume 71, Issue 4, Copyright © by the University of North Carolina Press. Used by permission of the publisher.

Conflict notions may apply under some circumstances, and consensus under others. Durkheimian theory suggests that certain conditions (such as war) can create social solidarity. Under certain political environments and idiosyncratic historical processes, then, a consensus perspective may be appropriate in explaining criminal justice phenomena. In other times and circumstances, the conflict perspective may better explain the same phenomena. An integrated theory would develop a framework for predicting when conflict and when consensus concepts would more powerfully explain our response to potentially criminal behavior. Objective and subjective perspectives again seem too opposite to bring together, yet postmodernists have begun to do just this. For example, Giddens's (1979) theory of structuration proposes that we subjectively construct structures, but after this process occurs, these structures have objective properties that can in turn influence those who constructed them. Given that crime is partly subjective and partly objective, and that both behavior and our response to behavior feed off each other reciprocally, it seems that structurationism might be very relevant to our understanding of crime and criminal justice.

Criminal justice theories explain many different types of responses, but certainly these responses are related to each other, and these relationships can be explored in integrated theory. Attitudes, behaviors, ideologies, and decisions undoubtedly affect each other. As criminal justice theory progresses, it should begin to explore the relationships between multiple response types rather than just one response type at a time.

Criminal justice theorists are already bridging levels of explanation, as they develop contextual theories that use more than one level of independent variables. On the other hand, very rarely do theories examine the interactional relationships across levels. In other words, the magnitude and nature of an effect of individual level attributes on some response might depend on where that individual is positioned in a higher-level context (such as group, organization, or society). For example, overzealous, aggressive police officers may behave differently toward potential suspects if they are in innovative and progressive police departments than if they serve in departments with organizational styles more compatible with their own.

Finally, we have already stressed the need to link institutional arenas when developing criminal justice theory. Of all the possible types of integration discussed above, this has probably been the most common in recent criminal justice theory. Much remains to be done.

This chapter has attempted to demonstrate how weak the state of criminal justice theory is, but also has suggested that it can be salvaged.

If criminal justice theory is to come into its own right, scholars who are highly motivated toward its furtherance must begin to organize, settling on parameters and basic definitions, and beginning to forge its future. The various chapters in this volume provide an exemplar for the stages of theory building in criminal justice.

NOTES

1. See also Akers (1992, 10), arguing that confusion between these fields of study may have impaired the academic standing of criminology among sociologists.
2. Several evaluations of criminal justice education in the early to mid-1970s noted that criminal justice curricula were too oriented toward professional training. Brandstatter and Hoover (1976, 47), for example, argued that criminal justice programs "include far too many professionally oriented courses" and "place undue emphasis on curricula designed to train students to perform specific operational tasks."
3. These perverse incentives can lead to interagency conflict, as is often portrayed by the media. As the Weasel, in Wambaugh's *The Glitter Dome* complained, "Times are pretty goddamn bad … when cops started using the same lies to each other that they should save for the real Enemies in the judiciary" (Wambaugh 1981, 142).
4. Some take this perspective one step further, arguing that because the ever-present conflict between the component institutions hinders the effective functioning of the justice process, the system should be reorganized. In *Organizing the Non-System*, Skoler (1977) argues that the separate criminal justice institutions should be unified and integrated so that they will coordinate more smoothly.
5. In some countries, such as Uganda and Zambia, the police are closely linked with the military force. Although this type of merger may enhance the crime control function of the police, it probably detracts from the due process functions.
6. The importance of informal relationships among groups of actors, both within and between organizations, now occupies a central role in organizational theory. The study of these informal relationships is known as network analysis. From a network perspective, the structure of an organization can only be fully understood by observing the numerous networks of relationships both within an organization, and with actors from other organizations (Nohria 1992). Of particular interest to criminal justice is the networking which occurs between actors at the *border* of different organizations that work together. From the network perspective, Nohria argues, "the environment consists of a field of relationships that bind organizations together." This environment, known in organization theory as an "interorganizational field" (DiMaggio and Powell

1983, 148; Warren 1967), is where actors from different organizations perform "boundary spanning" roles (Lipsky 1980; Reiss and Bordua 1967) which enhance the reliance of each organization upon the other.

7. From *Not Just Deserts: A Republican Theory of Criminal Justice* by J. Braithwaite and P. Pettit, 1990, pp. 756–57. By permission of Oxford University Press, Inc.
8. Or it may belong in that murky area of "normative theory" which is valid theory but not traditional scientific theory, and is best organized under "philosophy" or similar nomenclature.
9. For a review of different versions of conflict theory, and for an integrated conflict theory, see Vold, Bernard, and Snipes (1998).
10. Berger and Luckman's (1966) *Social Construction of Reality* is often hailed as the seminal piece spurring much discourse and theory in this area.
11. Although this is probably not a comprehensive list of potential outcomes for legitimate criminal justice theory, it probably covers at least nine-tenths of existing theory.
12. Black calls these dimensions stratification, organization, culture, morphology, and social control. His book consists of a number of hypotheses between various aspects of each dimension and the amount of law.
13. From *Social Forces*, Vol. 71: Issue 4. Copyright © by the University of North Carolina Press. Used by permission of the publisher.

3

DURKHEIM'S COMPARATIVE METHOD AND CRIMINAL JUSTICE THEORY

Gregory J. Howard and Joshua D. Freilich

INTRODUCTION

It has become quite clear that globalization has had considerable effects on matters of crime and justice around the world. Consequently, many now clamor that criminology and criminal justice should explicitly attend to the international dimensions of their subjects. In *Comparative Criminal Justice*, for instance, Charles Fields and Richter Moore (1996, xi) contend: "Although the world has gotten smaller, the crime problem has not. More so than ever before, it is vital that criminologists, and others whose studies include crime and criminality, move into the comparative and 'global' arena." In the same book, and perhaps with a bit more ethnocentricity, Gerhard Mueller and Freda Adler (1996, x) proclaim: "Comparative and international criminal justice, once regarded as an esoteric subject, now is central to American criminal justice because we are part of the world — maybe the center of the world — as receivers of and contributors to crime and justice worldwide." In short, as boundaries of space and time are removed by the rapid advancement of global communications, transportation, and commerce, the production and maintenance of social order has become increasingly problematic and the institutions of crime and justice have assumed a stronger role in the articulation and defense of such order.

A number of reasons are generally trotted out to justify the pursuit of comparative crime and justice studies. We will briefly address five reasons for engaging comparative studies of crime and justice. First of all, comparative studies promise to illuminate the contours of other societies. Since one can only appreciate a police practice or a punishment policy in the light of a society's economic and social history, a serious student of comparative criminal justice will achieve an informed perspective on world history, one that is likely to stimulate an appreciation of diversity and yet also a recognition of certain universals in society (i.e., rules and laws, police, punishment, and so forth) (Fairchild 1993). Second, as the process of globalization continues apace and new transnational crimes proliferate (e.g., human smuggling, financial fraud, drug trafficking, nuclear arms sales, cyber attacks, terrorism), innovative and effective criminal justice responses will be sought. Comparative crime and justice studies offer the chance to inform these responses with knowledge about practices and policies found around the world. Such knowledge might also help societies improve their responses as well to more traditional crimes such as murder, rape, assault, and theft (Fairchild 1993; Moore and Fields 1996; Howard, Newman, and Pridemore 2000). Third, because students of crime and justice harbor a native understanding of their home country's response to crime and justice, comparative studies can reveal previously hidden assumptions about the subject matter and expose advantages and disadvantages associated with native responses (Fairchild 1993; Moore and Fields 1996). Fourth, a society's crime and justice response is likely to be costly both in terms of financial commitments (i.e., salaries of police officers, judges, prosecutors, probation officers, and prison guards, to name only a few functionaries of criminal justice, as well as expenditures on patrol cars, computers, laboratory analysis, training, buildings, and other hardware) and human rights (i.e., discrimination in the enforcement of laws, freedom of expression, security, freedom of movement). Comparative criminal justice studies provide a mechanism for assessing the performance of various criminal justice complexes and ensuring accountability for criminal justice policy and practice (Maguire, Howard, and Newman 1998). From this position, comparative criminal justice scholars act in the role of Ralf Dahrendorf's (1970, 50) "fool," in that they "doubt everything that is obvious, make relative all authority, ask all those questions that no one else dares to ask." While raising their voices in spirited and informed criticism of criminal justice policy and practice, these students of comparative criminal justice should not be seen as troublesome naysayers but rather as checks on error and outright abuse of authority (Howard, Newman, and Pridemore 2000).

Fifth, comparative criminal justice studies, as this chapter hopes to demonstrate, offer significant opportunities to test and elaborate theories of criminal justice (Moore and Fields 1996; Howard, Newman, and Pridemore 2000).

Although the development of theory is listed as one justification for comparative studies of crime and justice, it seems a fair generalization to say that most comparative studies of criminal justice are descriptive in nature. This should not be read as an assault on descriptive studies; they are essential to a vibrant field of comparative criminal justice as they service such other demands of comparative criminal justice studies as critique and cultural awareness. Still, a well-rounded comparative criminal justice also needs theoretical attention. The purpose of this chapter is to point the way toward a more explicit and serious effort to test and elaborate criminal justice theories with Emile Durkheim's comparative method.

ON DURKHEIM'S COMPARATIVE METHOD

To begin our discussion of Durkheim's comparative method, we should indicate immediately that there is no need to use a particular theory with the comparative method, which can be used to test and elaborate any theory. It is true that the comparative method is sometimes conflated with particular theoretical approaches (i.e., social evolutionism and structural functionalism), but this conflation is not necessary and, given the disparagement of these two theoretical perspectives, probably has stunted its development and practice (Payne 1973). Moreover, the comparative method is not limited to particular substantive interests, as Richard Tomasson (1978, 2) observes:

> Comparative sociology is not, though it is frequently so regarded, a "field" of sociology. Rather it is a methodological orientation which is, or at least should be, warp and woof of the approaches of all the substantive areas of sociology. Looking about our disparate discipline we find marked differences in the use of the comparative perspective. It is well-developed in demography and political sociology, less so, for example, in the family and criminology.

Since the comparative method can be applied to a whole range of theories addressed to a host of dependent variables relevant to many disciplines, it should be useful to criminal justice scholars interested in promoting theory development. In order to see how Durkheim's comparative method might be useful, however, we should first be more explicit about its logic and procedure.

The comparative method has a long history in sociology because "virtually all of the nineteenth and early twentieth century 'pioneers' ... of modern sociology, at least all of those in the macrosociological tradition, were comparativist" (Tomasson 1978, 3). Still, of all the so-called "pioneers" of sociology, perhaps no one had more to say about this method of study than Emile Durkheim (1982) in *The Rules of Sociological Method* (Kapsis 1977).

The bedrock upon which Durkheim's comparative method rests is the concept of social fact. According to Durkheim (1982, 52), social facts are "manners of acting, thinking, and feeling external to the individual, which are invested with a coercive power by virtue of which they exercise control over him." As this definition makes clear, social facts exist outside of any given individual and exert a compelling influence on that person. While it is always possible for an individual to resist social facts, for Durkheim does not deny individual consciousness and will, the objective existence of social facts can only be denied at one's own peril. Thus, Durkheim (1982, 51) writes:

> I am not forced to speak French with my compatriots, nor to use the legal currency, but it is impossible for me to do otherwise. If I tried to escape the necessity, my attempt would fail miserably. As an industrialist nothing prevents me from working with the processes and methods of the previous century, but if I do I will most certainly ruin myself.

To draw this point closer to our own time, nothing prevents us from preparing this chapter on an electric typewriter, but social facts dictate that our efforts to submit the manuscript over the Internet with such an instrument will be an exercise in frustration. In short, a social fact can be detected by the "power of external coercion which it exerts or is capable of exerting upon individuals," a power which is recognizable in the consequences and sanctions visited upon the recalcitrant individual (Durkheim 1982, 56). Hence, social facts are most discernible when they are resisted, which is one reason why deviants play such a vital role in community life.

As for the origins of social facts, Durkheim (1982, 56) maintains that they are a product of a collectivity; they are an outgrowth of a "shared existence, of actions and reactions called into play between the consciousnesses of individuals." On this view, association between individuals, and not the individuals themselves, is central to the constitution of society and the social facts that characterize it. Resorting to a biological analogy, Durkheim (1982, 128–29) explains his position in this way:

It is indeed certain that in the living cell there are only molecules of crude matter. But they are in association, and it is this association which is the cause of the new phenomena which characterize life, even the germ of which it is impossible to find in a single one of these associated elements. This is because the whole does not equal the sum of its parts; it is something different, whose properties differ from those displayed by the parts from which it is formed…. By virtue of this principle, society is not the mere sum of individuals, but the system formed by their association represents a specific reality which has its own characteristics. Undoubtedly no collective entity can be produced if there are no individual consciousnesses; this is a necessary but not a sufficient condition. In addition, these consciousnesses must be associated and combined, but combined in a certain way. It is from this combination that social life arises and consequently it is this combination which explains it.

As Durkheim makes clear in this passage, society and social facts take on a life of their own, distinct from the varied lives of individuals. Because social phenomena are distinctive in this way, they can only be explained with reference to other, antecedent social facts and "not among the states of individual consciousness" (Durkheim 1982, 134). Moreover, because social facts are determined by the fact of association, it follows that social facts vary with the form of association or "according to how the constituent elements in a society are grouped" (Durkheim 1982, 135). It is in this manner that social morphology, or social types, take on particular importance for Durkheim's comparative method.

For Durkheim, then, the scientific study of society means that one is engaged in the search for covariation among social facts. Put most simply, a sociologist may wish to explain the variance in some dependent variable (social fact "y") with variation in some independent variable (social fact "x"). Of course, societies are very complex phenomena filled with many very interesting social facts, and these social facts and the relationships between them can vary with forms of association. Indeed, this embarrassment of riches can leave the student of society more confused than informed in the end, much like Dostoevsky's (1864/1974) underground man whose bout with excessive consciousness left him sick and spiteful. As an antidote, Durkheim suggests the restraint of a comparative method that proceeds through three stages. Because societies can fluctuate greatly and this variation can confound the search for regularities between x and y, one begins the comparative method by considering a particular instance of society and searching for covariation between the two variables in that limited venue. If the student of society is fortunate and makes good use of rich evidence within this single society, some relationship between x and y might be hypothecated. In an effort to test and elaborate this theoretical proposition, the student might next engage the second stage of the comparative method which involves examining the relationship between x and y in societies similar to the one in which the hypothesis was first excavated. If the relationship between x and y is not unique to the first society examined, then it also should hold in all societies of a similar type. To the extent that the hypothesis is refuted by the evidence produced in this second stage of the comparative method, then the theoretical statement can be elaborated in order to take account of various limiting circumstances (i.e., the who, where, and when elements of Dubin's [1978] theoretical structure). Only when a theoretical account for the relationship between x and y holds within similar societies does the comparative method of investigation move to the third stage. In these third stage studies, the student examines the relationship between x and y in dissimilar societies. If the relationship between the two variables of interest differs by type of society, then a search for conditional statements can ensue with which to elaborate the initial theoretical stance. In short, while the comparative method does not require that one begin with a particular theoretical approach, it does promise to systematize efforts at theoretical elaboration.

One central theme of the present book is that criminal justice studies are theoretically impoverished, and we maintain that Durkheim's comparative method might serve as one crucial remedy to this sorry situation. Starting with a single case, the comparative method provides guidance on how to articulate and elaborate theoretical propositions through a systematic study of an increasing constellation of cases. In other words, the method encourages theory elaboration through a recursive exchange between observing and hypothecating, the very stuff of the scientific method, accomplished in the only way possible with studies of society, indirect experimentation, as artificial manipulation of social facts is not possible (nor ethical).

While the possibilities are legion for Durkheim's comparative method to contribute to the development of criminal justice theory, we need also to be mindful of a number of vexing problems with the practice of this method. For one thing, the comparative method as borrowed from Durkheim requires that a definition of society be proffered. In other words, what is the unit of analysis (see Ragin [1981] for an important distinction between "observational units" and "explanatory units")? While defining society may seem easy enough, when one gets down to brass tacks, it is rather difficult to do (Marsh 1967; Etzioni and Dubow 1970; Ragin 1981). Instead of laboring over the issue, most studies of comparative criminology and criminal justice simply accept nation-states as the unit of analysis, and therefore as the definition of society, although this practice need not be followed, even if the availability of data for this unit encourages it. Moreover, a criminal justice scholar might not want to study societies at all, preferring along with Duffee (1990) to consider communities, in which case data about the nation-state would be less tempting. The point is that the comparative method, when pursued regally, forces a confrontation with the meaning of society (or community). Reaching a tolerable and practical definition of either concept is a main challenge to the comparative method.

Related to this problem of defining society is the requirement of the comparative method that societies be typified as well. In other words, after the first stage of the method in which the investigator is charged with the examination of a single society, he is then sent off to consider, first, similar societies and, then, dissimilar societies. Of course, this mission presupposes some conception of society as well as a division of instances of society into particular types (e.g., industrialized, tribal, adherents to adversarial justice schemes, democratized, and so forth). It requires one to posit a universe of societies and to identify relevant species of society, for as Durkheim (1982, 157) presses "*one cannot explain a social fact of any complexity save on condition that one follows its entire development throughout all social species*" (italics in original). So in a sense, the comparative method requires a metatheory of society before it can proceed, although as noted previously the lazy tendency to equate nation-state with society largely ignores this responsibility (Ragin 1981). As Ragin (1981, 109) puts it, the main problem with classifying societies "is that there is a limited number of societies and that any ranking or categorization of them can be described conceptually in a variety of ways." In other words, "listings of industrial and nonindustrial societies might perfectly reproduce the listings of meritocratic and not meritocratic societies" (Ragin 1981, 109). When concepts are articulated at high levels of abstraction, empirical links can be tenuous at best.

Another important limitation of Durkheim's comparative method, which derives from the definition of society as well, is that processes of globalization, in which societies become increasingly interpenetrated, threaten to undermine the independence of observations. In other words, Durkheim's method presupposes that societies can be delineated and hermetically sealed off from one another, that social facts in one society are not influenced by social facts in another society. However, as global communications and commerce, as well as the movement of people, accelerate between societies, the assumed independence of these units becomes increasingly untenable. This problem has led some sociologists to reject the idea of distinct societies altogether in favor of world systems theory in which one overarching social unit is posited and studied (McMichael 1990).

A final difficulty concerning the practice of Durkheim's comparative method to be discussed here is the collection of valid and reliable observations. In order to study the relationship between x (crime) and y (punishment) in two types of societies (i.e., industrial and nonindustrial), one must proceed under the assumption that both social facts (i.e., crime and punishment) exist in the two types of societies. Moreover, one must also take for granted that crime or punishment in one type of society is coterminous with that in the other. Of course, it is well-known that the definition of crime varies dramatically from society to society and that the recording practices of various police agencies, for example, are more or less rigorous. As a result, what counts as crime in one society, as a result of cultural differences in prohibitions as well as organizational differences in police institutions, among other possibilities, may be much different from what is counted in another, perhaps even "similar," society. The same goes for punishment, as Newman (1978) explains in *The Punishment Response*. In short, cultural differences in the measurement of crime and justice variables may leave comparative scholars with observations that are more or less valid and reliable.

Sources of data for testing theories of criminal justice with Durkheim's comparative method are varied (Newman and Howard 1999). Crime and justice data can be obtained from a number of official sources, and victimization data are now collected through the auspices of the International Crime Victimization Survey as well as a limited number of national victimization survey projects (e.g., the Crime Victimization Survey in the United States and the British Crime Survey, among others). While self-report surveys have been undertaken only haphazardly at the international level, they also represent another possibility for data collection about matters of crime and justice around the world. As for measures of independent variables of potential interest, criminal justice theorists can call upon a host of international agencies for assistance, such as the United Nations, World Bank, International Monetary Fund, Amnesty International, and more (Newman 1999; Howard, Newman, and Pridemore 2000).

Since official crime and justice data are commonly used in comparative criminology and criminal justice studies, we wish to say a few words about them in particular. Official sources of crime and justice data include the United Nations, Interpol, and for a limited selection of countries, the European Sourcebook. These official sources of data all derive from the records of police agencies and include figures on reported crime, criminal justice resources, convictions, sentencing practices, and so forth. The World Health Organization is another source of official data on crime and mortality in a nation, with figures produced by medical personnel, but this data source is likely to be limited in value for criminal justice theorists as it does not cover the behavior of criminal justice institutions. While there are well-known problems associated with the collection of official data at the national level, these potential sources of error are exacerbated at the international level by the disparate quality of national data collection systems, efforts of national governments to massage their representation of crime and their official response to it for international consumption, and differences in definition for many concepts central to the study of criminal justice (e.g., police, arrest, conviction, punishment, and so forth).

Responding to the problems of data collection associated with official records, victimization data from the International Crime Victimization Survey and certain national level victimization survey projects are another viable source of crime and justice information. While the sources of error in victimization surveys are different from those found in official reports, there are certainly threats to the reliability and validity of the representations of crime and justice in these figures as well, such as cultural differences in perceptions of crime, memory lapses, reactivity, and so forth (Zvekic 1996). Moreover, while relevant to studies of criminal justice, these victimization surveys do not provide information about variations in criminal justice behavior.

One glaring need for the advancement of comparative studies is investigations into the triangulation of various sources of crime and justice data. That errors will be present in each source of data is widely understood, but it would be useful to know whether the different crime and justice reports converge on a singular depiction of crime and justice. In lieu of confirmation about the validity and reliability of crime and justice data available from official and victimization sources, criminal justice scholars can begin to move theory testing and elaboration along with Durkheim's comparative method by accumulating their own observations. Such bootstrap efforts to collect one's own observations will also more likely ensure a tight fit between concepts and content. As efforts at data collection are never cheap nor easy, the best way to begin this exercise is with the beacon of theory.

ORGANIZATIONAL THEORY AND
THE CRIMINAL COURTS

The purpose of this section of the chapter is to study a theory of criminal justice that attends to courts, with an eye on the possibilities for elaboration of this theory that Durkheim's comparative method affords. While there is no denying that criminal justice theory has been deployed to explain variations in criminal justice behaviors across societies (e.g., Bayley 1985; Nadelmann 1993; Huggins 1998; Maguire, Newman, and Howard, 1998; Maguire and Schulte-Murray 2001; Banks 2001), we think that advancement in comparative criminal justice theory will benefit most from a systematic and detailed consideration of specific criminal justice theories directed to different aspects of the criminal justice response. The study of an organizational theory of criminal courts that follows is an effort in this direction.

Here we focus on Malcolm Feeley's (1979) *The Process is the Punishment*. Drawing upon an organizational perspective consistent with the one presented by James Eisenstein and Herbert Jacob (1977) in *Felony Justice*, Feeley's volume presents a systematic effort to develop an organizational theory about criminal justice behavior in a lower criminal court. While Feeley's investigation of court process is limited to a single United States city (New Haven, Connecticut), the organizational theory developed in his book offers myriad possibilities for extending and elaborating comparative studies of criminal courts. Our discussion will be methodical in that after first contextualizing Feeley's research and demonstrating how organizational theory moves beyond a bureaucratic view of criminal courts, we will then seek out the structure of organizational theory and then indicate how the theory might be tested and elaborated through the comparative method described above.

Contextualizing Feeley's Research

As we have already noted, Feeley conducted a study on one lower court (the Court of Common Pleas) in New Haven, Connecticut. Although the time frame of the study is not explicitly stated, it appears to have been conducted in the 1970s. Feeley's examination of this lower court consisted of observing and interviewing courtroom participants as well as surveying over 1600 criminal cases. While Feeley did utilize some quantitative analyses, the bulk of his study is based upon qualitative findings. Since this court only processed misdemeanors or lesser felonies (in which the maximum sentence was a year or less in jail), Feeley maintains that his findings are not necessarily applicable to more serious cases (although the organizational theory employed by Feeley was earlier applied to felony courts in Baltimore, Chicago, and Detroit by Eisenstein and Jacob [1977]). Feeley explains that he examined a lower court as opposed to a court that exclusively handled felony cases since "next to the police, the lower criminal courts play the most important role in forming citizen impressions of the American system of criminal justice" (Feeley 1979, xxvii).

"Why New Haven?" one might ask. As Feeley (1979, xx) explains, it was convenient since:

> I was at Yale during the period I conducted this research, and the courthouse was just a few blocks away from my office. This proximity allowed me to spend a great deal of time in the courthouse, maintaining close connections over a long period....

While the location of the courthouse allowed Feeley to observe judicial proceedings regularly and his close connections permitted behind the scenes access that enriched his understanding of this court, one will surely ask straight away: "Yes, but are the findings generalizable?" In other words, one wonders whether the theory of courts developed by Feeley from his study of a single court in New Haven can be usefully applied to understanding judicial behavior in other courts. Feeley (1979, xxxii) argues that the observations are generalizable to other lower courts because New Haven "is not so atypical as to be unique." Of course, this question of generalizability is an empirical one and is attuned to the fourth element of the structure of theory presented by Dubin (1978), the who, where, and when limitations. As we have observed previously, the comparative method can help to answer this question.

Problems with Bureaucratic Views of Criminal Courts

When James Eisenstein and Herbert Jacob (1977) and later Malcolm Feeley (1979) published their books on criminal courts, they were responding in large measure to a prevailing view of criminal courts as bureaucracies. This bureaucratic view of criminal courts naturally has its foundations in the sociology of Max Weber and is linked especially to the work of Abraham Blumberg (1967) in his book *Criminal Justice*. The image advanced by Blumberg pictures an assembly line process of justice in which specialized legal workers apply the law in a routine manner in order to dispose of an unseemly mass of cases. In other words, the crush of burgeoning caseloads leads actors in criminal courts to apply bureaucratic logic in order to increase their efficiency. On this model, the ideal of adversarial justice is replaced by a stale application of generalized procedures for resolving cases that might as well be carried out by computers rather than human actors.

Of course, both Eisenstein and Jacob as well as Feeley reject this bureaucratic view as inconsistent with actual behavior in the criminal courts. Accordingly, Eisenstein and Jacob (1977, 9) write:

> We do not agree that courts constitute a bureaucracy; they lack the hierarchy of bureaucratic organizations. Moreover, we do not think courtroom dispositions are assembly line operations. Although many cases flow through courtrooms, and most are given little time on any particular day, each receives a remarkable amount of individualized treatment. As we shall show, one could not substitute a computer for the courtroom as one can for most assembly line operations.

For his part, Feeley (1979, 16) raises similar objections:

> But to conclude that courts are bureaucracies because they handle large numbers of cases and depend heavily on the guilty plea is to draw a premature, and I think improper, conclusion. Bureaucratization implies much more than the rapid performance of repetitive tasks. It implies hierarchy, relatively clear agreement on organizational goals, the existence of efficacious means for securing compliance to these goals, and a substantial degree of organizational autonomy from the larger environment.

Taken together, Eisenstein and Jacob as well as Feeley maintain that empirical scrutiny of criminal courts shows that they are hardly hierarchical outfits; rather, the courtroom is a scene where actors from a number of relatively independent agencies come together to do business. Thus, in any given courtroom, the judge, prosecutor, and defense attorney respond to different bosses; they are subject to different rules, pressures, and demands according to the organization to which they belong. As we shall see shortly, the organizational theory of criminal courts seeks to explain how actors from relatively independent institutions arrange their interactions so as to achieve their common goal of resolving cases.

Before turning to a consideration of the structure of organizational theory, it is important to note that Feeley replaces the bureaucratic model with a view of criminal courts as marketplaces. Key to this marketplace view is the notion that the criminal court is a self-regulating organization based upon the self-interest of its multiple actors. The criminal court on this view is "a complex bargaining and exchange system, in which various values, goals, and interests are competing with one another" (Feeley 1979, 2). In this marketplace that is the criminal court, prosecutors, defense attorneys, judges, and to a certain extent defendants haggle over the terms of justice. What is it worth to an actor to resolve a case? What is fair? What will one give up in exchange for a resolution to a case? What will one risk on principle? What does justice demand in a specific case? Unlike in a bureaucracy, there is no central-ized formula for resolving these questions and certainly a straightfor-ward application of concrete rules to the facts of a particular case is out of the question. As in a marketplace, decision making is decentralized among the various actors, with each determining the benefits and costs of particular courses of action. This marketplace metaphor therefore posits courtroom actors as rational calculators who are intimately con-cerned with the transaction costs associated with their every move. As we shall now see, the organizational theory developed by Feeley uses this marketplace model to characterize the disposition of criminal cases in lower courts with a guilty plea as a function of court organization, conceptions of substantive justice, and the transaction costs associated with the invocation of due process.

The Structure of Feeley's Organizational Theory

Before discussing the structure of Feeley's organizational theory proper, it would be useful to address at this point the general and spe-cific research questions with which Feeley engaged his project. Feeley (1979, xxiv) writes that:

> The central question is: How is the criminal sanction adminis-tered? As it is explored, this question assumes various forms: How is the criminal sanction administered in a lower court in light of its low visibility and vast powers of discretion? How are rules used in this process? How does a concern with substantive justice shape the process? How does a legal system cope with high volume of "low stakes" cases? How do transaction costs affect the process?

Linked to this general question about the administration of the criminal sanction is a still more specific one. Speaking to this narrower question, Feeley notes that even though since the 1960s defendants in the United States have gained a large number of procedural due process protections (e.g., a right to counsel for any charge that might result in jail time), the operations of the lower courts have not changed all that much. Indeed, very few defendants actually invoke their right to a jury trial. In fact, out of the over 1600 cases surveyed by Feeley, not one was decided by a jury; instead, most were decided by joint agreement of the parties to have the defendant enter a plea of guilty. In addition, Feeley found that not only do many defendants fail to invoke their right to an attorney, but in the lower criminal courts most cases are so quickly processed that the "typical" case is usually decided in a matter of minutes if not seconds. The more specific question, therefore, is: Why has the expansion of due process protections in the lower criminal courts of the United States failed to modify its workings and operations?

Feeley begins by rejecting the claim that increased caseloads are responsible for the failure of most defendants to invoke their right to trial. After reviewing historical evidence, he claims that criminal courts in the past also suffered from high caseloads. He also compares the court in New Haven to another lower criminal court in Connecticut that had a much lower caseload to see if the difference in caseloads influenced the operation of the court. Feeley eventually concluded that since operations of these two courts were so similar, despite pronounced differences in the levels of their caseloads, caseload differentials could not be viewed as the cause of the current practice of plea bargaining in the lower criminal courts (see also Heumann 1978). Instead, Feeley resolves that there are three basic factors that determine how the lower criminal courts conduct their business and explains why, despite the due process revolution, the behavior of lower courts has not changed all that much. Taken together, Feeley maintains that guilty pleas (his primary dependent variable) are entered in lower criminal courts owing to three factors: (1) court organization; (2) conceptions of substantive justice; and (3) transaction costs associated with the exercise of due process. We now briefly consider each of these independent variables in turn.

ON COURT ORGANIZATION

In order to understand the behavior of lower criminal courts, Feeley asserts that we need to understand the organization of the courts. A court is not an isolated bureaucratic entity. Rather, it is composed of a number of distinct, and quite often competing, institutions (e.g., the prosecutor's office, the public defender's office, and the judiciary) which may not have the same interests or goals. Each of these institutions is not only linked to the others, but they are all also linked to the wider social structure and society that at times exert various pressures upon them. Students of the criminal courts need to take all these factors into account. For example, an individual prosecutor has a certain type of working relationship with an individual defense attorney. Both of these actors, as they navigate the intricacies of a case, must not only take into account their relationship to each other as members of the courthouse workgroup, but also to the judge and to other courtroom personnel (e.g., auxiliary staff, bail bondsmen, bailiffs, and news reporters). Moreover, they must also consider the interests of their own sponsoring agencies, as well as larger societal pressures. Taken together, students of criminal courts are advised to recognize the complexity of court structure and process. As Feeley (1979, 21) puts it, criminal courts are "open systems" in which decisions of courthouse actors result from "the balancing of the individual and collective interests in the courthouse workgroup, with the constraints and goals of their sponsoring organizations, and the influences of the environment."

ON THE PURSUIT OF SUBSTANTIVE JUSTICE

At times the law on the books is not the only factor utilized in adjudicating a specific defendant. Sometimes the law may be unclear, or the actors may be uncertain as to which law is applicable, or there may be unique facts that appear to argue against an unthinking application of the law to the particular case at hand. Feeley contends that the values (i.e., one's own unique sense of justice) held by individual actors involved in the case often play a role in resolving the case. Sometimes, according to Feeley, the substantive justice espoused by the participants in the process may conflict with the formal statute. In any case, choices always have to be made in the adjudication of criminal cases and personal dispositions play a more or less central role in these determinations. It is important that observers of the court pay attention to the inherent discretion that is present in the functioning of the court system.

Feeley explains that most cases are decided quickly as the prosecutor and defense attorney discuss the case moments before the case is called. For the most part the sentence imposed by the judge is based upon what the prosecutor and defense attorney already decided. Their decision is based upon their joint agreement as to what that particular case is "worth." Feeley (1979, 159) states that prosecutors and defense attorneys agree that for the most part they know what a case is worth: "The worth of a case is established by considering a host of factors, and different types of cases call forth different rules of thumb." Feeley points out that in most cases both the prosecutor and defense attorney heavily rely upon the official description of the charges. As the long day unfolds before them, the prosecutor and defense attorney, rather than considering each case alone on its merits, sometimes lapse and allow one case to influence another. While the dictates of an adversarial model call for a pitched battle between the prosecutor and the defense attorney, observed diligently by an impartial judge to ensure conformity to the rules of due process, Feeley's observations reveal more cooperation than contestation, a cooperation achieved through a joint abandonment of the presumption of innocence. In short, the exercise of discretion is central to the processing of criminal cases in lower courts. This discretion is channeled by, among other factors, the language of the law, norms of the courtroom workgroup, official descriptions of the case in police reports, experiences of the court actors in previous cases, and perhaps most significantly a cooperative spirit based on a presumption of guilt.

THE PROCESS IS THE PUNISHMENT

Most importantly, there are numerous costs imposed by the system upon defendants while the process is unfolding before conviction and sentencing. Feeley maintains that because the presentencing costs, in combination, are so high, and the actual sentences distributed by lower criminal courts are normally so low, for most defendants the pretrial process imposes the greater cost. For these individuals, Feeley concludes that, paradoxically, the actual punishment is really not that much of a burden. In other words, in most of the cases handled by the lower criminal courts, Feeley observes that the process is the punishment.

Many offenders are not concerned with any stigma that may be attached to a criminal conviction since: (1) they may have prior convictions; (2) they may be part of a subculture which does not view conviction as a stigma; and (3) missing work today to go to court may be viewed as a more severe cost than any stigma that may be attached to the offender in the future. Feeley states that from the offender's point of view it makes sense for the offender to plead guilty. In fact, if the offender invoked all of the rights available to him, he would prolong the process and thereby increase the length of the process and consequently his costs. After all, extending the process would result in more court appearances, which translates, through missed work, into smaller salaries.

ELABORATING AND EXTENDING ORGANIZATIONAL THEORY WITH DURKHEIM'S COMPARATIVE METHOD

While Feeley asserts that his findings are generalizable to other lower criminal courts across space and time, he does not provide explicit empirical support for this claim. However, as we have stated many times, Durkheim's comparative method is well suited to address issues of generalizability. For instance, although expensive, there is no scholarly reason to prevent researchers from attempting to observe a number of lower court systems simultaneously across the United States, or across national borders (i.e., examine other countries with common law, adversarial systems), to determine if the three themes (i.e., court organization, substantive justice, and transaction costs of the process) elucidated by Feeley play a significant role in explaining adjudication. Studies of this variety would fall into the second stage of comparative studies outlined by Durkheim in which similar societies are compared in order to ascertain whether the observed relationship between social facts in a single case hold under wider circumstances. Moreover, one might compare common law, adversarial societies with civil law and inquisitorial societies in order to determine whether the relationship between adjudication and court organization, substantive justice, and transaction costs stands in both types of societies. If the relationship is not borne out in civil law societies, then the researchers might identify qualifications to the organizational theory specified by Feeley to account for this discrepancy. Finally, particular attention could be paid to Feeley's third theme in which transaction costs (the process is the punishment) are thought to influence defendant plea bargaining. Investigating this issue opens up several possibilities for comparative consideration. Are defendants of societies that extend numerous procedural protections to defendants more likely to plead guilty as compared to defendants who reside in societies that extend fewer procedural protections? If they are more likely to plead guilty, is this because of the transaction costs exerted on them by the process itself?

In any case, the findings from such comparative studies promise to be quite useful in further refining and elaborating Feeley's work. For example, if Feeley's thesis is not found to be applicable to particular locations, cultures, or time periods, then the comparative method would have narrowed the relevance of Feeley's work. In other words, the comparative method is useful in specifying the exact contours of a theory's reach. In addition, such negative findings would almost certainly lead to attempts to figure out why Feeley's thesis was not supported. It is altogether possible that modifications could be made to the theory in order to further its applicability. Such modifications should encompass both theoretical and methodological issues. As Professor Alissa Worden astutely points out in this volume (chapter 8), "theory forces us to discipline our thinking about core concepts, and about cause and effect." Such disciplined thinking is even more likely to occur, we maintain, when the researcher must ponder concepts, indicators and relationships in "other, different" contexts. The comparative method, when properly used, appears adept in "forcing" scholars and researchers to engage more seriously theoretical and methodological issues.

PROMOTING THEORY DEVELOPMENT IN COMPARATIVE CRIMINAL JUSTICE

In this chapter, we discussed the implications for the development of criminal justice theory that attend the use of Durkheim's comparative method. As asserted elsewhere in this volume, we proceeded from the premise that criminal justice theory is woefully underdeveloped and argued that Durkheim's comparative method can be used to test and elaborate theories concerned with criminal justice behavior. Given the dearth of comparative criminal justice theory, this chapter then analyzed Feeley's organizational theory of criminal courts, seeking to outline the possibilities that the comparative method affords for testing and elaborating this particular theory. Our intention was not to be definitive in our statements about comparative criminal justice theory; rather, we have only sought to identify some fruitful avenues for moving forward this important area of investigation.

One final question that we would like to address is: How can theory development be promoted in comparative criminal justice studies? For one thing, theory should be taken more seriously in criminal justice education (Willis 1983; Henderson and Boostrom 1989; Bernard and Engel 2001), but so too should method and matters of research design. Far too many research design courses in criminal justice education fall more accurately into the "applied statistics" crowd. Consequently, too few students of criminal justice are informed about Durkheim's comparative method and its promise for theoretical elaboration. Second, because the comparative method requires that scholars of society define the unit of analysis in all its known variations, a deep appreciation of social and evolutionary history would be invaluable for carrying forward an informed comparative study of crime and justice. Finally, comparative criminal justice studies could be strengthened through a concerted effort to promote foreign language fluency in university education. Given the cultural variations in criminal justice response, comparative investigations would greatly benefit from the presence of multilingual observers in the field, folks who can understand the nuances of criminal justice responses as they are observed by citizens and investigator as well as recorded in official documents.

Perhaps the most certain way to advance comparative work with criminal justice theory is the development of reliable and valid data and observations. Given the reluctance of the United Nations to take this task seriously and the difficulty of the International Crime Victim-ization Survey to field its investigation regularly in a healthy sample of countries around the world, as well as the limited coverage of crimi-nal justice behavior in each instrument, it would seem that competent data collection will be left more to the industrious efforts of individ-ual scholars and grant supported research teams. Of course, as David Bayley (1985) has made abundantly clear, the task of data collection is time-consuming, fraught with problems of accessibility, and expensive to conduct, especially if efforts are to be made in the tradition of direct observation, which is one of the most promising paths toward reliable and valid criminal justice data.

While these challenges to data collection are formidable, indeed, they highlight the promise ahead for informed efforts at theoretical development in criminal justice. As the editors have observed in the proposal for this volume, "theory has to guide measurement because theory defines what is to be measured or observed." In other words, smart theory will permit investigators to deploy scarce resources more efficiently. Moreover, data collection guided by explicit articulations of theory and hypotheses provides the possibility for further development of theory through the virtue of disproof. This openness to disproof nat-urally requires some measure of courage on the part of criminal justice scholars. Whether this attribute is something academic departments are prepared or able to teach today is, unfortunately, an open question.

4

NEGLECT OF JUSTICE IN CRIMINAL JUSTICE THEORY

Causes, Consequences, and Alternatives[1]

Thomas C. Castellano and Jon B. Gould

INTRODUCTION

Criminal justice science faces many significant issues and challenges. Despite its remarkable growth and progress — as reflected by high student demand, a rising academic reputation, fine opportunities for funded research, and maturing professional organizations — the vitality of the field can be rightly questioned. A major reason, unfortunately, is the current nature of criminal justice theory. As suggested by Duffee and Allan in chapter 1 of this volume, and reinforced by Snipes and Maguire in chapter 2, criminal justice theory tends to be undeveloped, misunderstood, fragmented, narrow, and sterile.

If criminal justice theory is to meet its potential, the discipline must focus more attention on justice and less energy on crime. Up until now much of the criminal justice scholarship has either ignored justice as a legitimate concern or treated the measure as an exogenous influence. Yet the criminal justice system must be about justice — about just processes, just outcomes, and the just use of state power. Throughout the chapter we suggest that justice-based factors explain criminal justice behavior more accurately than does crime, a contention that calls on criminal justice scholarship to develop more powerful theory. In the end, we ask a central question: whether the American criminal justice system — and in particular criminal punishment — serves justice. There are many reasonable answers to this query, but it is essential that scholars and practitioners alike orient their thinking to what is fundamental to criminal justice, the concept of *justice*.

THE STATE OF CRIMINAL JUSTICE RESEARCH

Duffee and Allan define criminal justice science as the "study of governmental social control premised on punishment or blameworthiness" (chapter 1 in this volume). Under this definition, the object of criminal justice inquiry is to explain variations in the nature and amount of social control, for a wide variety of social institutions and governmental agencies are in the business of fostering social control. But one would not get a sense of this breadth by reading criminal justice scholarship. The majority of criminal justice research focuses on government "agencies involved in law enforcement, prosecution, and punishment" (Duffee 1990, 1), with much of the scholarship taking functional, objective, or instrumental perspectives. Researchers accept that crime and disorder remain serious public problems and focus their energies on the evaluation of policies or interventions advanced to "solve" these problems. Little attention is devoted to the structural or cultural bases for differentiated implementation processes and results. Instead, researchers study the outcomes of criminal justice policy — outcomes usually measured by crime rates — and assess whether the desired results have been achieved. All too often policy "failures" are identified, which generally spur calls to tighten the system, reduce discretion, throw more money (and usually punishment) at the problem, or "chase the rascals out." Old problems continue unabated or new problems are discovered; the legitimacy of the system is questioned; policy reforms take place; and so on (e.g., Rosett and Cressey 1976). Throughout, the rather mechanical business of criminal justice research continues.

Unfortunately, this policy-oriented research process is often uninformed by theory. Such research is particularly unproductive because the complex, fuzzy, and nonlinear relationships between crime, law, policy, and justice system behavior are not widely recognized, nor are they included in the development and testing of criminal justice theory. The worlds of crime, law, justice, and social control are simplified, with chaotic, unbalanced realities replaced by orderly but erroneous models of how and why criminal justice systems operate as they do.

WHY IS CRIMINAL JUSTICE THEORY LACKING?

It is important to recognize that criminal justice is still a relatively new discipline, and unlike some other fields, has but a modest tradition of theorizing. Part of the reason may be the discipline's roots as an applied field, but criminal justice scholarship also tends to isolate elements of the justice system rather than weaving them together into a larger understanding of social behavior and control. The fact that much of the research is dependent on government funding only reinforces the concept of crime as the core domain of criminal justice inquiry.

Criminal Justice is a Developing Discipline

The notion of criminal justice as a distinct discipline was relatively unknown before the late 1960s, when federal funding under the Law Enforcement Education Program was widely distributed to support the higher education of law enforcement officers (Sherman and the National Advisory Commission on Higher Education for Police Officers 1978). Indeed, the concept of a unified system of criminal justice is itself relatively new, having emerged only with the final report of the 1967 President's Commission on Law Enforcement and the Administration of Justice. If we seem overly critical of criminal justice theory it is not because we seek to unjustly accuse an embryonic field of study. We well recognize that academic disciplines have their growing pains, especially a field like criminal justice that reflects political and popular, rather than scientific, origins (Duffee 1990). But it is the field's very infancy (or perhaps now adolescence) that merits close scrutiny. If criminal justice is to be an accepted social science, its research must be based on theory — solid justice theory — and not simply the needs, interests, or concerns of those preoccupied with crime.

Missing the Forest for the Trees

Snipes and Maguire contend that a primary test of criminal justice theory is whether variation in some aspect of social control is the dependent variable in the theory (chapter 2 in this volume). Thus, criminal justice theory need not deal with the entire system. While this position is entirely reasonable, especially in light of the highly fragmented, variable, and loosely coupled nature of the criminal justice system, the consequences for criminal justice theory are great. Extant criminal justice theory tends to be narrow as a result; there are few theories developed within criminal justice that attempt to explain phenomena that transcend boundaries of particular components of the system. Most theoretically informed studies of criminal justice behavior are limited in focus and consequence, with the limits of theory (who, what, when) dwarfing the explanatory reach of theory (what, how, and why). Research tends to address individual behavior (e.g., police officers), rather than organizational (police departments), institutional (policing), or system-wide behaviors and outcomes (overall punishment processes and outcomes within a jurisdiction). As a result, we risk missing the macro issues at work in the criminal justice system by focusing so narrowly on the individual parts of the process.

State Sponsorship of Criminal Justice Research

This neat model of criminal justice research did not develop on its own but is heavily supported by government funding. Fostered by a federal research agenda focused on the nexus between crime and punishment, criminal justice scholars have largely ignored the bases and processes by which public policy is made. Researchers presume that justice policy is dictated by crime control and fail to question policy choices in ways threatening to the government, the chief benefactor of criminal justice research in the United States and the gatekeeper to criminal justice data.[2] As Duffee and Allan succinctly explain, criminal justice science "gains research resources in exchange for limiting theory to models that cannot threaten the legitimacy — or the presumed rationality — of the policy-making system" (chapter 1 in this volume).

PUTTING JUSTICE BACK INTO CRIMINAL JUSTICE

Criminal justice cannot let its research agenda be dictated by funding sources, nor can the discipline fully conceptualize the criminal justice process unless it addresses what must be one of the fundamental purposes of social control — the pursuit of justice. Certainly, justice is an organizing principle of American government, the Constitution itself declaring that the pursuit of justice is a cornerstone of the Republic. Many courthouses and the U.S. Department of Justice include a statue of "Lady Justice," a larger-than-life figure proclaiming that the courts and justice agencies will act impartially. But what is justice? To the layperson justice is likely to be synonymous with fairness, suggesting that government processes and outcomes should be impartial. Justice is most often associated with the courts and legal processes, compelling legal actors to treat litigants fairly regardless of their resources or station in life. These protections are guaranteed by two constitutional doctrines. Under the Fifth and Fourteenth Amendments to the Constitution, Americans are guaranteed due (fair) process under the laws. Similarly, under the equal protection clause of the Fourteenth Amendment government may not treat individuals inequitably without good cause.

But justice extends outside of the legal world. Scholars tend to distinguish between three types of justice: procedural justice, distributive justice, and restorative justice. Procedural justice is just as it sounds, referring to the processes that organizations establish to resolve disputes. Although the concept has recently been raised in the business world, its roots are in the civil and criminal justice systems, reflecting the legitimacy that people assign to interactions with police or court processes. Do police officers give suspects a chance to explain their behavior before automatically detaining them? Do courts provide defendants with sufficient resources to mount an adequate defense? Each reflects a concern for procedural justice. Interestingly, most social science research shows that people are not influenced by the results of justice processes so much as they are affected by their impressions of whether the justice system was fairly administered. If people believe they have been "heard" — if the justice system has treated them with respect and dignity — individuals are more likely to accept substantive results from those processes that go against them (Tyler and Huo 2002).

Distributive justice is sometimes treated as an economic term, dealing with the allocation of resources in limited supply related to demand (Rawls 1993). In the world of criminal justice, however, the concept addresses the substantive results of justice processes — police stops, arrests, verdicts, and sentences — asking whether these results are legitimate or if state power is differentially applied to individuals on the basis of immutable or immaterial characteristics (Spader 1988). The many critiques of racial profiling or racial disparities in sentencing, for example, are premised on concerns for distributive justice (*New Jersey v. Soto* 1996; Ulmer 1997; Steffensmeir and Britt 2001). In these cases, critics question whether police officers, prosecutors, judges, or jurors are treating minorities unfairly on account of their race.

Restorative justice is still a relatively new concept in criminology and victimology, defined as "a process whereby parties with a stake in a specific [criminal] offense resolve collectively how to deal with the aftermath of the offense and its implications for the future" (Prison Fellowship 2000, 1). Advocates of restorative justice sponsor victim-offender mediation, counsel ex-offenders, and generally recommend restitution over jail time, all as part of a larger agenda to change the response of the criminal justice system. As proponents say, "rather than measuring how much punishment is inflicted," the criminal justice system should "measure how many harms are repaired or prevented" (Prison Fellowship 2000). In many ways restorative justice is a policy response to crime and lawbreaking, not necessarily a measure of what justice is. Yet restorative justice is also a normative standard for assessing the results of justice processes. Just as distributive justice evaluates the proper apportionment of outcomes across individuals, restorative justice asks if the actions taken against offenders will prevent future wrongdoing or alleviate the existing harms.

Defining the elements of justice and evaluating them throughout the criminal justice system are two very different challenges. The former, while based on practical experience, is still essentially theoretical. The latter is a complicated process requiring researchers to select a part of the system to study — police stops, interrogations, charging decisions, or sentences, for example — and then construct variables to reflect the several constructs of justice. Researchers might evaluate the racial division of traffic stops (distributive justice), the appointment of competent defense counsel (procedural justice), or victim satisfaction with justice processes (restorative justice). Indeed, many criminal justice scholars are *already* doing this. Tom Tyler (1997), for example, has written extensively on procedural justice, and many other scholars have examined the distribution of, and disparities within, criminal sentencing (e.g., McDonald and Carlson 1993; Ulmer 1997; Steffensmeier and Britt 2001). Others have begun to systematically examine the implementation and outcomes of practices guided by principles of restorative justice (e.g., Umbreit and Bradshaw 1997; Braithwaite 1999; McGarrell 2001; Karp 2001).

If criminal justice scholarship has begun to examine justice concerns, there is still more that can be done. Initially, the field must address whether justice is a dependent variable, an independent variable, or a combination of the two. That is, should justice be the aim of the criminal justice system, or is justice simply another concern that influences practitioners as they seek to control crime? Although we believe that justice should be the ultimate goal, we would consider it a step forward if additional researchers would consider the normative implications of their findings on justice. Consider, for example, the work of David Baldus et al. (1990) on capital punishment. If both black and white defendants who kill white victims are more likely to receive the death penalty than are those who kill black victims, is the system unjust? How do officials justify capital prosecutions in light of these findings, and what, if any changes should or do they undertake? Perhaps we should leave such questions for the courts to answer, but for an academic discipline focused so heavily on the practical application of state power, it seems essential to evaluate the proper exercise of that authority.

THE FAILINGS OF CRIME-BASED CRIMINAL JUSTICE THEORY: THE CRIME–PUNISHMENT NEXUS

One of the overriding questions for criminal justice theory must be whether the American system of criminal justice is fair and unbiased — whether it is, in fact, just. We will resist the temptation to give an absolute, normative answer, for again, one of our points is that such matters must be examined empirically. We seek to raise questions for analysis, issues that students and scholars of criminal justice ought to keep in mind as they consider this matter for themselves. Accordingly, we examine the purpose of the criminal justice system, beginning with what we believe is a myth of criminal justice education — that the system is designed to prevent and control crime. If, as we contend, other motives drive criminal justice organizations and policy, how does one justify criminal justice policy?

MYTHS OF CRIMINAL JUSTICE

A variety of powerful myths exist about the purported purposes of criminal justice. These myths are reinforced in a number of ways, particularly within formal systems of criminal justice education.

The Prevention and Control of Crime Is the Bottom Line

One leading textbook in criminal justice actually defines criminal justice as "the management of police, courts, and corrections, and the study of the causes of and treatment for crime" (Albanese 2002, 17). Another textbook introduces itself by stating, "To provide solutions to the crime problem and to shape the direction of crime policy, we turn to the agencies of the criminal justice system" (Senna and Siegel 2002, 4). These, and almost all other introductory textbooks on criminal justice, frame their orientation to students in terms of the crime problem and the attempts of the criminal justice system to prevent and control crime. This itself not only fuels the lack of distinction between crime and criminal justice behavior, but also helps perpetuate a myth that the primary purpose of criminal justice is to "solve" the crime problem.

A variety of historical and cross-cultural evidence on the origins and evolution of criminal justice systems suggests that the emergence and functioning of formal systems of criminal justice were not solely or even primarily based on preventing and controlling crime, but on a variety of other concerns and functions. Evolving slowly and unevenly, early systems of informal justice were designed to resolve interpersonal and interfamily conflicts by interjecting "neutral" actors into the dispute resolution process. Conflict and dispute resolution appeared much more central to justice processes than formally sanctioning offenders to reduce aggregate levels of misconduct in the future (Vago 1988; Braithwaite 1999).

With the emergence of centralized authorities and increased stratification and heterogeneity in transitional societies, justice systems focused on consolidating and strengthening the power of monarchs (Morton 1938). As societies became more urbanized and industrialized, justice systems evolved to maintain and support class-based relationships between ruling and working classes (Chambliss 1964), urban elites and immigrant classes (Richardson 1970; Harring 1983), landowners and slaves (Platt and the Global Options Staff 1982), industrialists and union members (Harring 1981). Thus, it is inarguable that justice systems emerged and functioned to support structural sources of inequality based on factors such as class, race, and gender. If anything, justice systems were designed to control those groups considered threatening to prevailing social orders. Yet, the prevention and control of crime is only one aspect of social control, and historically, most likely only a secondary reason for the emergence of modern justice systems.

Likewise, a wealth of research indicates contemporary criminal justice systems have multiple functions within social systems, and that these functions vary greatly across space. They may support the production-distribution-consumption functions of communities or provide mutual support and services that other social institutions do not (for a detailed review see Duffee [1990]). Thus, criminal justice functions go well beyond the prevention and control of crime.

In some instances, if not many, the behavior of criminal justice agencies would be much better understood if the concept of crime was actually excluded from the analytic framework. In Illinois, for example, budgetary concerns led officials to consider closing a well-known prison, the largest employer in an economically depressed rural county. In response, officials heard strong and vocal opposition from local residents, many of whom warned of disastrous economic consequences for the region, not to mention the likely disruption to staff and inmates. State officials eventually decided not to close the prison, but concerns for crime control or the public's safety were nowhere in the decision calculus; the outcome was determined primarily by the nature of the local political economy. This is not uncommon.

Criminal Justice Behavior is Instrumental

It should also be recognized that much of the behavior of the criminal justice system is largely symbolic. Criminal justice scholars have come to recognize this point, but it has not yet become a staple of criminal justice theory. This is true whether one examines theory on microlevel decision making and processes (e.g., the status degradation functions of arrest, booking, prosecution, and trial processes) or macrolevel decision making (e.g., the passage of new laws). For example, when assessing the implementation or impact of a new regulation or piece of legislation, scholars often assume that legislators acted in a rational manner. Yet this approach fails to recognize that policy may be directed at different, symbolic, or implicitly stated goals. Indeed, even ostensibly clear goals and objectives may mask vague, hidden, or undefined policies (e.g., Casper and Brereton 1984). For example, Zalman's (1982, 61) analysis of the legislative process behind Michigan's 1976 Felony Firearm Law is quite illustrative:

> While legislatures do not set out to act in irrational ways, they often do not pursue a policy-rational process. In other words, the short- and long-range goals of legislation, as viewed by the legislature, may and often [do] include goals other than the most efficient and effective implementation of the statute's manifest ends....

Taking the advice of Berk et al. (1980) that implementation analyses of a law must go back to the text, goals, and politics of the legislation, Zalman (1982) concluded that the Michigan Felony Firearm Law reflected primarily symbolic goals. That is, the prime objective of the Michigan Felony Firearm was to show that the legislature was tough on crime rather than to enhance crime control efforts.

"Get tough" legislation may generate advantages for policy makers almost regardless of the legislation's actual implementation or impact. Policy makers are aware that the "bark" of legislation is often more pronounced than its "bite" — that the activities of prosecutors, judges, and others may mean that actual penalties are substantially reduced from the enhancements prescribed by the law (Casper and Brereton 1984, 124–25).[3] Yet, even if policy implementors "flout" the law, policy makers may still be pleased, the desired advantages of legislation having accrued merely from a statute's passage. In this respect, much criminal legislation manifestly intended to reduce violence is symbolic, with the successful achievement of legislative goals having little to do with the future behavior of criminal justice officials or potential criminal offenders.[4]

THE (IN)JUSTICE OF CRIME AND PUNISHMENT

If American criminal justice is driven by more than the wish to reduce crime, its effects are not always as easily defended either. Nowhere is this more problematic than in the imprisonment boom since the mid-1970s, a phenomenon that raises questions of procedural, distributive, and certainly restorative justice.

In fact, the United States has been on a well-documented and widely lamented imprisonment binge (Austin and Irwin, 2001). Between 1980 and 2001, the prison population increased from 315,974 to 1,405,531, an almost fivefold increase (Maguire and Pastore 1998, 490; Bureau of Justice Statistics 2002). Today, the United States imprisons a greater percentage of its population than ever before. Historically, from about 1850 to 1970 the U.S. imprisonment rate was remarkably stable — about 100 inmates per 100,000 U.S. residents. This remarkable stability occurred despite a number of great shocks to the political and economic systems of the nation — despite the Great Depression, two world wars, and massive population movements. It also prompted theorizing on the nature of homoeostatic processes that may underlie the stability (Blumstein and Cohen 1973). However, any notion that punishment might be stable was short-lived. Beginning in 1972 the U.S. imprisonment rate increased yearly so that by the middle of 2001, 690 of every 100,000 Americans were locked up in prisons or jails (Bureau of Justice Statistics 2002).

This dramatic and unprecedented increase has resulted in an imprisonment rate far exceeding those of other industrialized and Western nations. Moreover, except perhaps for Russia, the United States has the highest imprisonment rate of any other nation, even a number of nations without extensive democratic traditions (e.g., South Africa, Cambodia, and Poland; see Mauer [1997]). According to several prominent criminologists, neither recent increases in the American imprisonment rate nor the high level of incarceration in the United States relative to other nations can be rationalized by national crime rates (Christie 1994; R. D. King 1998). If anything, the American imprisonment boom is explained by the willingness of governmental officials to combat a variety of "old" and "new" societal problems with criminal sanctions.

"Old" social problems include traditional street crimes (e.g., murder, rape, robbery, assault, theft). Some observers might also include illicit drug use, domestic violence, child abuse, and white-collar crime within this category. Persons engaged in these behaviors, except for white-collar offenders (Szockyj 1999), receive harsher punishments today than they did for similar offenses in the past (Bureau of Justice Statistics 1998). "Newer" social problems, in some cases involving novel substantive offenses such as "drug loitering," "gang loitering," and "nuisance violations," have also been the subject of criminal sanctions in recent years (Steiker 1998). Coupled with the more stringent enforcement of preexisting laws against drunk driving, disorderly conduct, underage drinking, and the like, the reach and punitiveness of criminal sanctions have expanded mightily in recent years. In effect, an increasingly large criminal justice system has become much more productive in applying punitive sanctions to a broader population.[5] Unfortunately, scholars have offered relatively little theory to explain this growth.[6]

PUBLIC DEMANDS FOR PUNISHMENT: UTILITARIAN AND RETRIBUTIVE CLAIMS

The rise in punitive outcomes stems from a variety of interrelated beliefs about the American crime myth (Scheingold 1984). In traditional terms, criminal punishments are justified both on the basis of retributive and utilitarian rationales (Packer 1968). The contemporary era in the United States has been termed the "Just Deserts Era" by a number of observers (e.g., Clear and Cole 1999), with the term implying a retributive basis to current punishment policies. It may be more appropriate to view the current "penal harm" movement (Clear 1994) as being driven more by utilitarian demands than retributive impulses. That is, the primary engine behind the expanded use of criminal sanctions is the common belief that applying frequent and harsh levels of punishment prevents and controls crime through the mechanisms of deterrence and incapacitation. While the rehabilitative function of criminal sanctions is utilitarian in nature, it would be silly to emphasize its role in shaping contemporary penal policy. It is widely but erroneously believed that criminal sanctions have little value in rehabilitating offenders (Andrews and Bonta 1998). The effect has been a widespread dismantling of rehabilitative programs in correctional settings (Haney and Zimbardo 1998; Austin and Irwin 2001).

Contemporary punishment practices are more consistent with deterrent and incapacitative rationales than retributive demands. For instance, such responses as the "drug war," "quality of life" ordinances, "three strikes" legislation, and the like — all of which, to some degree, are the foundations of increased punishment rates — square more clearly with the preventive purposes of the criminal law than with its retributive purposes. The life terms imposed on 192 persons "striking out" for marijuana possession in California in 1994 under its "Three Strikes" law (Patch 1998), and the federally mandated long-term imprisonment of small-scale crack dealers throughout the nation (Tonry 1994), can hardly be justified by any set of retributive principles. In such increasingly common cases, the demands of deterrence and incapacitation are at odds with the demands of retribution. As a result, fundamental legal values such as proportionality, substantive due process, and basic fairness are compromised.

Crime, Fear, and Public Demands

Why are we witnessing this imprisonment binge? Many mainstream observers of criminal justice believe that the public demands as much. It is assumed that as crime increases so does public fear, and thus officials respond by strengthening the criminal justice response to ensure that criminal offenders are punished certainly, severely, and efficiently. Other observers, however, question these simple cause and effect relationships (e.g., Scheingold 1984). There is a great deal of data to suggest that the purported links between crime, fear, and punishment are tenuous and weak. As crime goes up, fear of crime does not necessarily increase. Persons in high crime areas and persons at greatest risk of victimization are generally not those who fear crime the most. Although the precise linkage between crime and fear of crime has yet to be determined with any degree of consensus (Roundtree 1998), there is little evidence to suggest that objective levels of crime strongly affect the public's fear of crime or that previous victimization conclusively creates greater crime fears. In general, the relevant research indicates that the crime–fear linkage is extremely complex, influenced by a number of mediating, conditioning, and confounding factors (Roundtree 1998).

One such factor is local media coverage of crime. A number of studies have suggested that media reports of crime may have more to do with fear of crime than with the level of crime itself (Liska et al. 1988; Liska and Baccaglini 1990). It is apparent that the mass media can stoke the fires of fear and divisiveness. Viewers may feel vicarious victimization, especially when they are exposed daily to the "body count" journalism that is so pervasive on television. While some viewers may enjoy this type of news, and journalists respond to what promotes ratings, many contend that this type of journalism increases fear of crime and constrains responsible public dialogue on crime policy (Donziger 1996).

The ability of the mass media to raise fears seems especially great when people have widespread concern about the quality of life and related economic conditions. These relate to two differing models of crime fears highlighted in community-based research on the topic. The first is called the "disorder" or "social control" perspective, which suggests that fear of crime represents a broader concern about social conditions than simply crime rates (Garofalo and Laub 1978; Lewis and Salem 1986). In this model, the attenuation of social control, or the fear that it is occurring, is a greater source of fear than the objective risk of victimization. The second model, receiving relatively little attention, has been termed the economic viability model, and posits that fear is heavily anchored in the economic conditions of the resident's neighborhood. When personal and neighborhood economic conditions are perceived as decreasing or in jeopardy, fear increases (Taub, Taylor, and Dunham 1984). Under these conditions, then, the mass media are able to foster "moral panics" about crime and to generate heightened demands for punitive crime policy (McGarrell and Castellano 1991; Chiricos 1998).

Such agitation aside, the relationship between rates of crime and rates of imprisonment is actually quite weak. As noted earlier, rates of serious crime in the United States have been decreasing steadily for some time. Nonetheless, more and more people are being incarcerated. As Austin and Irwin (2001) have found, increases in state-level incarceration rates between 1980 and 1991 were not strongly related to changes in state crime rates. These and a host of other data (see R. D. King 1998, 597–606) suggest not only that crime rates have a weak influence on imprisonment rates, but also that massive increases in incarceration during the 1980s and 1990s produced a scant reduction in crime rates (Spelman 2001; Austin and Irwin 2001). It is surprising, then, that many political leaders believe they have little flexibility in responding to crime. In truth, citizens are not monolithically punitive in their values or policy preferences. While most people want punishment for convicted criminals, they also favor the delivery of correctional treatment programs that work, even programs delivered in the community (Sundt 1999).

THE POLICY CHOICE TO SELECT PUNISHMENT: GOVERNING THROUGH CRIME

Penal policies reflect the deliberate policy choices of a people and have to be understood as an integral part of the entire social system (R. D. King 1998). Whether one contends that punishment systems are driven by the division of labor in a society and related demands of the labor market (Rusche and Kirchheimer 1939), or that cultural values allow for greater levels of tolerance (Downes 1988), it is fairly clear that the use of imprisonment is not simply an automatic response to crime, but rather a policy choice to respond to crime levels in a particular way (Rutherford 1985). Crime policy reflects deeper formulations of social problems and related public policies. For instance, Christie believes that "high incarceration rates reflect a society's choice to define the problems of inner cities, such as 'wife-abuse, selling sex, selling crack, killings, crime' as 'targets for war' rather than targets for drastic social reform" (1994, 198).

In terms of modern America, many "social troubles" are currently defined as crimes. However, several of these could be defined differently and addressed outside the criminal justice system. Consider the dichotomy between business fraud and sexual fraud. Although prosecutors are willing to charge executives who defraud investors, they pointedly refuse to handle cases in which men openly lie to woo sexual partners (Larson 1993). At best, sexual fraud is relegated to shaming, in which informal but collective disapproval replaces government enforcement of community or legal norms (Gould 2002). Drug use, too, is an example of a penal issue that almost as easily could be defined as a public health problem. Yet penal definitions have been constructed, with the concurrent effect of further politicizing public discussion of such topics. Indeed, several observers, including most notably the National Criminal Justice Commission, attribute the growth in imprisonment to this heightened politicization of crime issues. Explains R. D. King (1998, 604),[7*] we have witnessed:

> the heightened political sensitivity on criminal justice issues in which politicians have either capitalized on, or been constrained by, a national fear of and obsession with crime. The result has been a national hoax in which politicians have talked tough and public debate has been reduced to sound-bite slogans in which real risks to the public, and the actual operation of the criminal justice system, are never exposed to proper analysis. Meanwhile, the true causes of crime, and the underlying social problems associated with it are ignored, and resources are diverted from educational and welfare programs into an ineffective, and even counterproductive, war on crime.

This phenomenon of "governing through crime" has been seen across many Western democracies in recent years (Caplow and Simon 1999, 79). Understanding these processes should be a primary aim of criminal justice theory.

PUNISHMENT AND JUSTICE THEORY: A CALL FOR A TRUE EXAMINATION

The preceding discussion of the American punishment binge presents a number of lessons that should be explicitly heeded in the development

---

* Chp. 22 "Prisons" by Roy D. King from "The Handbook of Crime and Punishment" edited by M. Tonry (2000). By permission of Oxford University Press, Inc.

of criminal justice theory, but at its most basic level it calls for a reemphasis of the concept of justice within the criminal justice system and a reduction in the emphasis on the criminal. Perhaps the greatest failure in the recent rage about the preventive state, and the related expansion of functions involving the criminal justice system, is the attenuation of principles derived from retributive rationales for criminal punishment. It may sound ironic to some that a "just deserts" model of punishment is spoken of favorably because the retributive model is often demonized as being repressive and alien to progressive impulses. Some contend that the inability to effectively scale punishments within a just deserts model, and the ease by which punishments in law can be erased and subsequently increased, are major culprits responsible for the contemporary imprisonment binge. In actuality, the retributive model has much greater potential to effectively constrain punishment practices than do alternative, utilitarian-based models. Linking criminal justice responses to the harm caused by an offender, even within the most draconian of sentencing schemes, bridles responses more effectively than does sentencing based solely on utilitarian rationales. Without a proper emphasis on proportionality and basic fairness, the demands of crime control have allowed us to impose life sentences on marijuana smokers.

Of course, one person's critique of unjust sentencing is another's ideological argument, but ideology is not the antithesis of empiricism. Empirical theory must incorporate into the theory-building and testing process, the ideological and power-based conflicts that greatly shape the contours and outcomes of criminal justice behavior. Indeed, as Walter Miller (1973, 142) reminds us, "ideology is the permanent hidden agenda of criminal justice." Such ideologically laden concepts and values often become the source for popular prescriptions for criminal justice behavior. A sterile criminal justice theory, one that fails to account for normative concepts and their consequences for social behavior, ultimately explains little.

In our view, a more detailed incorporation of goal and value structures into criminal justice theory would advance the field. Extant criminal justice theory, except perhaps in the court area — see Worden (chapter 8), and Kautt and Spohn (chapter 7) in this volume — tends to minimize an in-depth and critical realistic assessment of goal and value structures as determinants of criminal justice behavior. Instead, most criminal justice theory uncritically accepts the assumption that utilitarian values associated with the prevention and control of crime actually drives criminal justice behavior. This, however, is not the case.

To understand the full workings of the criminal justice system, critical justice theory needs to pay closer attention to at least four other factors: (1) retributive impulses; (2) mechanisms of repression aimed at the "dangerous" classes; (3) latent goals of criminal justice organizations that have more to do with organizational survival and growth than their stated intentions to prevent and control crime; and (4) the political and organizational benefits that derive from "governing through crime" strategies (Caplow and Simon 1999, 111).

Definitions of justice in a social setting will tell us much about the four elements identified above. Retributive impulses and their expressions in state-sponsored punishment of individuals are inextricably intertwined with definitions of "justice." The balance between governmental powers to deny one's life, liberty, or property and individual rights to withstand unwanted governmental intervention likewise is an essential indicator of how justice is defined in any polity (Packer 1968). This balance also speaks to the power of governmental agencies to engage in repressive actions against citizens, particularly those associated with the dangerous classes. For instance, in recent years we have seen many policing organizations engage in aggressive order-maintenance policing, proactively focusing on "quality of life" issues rather than reactively respond to crime. The result has been massive increases in arrest rates, especially among persons identified with the "dangerous classes." Why have some city police departments gone down this path (e.g., New York City) while others have engaged in more collaborative problem-solving activities with its citizens (e.g., San Diego; see Greene 1997)? Can these differences be explained by reference to local variations in definitions of justice? Would more expansive, constitutionalized definitions of due process constrain the ability of local governments to decide on their own what the balance should be between governmental powers and individual liberties? These are important questions to be addressed by criminal justice theory.

Criminal justice scholars should not only ask how and why social control is exercised differentially across peoples and places based on competing definitions of justice, but also how criminal justice behavior is influenced by the goal structures of criminal justice organizations. One would find that latent organizational goals (those related to organizational survival and growth) are often more important than manifest goals (stated goals, often associated with public safety) (e.g., Tonry 1990).[8] Finally, if criminal justice agencies were to focus on doing justice rather than fighting crime, would politicians find less institutional support for the type of "law and order" campaigns that often become polemical? Thus, in many respects, bringing justice to the center of criminal justice inquiry would not only enhance the explanatory value of criminal justice theory, it might also keep criminal justice organizations better focused on the true needs of the people they are supposed to serve.

Thus, we encourage criminal justice scholars to utilize justice as the central organizing concept of their theorizing and research. How can criminal justice theory incorporate justice into methods? How can scholars and policymakers apply principles of justice when evaluating the criminal justice system? Ultimately, the method must be holistic, for a theory of justice seeks to connect two different concepts — an understanding of the bases behind given policies or behavior and an evaluation of whether those measures make the criminal justice system more or less fair. Fairness in this context is multidimensional, incorporating the three branches of justice mentioned earlier: Are the policies or behaviors of the criminal justice system procedurally acceptable, creating public confidence in the system's legitimacy? Are their distributive outcomes appropriate? Do they help to restore society? These are some of the central questions that should be posed and addressed by criminal justice theory. Until the field of criminal justice moves more systematically in these directions, criminal justice theory will continue to remain underdeveloped, fragmented, and sterile.

NOTES

1. The authors would like to thank David Duffee, Edward Maguire, Julie Willis, and Anna Randolph for their helpful comments on earlier drafts of this chapter.

2. In the mid-1990s Professor Castellano had the good fortune to receive a Visiting Fellowship from the National Institute of Justice (NIJ), the research arm of the U.S. Department of Justice. While there he was able to watch decision-making processes up close, and to assess the nature of the agency's research portfolio. In time, he became convinced that the name of the agency was a misnomer; the more appropriate term for NIJ would be the National Institute of Crime Control.

3. A very interesting set of questions for criminal justice theory relates to recent changes that have apparently occurred with regard to the criminal justice system's historic willingness to neutralize severe penalties found in the law. Patterns of justice system adaptation to external demands for change have commonly resulted in the maintenance of preexisting legal norms, including going rates of punishment. These well-documented adjustments have led Sam Walker to come up with the concept of "the law of criminal justice thermodynamics" (1994, 51–52). A useful focus of systematic inquiry could focus on the reasons why legal officials seem

to be more willing today than in the past to apply draconian calls for punishment (rather than neutralizing them). Answers to this and related questions might go a long way toward helping us better understand the contemporary imprisonment binge, which is discussed subsequently.

4. This does not suggest that there is a rigid dichotomy between instrumental and symbolic purposes of the criminal law. As Carson (1974, 136) has observed:

> Although the distinction between the instrumental and symbolic import of a legal norm is an important one, analysis in terms of a mutually exclusive empirical dichotomy between the two is likely to be misleading. Such an approach not only glosses over the fact that, in practice, most attempts to make law probably contain elements of both, but also neglects the vital possibility of a dynamic interplay between them.

5. Between 1982 and 1999, national expenditures for the operations and outlay of the U.S. justice system increased 309 percent, moving from $36 billion to $147 billion in that time period (Bureau of Justice Statistics, 2002). Expenditures by the federal government grew faster (514%) than for state (393%) and local governments (257%); and by 1999 the federal share of justice system expenditures was 19 percent, compared to 12 percent in 1982. The increase in expenditures was highest for corrections (653.2%), while police protection exhibited a more modest, yet still large increase (485.5%). Justice spending outpaced growth in the Gross Domestic Product; in 1982 the ratio of justice expenditure to GDP was 1.10 percent but by 1999 it had risen to 1.58 percent.

6. For an exception see Clear (1994). The best work in this area has come from sociologists such as David Garland (2001).

7. From chapter 22 of *The Handbook of Crime and Punishment* by Roy D. King, edited by M. Tonry (2000). By permission of Oxford University Press, Inc.

8. Many studies across the range of criminal justice operations illustrate this basic point. For example, Langworthy (1989) has discussed the ability of sting operations to promote police organizational goals, including transitive and reflexive goals. Transitive goals are "intended effects on the organizational environment" (e.g., the prevention and control of crime) while reflexive goals are "goals for organizational survival" (1989, 29). As Langworthy (1989, 29) observed:

> Without question, sting operations are effective means of reflexive goal achievement. It is no accident that police departments engaged in sting operations contact the media when they begin their nighttime roundup of those who have done business with police fences. The high visibility of the roundups and the smile that crosses our faces as we ponder the situation of the unwitting criminals duped by the clever police sting can only enhance police organizational stature both with funding agencies and with the public.

Part II
Theories of Policing

The police are in many ways the gatekeepers of the criminal justice system. Once the police make an arrest or issue a citation, they invoke the remaining elements of the criminal justice process. A fruitful body of criminal justice theory has focused on the police. These theories have been developed at many levels, from those designed to explain the behavior of individual police officers, to those meant to explain the development of policing as an institution. Part II features two chapters on policing. In both cases, the unit of analysis is the police organization, and the important research question is why police organizations differ from one another. In chapter 5, Maguire and Uchida explore this question from a bird's eye view, showing how police organizations vary in many ways, and considering a variety of explanations for why this is true. In chapter 6, Renauer takes a much closer look, focusing in on one element of policing that varies across agencies — the implementation of community policing — and one theory that can be used to explain that variation — institutional theory. Inherent in both chapters is the important idea that policing is not a monolith; it varies across police organizations. The important question, of course, is why.

In chapter 5, "Explaining Police Organizations," Ed Maguire and Craig Uchida survey the landscape of theory and research on police organizations. The chapter begins by demonstrating that police departments differ from one another in many ways: in structures, policies, processes, and outputs. For example, some arrest offenders aggressively while others may rely on different, less formal methods for achieving compliance with the law. A large body of research has developed to explain these variations. Maguire and Uchida review this research, showing how these approaches contribute to a theoretical understanding of police organizations and the factors that influence, shape, enable, and constrain them. Theories explaining police organizations are an important element of criminal justice theory, and scholars have been conducting tests of these theories for nearly four decades. These theories have enabled us to learn a great deal about police organizations and the factors that influence them, though as Maguire and Uchida conclude, much remains to be learned.

In chapter 6, "Understanding Variety in Urban Community Policing: An Institutional Theory Approach," Brian Renauer presents a theory that attempts to explain variation in one particular kind of police effort: the adoption of a particular kind of community policing. In particular, he focuses on those elements of community policing that are designed to stimulate community building activities with the intention of enhancing sustainable neighborhoods. Renauer argues that there are important variations in the adoption of the community building components of community policing in urban police organizations, and more importantly, that these variations are both measurable and explainable.

To explain variation in the implementation of community policing, Renauer draws on institutional theory, a specific organizational theory which has been applied to many different types of organizations, and which was introduced briefly by Maguire and Uchida in chapter 5. According to Renauer, institutional theory provides a number of insights about variation in urban community policing. First, it focuses attention on the different levels that influence police organizations: "centrist" forces such as government agencies and national police professional organizations (such as think tanks focusing on policing issues); "local" forces, such as mayors, city councils, and the citizenry; and "internal" forces, such as police unions, organizational culture, and tradition. Second, it focuses attention on the routes through which organizational change efforts arrive at and are introduced into police organizations. Government agencies, police professional organizations, and other police departments all play a role in stimulating organizational change in policing, as do more localized forces internal and external to the agency. Running throughout these mechanisms for influencing organizational change is the central idea that organizations change to maintain the appearance of legitimacy. Renauer explores how variation in the implementation of community policing results from the intersection of these various forces at different levels, all with the goal of enhancing the perceived legitimacy of the organization. Renauer concludes by outlining several ways that researchers can collect data to test the hypotheses he has outlined.

Together, the two chapters in part II illustrate rather pointedly that while police organizations share many characteristics, they also differ from one another in a number of important ways. Due to space limitations, we were unable to present examples of criminal justice theories that have been applied to policing at other levels, both smaller and larger than police organizations. But such work exists, and it falls well within the legitimate territory of criminal justice theory. For example, some theories explain differences in the behavior of individual police officers, exploring why some officers make more arrests and use more force, while others adopt a gentler or less formal orientation. At a more macrolevel, some theories explain why different nations employ fewer numbers of police officers than other nations, or why some nations adopt different policing structures. In sum, explaining different facets of policing at different levels is all within the purview of criminal justice theory. Chapters 5 and 6 present two examples of criminal justice theory applied to police *as organizations*.

DISCUSSION QUESTIONS

1 Both chapters in this section make the claim that police departments differ from one another in many ways. Think about one or two ways in which they might differ, and generate a potential explanation for these differences.
2. Both of the chapters in this section discuss a specific theory that has been applied to policing: institutional theory. In a nutshell, this theory argues that organizations are heavily influenced not only by the technical requirements of the work they perform, but also by widely held beliefs of certain individuals and groups about how they *should* do their work. Some institutional theorists have made the argument that if the theory is true, organizations within a certain sector (such as all police organizations) will grow to resemble one another more and more over time after repeatedly trying to conform to expectations about what they should look like. We know from the history of policing that experiments with alternative types of police uniforms (such as blazers, or those without traditional police insignias) have failed and resulted in a return to the traditional police uniform. The same has occurred when departments have attempted to eliminate in a wholesale fashion the typical rank structure of police departments.

- What kinds of specific forces might influence a department's inability to change its uniforms, its rank structure, or other elements of traditional policing?
- Do the forces you have just identified act only as restraints, in the sense that they only inhibit change in police organizations? Or, might these same forces also act as enablers, supporting some changes in policing while trying to thwart others?
- Recent research has demonstrated that many police organizations have begun to adopt gang units to focus specifically on youth gang problems. However, many police organizations without a gang problem have also adopted gang units. What kinds of forces might lead a police organization in a community without a gang problem to adopt a gang unit?

3. Both chapters in this section have chosen police organizations as their units of analysis. Both are premised on the assumption that police organizations vary in important ways, and that understanding why they vary is important. But theories of policing need not just explore variation across police organizations. They can also explore variation in policing across police officers, across geographic districts within police departments, across states, or across nations. In other words, there are many potential units of analysis in criminal justice theories that focus on policing. With this in mind:

- Select a unit of analysis other than police organizations.
- Select a dependent variable; something that varies across the unit you have chosen.
- Select one or more independent variables that you believe plays a role in influencing the variation in your dependent variable.

4. Once you have answered these questions, you have started to generate a theory about some aspect of policing. When you read chapters 7 and 8 in part III, return to this police theory and ask yourself what steps you should take before you would go to all the time and expense of gathering data about your theory. What suggestions do Kautt and Spohn and Worden have to assist you in determining whether your theory is worth pursuing, or how it can be modified to make it stronger?

5

EXPLAINING POLICE ORGANIZATIONS[1]

Edward R. Maguire and Craig D. Uchida

INTRODUCTION

The introductory chapters in this volume have established the basic boundaries of criminal justice theory. This chapter examines one tradition of research and theory in criminal justice: efforts to identify the factors responsible for producing departmental variations in policing. We explore the ways that various features of police organizations have been explained over time and place. Police organizations share much in common, but they also exhibit tremendous variation. Some are large, but many are quite small; some patrol aggressively, arresting offenders for minor public order offenses, while others enforce the law with less vigor; some have tall hierarchies and formal command structures, while others are less formal, with only a handful of separate levels; some work closely with communities and spend time formulating customized solutions to local problems, while others shun community involvement and provide more "traditional" police services. This variation in both what organizations *do* and what they *are* is not unique to police agencies. As W. R. Scott (1992, 1) notes, "while organizations may possess common, generic characteristics, they exhibit staggering variety — in size, in structure, and in operating processes." This chapter explores efforts to explain variation in American police organizations: variation in what they are and what they do; variation in form and function, in structure and process, in policy and practice.

The subject of this chapter is police *organizations*. The study of police agencies as organizations is a growing field, owing its theoretical roots to the sociological and social psychological study of organizations more generally.[2] This focus on police as organizations is the common thread linking each section of the chapter. Thus, we do not examine other frequently studied features of policing, including police culture, police discretionary behaviors (and misbehaviors), individual police officer attributes, and many other important phenomena occurring at units of analysis that are larger (e.g., states or nations) or smaller (e.g., officers or workgroups) than police organizations.[3]

Furthermore, the focus of this chapter is on broad organizational properties rather than particular policies, programs, activities, or structural features. Researchers have produced a wealth of valuable research on particular features of police organizations such as pursuit policies; DARE programs; the use of one- and two-officer patrol cars; and the establishment of special units for various tasks, such as narcotics, child abuse, or gangs. The line between general and specific organizational properties is admittedly arbitrary. Nevertheless, the focus of the chapter is to draw together a diverse body of scholarship on American police organizations. Research on very specific (and sometimes esoteric or idiosyncratic) organizational properties will make it much more difficult to consolidate this vast body of theory and research. Thus, while we do not discuss the prevalence of specialized bias-crime units, we do discuss specialization more generally; we do not discuss the implementation of various new technologies for processing offenders, but we do examine the adoption of innovation; we do not discuss drunk driving enforcement or use of force, but we do discuss aggressive patrol strategies and styles of policing.

There is some ambiguity over what constitutes a police organization (Maguire, Snipes et al. 1998). As Bayley (1985, 7) notes, "police come in a bewildering variety of forms ... moreover, many agencies that are not thought of as police nonetheless possess 'police' powers." To reduce the scope of our task, we shall focus on public police organizations in the United States whose primary purpose is to provide generalized police service, including responding to calls-for-service for a distinct residential population.[4]

Even after narrowing the focus in this way, there remain considerable variations among police organizations over time and place.[5] A substantial body of theory and research has developed to measure and explain these variations. As one way to organize the large body of scholarship on police organizations, we draw an important distinction between what they *do* and what they *are*. These categories sometimes overlap in practice, but there is some precedent in the development of organization theory for treating them separately.

WHAT POLICE ORGANIZATIONS DO

Like corporate America, police organizations do many things. Most people are unaccustomed to thinking of *organizations* as doing things. After all, organizations are comprised of people, and it is the people within them who think, plan, act, decide, debate, respond, cooperate, and all of the other activities and behaviors in which *people* engage. Yet, as Maguire (2003, 9–10) has argued:

> Organizations are greater than the sum of their parts. They expand and contract, rise and fall, and generally take on lives of their own. Organizations, like individuals and social groups, do not only act, but are acted upon as well. They are influenced, shaped and constrained by a complex interaction of political, social, economic, cultural, and institutional forces. Organizations exhibit patterned regularities, and they can (and indeed should) be studied apart from the people within them (Blau et al., 1966; Blau and Schoenherr, 1971).

Work by King and his colleagues (1997) takes this argument one step further, using a biological or life-course perspective to study the birth, death, and aging processes of police agencies. Thinking about organizations as separate from the people within them — as "corporate persons"— is essential to understanding what they do (Coleman 1974).

Police organizations do many things: they make arrests, quell disturbances, respond to emergencies, solve problems, form relationships with the community, and other activities too numerous to summarize briefly. These activities constitute the output of police organizations. Systematic collection of data from large samples of police agencies has shown that there is considerable variation in the quantity and quality of these outputs over time and place. These data are used in many ways: arrest and clearance statistics, for instance, are frequently used as measures of a police organization's productivity. The use of these kinds of performance indicators is beginning to fall out of fashion as police executives, scholars, and reformers focus on alternative measures. These data are also used as indicators of a police organization's "style."[6] Some agencies may emphasize aggressive enforcement of panhandling ordinances, for instance, while others may tend to ignore such minor offenses. While the concept of organizational style is intangible and difficult to measure, researchers have attempted to draw inferences about policing styles by examining arrest patterns for discretionary offenses such as drunkenness or disorderly conduct (Wilson 1968b). While police organizations do many different things, data are systematically collected on only a handful of these activities. Organizational measures constructed from these data are therefore limited.

One focus of this chapter is to examine variations in police activities, processes, performance, and style over time and across agencies. We will trace efforts to explain what police organizations do, from the traditional focus on arrests and clearances, to more recent efforts to embrace problem-solving and community partnership strategies.

WHAT POLICE ORGANIZATIONS ARE

What a police organization *does* is external, typically taking place outside of the organization: in the community, on the streets, in residences. The features that define what a police organization *is* tend to be internal: administrative arrangements, processing routines, structures, communication patterns, and overall "corporate" personalities.[7] In short, what police organizations *do*, takes place within the framework (or context) of what they *are*. The social scientific study of what police organizations are has a much shorter history than the study of what they do. This history parallels a similar split in the study of organizations more generally. While outputs and performance have always been a primary focus of organizational research, it wasn't until the late 1950s that "researchers began to conceive of organizations as more than just rationally-derived mechanisms for the production of goods and services, but as entities worthy of understanding for what they *are* in addition to what they *produce*" (Maguire 2003, 9).

The internal features of police organizations vary considerably from one agency to the next. Researchers began to measure this variation using systematic surveys in about the late 1920s. Attempts to explain this variation came later, with theoretical explanations appearing in the 1960s and empirical studies beginning in the mid-1970s. Much of this research focuses on why we have the police organizations we have, seeking to isolate local contingencies (such as regional, historical, governmental, cultural, or demographic factors) that would lead to variations in police organizational form from one jurisdiction to another.

EXPLANATION

The first step in explaining why differences exist between police organizations (or any social entity, from people to nations) is to measure those differences. The problems in measuring the properties of police organizations are noteworthy, though there is not sufficient space in this chapter to explore measurement issues in detail (Maguire and Uchida 2000). Once researchers have measured variation in police organizations, the next natural step is to ask why such differences exist. That is the goal of explanation. Like measurement, explanation is one of the principal goals of social science research. Social scientists usually arrive at explanations for social phenomena through induction and deduction. Using the inductive method, they begin by collecting data and then analyze or search for patterns in the data. Based on their observations and analyses, they develop theories. Using the deductive method, they begin by specifying a theory, and then collect and analyze data to test the theory. In reality, these two processes tend to overlap. Frequently, social scientists begin by stating an explicit theory and collecting data to test the theory (deductive method). Upon finding only partial support for the theory in the data, they will often modify the theory accordingly (inductive method).

Police organizations, like many other units of analysis studied by social scientists, vary widely on some dimensions, and are very similar on others. When social scientists use the term *explanation*, they are nearly always referring to explanations for why some trait varies across time and place. For instance, some police organizations are steeped heavily in paramilitary culture, while others appear to be more democratic and less rigid. When social scientists try to "explain" paramilitarism in police organizations, they mean that they are trying to explain why some organizations are more paramilitary than are others. In other words, explanations in social science nearly always have the goal of *explaining variation* among units of analysis.[8]

If, for example, we believe police organizations in turbulent political climates are less productive (say, in terms of clearance rates) than others, then to properly test the theory, we must collect data from a sample of police organizations in different political climates. If we were to only study police organizations in hostile political climates, we could not test the theory because we would have nothing with which to compare them (in social science terms, this test would be flawed because the independent *variable* does not *vary*). A similar logical flaw, in which the dependent variable does not vary, is present in much of the current popular management literature. Many of the books in this genre study successful companies, identifying attributes that are common across each. The flaw, of course, is that these same attributes might be present in unsuccessful companies, but we cannot know for sure because they were not studied (Aupperle et al. 1986; King 1999, personal communication to Maguire).[9]

Thus, the key to developing, testing, modifying, and understanding social science explanations is *comparison*. The comparative method has come to be associated with multinational research, but comparative research can focus on many types of organized collectivities, from police departments and schools, to nations and societies (Blau et al., 1966; Ostrom 1973; Ragin 1987). It is a cornerstone of sociological research on organizations (Langworthy 1986; W. R. Scott 1992). The comparative method is featured prominently throughout this volume.

The selection of a unit of analysis within which to conduct comparisons depends heavily on the research question. If our research question focuses on why some police organizations are more effective than are others, our unit of analysis is police organizations. If, on the other hand, our interest is in how a single organization changes over time, our unit of analysis is the organization at specific points in time (like the month or year). Sometimes the unit of analysis is more complex, combining cross-sections (organizations) and times (years). For instance, if we want to determine whether changing the number of officers in municipal police departments has an effect on clearance rates, we would need to collect and analyze data from multiple organizations at multiple times. Whether we are comparing multiple organizations, the same organization at multiple times, or both simultaneously, comparison is central to understanding social science explanations.

This section examines how social scientists have sought to develop explanations for various features of police organizations. Throughout this section, the concepts we have just discussed — explaining variation, units of analysis, and comparison — will appear over and over again as central and important themes. The most common unit of analysis in our discussion is the individual police organization, and the studies we discuss usually allow for comparisons by including observations from a sample of such organizations. Nearly all of these studies are focused on explaining why some police organizations are different from others, isolating the causal factors thought to be responsible for these variations. One thing that should become very clear throughout the remainder of this chapter is how measurement is inextricably linked with explanation (Maguire and Uchida 2000).

EXPLAINING VARIATION IN POLICE ORGANIZATIONS

The scholarly study of variation in police organizations was born in the early 1960s. Following a trend in the sociology of organizations and the administrative sciences more generally, policing scholars began to devote serious attention to the role of the environment in determining the nature of a police organization. Organizational scholars of that era were profoundly influenced by a series of studies stressing the importance of the environment on organizations. Burns and Stalker (1961), Eisenstadt (1959), Emery and Trist (1965), and Lawrence and Lorsch (1967) introduced a new way of thinking about organizations and their problems. Based on their influence, scholars, managers, and others interested in organizational life could now be heard talking about the "fit" between an organization and its environment. The environment consists of everything external to an organization that is important for its functioning and survival. "Funding agencies, raw materials, clients, potential employees, the media, politicians, rumors, legislation, and employees' unions all reside in an organization's environment" (Maguire 2003, 26).

Initial discussions of the linkage between police organizations and their environments were both subtle and implicit. For instance, Stinchcombe (1963) argued that the distribution of public and private spaces within a community has important effects on administrative practices and aggregate patterns of police behavior. Of particular importance here is his notion that different concentrations of public places within communities might account for differences between urban and rural policing. At around the same time, Wilson (1963) developed a theory linking the professionalism of police agencies to local government structure and political ethos. Though both of these early works seem to have disappeared from the landscape of modern police scholarship, they helped to plant the seeds for a growing wave of police research and theory.

Presumably influenced by these earlier works both inside and outside the study of policing, Reiss and Bordua (1967) highlighted some of the effects that the environment might have on police organizations.[10] They argued that the environmental perspective was especially important for police organizations, since "the police have as their fundamental task the creation and maintenance of, and their participation in, external relationships" (Reiss and Bordua 1967, 25–26). Reiss and Bordua described the "internal consequences" of three broad environmental features: the nature of the legal system, the nature of illegal activity, and the structure of civic accountability. They also noted several other environmental features that might be important in shaping police organizations. It is perhaps one indicator of the halting progress in the study of police organizations since the mid-1970s that important theoretical propositions outlined by Reiss and Bordua still have not been empirically tested.[11]

These early works had the effect of focusing attention on some of the factors responsible for variation in police organizations — both what they are and what they do — across time and space. Yet, the appearance in 1968 of James Q. Wilson's *Varieties of Police Behavior* signified the first attempt to formulate a theory of police departments *as organizations* and test the theory using a variety of qualitative and quantitative methods (Langworthy 1986; Maguire 2003). Wilson's book continues to influence police scholarship today, though sadly, empirical research has yet to test the full range of Wilson's propositions (Slovak 1986).[12] Nevertheless, these early works set the stage for three decades of research on interagency variation in police organizations. With this brief historical backdrop in mind, we now discuss the evolution of this body of research, starting with what police organizations do.

EMPIRICAL RESEARCH ON WHAT POLICE ORGANIZATIONS DO

In this section, we discuss various efforts to explain some of the external features of American police organizations, including their outputs, styles, and performance. *Varieties of Police Behavior* (Wilson 1968b) was the first and most influential attempt to explain the outputs and behaviors of police agencies (their arrest rates and styles of policing). Wilson's theory essentially posited that local contingencies such as characteristics of the population, the form of government, and political culture, shape agency behaviors (and therefore outputs). Wilson's work was the first in a long line of research on the causes and correlates of police organizational outputs, which are most frequently operationalized as aggregate-level arrest rates for various offenses (Crank 1990; Langworthy 1985; Monkkonen 1981; Slovak 1986; Swanson 1978).[13] More recent research extends these traditional output measures to include community policing activities, attempting to generate theoretical and empirical explanations for interagency variation in these activities (Maguire, Kuhns et al. 1997; Zhao 1996). Overall, this body of research seeks to determine whether the environmental, historical, and other contextual circumstances (known in organization theory as contingencies)[14] of police organizations play a role in shaping their outputs and performance. This literature includes a broad range of theoretical explanations that have not yet been tested empirically (e.g., Crank 1994; Crank and Langworthy 1992; Duffee 1990). In addition, there is a large body of empirical research in this area that ranges from being nearly atheoretical to almost wholly guided by theory.

Maguire and Uchida (2000) identify twenty studies seeking to explain variation in what police organizations do. All of these studies meet several criteria: (1) the dependent variable is an organizational property; (2) there is at least one explanatory variable; (3) the study is based on quantitative data; (4) it reports the results of a statistical analysis (loosely defined) of the data; and (5) the total number of observations in the analysis is at least twenty (to allow for adequate comparison). In addition, since their focus is on what police organizations do, they do not include studies in which the dependent variable is a measure of crime. Although police organizations may have an effect on crime rates, crime is not necessarily an organizational property; in the parlance of performance measurement, it is an *outcome* rather than an *output*.[15] The remainder of this section explores some of the issues that Maguire and Uchida (2000) identify based on these twenty studies.

Wilson (1968b) was the first to use quantitative data from a sample of police agencies in an attempt to explain what police organizations do. This analysis was separate from the well-known details of his taxonomy of police styles (legalistic, watchman, and service). Wilson's theory was that local political culture constrains (but does not dictate) the style of policing within a community. Wilson argued that measuring both style and political culture would be "exceptionally difficult if not impossible" (p. 271). Nevertheless, considering it to be a worthwhile exercise, he constructed a "substitute" measure of political culture focusing on the form of government, the partisanship of elections, and the professionalism of city managers (based on their education and experience). Nodding to the presence of measurement error in his constructs, Wilson concludes: "the theory that the political culture of a community constrains law enforcement styles survives the crude and inadequate statistical tests that available data permit" (p. 276).[16]*

A number of empirical studies of police organizational style have appeared since 1968. All of them measure police style using arrest rates for some mix of offense types, usually less serious offenses thought to be subject to greater discretion. Most of these studies find that organizational and environmental characteristics play a significant role in shaping police style, though there is little consensus or uniformity about what kinds of explanatory variables are important. Several other studies use arrest rates as a dependent variable but do not treat them as

---

* Reprinted by permission of the publisher from *Varieties of Police Behavior: The Management of Law and Order in Eight Communities* by James Q. Wilson, p. 276, Cambridge, Mass.: Harvard University Press, Copyright © 1968, 1978 by the President and Fellows of Harvard College.

measures of police style. They are usually referred to more generally as indicators of organizational activity, behavior, or productivity.

Other empirical studies have focused on effectiveness or performance, which is usually measured using objective criteria such as clearance rates or subjective criteria such as citizen evaluations of local police performance (Alpert and Moore 1993; Bayley 1994; Parks 1984).[17] One issue these studies address, in part, is whether bigger police departments are necessarily better, as some critics of American policing have claimed (e.g., Murphy and Plate 1977). Subjective studies of police performance conducted by Elinor Ostrom and her colleagues suggest that bigger is not necessarily better.[18] Cordner's (1989) examination of investigative effectiveness in Maryland found that the region of the state (a proxy for urbanization) was an important predictor, but that crime, workload, and department size were generally insignificant. Davenport (1996) is the only scholar to test a model in which the environment has a direct effect on department performance, and an indirect effect on performance through organization structure. His findings are too numerous to summarize, but the most import predictor of department performance was the complexity of the environment. Probably the most consistent finding is that larger police organizations are not necessarily more effective, and in many cases they are less effective than smaller agencies.

In the past few years, responding to the need for better measures of what police organizations do, researchers began to focus their attention on measuring other facets of police behavior. Using data from a national survey of police organizations, Zhao (1996) was the first researcher to test an empirical model explaining community policing. Zhao divided community policing into external and internal components, measuring and estimating models for each one separately. Zhao's findings span the sections of this chapter, since his findings regarding externally focused change refer to those community policing activities that occur outside the police organization and in the community, while his results for internally focused change consist primarily of administrative reforms. All of these studies construct measures of community policing using various methods, and then try to explain interagency variations in these measures. Probably the most consistent finding in these studies is the important role of region and department size in shaping community policing.[19] Emerging research continues to address the causes and consequences of the adoption of community policing. In chapter 6, Renauer presents a new theory to explain variation across American cities in urban community policing, particularly in those activities related to community-building.

EMPIRICAL STUDIES SEEKING TO EXPLAIN WHAT POLICE ORGANIZATIONS ARE

The topic of this section — explaining what the police are — has received less attention from researchers and theorists than the study of what the police do. The reason, as in organizational studies more generally, is probably that most people are far more interested in how organizations behave and what they produce than in more mundane administrative details like how they are structured. This is especially the case in policing, where the "bottom line" is typically considered to be crime, a subject of endless fascination to the American populace. While reams of paper have been expended by reformers trying to convince police administrators to change the structures and internal operating processes of police organizations, scholarly progress in producing theory and research on these organizational features has been slow. In this section, we trace the development of research on internal variation in police organizations, including structure, policy, and other administrative attributes.

We find ourselves once again returning to Wilson's (1968b) *Varieties of Police Behavior*. Wilson's analysis did not explicitly consider internal organizational attributes as an object of study, but throughout the book he makes references to the structural correlates of police style. Langworthy (1986) considered Wilson's work "the only empirically derived theory of police organization to date." Langworthy (1986, 32) summarized Wilson's implicit linkage between style and structure as follows:

> Watchman police departments were said to emphasize order maintenance, to be hierarchically flat, unspecialized, and decentralized. Legalistic departments were characterized as oriented toward vigorous law enforcement, hierarchically tall, specialized in law enforcement function, and centralized. Service-style departments were described as responsive to requests for aid or action, highly specialized across a broad range of functions, decentralized in operations, and centralized administratively.

Thus, although Wilson's work is best remembered as a theory of police style, it also contains an implicit theory of police organizational structure.

The first empirical studies in this genre didn't appear until the mid-1970s, emerging, like Wilson's work, from political science and urban studies. In 1975, T. A. Henderson published a study on the correlates of professionalism in sheriffs' agencies. The study falls within the class of theory and research that Langworthy (1986) classifies as normative, since defining and measuring police professionalism requires the researcher to make personal judgments about what it means to be professional.[20] It was the first (and perhaps only) study to treat professionalism as an organizational, rather than an individual, attribute. In 1976, Morgan and Swanson examined a number of organizational attributes. With little regard for theory, the researchers used exploratory factor analysis to construct both their independent and dependent variables.[21] According to the Social Science Citation Index, neither study has been cited very often (7 for Henderson and 1 for Morgan and Swanson), suggesting that the birth of empirical research on the causes and correlates of police organization was rather anonymous.

During the 1970s, Elinor Ostrom and her colleagues collected considerable data on American police organizations. They examined policing as an "industry," focusing on patterns in the production and consumption of police services. In a number of publications, Ostrom, Parks, and Whitaker (see 1978a) described and explained how police organizations in metropolitan areas rely on one another for mutual support and to provide various specialized services. Their work defied critics who argued that American policing was a loosely connected patchwork of small and untrained police agencies, often consisting of only a handful of officers (Murphy and Plate 1977; Skoler and Hetler 1970). While the work of Ostrom and her colleagues made enormous contributions to the study of policing in general, the unit of analysis in nearly all of their publications was the metropolitan area and its patterns of service production and consumption, not police organizations.[22] For that reason, most of their work falls outside the scope of this chapter. Their focus on the internal consequences of police organizational size, however, was one of the earliest studies seeking to explain variations in police organizational structure (Ostrom et al. 1978b).

Probably the most influential work in this area is Robert Langworthy's 1986 book, *The Structure of Police Organizations*. Langworthy argued convincingly that with the exception of James Q. Wilson's work, scholarly attention to police *organizations* had been restricted to normative theories and prescriptions about how they *should* be structured and what they *should* be doing. This tendency to focus on prescription rather than description and explanation, on what police *should* be doing rather than what they *are* doing and why they are doing it, left a large empirical gap in our understanding of police organizations.[23] As a first step toward filling this gap, Langworthy borrowed a series of propositions from organization theory (and once again from Wilson's work), constructing his own unique theory to explain variation in the structure of police organizations. Using data from two national surveys (including data from Ostrom and her colleagues and the Kansas City General

Administrative Survey), Langworthy then tested his theory empirically. His analysis was the first comprehensive comparative empirical study to treat the structure of police organizations as a dependent variable. He concluded that the causal forces in his study did not appear to exert a significant constraint on organization structure (136):

> It seems plain that the explanations, size, technology, population mobility, population complexity, and type of local government, although theoretically significant determinants or correlates of agency structure, explain very little of the variance in agency structure. The constraints, when they are suggested by the data, do not appear insurmountable.

These findings suggest that American police executives are, by and large, free to design police organizations as they see fit.

Research studies on the causes and correlates of police organizational structure continue to emerge. Crank and Wells (1991) found that size exerts a nonlinear effect on structure. King (1999) found that older police organizations employ fewer civilians that younger ones. Davenport (1996) found that violent crime, resource capacity, and environmental turbulence have mixed effects on measures of structure. Maguire's (2003) replication and extension of Langworthy's study found a series of mixed effects of age, size, technology, and environment on structure. Maguire divided the structure of police organizations into two domains: (1) structural complexity, and (2) structural coordination and control mechanisms. Structural complexity is the extent to which the organization divides itself into vertical or hierarchical levels (such as different levels of command), functional divisions (such as special units or teams), and spatial divisions (such as different precincts). Those organizations with many vertical, functional, and spatial divisions are more complex. Structural coordination and control mechanisms are elements that are built into the structure of the organization to help managers and administrators maintain coordination and control. Maguire considered three such mechanisms: the use of administrative staffs, formal written policies, and centralization of command. Maguire found strong evidence that the context of police organizations exerts constraints on structural complexity (vertical, functional, and spatial divisions), but not on structural coordination and control (administration, formalization, and centralization). Overall, the study of police organizational structure has entered a stage of incremental development.

Other studies in this genre examined the environmental and organizational correlates of police innovation and various internal (administratively oriented) community policing reforms. Based on the literature on "innovation diffusion," Weiss (1997) examines two questions: do police organizations rely on informal communications with other agencies (peer emulation), and if so, do these contacts result in the diffusion of innovation across agencies? Diffusion of innovation is the general notion that innovative practices, whether new vaccines to cure the sick or new managerial practices in policing, tend to spread in predictable ways. Weiss found that agencies do engage in informal information sharing, and that peer emulation and cosmopolitanism both shape the adoption of innovations. King (1998) also examines the sources of innovation in police agencies, but his research is rooted more in traditional organizational theory than the diffusion literature. King found that innovation is a multidimensional concept consisting of at least five separate dimensions: radical, administrative, technical, line-technical, and programmatic. Furthermore, he found additional evidence that at least some of these dimensions can be further reduced into multiple subdimensions. The findings are too numerous to summarize here, but overall, organizational factors played a stronger role in shaping innovativeness than environmental or "ascriptive" factors.

Several studies have examined just one category of innovativeness: the various kinds of administrative changes occurring under the banner of community policing. Zhao (1996) was the first researcher to examine the causes of "internally-focused" changes occurring under community policing. He constructed a measure of internal change and then sought to explain variation in the measure using a number of organizational and environmental predictors. His models were able to explain more of the variation in externally focused change than in internally focused change. In their evaluation of the Justice Department's COPS Office, Roth and Johnson (1997) found that while federal funding may have affected external elements of community policing, agencies receiving the funding were not more likely than nonfundees to have made internal organizational changes. Finally, in a study focusing on measurement rather than explanation, Maguire and Uchida (2000) developed reliable measures of internal change which they referred to as "adaptation." Although region and department size were only included in the model as predictors for statistical reasons, once again, both were found to exert a significant effect on adaptation.

Explaining what the police are — their policies, structures, programs, and other elements — represents the next frontier of research on police organizations. The research in this area is relatively undeveloped and there is an untapped pool of theories to test. For instance, promising theories that were developed in the 1960s have still not been fully tested. These include the work of Reiss and Bordua (1967) and a number of propositions about police agency structure implicit in Wilson's (1968b) theory of police behavior (Langworthy 1986). In addition, there have been a number of recent theoretical contributions in the areas of contingency theory (Maguire 2003), institutional theory (Crank 1994; Crank and Langworthy 1992; Katz 1997; Mastrofski and Uchida 1993), resource dependency theory, and various combinations of these theories (Maguire, Zhao, and Lovrich 1999; Mastrofski and Ritti 2000). Below, we describe these theories and their promise for helping us to understand police organizations.

WHAT FACTORS SHAPE POLICE ORGANIZATIONS?

Many of the same variables are used to explain interagency variation in both what police organizations do and what they are. One reason for this is undoubtedly the availability of these measures in common sources such as Census Bureau publications and data or the Municipal Yearbook. Another reason is that many of the same theories are used to explain differences across police agencies.

If we were to isolate the factors that shape police organizations with any degree of certainty and rigor, we would require a full-length book to do so. The studies listed by Maguire and Uchida (2000) contain at least eighty-five separate independent variables, even after combining those that are similar but not exactly the same (two different measures of political culture, for instance). The following list contains the fourteen measures that had at least one statistically significant effect in at least three separate studies. They are sorted in descending order by the number of studies in which they demonstrated a significant effect:

- Organizational Size (18)
- City Governance (5)
- Region (5)
- Concentration (4)
- Crime Patterns (4)
- Organizational Age (4)
- Political Culture (4)
- Population Size (4)
- Population Heterogeneity (4)
- Poverty/Income (3)
- Urbanization or Ruralization (4)
- Span of Control or Supervisory Ratio (3)
- Time (3)
- Vertical Differentiation (3)

We are careful not to make too much of these findings. This list is intended to simply illustrate the kinds of variables that researchers have used to explain differences in police organizations, and those that have been found important. These findings pertain to several different dependent variables, and neither the direction of effects nor the quality of the studies is considered. Nevertheless, this list illustrates some of the factors commonly thought and found to influence police organizations.

The most frequent and consistent finding in organizational research on police is the importance of organization size. The effects of size are not universal, as Ostrom and her colleagues have repeatedly demonstrated; the research suggests that size has an important effect on style, structure, and processes, but not necessarily on effectiveness and efficiency. Region also continues to exert significant effects on the administration of public organizations. Yet, to date, researchers have not done a very good job in isolating the theoretical reasons for these effects, though many possibilities have been suggested (Maguire et al. 1997). The structure of city governance, together with local political culture, also exerts significant effects on police organizations, suggesting that any comprehensive theory of police organizations needs to account for political effects. Another particularly noteworthy finding is the presence of two variables suggesting a historical effect on police organizations: the department's age and the passage of time. Police organizations constantly change. The appearance of time and age in this list suggests that they change in ways that are sometimes predictable. Thus, any comprehensive theory of police organizations needs to account for historical effects. The remaining variables are all elements of the organization or its environment, and most are represented in traditional organizational theories.

FUTURE PROSPECTS

The scholarly study of police organizations has not evolved in a progressive, orderly fashion. Much of the research contains methodological and theoretical shortcomings, and for that reason it has been of limited utility for understanding police organizations and the forces that shape them. A byproduct of this limitation is that this research has been of little practical use for police executives and policy makers. More than two decades ago, Dorothy Guyot (1977) bemoaned the lack of empirical research on police organizations, citing Wilson's *Varieties of Police Behavior* as the lone exception. Nearly a decade later, Robert Langworthy (1986, 32) echoed Guyot's complaints, arguing that Wilson's work "remains the only empirically derived theory of police organization to date." Through the mid-1980s, police organizational scholarship had not substantially evolved beyond Wilson's seminal work.

Langworthy's *The Structure of Police Organizations* was an important turning point in police organizational scholarship. It is among a handful of studies that have blended theory and research in an effort to further our understanding about the structure and function of American police organizations. Perhaps even more importantly, it inspired a new generation of police organizational scholarship (Crank and Wells 1991; King 1999; King, Travis, and Langworthy 1997; Maguire 1997, 2003).

Thus, we cannot complain as forcefully as our predecessors about the status of the scholarship regarding police organizations. Since the mid-1990s, there have been a number of improvements in theory, data, and method, though certainly much remains to be done. This section has two simultaneous goals: to diagnose some of the weaknesses in this line of research, and to suggest some ways that researchers might continue to breathe into it some new life. We will consider three primary areas: theory, research, and policy.

Theory

Throughout this chapter we have made reference to theories used by scholars to explain interagency variation in police organizations. Some of these theories have received empirical support, others have not, and others remain untested. This section briefly reviews the state of theoretical explanation in the study of American police organizations.

We begin by restating contingency theory, since it is an inclusive theory of structure, process, and performance. Briefly stated, contingency theory holds that organizations will only be effective if they remain dynamic, adapting to changes in technology and environment. Technology here is used in the broadest sense, referring to the tools and strategies used by the organization to process raw materials. Thus, in addition to the material technologies that are having such a profound influence in policing (Ericson and Haggerty 1997; Manning 1992), it also includes the social technologies used by the police to process and change people and communities (Maguire 2003; Mastrofski and Ritti 2000). Contingency theory focuses predominantly on the "task environment" — those elements of the environment with direct relevance for the work of the organization. In policing, the task environment would include citizens, courts and other parts of the criminal justice system, patterns of crime and criminality, the sources available for recruiting and training officers, the physical and social attributes of the community, and numerous other external forces that shape the structure and function of police agencies.

Contingency theory is the foundation of nearly every study of police organizations. It is the implicit source of most of the explanatory variables used in models explaining organizational features: size, technology, and the various elements of the environment. It assumes that effective organizations are rational entities seeking to maximize their levels of effectiveness and efficiency. It also assumes that organizations failing to adapt to changes in technology and environment will be ineffective, fail, and be replaced by others (Langworthy 1992).[24] This inherent rationality is why many organizational scholars have abandoned contingency theory (Donaldson 1995). Most of the people who study police organizations would probably not describe them as rational, dynamic, or adaptive. The failure of contingency theory to effectively explain the structure and function of organizations has led to the development of numerous other theories. We now discuss three alternative perspectives on the role of organizational environments: as sources of legitimacy, resources, and information.

Institutional theory has its roots in the early study of organizations by such influential theorists as Talcott Parsons and Philip Selznick. For example, Selznick described institutionalization as the process by which organizations develop an "organic character" (Perrow 1986) and become "infused with value beyond the technical requirements of the task at hand" (Selznick 1957, 17). Selznick was fascinated by the paradox that organizations are created for rational action, but that they never quite succeed in conquering irrationality. Institutional theory has experienced a revival since the mid-1980s, a trend that many attribute to an influential article by Meyer and Rowan in 1977. Meyer and Rowan argued that the environment is not just a source of raw materials, clients, technologies, and other technical elements essential to the function of an organization. Environments are also the source of such intangible elements as standards, norms, rumors, myths, symbols, knowledge, ceremonies, and traditions. These elements constitute the institutional environment, and though they are often less rational than elements in the technical environment, they are nonetheless essential sources of organizational legitimacy. Since organizations require legitimacy to survive and prosper, they are often more responsive to institutional concerns than they are to technical concerns. Institutional theory has begun to occupy an increasingly important role in the study of police organizations (Crank 1994; Crank and Langworthy 1992, 1996; Maguire 2003; Maguire and Mastrofski 2000; Maguire, Zhao, and Lovrich 1999; Mastrofski 1998; Mastrofski and Ritti 1996; Mastrofski, Ritti, and

Hoffmaster 1987). Enough has been written about institutional theory now, that finding ways to test it in policing is an important next step.

While institutional theory is based on the role of the environment as a source of legitimacy, credentialing, and support for the organization, resource dependency theory focuses on the environment as a source of valuable resources. The principal statement of resource dependency theory is Pfeffer and Salancik's (1978) *External Control of Organizations*. Resource dependency theory is essentially a theory of power and politics that focuses on the methods used by organizational actors to secure the flow of resources. Because organizations are frequently dependent on securing resources from the environment, they are to a certain point "externally controlled." Resource dependency theory has not yet been applied to policing in a comprehensive way, though two recent papers have described its relevance to police organizations (Katz, Maguire, and Roncek 2002; Maguire and Mastrofski 1999).

While the first two theories focus on the environment as a locus of resources, the third sees it as a source of information. Weick (1969) and Duncan (1972) have both demonstrated how various sectors of the environment contain "pools" of information that are critical to the organization, which then processes this information in such a way as to decrease "information uncertainty." As the pace of computerization in police agencies continues to grow, the role of information may become even more relevant. Two discussions have focused on the centrality of information to police organizations. Manning (1992) outlines the link between organizations, environments and information-processing technologies such as computer aided dispatch (CAD) systems, centralized call collection (911) mechanisms, "expert" systems, management information systems, and other tools designed to increase the organization's capacity to intake and process information. Manning concludes by suggesting that information technologies have "an indeterminate effect on the organizational structure of policing; technology is used to produce and reproduce traditional practices, yet is slowly modifying them" (1992, 391). Ericson and Haggerty (1997) explore similar themes in *Policing the Risk Society*. They view police organizations as part of a larger network of institutions responsible for the identification, management, and communication of risks. They argue that policing (at multiple levels) is shaped by external institutions and their need for information about risks. Theories of the environment as a source of information are not very well developed at this point. In addition, they contain a host of ambiguities about the proper unit of analysis.[25] Nonetheless, given the emergence in policing of sophisticated technologies for collecting and processing information, this perspective deserves further attention.

While all of these theories offer substantial promise for understanding police organizations, we cannot ignore classical explanations. Stinchcombe (1963) made a series of early propositions in which the distribution of public and private spaces within communities serve as important sources of variation in police practice administration. His work foreshadowed the emergence of large private spaces policed by private entities, such as malls, amusement parks, and gated communities. Other classic theoretical statements appearing in the 1960s (Bordua and Reiss 1966; Reiss and Bordua 1967; Wilson 1963, 1968b) have still not been adequately tested. These classics need to be dusted off and revived.

Many of the studies reviewed earlier in this chapter have not been adequately rooted in theory. In diagnosing the current state of police organizational scholarship in the United States, we find little reason for concern about the nature or volume of theories upon which to base solid empirical research. One area for improvement that should be explored is how a good theory of police organization might differ from a theory of organizations in general, or of public service organizations in particular. There is already some evidence that theories designed to explain private organizations, especially those in manufacturing rather than service industries, are inadequate to explain police organizations (Maguire 2003). The answer may exist in either the artful blending of existing theories, or the emergence of new and better ideas.

RESEARCH

Data Collection

Data collection in policing is currently in an exciting and rapid state of development. Much of this can probably be attributed to the emergence of new technologies for recording, collecting, processing, and distributing data. Police organizations are now experimenting with technology at a record pace, implementing or updating their management information systems, computer-aided dispatch centers, geomapping and other modern forms of crime analysis, mobile data terminals in patrol cars, and many other advances emerging in the past decade. One consequence of the proliferation of information-processing technologies is that police agencies now contain vast archives of data. While much of this data is not very useful for national comparative research, it is changing the face of policing in important ways.

National data collection on police organizations is not in a state of crisis. Police agencies are now more open than ever. Careful surveys conducted by researchers, government agencies, and survey firms routinely obtain response rates of 70 to 90 percent. There are numerous sources of data, and although most could be improved, they are, on average, of decent quality. We have criticized some of the data inventories used by government agencies for counting the number of police agencies and officers in the United States over the past several decades (Maguire et al. 1998). Many of the problems cited in that article have been rectified, though some remain. Consequently, current efforts to enumerate the American police are more accurate than ever. Finally, several agencies within the Justice Department now routinely include in their police agency databases a unique agency code, thus enabling researchers and policy makers to link separate databases and test interesting new hypotheses. While there is always room for improvement in the kinds of data that are collected, the methods used to collect data from police organizations tend, on average, to be fairly good.

Our optimism here is not meant to suggest that there remain no challenges. For instance, in response to the 1994 Crime Act, the Bureau of Justice Statistics (BJS) and the National Institute of Justice (NIJ) have undertaken efforts to measure the use of force by police agencies throughout the nation. BJS has added supplemental questions on police use of force to its national household survey. While this strategy is useful for some purposes, it undercounts at least three classes of people who may be more likely to have force used against them by the police: the homeless, the incarcerated and institutionalized, and those without telephones.[26] A second strategy, undertaken by the International Association of Chiefs of Police (IACP) with funding from BJS and NIJ, attempted to develop a national Police Use of Force Database based on confidential reporting by police departments of use-of-force incidents. This method, too, contains a number of problems. Most importantly, it relies on official records that may reflect as much about the organization's willingness to record use-of-force incidents as the actual number of incidents that take place. Other agencies, including the Police Complaint Center and the American Civil Liberties Union, collect data on excessive force and patterns of discrimination from citizens alleging to be victims of these offenses. While these may serve a useful social purpose, neither attempts to (nor claims to) carefully enumerate use-of-force incidents nationally.

Police agencies face new challenges with regard to "racial profiling" data: collecting detailed information on the characteristics of those who are stopped and the reasons for conducting searches. This enterprise is fraught with the potential for error (and possibly subversion) and will be very difficult to implement nationally. The demand for these kinds of measures reflects a point we raised throughout the chapter — policing doesn't have one bottom-line — it has many. The demand for these new data collection efforts reflects a concern for something other than the war on crime and drugs. It reflects a growing concern for equity and fairness on the part of the police. Once again, data collection will play a central, if challenging, role.

Explanation

The methodologies used in the comparative study of police organizations have improved over the past three decades. Yet, many of the studies we examined are flawed in both theory and method. If we had to identify the single most serious problem in the entire line of research, our choice would undoubtedly be the failure to consistently root empirical studies in theory. Some of the studies with the worst methodological flaws contained flawless reviews of the relevant literature and theory. The indiscriminate use of statistical methods without proper attention to theory is common in much of the research. Judging from this literature alone, it appears that a crucial point in the research process that many people either ignore or find difficult is the translation of a theoretical model into an empirical one. Our goal here is not to denigrate past researchers, but to point out some of the flaws in the research in the hope of steering future researchers away from making the same mistakes.

A Modest Vision for Future Research

Sometimes it seems that empirical research on police organizations is a lot like making minestrone soup: in the absence of a good recipe (theory), find whatever vegetables that happen to be convenient (the data), toss them into the pot (the model), cook it (execute the statistical program), and see if it tastes good (check the statistical results). Continue to make adjustments (capitalizing on statistical chance) to the soup until you like the way it tastes.

Our vision for the future of police organizational research is rather simple. Begin by explicating a reasonable theory, spend a considerable amount of time translating the theory into an empirical model, collect reasonably good data that are useful for testing the theory, spend some additional time turning those raw data points into theoretically meaningful and reliable measures, and then test a model that posits some type of causal order among the measures. Don't capitalize on statistical chance by endlessly tinkering with the model if it doesn't fit. If this is the case, return to step 1 and modify the theory. Recent advances in statistical modeling techniques and the software packages in which these techniques are implemented make it easy for most social scientists to become skilled and careful theory testers. This is our "recipe" for achieving incremental progress in the study of police organizations.

Policy

Police executives and policy makers are concerned with the day-to-day realities of their worlds. They want measures that assist them in making decisions and policy. They want explanations for why things occurred. In the academic world of theories and data, researchers want precision and statistically significant findings. They want analysis driven by theory. Coming to grips with both of these worlds is difficult but not insurmountable. The policy implications that derive from theory and analysis need to be made explicit by researchers. Our experience suggests that police executives and policy makers want good measures and explanations, but they want them in ways that are much more understandable. They want direct answers to questions about "How does my department compare to others in terms of community policing or officer performance? If there are differences, how can we overcome them?" As researchers, at least one of our jobs is to assist policy makers in answering these types of questions. Balancing all of these competing interests — using adequate theory, collecting good data, formulating accurate measures, developing sound explanations, and isolating the implications for policy — is no small task. Pulling them all together is a worthwhile challenge.

CONCLUSION

This chapter is meant to serve as an introduction to research and theory on the comparative study of American police organizations. Police organizations differ, and understanding those differences is an important area of focus for both research and theory. We have tried to escort readers on a journey from the early research on why police organizations vary and the birth of scholarly theories meant to explain these variations, to the more sophisticated research that is now taking place. Along the way there have been many pitfalls: insufficient attention to conceptualization and theory, unrealistic measures, inadequate statistical methods, and an overall lack of appreciation for previous research. While looking back upon the classics in the field provides a sense of foundation, with perhaps a touch of nostalgia, there remain countless avenues for refinement and rediscovery. Chief among these are two responsibilities that may seem at first glance like strange bedfellows:

doing research that (1) is based firmly in existing or new theories, and (2) contributes to the understanding or practice of policing. By tracing the evolution of research on police organizations from past to present, bumps and all, we hope this chapter provides a clear road map for what is to come. As we progress through the twenty-first century, much remains to be learned.

NOTES

1. Portions of this chapter appeared in Maguire and Uchida (2000).
2. This research also grew out of the political science tradition of exploring variations in local government policies and structures (Meyer and Baker 1979; Wilson 1968a, 1968b).
3. Several different levels of analysis are commonly used within organization studies. The level of analysis used in this chapter is called the "organization set," which "views the environment from the perspective or standpoint of a specific (focal) organization" (Scott 1992, 126). This is an important detail because it limits the scope of the chapter to a particular analytical framework. Many studies of police organizations are implicitly based on a different level of analysis. For instance, Ostrom, Parks, and Whitaker (1978a) used an "areal organization field," while Bayley (1985, 1992) used the "organizational population" (Scott 1992).
4. This definition purposely excludes agencies that are specialized by function (e.g., fish and wildlife police) or territory (park or airport police), including most federal law enforcement agencies, many county sheriffs and state highway patrol agencies, and private security firms. While using such a restrictive definition reduces the overall level of variation across the organizations under study, it defines a common set of core tasks and functions.
5. There are also numerous similarities among police organizations. As Wadman (1998) points out, all of the largest municipal police agencies have hierarchical rank structures (though some may be flatter than others), they all have divisions for patrol, investigations, and administration, and they all devote a disproportionate share of their resources to motorized patrol. Wadman overstates the similarities between police agencies, but his point is well-taken. There is variation among police agencies, but it is variation "within a theme." We are grateful to Graeme Newman for this observation.
6. Although there is some overlap, the style of a police organization is conceptually different from the style of an individual officer (Talarico and Swanson 1979; Wilson 1968b).
7. We are careful to distinguish what an organization does from what it is by the location of the activity, behavior, or program, rather than its degree of visibility to the public. Much of what the police do *externally*,

as Goldstein (1960) has argued, occurs in low visibility settings. On the other hand, Marshall Meyer (1979) and other organizational theorists have shown how *internal* features of organizations (such as their structures) are sometimes designed to serve as visible signals to external constituents that the organization is doing the right things.

8. Most serious organizational scholars would probably agree that much of what goes on in organizations is random or unexplainable. Weick (1976) suggests that explaining the regularities across organizations is less interesting than explaining this seeming randomness. He suggests using alternative methods that enable researchers to understand the "loose coupling" or unexplained variance in organizational relationships.

9. A similar issue arises in mortality studies. Studying only the dead to learn about causes and correlates of death is a flawed strategy because we cannot know whether these same conditions are present in people who lived (Kaufman 1976; King, Travis, and Langworthy 1997).

10. Bordua and Reiss (1966) explore these same themes (to a lesser extent) in an earlier article.

11. For example, Reiss and Bordua (1967) discussed two environmental variables that are important to the organization: the security of the police chief's tenure and the degree of accountability that the government executive demands from the chief. Cross-classifying these two variables, they formed a crude taxonomy of four department types that might reflect variation in political interference into police department affairs. They suggested that these and other environmental variables were important because they "structure the effective range of command and control" (p. 49) in municipal police departments.

12. Slovak (1986) laments that "there is a very real sense in which the promise offered by Wilson's original analysis has gone unfulfilled" (p. 5).

13. Aggregate-level arrest rates for various offenses are frequently used as an indicator of police style. Note that these studies focus on organizational style (or some other aggregate), not the style of an individual officer (Slovak 1986).

14. In general, structural contingency theory suggests that no single organizational form is ideal for all circumstances (Donaldson 1995; Lawrence and Lorsch 1967). Successful organizations survive by adapting to the contingencies of their specific tasks and environments.

15. This is not meant to imply that police organizations have no effect on crime, because crime is the product of numerous social forces, including the police and other institutions. Therefore it is awkward to think of the volume of crime within a community as an organizational measure that describes the police. For a recent review of the available research evidence in this area, see Eck and Maguire (2000).

16. Reprinted by permission of the publisher from *Varieties of Police Behavior: The Management of Law and Order in Eight Communities* by James

Q. Wilson, p. 276, Cambridge Massachusetts: Harvard University Press, copyright © 1968, 1978 by the President and Fellows of Harvard College.

17. We have chosen not to examine studies that use measures of organizational properties (such as performance) that are aggregated based on individuals' subjective impressions or opinions. For instance, if we ask one thousand citizens in each of ten cities to rate their local police, and then compute a summary measure of citizen ratings for each agency, we would be forming an aggregate subjective measure. Such measures are not considered here, though they are clearly important.

18. Ostrom and Parks (1973), for instance, found curvilinear relationships between city size and citizen ratings of police performance in their secondary analysis of data from 102 cities. For central cities, performance ratings increased as city size approached 100,000 residents, after which ratings decreased; the same curvilinear relationship was found for suburbs, but the population threshold was only 20,000 residents. Whitaker (1983) also concludes that the size of the police organization is more important than the size of the political jurisdiction, thus lending support to reform strategies that seek to simulate the feel of small-town policing in large cities through the use of precinct stations, substations, and other decentralization and spatial differentiation strategies. Whitaker's (1983) chapter contains the most comprehensive (though dated) review of the effect of department size on police organizations.

19. There is a shortage of theory to explain either of these consistent findings. Region may simply be a proxy for any number of political, historical, economic, or demographic differences between regions. Organizational size seems to affect nearly every aspect of what organizations do. One possible reason that larger police agencies may report engaging in more community policing activities is simply that they have more employees to assign to such functions.

20. This point is controversial. Some might argue that measuring any concept involves normative judgments. Our view is that the concept of professionalism is inherently normative because it implies a rank-ordering and a value judgment: more professionalized organizations are better than those that are less professionalized.

21. Exploratory factor analysis is a method used by researchers to combine multiple variables into a single measure. Like any other tool, it can be, and is often, abused. One way that it can be used in an atheoretical manner is to combine variables that are seemingly unrelated into a single measure for statistical rather than theoretical or conceptual reasons.

22. Clark, Hall, and Hutchinson (1967) treat interorganizational relationships as "contextual" variables rather than organizational variables in their study of police performance.

23. According to Duffee (1990), this problem is rampant in all sectors of criminal justice. His advice to criminal justice scholars is particularly appropriate — we should focus on describing and explaining what criminal justice organizations *do*, rather than what they *should be doing*.
24. Conventional wisdom in policing is that police organizations do not "go out of business" (Travis and Brann 1997). Recent work by William King and his colleagues (King 1999b; King, Travis, and Langworthy 1997) challenges this assumption. Based on a survey of county sheriffs in Ohio, King documented the death of 104 police agencies (and the birth of an additional 15). King is now replicating this study in several other states.
25. Weick's (1969) discussion is inherently social psychological, while Manning (1992) and Ericson and Haggerty (1997) span levels from the individual to the institution.
26. We are grateful to Paula Kautt for this observation.

6

UNDERSTANDING VARIETY IN URBAN COMMUNITY POLICING
An Institutional Theory Approach[1]

Brian C. Renauer

INTRODUCTION

Numerous police agencies in the United States report involvement in community policing strategies (Maguire, Kuhns, Uchida, and Cox 1997; Maguire and Mastrofski 2000; Zhao, Lovrich, and Thurman 1999; Zhao, Thurman, and Lovrich 1995). The 1999 Law Enforcement Management and Administrative Statistics survey, based on a representative sample of 13,000 local police departments, estimates that more than 90 percent of departments serving 25,000 or more residents had some type of community policing plan in operation (Hickman and Reaves 1999). Sixty-four percent of local police departments report having full-time community policing officers (Hickman and Reaves 1999). No one doubts there is a proliferation of police departments that claim to do community policing. The term *community policing* has evolved into a "household phrase" recognized by many (Maguire and Mastrofski 2000).

There continues to be speculation over the activities that characterize "ideal" community policing, the accuracy of department claims regarding their involvement in particular community policing activities, and how to assess the "dosage" or intensity of community policing efforts (Bayley 1994; Crank and Langworthy 1992; Maguire and Mastrofski 2000). The effectiveness of community policing strategies at lowering

121

crime, reducing fear, and building strong neighborhoods is still unclear — although we are exposed to numerous community policing success stories (University of Maryland 1997; Walker 2001). Nonetheless, community policing continues to be implemented under a variety of strategies and activities, without a universally agreed upon definition or theory of crime prevention (Cardarelli, McDevitt, and Baum 1998; Maguire, Kuhns et al. 1997; Maguire and Mastrofski 2000; Zhao, Lovrich, and Thurman 1999; Zhao, Thurman, and Lovrich 1995).

This chapter proposes that there are important measurable variations in urban community policing implementation efforts. In particular, community policing as implemented in one city may take on a more "community building" style than other cities (described in next section). Institutional theory is employed to make sense of such variation and investigate why community policing may involve more community building efforts in some cities, than in others. By attempting to explain variation in community policing, an official criminal justice response to behaviors labeled as criminal, this chapter falls squarely within the domain of criminal justice theory as described in chapter 2 (Snipes and Maguire).

Institutional theory perspectives describe institutionalizing forces that cause structural, strategic, and policy innovations in an organizational field, such as the innovation of community policing, and its adoption by police organizations. Institutional theory also explains how strategic innovations may be molded or changed to fit a particular organization's operating context or "task environment." A simple analogy for institutional theory is the children's game "telephone." Children in the game are supposed to verbally pass along to the next child an *original message*, yet as the message is passed from child to child it inevitably changes. The original message of community policing can be changed and adapted to be congruent with the institutionalizing environment of any specific urban police department. This chapter develops multiple propositions regarding the institutionalizing forces and contexts of urban police departments that are likely to create a "community building" style of community policing implementation. Empirically testing these propositions will help in identifying the conditions that support or resist a certain style and intensity of policing operation. An empirical test of these propositions is not undertaken here, but a heuristic device to further theoretical elaboration and eventual empirical examination of community policing variation is developed.

POLICE COMMUNITY BUILDING

Bayley (1994) and Kelling and Coles (1996), early proponents of community policing, agree that community policing activities should contribute to the formal and informal institutions within urban neighborhoods and not negatively interfere with their functions (Duffee, Fluellen, and Renauer 1999). Bayley (1994, 145)[2]* states:

> The challenge is to find ways of using the police for crime prevention without ... discouraging the strengthening of other social processes that are critical to the enterprise ....

Kelling and Coles write:

> [Policing should] help to create conditions in neighborhoods and communities that will allow other institutions — the family, neighborhood, church, community, and government and commerce — to deal with these basic problems of society.

The comments of Bayley (1994) and Kelling and Coles (1996) suggest that the police and groups in the communities in which the police work can "jointly produce" certain public safety outcomes, such as feelings of safety or fear, levels of disorder and crime, and levels of trust and cooperation. Their research and other studies indicate that police alone cannot maintain temporary improvements in communities unless something else occurs in the neighborhood. Thus, the ultimate goal in police–community collaboration is getting "something else" to transpire that will sustain a community over the long-term. That something else is commonly referred to as "community capacity." Community capacity is, "the extent to which members of a community can work together effectively, including their abilities to develop and sustain strong relationships, solve problems and make group decisions, and collaborate effectively to identify goals and get work done" (Mattessich and Monsey 1997).[3] Another way of thinking about community capacity is the old saying about the hungry peasant, "give him a fish, and he is full today but hungry again tomorrow; teach him to fish, and he need never be hungry again." Neighbors who *observe* that the police reduce crime do not represent the same situation as neighbors who gain *experience in controlling crime* with the police. Some things that the police do to reduce or prevent crime may promote dependency of the citizenry on the police and thereby reduce the strength of civic institutions, even if they have short-term positive effects on crime. Other things the police

---

* Pp. 145 from *Police for the Future* by Bayley, D. H. (1966). By permission of Oxford University Press, Inc.

may do to reduce or prevent crime may promote neighborhood resident experience in civic engagement that strengthens civic institutions and allows residents to solve other problems in the future. When police make this contribution to civic engagement, we can talk about police community building. "Community building" processes are community activities that build community capacity. In contrast, Lyons (1999) and DeLeon-Granados (1999) indicate police activities (under the guise of community policing) have in fact neutralized neighborhood independence, reasserted centralized policing after initial decentralized partnering, and increased community divisiveness, distrust, and ill-feeling.

The theoretical ideal that community policing should contribute to important processes that build neighborhood efficacy or community capacity has been developed elsewhere (Bennett 1998; DeLeon-Granados 1999; Duffee 1996; Duffee, Fluellen, and Renauer 1999; Duffee, Fluellen, and Roscoe 1999; Lyons 1999). One particular research effort, the Police Community Interaction Project (PCIP), has identified general processes of community building and asked how the police might be involved in such community processes (Duffee, Scott, Renauer, Chermak, and McGarrell 2002). PCIP has defined five major community building dimensions in which the police are often active. These dimensions recognize different ways in which the police can interact with community groups that improve community capacity. For the purposes of this study only three police community building processes will be discussed.

Steps to Identify with Neighborhoods

Definition: the manner and extent to which a neighborhood is recognized as a unique place to be considered separately from other neighborhoods in the city by agencies making policies that affect the neighborhood or providing services to the neighborhood. In terms of policing, steps to identify with neighborhoods would measure the broad steps that provide for *police presence* in the neighborhood, for increased *knowledge* about the neighborhood, for *accessibility* of police to residents, and for police *responsiveness* to residents' concerns. Police steps to identify with neighborhoods would include levels and dispersion of (1) physical decentralization; (2) permanency of personnel assignment; (3) aligning patrol with place boundaries; (4) place specific information gathering and analysis; (5) regular foot and bike patrol; and (6) a policy of police attendance at neighborhood meetings.

Steps to Encourage Resident Efforts

Definition: the types and levels of activities to encourage residents in a neighborhood to contribute their efforts to concerted or collective action to improve the neighborhood. In terms of policing, encouragement consists of five activities including: (1) disseminating information about neighborhood problems, common bonds among neighbors, and the importance of collective action; (2) taking active steps to recruit any willing individuals in the neighborhood to work on projects; (3) helping to design and structure neighborhood organizations or collective endeavors; (4) suggesting to specific groups or individuals (e.g., to persons already identified as willing and available) particular actions or tactics; and (5) providing material resources, transportation, equipment, or other supports that either enable citizen participation to proceed or increase the level of participation.

Steps for Resident Participation

Definition: the forms and degree of resident involvement and decision making about the collective interests in a neighborhood. In terms of resident interactions with the police, this measure would entail assessing: (1) resident involvement with police on problem/goal identification, solution/means identification, and division of labor; (2) resident levels of decision-making input based on their ability to raise issues, discuss issues, and make final decisions over issues in interaction with the police; (3) balance in the decision-making process — with decisions among the police, residents, and other organizations participating in the community endeavor.

VARIATION IN POLICE COMMUNITY BUILDING

There is evidence that police do engage in the above "community building" activities (Duffee, Fluellen, and Renauer 1999; Duffee, Scott et al. 2002; Renauer, Duffee, and Scott 2003; Scott, Duffee, and Renauer 2003). Police often *identify with neighborhoods* by having a physical presence there in terms of a storefront station, permanent officers, and neighborhood planning (Giacomazzi, McGarrell, and Thurman 1998; Skogan 1990). Police often *encourage residents in a neighborhood* toward collective efforts by distributing newsletters describing neighborhood problems and passing around signup sheets so neighbors can become involved in a project (Skogan 1990; Skogan and Hartnett 1997). Many community policing initiatives allow *participation of neighborhood residents* in decision-making processes (Renauer et al. 2003; Skogan 1995; Skogan and Hartnett 1997). Sometimes resident participation only comes in the form of identifying neighborhood problems, but in other neighborhoods residents may also be involved with police in the formulation of problem solutions and the actual carrying out of crime prevention tasks (Duffee, Scott et al. 2002; Skogan 1995).

A crucial component to researching the propositions presented in this chapter is that the above police community building processes exhibit variation across locales and there exist measurement tools to examine such variation. Thus, there is a need to classify departments according to the *intensity* of their involvement in these three community building processes (Renauer, Duffee, and Scott 2003). Detailed measures of police community building will be needed to classify a police department as exhibiting a high or low strength (dosage) of community building (see Scott et al. 2003). For example, a high measure of community building by police would indicate police involvement in most of the six steps to identify with neighborhoods and five steps to encourage resident efforts. Police attempts to encourage resident efforts should also be consistent over time, not a single encouragement attempt. A high measure of community building would occur if residents are involved in all areas of decision making, not just problem identification, and residents have an equal balance of participation with other organizations. A high measure community building would entail large turnouts of resident participants at neighborhood meetings, by residents who are representative of the neighborhood population and its concerns. Throughout this chapter, propositions are developed that connect descriptions of police community building to the institutional forces that are likely to produce them.

VARIATIONS IN POLICE COMMUNITY-BUILDING ACTIVITIES: AN INSTITUTIONAL THEORY APPROACH

Community policing is considered an organizational and strategic innovation, just as the professional model of policing, which advocated for motorized police forces and rapid responses to calls for service, was a predecessor innovation. Organizational and policy innovations spread or diffuse (i.e., are adopted by organizations) through society at particular rates and forms, and this is no different for the diffusion of policing innovations (DiMaggio and Powell 1983; Walker 1977). The ideal descriptions of community policing philosophy contained in academic books or government documents may be molded into different types of community policing implementations (Maguire and Mastrofski 2000). One form of community policing implementation would be strong police department involvement in neighborhood community building

as described above. Other departments may interpret community policing as the implementation of an aggressive order maintenance style of
policing, or as the use of police-controlled problem-solving strategies,
or as a community relations program (Maguire and Mastrofski 2000;
Zhao, Thurman, and Lovrich 1995). This chapter describes the contexts
and institutionalizing processes that are likely to create *a certain form*
of community policing adoption: *police departments highly involved in
community building*. Institutional theory is introduced in this section
to help us understand how such innovation diffusion could take place.

INSTITUTIONAL THEORY: LOCAL CONTROL
VS. FIELD AND CENTRIST CONTROL

Institutional theory attempts to develop a greater understanding of
organizational–environment relations (Kraatz and Zajac 1996). Thus,
it essentially addresses the question of how an organization's environment (which is comprised of other organizations, resources, and clients) influences its operations, structure, and service delivery. There
exist two "camps" or competing institutional theory perspectives: "old"
institutional theory and "new" institutional theory (Kraatz and Zajac
1996). The traditional or "old" institutional perspective is often referred
to as adaptation theory, contingency theory, or resource dependency
theory (Kraatz and Zajac 1996). Old institutional theory proposes
organizational change as a direct response to technical environmental demands. In other words, rational leaders of organizations choose
operational strategies that address customers' demands and competition from other organizations, or other factors in their immediate task
environment (Kraatz and Zajac 1996). Therefore, police departments
should seek to implement organizational structures and operations that
will accomplish goals desired by their clients, such as reducing crime
and fear of crime. According to the traditional institutional theory perspective, an organization's structure and operation *is highly influenced
by the local or immediate context in which services are delivered.*

The recognition that innovations in criminal justice are influenced
by the local context and implemented in a variety of forms at the local,
municipal level is not a new insight. Maguire and Mastrofski (2000)
use the term *refraction* to describe localized filtering and adaptations
of nationally promoted and funded criminal justice innovations.
Thus, criminal justice organizations often shape operational strategies promoted (or demanded) by other organizations or law to fit the
demands of their local context (Walker 2001). Good examples of local
adaptations of criminal justice policy can be found in the studies that

evaluated the administration of federal money and grant programs by the Law Enforcement Assistance Administration (LEAA) in the 1970s. These studies revealed that conceptual uncertainty of goals and strategies, lack of coordination, and distance between coordinating agencies resulted in distortion, misinterpretation, and "willful avoidance" of the national program ideals and strategies promoted by LEAA (Duffee 1990; Feeley and Sarat 1980; Gray and Williams 1980). Feeley and Sarat (1980, 33) in their review of federal funding for LEAA law enforcement initiatives have cautioned: "The success and failure of a policy is determined, in the first instance, by the conceptual, technical, and political constraints within which the policy delivery system must work."

The new institutional theory perspective differs from the traditional in two important ways: (1) the source of organizational change and stability is primarily from a broad "organizational field" rather than the local level, and (2) the mechanism that influences organizational change and stability is maintenance of organizational legitimacy rather than constant improvement of technical efficiency and service delivery to meet customer or local demands (Crank and Langworthy 1992; DiMaggio and Powell 1983; Maguire and Mastrofski 2000). New institutional theory proposes that an "organizational field" composed of organizations with similar purposes and goals, and spanning many locales is a primary source that stimulates organizational change (DiMaggio and Powell 1983; Scott 1995). It follows that police department structures and operations are often the result of copying what other police departments are doing around the nation. Police are also influenced by the ideas of police professional organizations and national powers (Police Foundation, PERF, IACP, U.S. Department of Justice programs). Thus, police departments are part of a national field of like organizations with similar concerns that collectively exert a powerful influence over the direction of policing.

According to new institutional theory, if an organizational field is highly structured and cohesive, the national organizational field will have a greater influence on organizational change and operational strategies than the local technical environment of an organization (Kraatz and Zajac 1996). In order to understand variation in community policing implementation across this nation, we must explore how the national policing field intersects with the local context of police departments simultaneously creating a certain community policing style.

POLICE ORGANIZATIONAL RELATIONSHIPS

This chapter utilizes a similar perspective for understanding policing described by Langworthy and Travis (1998) — police department structures and operational strategies result from a "balance of forces." Hence, a variety of relationship networks can influence urban policing forms (Crank and Langworthy 1992; Maguire and Mastrofski 2000). Ideas, norms, rules, laws, and resources generated by other organizations or institutions influence urban police departments (Crank and Langworthy 1992). Urban police departments are also influenced by their own internal policies, culture, and leadership (Greene, Bergman, and McLaughlin 1994; Guyot 1991; Langworthy and Travis 1998). This study proposes that there are three important relationship networks that influence the diffusion of community policing into different forms of implementation. These three networks are as follows:

1. *Centrist Level:* This level is concerned about the relationships between local police agencies and national and state organizations which have an influence over policing operations (e.g., legislatures, judiciary bodies, administrative bodies, professional policing organizations, university research). A good example of a centrist relationship in policing would be the link between a police department and services offered by the Office of Community Oriented Policing Services (COPS) run by the U.S. Department of Justice. The COPS program has been integrally involved in promoting the spread of community policing through the provision of financial and technical resources to thousands of local police departments (Office of Community Oriented Policing Services 2001). The Police Executive Research Forum and the Police Foundation, which hold national conferences and publish policing research and training materials, are also examples of centrist influences on policing (Maguire and Mastrofski 2000). An equally important centrist influence would be an organization's perception of a national trend among like organizations in their "organizational field" or "policy sector" (Scott 1995). Thus, police departments may look to see what strategies other departments are implementing or stay abreast of the operations used by "cutting edge" departments.

2. *Local Level:* The important relationships in a police department's local context are relations with local political leaders, government agencies, businesses, and organized resident groups. It is important at this network level to understand how

police department operations intersect with the urban vision and policy-making approaches of the city executive and his or her regime. Cities that strongly support neighborhood decision making and even offer monetary support to resident-based neighborhood organizations are perhaps more likely to pressure police departments to engage in a community building style of policing. In contrast, community policing in Seattle was an outgrowth of business and chamber of commerce pressures, not resident-based organizational pressures (Lyons 1999).

3. *Internal Police Department Level:* The importance of internal police department influences on organizational change toward community policing is illustrated by Greene, Bergman, and McLaughlin (1994). They state, "organizational adaptation in police bureaucracies has tended to be one way: the change efforts adapt to the organization, rather than the organization adapting to the intended change" (93). Based on their experiences with Philadelphia's move toward community policing, Greene et al. (1994, 93) suggest that the police internal culture will, "greatly shape the success or failure of community policing implementation efforts." To understand police operational choices it is important to examine the relationships between the chief of police and the city executive (mayor or city manager), and also the relations of the chief with the internal police culture, especially organized police unions or fraternal police organizations.

INSTITUTIONALIZING FORCES: MIMETIC, NORMATIVE, AND COERCIVE

Scott (1995) and DiMaggio and Powell (1983) describe three mechanisms (institutionalizing processes) that support or constrain organizational activities, and influence organizational change and stability. These institutionalizing processes are as follows:

1. *Mimetic Forces:* Organizations, especially those in the same field, often mimic, copy, or imitate one another (Maguire and Mastrofski 2000). Another term for such "copy cat" behavior by organizations is "isomorphism" (DiMaggio and Powell 1983). Organizations often change operational policies to mirror organizational models they perceive as superior or prevalent in their organizational field. In order to maintain organizational legitimacy, organizations often perceive a need to do what

others are doing ("jump on the bandwagon"), especially when an organizational change is widely considered the "right" thing to do. Thus, police departments may develop a community policing program because they recognize most other police departments are doing so. Imitating other organizations' operations is usually done with haste, often disregarding whether such operations are actually proven to produce desired outcomes or whether they are technically efficient activities (Mastrofski 1998). Isomorphic organizational changes are often just symbolic gestures to look progressive and legitimate on the surface, with perhaps little substantive change occurring in actual implementation (Crank and Langworthy 1992; Maguire and Mastrofski 2000; Mastrofski 1998). Thus, police organizations may appear to be doing community policing, but only on paper, on a website, or in a survey questionnaire. Mimetic forces are part of the new institutional theory perspective.

2. *Normative Forces:* Organizational structures, policies, and behaviors can be based on norms that define the proper social purposes (goals) of organizations and strictly prescribe the legitimate activities (means) needed to fulfill social purposes (Crank and Langworthy 1992; Meyer and Rowan 1977). Organizations in the same field will often create standards for themselves (Maguire and Mastrofski 2000). An organization's conformity to norms and values that define proper organizational goals and means is based on the affective ties an organization develops with other organizations, not a fear of coercion or punishment (Scott 1995). Sometimes diverse organizations within the same locale can develop shared meanings and a collaborative purpose, thus feeling obliged to make organizational changes in accordance with such shared beliefs.

3. *Coercive Forces:* (called "regulatory institutionalizing elements" by Scott [1995]) Coercive forces involve an organization's capacity to create rules and laws, monitor others' conformity, offer incentives, and impose sanctions when needed (Scott 1995). Organizations that are attempting to stimulate change and conformity toward new (or old) operations exert coercive forces upon other organizations in hopes they will adopt or adhere to such operations. For example, police are offered numerous monetary incentives to innovate, implement new strategies, and change organizational structures (e.g., grant monies to hire community policing officers, or engage in crime mapping). Coercive forces can be effective in producing change

because rational organizational leaders make decisions that will maintain organizational stability and avoid resource punishments or adverse publicity (Scott 1995).

POLICE INSTITUTIONALIZING ENVIRONMENT

Figure 6.1 provides an illustration of the institutionalizing environment. Urban police organizations are imbedded in multiple relationships involving centrist, local, and internal level forces. Each relationship network simultaneously influences the range of operational choices a police department can engage in by exerting mimetic, normative, or coercive institutionalizing forces. Police departments are offered incentives to engage in certain strategies and constrained by rules, laws, and potential sanctions. The operational choices of police departments are also influenced by their desires for organizational legitimacy, their shared beliefs with other organizations, and their recognition of progressive ideas. Police responses to organizational influences can range from complete compliance, refusal, mirroring actions (isomorphism), negotiation, adaptation, to deception (Scott 1995). In the next section of the chapter, propositions are developed that characterize institutional relationships that would foster strong police community building efforts by an urban police department.

PROPOSITIONS

Since the International Association of Chiefs of Police meetings in 1893, the enactment of civil service laws, and increased federal funding for criminal justice national and state organizations have utilized a variety of institutionalizing forces to stimulate change in urban police department operations and policies (Crank and Langworthy 1992; Walker 1977). For example, laws and court rulings have established regulations on police practices and behaviors (e.g., search and seizure, use of deadly force). Police departments are baited with a variety of technological and monetary resources/grants in exchange for applying new strategies and techniques of law enforcement (Feeley and Sarat 1980; Gray and Williams 1980). Experts and think tanks describe legitimate police goals and provide the training necessary for police departments to adopt new styles and missions (Crank and Langworthy 1992). National and state interests can extend or withdraw political support and resources to police departments. Thus, a broader organizational field, which extends beyond the local environments of police departments, can influence the direction of policing.

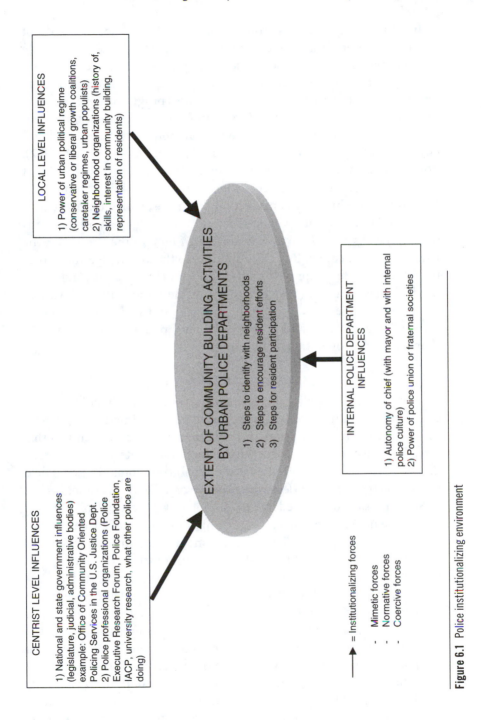

LOCAL LEVEL INFLUENCES

1) Power of urban political regime (conservative or liberal growth coalitions, caretaker regimes, urban populists)
2) Neighborhood organizations (history of, skills, interest in community building, representation of residents)

CENTRIST LEVEL INFLUENCES

1) National and state government influences (legislature, judicial, administrative bodies) example: Office of Community Oriented Policing Services in the U.S. Justice Dept.
2) Police professional organizations (Police Executive Research Forum, Police Foundation, IACP, university research, what other police are doing)

EXTENT OF COMMUNITY BUILDING ACTIVITIES BY URBAN POLICE DEPARTMENTS

1) Steps to identify with neighborhoods
2) Steps to encourage resident efforts
3) Steps for resident participation

INTERNAL POLICE DEPARTMENT INFLUENCES

1) Autonomy of chief (with mayor and with internal police culture)
2) Power of police union or fraternal societies

= Institutionalizing forces

- Mimetic forces
- Normative forces
- Coercive forces

Figure 6.1 Police institutionalizing environment

Institutionalizing forces from national and state sources are not exclusively directed at influencing local policing. National and state institutionalizing forces also influence city governments, community organizations, and the characteristics of urban space. National and state efforts to promote urban renewal, model cities programs, revenue sharing, interstate highway construction, improved social services, and civil rights have had enormous impacts on urban politics and neighborhood environments (Judd and Swanstrom 1998; Logan and Molotch 1987). For example, the federal government in the 1950s and 1960s agreed that cities should become more accessible to the automobile age and thus funded massive highway construction programs, which unfortunately displaced large minority populations that were in the path of the highways (J. Jacobs 1961; Judd and Swanstrom 1998). In the late 1960s, the federal government felt that cities should tap the knowledge and expertise of citizens for improved public service delivery so it funded the Model Cities Program (Warren, Rose, and Bergunder 1974). A variety of historic policies have shaped the physical and social environments that police operate in, and new centrist level policies will continue to shape the police operational environment.

Centrist Level Influences

To understand how police involvement in community building can be connected to centrist institutionalizing forces two important linkages should be explored: (1) the structure of current financial incentives that directly connect a police department to national and state funding sources; (2) the policy direction and influence of the broader organizational field of policing (i.e., what are "legitimate" police organizations doing?).

Since passage of the Federal 1994 Violent Crime Control and Law Enforcement Act there have been numerous financial incentives for municipal police departments to implement community policing. As of November 2001, the Office of Community Oriented Policing Services (COPS), established in the 1994 Crime Act, has funded 114,121 police officers nationwide (COPS 2001). Officers funded by the COPS universal hiring program are supposed to be engaged in community policing activities. The COPS program has also supported a variety of local problem-solving policing partnerships. In order to understand the potential influence that COPS and other centrist funding agencies could have on police department involvement in community building, the following links need to be examined: (1) the level of monetary input from national/state funding agencies relative to a department's total budget; (2) the amount of expert guidance and training in community policing received as a result of the grant; (3) the clarity of community policing goals and strategies and their connection to community building activities; and (4) the intensity of oversight mechanisms regarding the use of grant monies.

There is a general consensus that community policing still lacks conceptual clarity regarding its goals and strategies (Maguire and Mastrofski 2000; Zhao, Lovrich, and Thurman 1999). In fact, national survey data by Zhao et al. (1999) show that *departmental confusion over what community policing actually means* is one of the highest rated community policing implementation impediments reported by police chiefs. Confusion over the meaning of community policing remained a consistently expressed impediment across two waves of surveys in 1993 and 1996 (Zhao et al. 1999, 86). Can we therefore expect community policing to be the same everywhere? There is no contractual language in COPS universal hiring grants that describes how much community policing must be accomplished in a month or whether community policing must aggressively adhere to a community building style. Therefore, strong police–community building efforts are likely caused by interactions/coordination with neighborhood organizations and city organizations knowledgeable and supportive of community building processes and not as a result of federal guidance.

According to resource dependency theory ("old" institutional theory), organizations that provide the bulk of a target agency's resources are more likely to engineer an organizational change (Gray and Williams 1980). A rational organization will first and foremost appease organizations or clients that have the most influence over organizational resources (Gray and Williams 1980). Most urban police department budgets are *overwhelmingly locally funded*, thus their organizational policies (especially intensity of implementation) are more likely to be influenced by local politics (Gifford 1999; Scheingold 1991). Given that police department budgets are dominated by local funding sources and there exists little national guidance on how (and to what extent) police should help build community capacity in neighborhoods, high levels of community building by urban police will be largely determined by the structure of the local political context and relationships internal to police departments.

The phenomenon of local refraction or filtering of federally supported policies to fit the local policing environment suggests the following propositions regarding variation in police community building:

Proposition A: A lack of conceptual clarity in the goals, strategies, and activities of community policing provides an opportunity for the local political economy and internal police processes to reinterpret, misinterpret, or add idiosyncratic touches to community policing operations. Additionally, since municipal police department budgets are almost exclusively locally funded, their operations are more likely to be tied to the agenda of the local political context rather than the paper ideals of their centrist funding sources (see similar propositions by Crank and Langworthy 1992; Maguire and Mastrofski 2000).

Therefore, this chapter proposes that strong police community building efforts are more likely the result of influences from local and internal police department dynamics (old institutional theory), rather than the influences of centrist forces (new institutional theory). Such a proposition does not mean that centrist institutionalizing forces have had no influence on police involvement in community building; they have had a tremendous influence (at least on the surface). Police across this nation report the implementation of a number of community building activities (e.g., opening storefront stations, attending community meetings, increasing resident input into problem identification) (Hickman and Reaves 1999; Maguire and Mastrofski 2000; Zhao et al. 1999). Thus, there is some evidence of isomorphism toward a community building style of policing.[4] In the broader organizational field of policing, implementing community policing is considered a very legitimate operational choice. This chapter proposes that the national trend toward reported widespread involvement in community policing is more symbolic and the dosage of community policing implementation, especially a strong community building style, is very weak in many urban places (Crank and Langworthy 1992; Manning 1988).

Proposition B: Centrist forces have influenced police departments to copy other department's operations and experiment with many community policing components, some of which are related to community building. Police departments are experimenting with storefront stations, distributing neighborhood newsletters, and attending community meetings because such activities are considered legitimate and common in the broader policing field. Centrist forces only have the power to influence the experimentation with some community building components in urban locales. High levels of police community building are related to certain types of local contexts and internal police dynamics.

LOCAL LEVEL INFLUENCES

Police departments are also influenced by their relationships within a local interorganizational system (Crank and Langworthy 1992). Local relationships may solicit, reinforce, and often demand a particular style of policing. The relations between police and the local mayor/city manager are the most common political linkages recognized in policing literature (Andrews 1985; Fogelson 1977; Fraser 1985; Hudnut 1985; Murphy 1985; Walker 1977). This section proposes that local influence on police department operations is based upon the strength of a dominant political coalition, how the dominant coalition values urban space, and the strength of resident-based neighborhood organizations.

How Should Urban Space Be Valued? Exchange vs. Use Value

A common policy and political dilemma continually challenges city administrators in America: With an expanding world economy and mobile market, how can cities remain competitive with other cities and suburbs to maintain current economic investment and ensure future growth and stability, while satisfying residents' needs and securing a healthy fiscal balance (Judd and Swanstrom 1998; Swanstrom 1985)? A theory of growth politics has developed to explain the varied responses by city administrations to this continual dilemma (Logan and Molotch 1987; Swanstrom 1985). At the core of growth politics theory is the understanding of how urban space is valued. Urban space is comprised of different elements: land, natural resources, transportation systems, buildings, commerce, housing, neighborhoods, and residents. City administrators can value these urban elements in terms of their worth in an exchange relationship (*exchange value*) and improving *profitability* of urban space (Logan and Molotch 1987; Stoecker 1994; Swanstrom 1985). City administrations concerned with improving the exchange value of urban space coordinate with supporters (speculators, developers, city council, zoning boards, banks) to implement political strategies and policies that support urban development approaches that "increase the chances of further commodifying urban land and infrastructure toward making profit" (Stoecker 1994, 11). An example of an exchange value project would be supporting the construction of high-density apartment units in neighborhoods, which allow landlords to make more profit by bringing in more residents, yet increase anonymity and congestion.

Alternatively, city administrators may value urban elements in terms of their "usefulness in providing services, sustenance, and quality of life" (*use value*) (Stoecker 1994, 11). City administrations concerned with use values coordinate with supporters (neighborhoods, city council, zoning boards, environmental or social activist groups) to implement urban development strategies that preserve urban land, infrastructures, and policies that contribute to the convenience of neighborhood residents' daily round (Logan and Molotch 1987; Stoecker 1994). A use value orientation by a city government is concerned with supporting residents and neighborhoods, and ameliorating the costs of urban growth. A use value project would support the construction of low-density apartment units with playgrounds and increased public green space (e.g., parks) in neighborhoods. The advocates of exchange value policies are often in opposition to the advocates of use value policies.

Growth Politics and Institutional Theory

Although it appears this study is introducing a new theory, there are some strong similarities between theories of growth politics and institutional theory. It is arguable that theories of growth politics are really applications of institutional theory (Clingermayer and Feiock 2001). In other words, theories of growth politics explain the sources, both individual and organizational, that influence urban change and the mechanisms by which urban space is rearranged over time. Theories of growth politics use institutional theory language. For example, growth politics focuses on the power (coercive, normative, and mimetic influences) and coalition building used by city administrations to carry out their vision for urban growth and stability. City administrators need the help of other organizations and constituents to establish ordinances, laws, standards, resources, publicity, norms, and symbols in order to develop urban space or maintain quality neighborhoods (Logan and Molotch 1987; Stoecker 1994; Swanstrom 1985). Urban growth coalitions, *which have the power to influence policing resources*, may pressure police departments to change operations to be complementary with the urban policy agenda. The ways in which the urban growth coalition values urban space, either toward exchange or use values, will influence the range of policing strategies and operations considered locally legitimate.

TYPES OF URBAN GROWTH COALITIONS AND COMMUNITY POLICING

At a local level, the key to understanding variation in police community building is: (1) to examine the dominant type of urban growth coalition and its strength; (2) examine the connection between the police department and the agenda of the urban growth coalition; and (3) to examine how neighborhoods, organized or not, fit into local growth politics.

Todd Swanstrom (1985) has outlined a typology of urban growth coalitions based on their growth politics (exchange vs. use value interest) and strategies. The dominant urban growth coalitions found in American cities are labeled conservative growth coalitions, liberal growth coalitions, caretaker regimes, and urban populists (Swanstrom 1985). Logan, Whaley, and Crowder (1997) advocate a need for increased research on the social consequences — such as disparities in police and fire protection between and within cities, gaps between rich and poor neighborhoods, and racial segregation — that can be connected to different types of urban growth coalitions. This study proposes that the policies and values *of specific types of growth coalitions* are more likely to support and foster strong police community building initiatives.

The remainder of this section will detail Swanstrom's (1985) four growth coalition types and their potential influence on policing operations. The section ends with a discussion of how neighborhoods fit into growth politics and policing strategy.

The Conservative Growth Coalition and Community Policing

Conservative coalitions stimulate urban growth through promotion of the following exchange-value strategies: intensification of land usage, increasing rent levels, increasing tax base, tax abatement for corporations, cutting utility costs for corporations, and decreasing social service budgets. Exchange value strategies often require "risky" investment projects and policies that put all neighborhoods of the city in jeopardy or increase "collective liability" (Swanstrom 1985). Conservative growth coalitions argue that risky investment projects and policies are necessary to remain competitive in today's mobile economy. They believe that future benefits of these investments will trickle down to all city residents, who are left out of such decision-making arenas (Logan and Molotch 1987).

The key characteristic that separates the conservative growth coalition from the liberal growth coalition is the level of confidence placed in the belief that all increased economic activity and investment will eventually benefit every city resident and neighborhood (Logan and Molotch 1987; Swanstrom 1985). The conservative growth coalition will cut city and social services and lower taxes to attract or maintain corporate investment. Instead, the liberal growth coalition believes it must improve urban livability, which requires the enhancement of public services and taxes, in order to attract or maintain corporate investment. The liberal coalition recognizes urban growth often translates into costs for certain urban neighborhoods and residents (Swanstrom 1985).

In contrast to liberal coalitions, the policy development process of conservative coalitions is typified by a small, tight-knit group of professional politicians, bureaucrats, and investors (Swanstrom 1985). The conservative coalition attempts to ensure government actions and decisions are streamlined and efficient. Centralizing and "trimming" the decision-making processes over urban development translates into less recognition of the specific needs of urban neighborhoods and residents.

Police efforts to identify with neighborhoods, encourage resident efforts, and increase resident participation/representation (i.e., community building) appear antithetical to the values of conservative growth coalitions. A city administration concerned with governmental efficiency and tight centralization does not mix well with increased community participation and decentralized decision making. Therefore, the following proposition is made:

Proposition C: Police steps to identify with neighborhoods, encourage resident efforts, and promote resident decision making, will be uncommon and poorly developed (weak dosage) in conservative growth cities. The local legitimacy of engaging in such community building processes by a police department would be suspect and perhaps threatening to a conservative regime. Ultimately, there are more incentives for police administrators to adopt the centralized decision-making values of the conservative regime.

Urban growth projects initiated by conservative coalitions generally target the central business district (CBD), CBD adjacent land, and wealthy residential areas located within city boundaries (Swanstrom 1985). "Community policing" in conservative growth coalition cities is likely to include zero-tolerance enforcement within the CBD and its border neighborhoods. For example, the presence of a highly transient population and panhandlers in the CBD district would be considered a threat to city commuters and local businesses, thus requiring a quick removal or sanction by police. Such a strategy may be considered a successful partnership between police and local business. Police departments in conservative growth cities are likely to utilize problem-solving activities (e.g., hot-spot analysis) that don't require extensive citizen involvement, but produce increased arrests, crackdowns, stings, and patrol in target areas. Such tactics would be publicized and supported by growth coalition leaders in order to show the city's no nonsense approach to crime, protecting urban investors and business commuters.

Proposition D: Policing in conservative growth cities is more likely to include strategies and/or special units for identifying high problem areas and using aggressive, traditional law enforcement tactics that increase arrests. These activities would be classified as part of the department's community policing strategy.

There are no incentives for police departments to become a strong wedge between use value oriented neighborhoods, especially feisty ones, and a conservative political regime. Police departments in conservative coalition cities will not ignore neighborhoods but may stress that neighborhoods are the source of crime and advocate for residents to increase their reporting of crimes. The community partnership role stressed by police in conservative coalition cities would entail being the police's "eyes and ears" on the street and reporting all disturbances. Emphasizing such a community role conceals the broader political and economic forces impacting neighborhood crime and may not help foster the type of community capacity needed for revitalizing poverty-stricken neighborhoods and addressing root causes of crime (Duffee, Fluellen, and Roscoe 1999). Police partnership efforts are more likely to occur with homeowners, businesses associations, and chambers of commerce, who will embrace community policing as a method of increasing property values and commerce, and to keep undesirables out of the neighborhood (Crank and Langworthy 1992; Lyons 1999; Skogan 1990). In the short term, community policing may be perceived as useful by conservative growth coalitions because it can provide extra policing funds and political relief (e.g., announcing a new program that will address crime).

Proposition E: Police community building activities occurring in conservative coalition cities are more likely to happen in predominately homeowner neighborhoods and business districts. The scope of community policing activities in these cities will be narrow. Activities will be primarily focused upon increasing crime reporting and target hardening. Police are not likely to be involved in noncrime issues and will not actively encourage broader resident participation and decision making.

The Liberal Growth Coalition and Community Policing

The primary difference between the conservative and liberal growth coalition is how each goes about the process of urban development

(Swanstrom 1985). Liberal growth coalitions will devote extensive time to planning growth projects and researching the potential costs of development and growth (Swanstrom 1985). This sense of responsibility pushes liberal growth coalitions to accommodate collaborative decision making with neighborhoods on growth projects. The degree of neighborhood–government consultation will be dependent on the strength of neighborhood organizations and their pressure for involvement. Neighborhood organizations in liberal growth coalition cities may actually be funded by the city. In general, a liberal coalition city will embrace more use value concerns and attempt to sustain neighborhood livability. Development projects in liberal growth cities may include enhancing public green spaces, protecting and promoting unique neighborhood characteristics, improving public transportation and schools, and aiding less prosperous residents. The liberal growth coalition must persuade investors/partners that quality public services produce competent laborers, reduce neighborhood tensions, and increase the attractiveness of the city — not just higher taxes (Logan and Molotch 1987; Swanstrom 1985). Public services can be maintained by keeping risky investment strategies to a minimum (few tax or utility breaks for corporations), garnering federal and state grant monies for urban redevelopment projects, and seeking voluntary contributions to provide aid to economically disadvantaged areas (Stoecker 1994; Swanstrom 1985).

Since police department budgets are primarily locally funded, departments in strong liberal growth coalition cities are likely to share the dominant political concern for extensive neighborhood planning, improving neighborhood livability (especially enhancing the use value of space), and providing quality public services.

Proposition F: Community policing in liberal growth cities is more likely to be characterized by strong efforts to identify with neighborhoods, encourage resident efforts, and increase resident participation in decision making (i.e., community building). Police–community partnerships in liberal growth cities are more likely to respond to social issues outside of traditional law enforcement and involve extensive coordination efforts involving social service agencies, businesses, schools, faith-based groups, and neighborhood organizations. Thus, the scope of community policing activities is more likely to address broader social issues.

Police community building efforts in liberal coalition cities are more likely to involve numerous organizations with diverse interests and specialties. Unfortunately, such broad and complex coordination may cause intense conflict and slow implementation ("too many cooks in the kitchen"). The coordination of multiple organizations always sounds good in theory, yet unintentional consequences often occur in practice. Evidence from the Model Cities programs revealed that attempts at increasing resident collaboration are often resisted by entrenched public service agencies (Warren et al. 1974). Neighborhood organizations can easily become co-opted into the "clientelism" philosophy of public service organizations, at the expense of broad resident participation (Stoecker 1994). Often the representation of neighborhoods in broad coordination efforts is trivial (Hallman 1984; Judd and Swanstrom 1998).

Proposition G: Community policing in liberal coalition cities that lack the strong neighborhood organizations, which would fight for broad resident participation and decision-making powers, will be characterized by a "service-provider" mentality. Efforts will be made to bring to neighborhood residents a wide variety of programs and services carried out by professional service organizations, as opposed to developing grass roots programs and strategies carried out by residents. These partnerships are not likely to be characterized by creative problem-solving processes, but are efforts to use, expand, and protect existing programs.

Caretaker Regimes, Urban Populism, and Community Policing

The final types of local political coalitions, caretaker, and urban populist regimes, are less likely to develop a strong presence in urban politics. Caretaker regimes are similar to the political machines that dominated urban governance from the mid-1800s to World War II, yet rarely occur today (Judd and Swanstrom 1998; Swanstrom 1985). Caretaker regimes tend to be antigrowth; their only concern is meeting the needs of the constituency that brought them into power (Haller 1976; Swanstrom 1985). In today's modern economy and complex urban environment, caretaker regimes are more likely to occur in small towns or university towns (Judd and Swanstrom 1998). Caretaker regimes tend to provide low quality services to their constituents, yet public services are more informal and personal in contrast to large bureaucratic institutions (Judd and Swanstrom 1998). As long as the interests of mobile corporate wealth in a city can coexist with the interests of the caretaker regime, and the service needs of voters are maintained, a caretaker regime may develop and stay in power (Swanstrom 1985).

The traditional police department in a caretaker regime city works closely with the representatives of the political party and is integrally involved in addressing all public service needs of residents (Fogelson 1977; Haller 1976; Judd and Swanstrom 1998). Thus, policing in caretaker regimes will exhibit strong neighborhood identification. Police–neighborhood identification would not entail encouragement of collective action or organizing, but entail listening to residents' personal problems. Caretaker regimes are always accessible to hear residents' problems, which translates into votes (Grondahl 1997). The goal of increasing resident participation in broad policy decisions or urban planning is foreign to caretaker regimes and their police departments; city services are already very personal. The biggest problems for caretaker regimes are appeasing local capital interests and maintaining a solid urban infrastructure. Caretaker regimes are often reluctant to apply for grants from state or federal agencies, which require oversight. Caretaker cities are unlikely to respond to centrist institutionalizing forces that attempt to mold the direction of policing (Grondahl 1997).

Urban populist parties are also a rare occurrence in cities today. The recent resurgence of urban populist parties was set off by the loss of manufacturing jobs, loss of family farms, civil rights movements, and religious movements (Boyte 1986). According to Boyte (1986, 8), "Populism is a language of inheritance. It grows from a sense of aggrieved 'peoplehood.'" Urban populist leaders are known for their rousing speeches that attempt to expose the bald political reality of society. Common populist spins exclaim how politicians and corporations are duping the American worker, or how American culture has lost its moral foothold. Urban populism thrives on the creation of belief systems through which urban problems should be viewed. Unlike conservative and liberal growth coalitions, urban populist parties are generally unable to develop strong coalitions of partner organizations and institutionalizing power in order to implement their urban agendas (Swanstrom 1985).

Swanstrom's (1985) analysis of Mayor Dennis Kucinich's urban populist movement in Cleveland in the late 1970s illustrates how an overly boisterous urban populist party can garner the popular vote, but quickly enrages necessary political and economic allies. Without the support of banks, corporations, the legislature, and police, the populist party, which advertised the abuses of power by these same institutions, was eventually voted out of office at the next election. Voters eventually perceived more harm than good being wrought because the populist party couldn't get anything accomplished (Swanstrom 1985).

If other urban institutions and key urban figures do not back a populist party, it is unlikely the party will be able to influence police strategies. The typical urban populist platform, which spotlights accountability of governance to citizen needs, would appear to favor many aspects of police community building, especially neighborhood decision making. If the local police have already gravitated toward a community policing strategy, the connection to an urban populist party may generate exemplary community building activities. It is more likely, though, that the police are a target of populist rhetoric, and would therefore support antipopulist political parties.

Neighborhood Organization and Community Policing

Neighborhood organizing efforts can differ in the attention given to community building (Cortes 1993; Hess 1999; Stoecker 1994). Thus, not every neighborhood organizing initiative aggressively attempts to build community, broaden resident participation, and train future resident leaders (Renauer 2000; Stoecker 1994). For example, Weingart, Hartmann, and Osborne's review of community antidrug efforts reports (1994, 12), "citizens do not always aspire to create robust and long-lasting institutions." Therefore, a neighborhood's existing community capacity and interest in community building will impact the level of police community building likely to occur in that neighborhood (Friedman 1994).

Proposition H: Organized neighborhoods, led by community building activists, are more likely to resist co-optation by police and other service agencies. These neighborhoods will struggle for an increased resident influence over the types of crime prevention strategies implemented in the neighborhood. Police departments may learn how to better identify with neighborhoods, encourage resident efforts, and increase participation from these organizations. The power of neighborhood organization influence over the direction of policing strategies will improve if neighborhoods form cross-neighborhood coalitions.

INTERNAL DEPARTMENT INFLUENCES

Despite all the external institutionalizing forces that impact police departments, the internal actions and beliefs of police leaders, police subcultures, and police associations are equally critical components in shaping police behavior and organizational structure (Andrews 1985; Bouza 1985; Crank and Langworthy 1992; Fraser 1985; Greene et al. 1994; J. B. Jacobs 1985). This section will examine two important relationships vital to the formation and implementation of policing operations. The first relationship is between the chief of police and the city executive (mayor or city manager). The second is the influence of police unions or associations on the direction and implementation of police operations.

The Police Chief and the City Executive

The independence and creative power of police chiefs exist in an unwritten, informal, political, and invisible state of nature (Andrews 1985). Sometimes city executives specifically inform police chiefs to take free rein over department structures, operations, and policies necessary to get the job done (Murphy 1985).[5] The relationships between police chiefs and city executives can also be tenuous and arbitrary, and may change according to political, economic, and crime emergencies (Andrews 1985). There are arguments for the complete independence of police chiefs from the city executive branch (Andrews 1985) and arguments for strong cooperation between police and city executives in order to successfully accomplish all urban policies (Hudnut 1985). In order to link the influence of a city's growth politics to policing operations, research must better understand the negotiations and shared values between police chiefs and city executives regarding the autonomy of chiefs and the role of policing within broad urban agendas.

Murphy (1985) provides a list of issues concerning the role of police chiefs and their autonomy. The following are Murphy's (1985) examples of negotiable issues: What is the role of the mayor and chief regarding media relations? Can the chief go directly to the mayor even when there is not a crisis? What are the lines of authority between the chief and the city's budget office regarding the police budget? Who decides personnel additions and changes, is the mayor allowed input? Who has ultimate control over discipline? Can there be a contract with the chief for a set number of years of employment? Does the mayor have any role in the deployment of personnel and organization of the agency? Gathering accurate information about the history of these issues within an urban setting and on the ability (or lack) of the police chief to negotiate with the city executive on these issues is integral to understanding the development of police structures, operations, and policies (Murphy 1985).

Police chiefs with set contracts and strong autonomy over operations are less likely to feel the overriding pressure to structure police operations to be consistent with the growth agenda of the city. If there is strong police autonomy in a conservative growth city, the chances of intense police community building efforts are improved, if the chief is attracted to such a style of policing. A reverse situation could happen in a liberal growth city, where an autonomous chief could maintain a more law-enforcement oriented and centralized style of policing in operation.

Proposition I: Police chiefs with set contracts and given free rein by city executives will not feel the overriding pressure to structure police operations to be consistent with the growth agenda of the city. These chiefs will follow their own vision and agenda for policing or adhere to an agenda consistent with the internal culture of the department.

Police Culture, Police Unions, and Collective Bargaining

Regardless of how a chief is connected to the city politics, if the chief is unable to garner support from top police administrators and middle managers, any community policing activities may be carried out in a haphazard or "loosely coupled" manner. Greene et al. (1994) feel the influence of the internal police culture, which is often organized in unions and associations, is the most important impediment to organizational change.

One of the major challenges to police administrators is dealing with police unions or associations and collective bargaining policies (Walker 1977). Police unions have spread across the nation at a varied pace and most are generally distinct from one another (Bouza 1985). Unions negotiate for patrol officers on employment contracts and specific grievances (Bouza 1985).

Efforts to change policing operations in Philadelphia toward community policing were strongly opposed by the police officers' bargaining unit, the Fraternal Order of Police, which resisted virtually all attempts at personnel changes (Greene, Bergman, and McLaughlin 1994). Police union reaction to greater resident involvement and decision making has also consistently been one of repugnance (Bouza 1985; Walker 1977). Local movements that have advocated civilian review boards and the introduction of volunteer or civilian officers have been strongly resisted by police unions (Bouza 1985; Perez 1994; Walker 1977). To engage in effective community building, police may have to work flexible hours, use different modes of patrol, attend community meetings, and be isolated from other officers. These are the same operational issues that many police unions have effectively addressed with institutionalized department policies.

Proposition J: Strong efforts by police to identify with neighborhoods, encourage resident efforts, and increase resident participation are not likely to occur when there are restrictive policies regarding officer duties and attendance at off-duty community meetings/events. Community building efforts will be hampered and short-lived if police–neighborhood collaborations are based exclusively upon overtime for officer involvement in such activities. Strong union cities are more likely to have small community policing subunits comprised of volunteer or new recruit officers funded by grant monies and focused on small target areas.

CONCLUSION

Hagan (1989b) argues that criminal justice theory would advance by seeking to predict where and when the couplings between policy goals and quality application would loosen or tighten. A fruitful avenue for this theory development is in the community policing area. Community policing is a sufficiently ambiguous and wide-ranging strategy, thus allowing several configurations or styles of implementation to occur. One potential style could involve strong police community building efforts that seek to identify with neighborhoods, encourage resident efforts, and develop broad resident participation and representation. This chapter proposes that the balance of institutionalizing forces (coercive, normative, mimetic) from centrist, local, and internal levels will determine the extent of police community building in urban neighborhoods (see Figure 6.1). Institutional theory is used to describe the characteristics of institutionalizing relationships that are likely to support a certain style of policing operation — police community building.

The propositions developed above suggest intense police community building is more likely to develop in liberal growth coalition cities, where there are organized neighborhoods concerned about community building, and support from police chiefs and internal police cultures. This chapter argues that the causes of police–community building are primarily from local level influences within a police department's immediate task environment and constituency. Local level and internal police department influences are more powerful because they have more severe impacts on police resources and organizational flexibility, and certain local forces are more experienced with community building. Centrist level influences ("new" institutional theory) can push police departments to experiment with police community building activities, but ultimately the strength and direction of local and internal influences ("old" institutional theory) will impact the extent of police community building actually carried out.

By understanding the various institutionalizing relationships influencing urban community policing implementation we can learn more about the obstacles, resistances, and achievements of community policing as a national movement and as a local project (Crank and Langworthy 1992). If these forces do influence community policing implementation toward (or away from) strong community building, there are important policy implications.

Since no data is presented here, it can only be hypothesized what the potential policy implications of research that may support such a theory of community policing variation would be. If centrist, local, or internal police forces advocate one form of community policing over another, they should be interested in such theoretical research. In point of fact, research on the balance of forces perspective presented here would point out where constraints against a desired policing agenda would occur and where certain policies could take a firm hold, thus decreasing the chances of a decoupling phenomenon or weak implementation. For students of criminal justice, recognition of the potential refraction and adaptation of criminal justice policies at the local level is an important lesson to take into their careers. Public pronouncements, websites, and training manuals do not have the institutionalizing power to translate criminal justice policies into aggressive, quality implementations everywhere — many other factors come into play.

The research propositions presented here are integrally tied to a need for measuring the extent to which police departments engage in community building (see Duffee, Scott et al. 2002). This chapter did not arbitrarily choose to explore why policing may involve more or less community building in neighborhoods. Community building is theoretically linked to the development of community capacity and hence long-term impacts on community safety and livability. It would behoove criminal justice research to explore not only where police community building is more likely to be manifested but also its connection to long-term public safety improvements.

NOTES

1. This chapter was made possible by the Police Community Interaction Project supported by Grant No. 97–IJ–CX–0052 awarded by the National Institute of Justice, Office of Justice Programs, U.S. Department of Justice. Points of view in this chapter are those of the author and do not necessarily represent the official position or policies of the U. S. Department of Justice.

2. From *Police for the Future* by D. H. Bayley, 1994. By permission of Oxford University Press, Inc.

3. We liken community capacity with "social capital" and "collective efficacy." All three concepts are concerned with social processes that increase the likelihood of residents' engaging in social action for the common good of their community. Despite the basic similarity, all three concepts focus on slightly different social processes and different measurement techniques have been used to indicate each (Renauer and Scott 2001).

4. Evidence of community policing involvement from national surveys may be tainted or lack validity because some surveys were tied to funding applications (Maguire and Mastrofski 2000).

5. Murphy (1985) states that this is the exception rather than the rule.

Part III

Individual and Community
Level Theories of the Courts

In both chapters in this section, the authors deal with explanations of "court" behaviors. The chapters share a broad concern for what happens in the middle of the criminal justice system and why it happens. Both chapters are also critical reviews of extant theory. That is, much like Maguire and Uchida in chapter 5 on police organization theory, these chapters attempt to assess a broad class of theories that seek to explain similar if not identical phenomena. In both chapters, the authors pose a framework for comparing theories and assessing what we know better and what we are less sure of. Both are concerned about using a framework for comparing explanations so that scholars of the courts can determine both what kind of research is most pressing in order to test developed but underresearched theory and, at the same time, what kinds of theoretical explanations need to be developed next to provide better guides to research.

The behaviors that are the focus of these two chapters are certainly related, since they both deal with why certain court outcomes occur. But these two chapters cover quite different theoretical territory. In chapter 7, Paula Kautt and Cassia Spohn develop a framework for assessing judicial sentencing decisions. In chapter 8, Alissa Pollitz Worden assesses the nature of theories that use community variables to explain court outcomes and court variables to explain community outcomes. The distinction between these two chapters, then, would often be described as the difference between microtheories about individuals, in chapter 7, and macrotheories about complex social systems in chapter 8. However, the understanding of the level of social units designated by the terms *micro* and *macro* is not fixed, as Snipes and Maguire point out in chapter 2.

The exact use of these terms varies by discipline. Deciding on the specific social levels and what to call them is less important than recognizing that there are distinctly different social levels that can perform quite differently, even if they are related. One of the most common examples of the importance of examining different social levels separately is the example of the "hung jury" concept. A hung jury is an indecisive group: it made no decision. But that group is comprised of individuals who have made firm decisions as individuals, but in conflicting directions. Consequently, it would be appropriate to call the group indecisive, but that would be an inaccurate description of the individuals in the jury. Different social levels behave differently.

Similarly, and probably of more importance in the court realm, we can conceive of (and find) a racially fair jurisdiction (or community or social system) that nevertheless contains some prejudiced individuals who make racially biased individual decisions. We can also conceive of (and find) a racially biased jurisdiction or community that contains individual decision makers who are not racially biased in their individual decisions. Certainly, society may want to eliminate or at least control injustice and bias at both levels. However, fixes at one level (such as controls on individual discretion) may not be relevant to problems at the higher level (such as criminal penalties that punish sale of one form of cocaine more severely than another form). Consequently, it is critical that we recognize the need for theories at multiple levels and encourage theoretically guided research at each appropriate level.

In chapter 7, Kautt and Spohn devise a framework for organizing different theories about individual judicial sentencing decisions. Their framework has two dimensions, a vertical dimension that identifies the level of the social phenomena that are expected to affect the decision (from attributes of the case at the low end to attributes of the jurisdiction at the high end) and a horizontal dimension that organizes the nature of the explanatory variables at any one level (such as physical attributes, internal commitments, perceptions, and experience of individual decision makers).

These authors argue that this means of organizing theories of decision making could be applied to any criminal justice decision. In other words, while Kautt and Spohn focus on explanations of judicial sentencing in this chapter, they assert that the framework proposed should also work for assessing theories of police arrest decisions, prosecutorial charging decisions, prison guard disciplinary write-ups, and so on. If they are correct, then this framework would also be useful in examining whether the same kinds of variables affect different decisions by different actors or whether different kinds of explanations are more relevant at different parts of the criminal justice system.

Kautt and Spohn cover five of the seven themes that Snipes and Maguire used to consider criminal justice theories in chapter 2. Chapter 7 considers organizational, sociopolitical, objective/subjective, type of response, and level of explanation themes. Like Howard and Freilich in chapter 3 and Castellano in chapter 4, Kautt and Spohn are deeply concerned with how to theorize. They suggest that understanding decision making can be advanced if we are very systematic in thinking about the placement of a theory in the universe of possible explanations of a phenomenon. They illustrate their framework by reviewing various theories of judicial sentencing decisions, beginning with those that examine attributes such as age, race, and gender of the judge, moving on to perceptual theories that explain judicial decisions as outcomes of the judge's internal assessment processes, and finally they examine some integrated theories that seek to use different domains of variables at the same time.

In chapter 8, Alissa Worden tackles an assessment of theories that try to link communities and courts. She begins by asking what we should consider "court theory." She briefly appraises the conceptual domains that are necessary to the court–community connection and how variations in these domains would affect the nature of those theoretical connections. She then asks how theorists should try to link the communities and courts. She proposes that current theories about this linkage can be divided into three broad categories: theories that examine how a constituency is represented in a public organization; theories that pose conflict among constituents; and theories that rely on organizational or working group "communities" to explain court processes and outcomes. She then asks what might be compatible or conflictual among these different approaches, with an aim, ultimately, of developing each more completely by combining or integrating them.

This critical review of theory utilizes five of Snipes and Maguire's "theoretical themes." Worden is concerned about the level of explanation embedded in a theory, the sociopolitical perspective or assumptions about society underlying a theory, the types of criminal justice responses that the theory sets out to explain, the organizational perspectives employed in typifying the criminal justice phenomenon, and the institutional arena to which the theory applies.

Worden clearly indicates that dividing the "system" up neatly into different institutional areas may be easier said than done (or too simplistic to carry us very far). From one point of view, the court is a local phenomenon influenced by a local "community." But as we add the institutional perspective about organizations and get involved in the symbolic politics of courts, theorists rapidly leave the "local" for broader concerns of culture and political structure. It would appear that a very difficult and intriguing part of court theory is how the local and the national or societal come together — a question that was also at the heart of Renauer's theory of police community building. On a somewhat more abstract plane, Worden's concerns about what is contained in the idea of community and how those ideas affect courts, and vice versa, is also similar to McGarrell and Duffee's investigation of state environments and correctional structures and Maguire and Uchida's review of police organization connections to their environments. It would appear that a great deal of criminal justice theory, whether it ostensibly deals with specific institutions or not, struggles to connect broader social, political, and cultural systems to the government control system called criminal justice. That these attempts are constantly wrestling with the local and nonlocal and how they mix is not surprising or unique to criminal justice. Perhaps the main theme of Warren's classic *Community in America* (1978) is precisely this: the variation in community that we seek to understand is often a product of the confluence of national forces that affect all communities and the local characteristics or filters through which those national forces become distinct in particular localities.

DISCUSSION QUESTIONS

1. Take Kautt and Spohn's challenge. See if you can take their schema for individual decision making and apply it to a different institutional sector or to different decision making within the court sector. Can their model for systematically varying the level and domain of explanation help with police use of force? Arrests? Decisions to charge? Release on bail? Prison disciplinary charges? Discretionary prison release? What about some less studied decisions: victims' decision to call the police? Legislators' decisions to treat a harm as a crime?
2. Examine Worden's proposed examination of court impact on community. Is this criminal justice theory, under the four tests proposed by Snipes and Maguire?
3. Castellano's and Gould's concern for justice as a dependent variable might be particularly relevant to studies of the court. Review the dependent variables proposed by both Kautt and Spohn and Worden. Which of these might be most consistent with a desire to explain justice rather than crime?

7

ASSESSING BLAMEWORTHINESS AND ASSIGNING PUNISHMENT

Theoretical Perspectives on Judicial Decision Making

Paula M. Kautt and Cassia C. Spohn

Dynamic theories of the judicial process ... picture the judge as a policy oriented decision-maker who derives ... premises both from within and without the courtroom and whose functions far exceed the mechanical task of applying settled rules of law to clear fact situations ... the judge operates in an institutional framework which places certain restraints on the pure expression of personal preferences, but which also allows significant latitude for such expression. (Grossman 1967, 334–35)

INTRODUCTION

More than other components of the criminal justice system, the criminal courts possess a certain mystique. There, defense and prosecution join in battle over the facts of a criminal case and the guilt or innocence of a defendant in order to achieve the ideal of "justice." The judge, physically and symbolically removed from the combatants, is the impartial primary arbiter of these adversarial proceedings: He or she weighs the evidence, interprets the rules of engagement, and metes out decisions from the lofty bench. Yet, when a decision of guilt is finally reached, how do judges, these supposed paragons of impartiality, decide the sentence to be imposed upon the convicted offender? Intuitively, the answer seems simple: the more serious the infraction, the harsher the punishment. In other words, the law and the interests of justice alone dictate sanction. All other factors are simply irrelevant. Such an idealized explanatory framework has been with us since ancient times. Its simplicity and symmetry have an intuitive appeal that evokes the ideals of equity and fairness while its longevity and tradition attractively cloak it in the fabric of historical "truth." Academically, this simple, commonsense explanation of criminal sentencing outcomes is also known as the legal metaphor (Eisenstein, Flemming, and Nardulli 1988).

However, despite its rich heritage, it seems clear that the legal metaphor's concept of courtroom actors who objectively apply the rule of law to each case is misleading. As indicated by the introductory quotation, factors deemed legally irrelevant do affect punishment. Consider, for example, the offender's income. Clearly, how much money someone makes is irrelevant as to whether or not he or she is factually guilty of a criminal offense or deserves punishment. Yet, one need only think of the expensive legal defenses mounted in recent high profile criminal cases to quickly recognize that this seemingly extraneous factor does indeed play a role in determining criminal sanction (or lack thereof). With brief additional reflection, one can readily conceive of a host of other factors that can influence judicial sentencing decisions. Personal biases, political influence, court resources, or past experiences might all play a role. As a result, common sense tells us that the legal metaphor does not accurately portray or comprehensively explain the realities of judicial decision making and criminal sentencing.

Existing empirical research bolsters this commonsense conclusion, indicating that a myriad of factors — many of which are completely independent of the case at hand — influence court decision makers (Jacob 1997; Ulmer 1997) and the sentences they mete out (Gibson 1977; Blumstein et al. 1983). For example, defendants who go to trial are more likely to be incarcerated and receive longer sentences than their nonjury counterparts (Uhlman and Walker 1980; Spohn 1992). Likewise, defendant gender (Steffensmeier, Kramer et al. 1993; Daly and Tonry 1997); age (Steffensmeier, Kramer et al. 1995); race (Steffensmeier, Ulmer et al. 1998; Spohn and DeLone 2000; Kautt and Spohn 2002); and socioeconomic status (C. E. Smith 1991) all have been shown to affect case outcomes. There also is evidence that judges are more likely to impose the death penalty in jurisdictions where they are elected rather than appointed (Bright and Keenan 1995) and that city political environments have a direct impact on judicial sentencing philosophy and behavior (Levin 1972). Such findings clearly indicate that factors from a wide variety of sources affect sentencing outcomes. As a result, perspectives more comprehensive and sophisticated than the legal metaphor are necessary to explain the punishments assigned to criminal defendants. Meeting this challenge is one purpose of court and sentencing theory.

While it has often been said that empirical investigations of the criminal justice system are atheoretical (see Snipes and Maguire in this volume as well as Hagan [1989b]), the notable exception to this is the arena of criminal courts — specifically, judicial decision making. There, substantive theories have rapidly developed over the past several decades. Collectively, these frameworks provide a global perspective for understanding the criminal courts, their function, and their outcomes. Yet, not all court theories are created equal. In fact, the theoretically relevant factors vary widely in the existing court perspectives. For example, some focus exclusively on a single level of influential factors — such as only case, organizational, or jurisdictional attributes — while others simultaneously account for multiple influential levels. Likewise, single-level theories (e.g., case) may address only one group of factors from that level — such as defendant characteristics — while others incorporate multiple factor categories from that same level (defendant characteristics in conjunction with offense and processing factors). Such variability clearly demonstrates how the explanations of the courts and their outcomes can differ radically by the vertical and horizontal dimensions they encompass.

While the existing theories exhibit numerous variations in the elements believed to have predictive and explanatory importance, such differences can be translated into an organizing framework for discussing and categorizing existing sentencing theories. The aforementioned vertical and horizontal dimensions are the key to this approach. The vertical element or *hierarchy* broadly refers to the level of the theory. This dictates both the level and unit of analysis for empirical investigation. Much more specific than micro, meso, or macro levels, hierarchy represents the level of the theory both in terms of which and how many levels are accounted for by a given perspective (see Figure 7.1 for a graphic representation). Conversely, different groups of influential factors that occur at the same level of analysis comprise the horizontal elements or *spheres* (see Figure 7.2). At the individual level, for example, and as illustrated by Figure 7.3, physical judicial characteristics (gender, race, age) comprise one sphere of influence, while nonphysical judicial characteristics (experience or education) comprise another.

Using hierarchy and spheres together, one can categorize court theories by the breadth and width of factors they incorporate. Practically speaking, theories can be labeled horizontally integrated, vertically

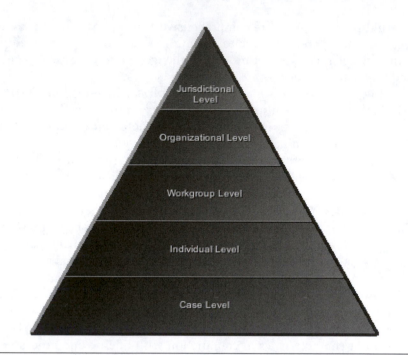

Figure 7.1 Vertical hierarchies

Figure 7.2 Horizontal spheres

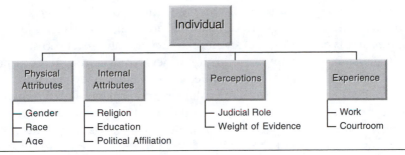

Figure 7.3 Horizontal spheres: The individual level

integrated, both, or neither. A horizontally integrated theory would capture multiple spheres of influence occurring at the same hierarchical level. Conversely, a vertically integrated theory would incorporate theoretical influences from two or more hierarchical levels. Beyond this categorization, theories can be differentiated further by which specific hierarchies or spheres they address. However, it is important to note that not all theories simultaneously incorporate vertical and horizontal dimensions or even all spheres from within the same level; in fact, most do not. Many theories are neither horizontally nor vertically integrated — although there has been movement toward this ideal since the late 1990s (Ulmer 1997; Ulmer and Kramer 1998; Henham 2001).

Although our initial model identifies several potential hierarchies and spheres, our current examination of judge-based theories of sentencing outcomes will cover only three major groupings representing a gradual theoretical evolution from simple or unidimensional theories to complex and integrated ones. These are: judicial attributes, judicial perceptions, and integrated theories. The judicial attributes section describes theories positing that two individual level spheres — physical (gender, race, age) and nonphysical (education, experience, and values) judicial characteristics — affect sentencing outcomes. This section also discusses the emergence of horizontally integrated individual level theories. The judicial perceptions section addresses theories concerning how judicial *views* of particular external factors (such as the defendant, case, workgroup, environment — which may be located on different hierarchical levels) affect the sentencing decision reached. Such theories represent a preliminary step that attempts to incorporate multilevel factors into individual level theories via individual *perception* of factors from other levels. Finally, the integrated theory section addresses theories that encompass multiple hierarchical levels — incorporating elements from several — to explain judicial sentencing decisions. Thus, addressing Snipes and Maguire's seven dimensions of criminal justice theories (chapter 2 of this volume), the frameworks reviewed in this chapter include the organizational, sociopolitical, objective versus the subjective, type of response, and level of explanation perspectives.

Obviously, our listing of examined hierarchies and spheres is not comprehensive — nor was it intended to be. Rather, they are chosen in a deliberate effort to reflect the evolution and range of judicial theory — from the flat one- or two-dimensional traditional frameworks to the modern multifaceted picture of judicial decision making. Moreover, they are illustrative of the utility of our proposed framework in discussing the existing judicial decision-making theories. We believe that this classification system can serve as a tool for categorizing existing research and theories. We also believe that it will facilitate the development of new models and theories by providing a precise framework for considering, organizing, and incorporating any theoretically relevant factors. Such theoretical innovations will produce more accurate depictions of reality as well as predictions of and explanations for sentencing outcomes. What follows is a discussion of each of the aforementioned theory groups.

JUDICIAL ATTRIBUTES AND JUDICIAL DECISION MAKING

Social scientists and legal scholars, who acknowledge that the legal metaphor is an inadequate explanation for sentencing decisions, have developed other theoretical perspectives for explaining how judges determine the appropriate sentence for any given offense and offender. Some scholars maintain that sentencing decisions are affected by the personal characteristics of the judge. As Myers (1988, 649) states, "The social background of judges is presumed to affect early and professional socialization experiences, which in turn are hypothesized to affect attitudes, role orientations, and ultimately, behavior." According to this perspective, judges' background characteristics, attitudes, and values influence — either directly or indirectly — the sentences they impose. This and other such theories are classic examples of the sociopolitical and the objective versus subjective perspectives as articulated by Snipes and Maguire earlier in this volume.

Early studies of judicial decision making suggested that the influence of the judge's personal characteristics was predicated on one of three theoretical concepts: *conversion, consensus,* or *rationality* (Grossman 1967). The most basic concept, *conversion,* refers to the direct translation of social background characteristics into judicial decisions (Goldman 1969). Sentencing theories based on conversion assume that individual thought and decision making are the products of one's social identity, which is shaped by physical attributes such as race, gender, and age. As a result, the sentences imposed by black judges will differ from those imposed by white judges and the sentencing decisions of male judges and younger judges will differ from those of female judges and older judges.

THE EFFECT OF THE GENDER, RACE/ETHNICITY, AND AGE OF THE JUDGE

Several theories have been put forth about the effect of specific physical attributes on judges' sentencing decisions. Many theorists, for example, contend that female judges will dispense a different type of justice than male judges as a result of differences in their outlooks, orientations, and experiences. In support of the argument that women judges "speak in a different voice," some point to the work of Carol Gilligan (1982), who claimed that women's moral reasoning differs from that of men: whereas men emphasize legal rules and reasoning based on an ethic of justice, women, who are more concerned about preserving relationships and more sensitive to the needs of others, reason using an ethic of care. Others, who counter that "the language of law is explicitly the language of justice rather than care" (Berns 1999, 197), claim that the differences women bring to the bench stem more from their experiences as women than from differences in moral reasoning. They maintain, for example, that women are substantially more likely than are men to be victimized by rape, sexual harassment, domestic violence, and other forms of predatory violence, and that their experiences as crime victims or their fear of crime shape their attitudes toward and their response to crime and criminals.

Although researchers generally agree that the attitudes and experiences of women and men on the bench are different, they disagree about the ways in which these differences will influence the sentencing patterns of female and male judges. Some researchers contend that, because females are socialized to be nurturing, sympathetic, and understanding, female judges will be more lenient than male judges (Gruhl, Spohn, and Welch 1981). Others suggest that the fact that women are more likely to be victims of sexualized violence and are more fearful of crime in general might incline them to impose harsher sentences than men, particularly for violent crimes, crimes against women, and crimes involving dangerous repeat offenders (Steffensmeier and Herbert 1999). A third school of thought holds that, because the presence of women in positions of authority — such as judges — is relatively rare, females in those positions will tend to view themselves as tokens. As a result, female judges will be uniformly harsher than male judges because of a psychological need to prove that they are not "soft on crime" and that they are "worthy" of judges' robes, despite so many years of formal exclusion from the profession (Kanter 1977). Still others argue that the life experiences of female judges — and particularly black or Hispanic female judges — will make them more sensitive to the existence of racism or sexism; as a result, they might make more equitable sentencing decisions than white male judges (Gruhl, Spohn, and Welch 1981).

Researchers who contend that the race of the judge will affect sentencing decisions advance similar arguments. Because the life histories and experiences of blacks differ dramatically from those of whites, the beliefs and attitudes they bring to the bench also will differ. Justice A. Leon Higginbotham Jr., an African American who retired from the U.S. Court of Appeals for the Third Circuit in 1993, wrote: "someone who has been a victim of racial injustice has greater sensitivity of the court's making sure that racism is not perpetrated, even inadvertently" (Washington 1994, 11–12). Welch and her colleagues make an analogous argument. Noting that blacks tend to view themselves as liberal rather than conservative, they speculate that black judges might be "more sympathetic to criminal defendants than white judges are, since liberal views are associated with support for the underdog and the poor, which defendants disproportionately are" (Welch, Combs, and Gruhl 1988, 127). Others similarly suggest that increasing the number of black judges would reduce racism in the criminal justice system and produce more equitable treatment of black and white defendants.

Regarding the age of the judge, researchers generally expect older judges to be more traditional and more conservative and hence to impose more punitive sentences than younger judges. Myers (1988, 654), however, speculates that older judges might be "selectively punitive" — that is, older judges might "impose harsher sanctions on certain offenders with whom, because of their age, they are least able to sympathize." Myers states that while drug offenders are the most likely candidates for harsher treatment by older judges, these judges also might impose more punitive sentences on "members of disadvantaged and potentially troublesome groups (e.g., black, young, single, unemployed)" (654).

Although several studies concluded that older judges sentenced defendants more harshly than younger judges (Cook 1973; Kritzer 1978; Myers 1988; Steffensmeier and Herbert 1999), the results of research examining the effect of the gender and race of the judge on sentencing decisions are inconsistent. While some research finds that female judges impose harsher sentences than do male judges in certain contexts (Spohn 1990b; Steffensmeier and Herbert 1999), most studies conclude that there are more similarities than differences between the sentences handed down by male and female judges (Gruhl et al. 1981; Myers 1988; Spohn 1990b; Laster and Douglas 1995). Moreover, the studies that do find a "judge gender effect" conclude that the relationship between the gender of the judge and sentence outcomes is neither simple nor straightforward. Rather, several studies find that contextual factors — such as defendant or case characteristics (Spohn 1990a; Steffensmeier and Herbert 1999) — interact with judge gender to affect both the incarceration and sentence length decisions. Recent research also argues that these varied gender effects are not the product of women's socialization patterns but instead reflect other factors such as the judge's professional background (Laster and Douglas 1995) or the judicial selection process (Songer and Crews-Meyer 2000). These results suggest a bridge between judges' physical and nonphysical attributes in the decision-making process.

The findings regarding the effect of the judge's race/ethnicity on sentencing decisions also are contradictory. Most researchers find few overall differences in the sentences imposed by black and white judges. Engle (1971) concluded that there were only minor differences in the sentences imposed by black and white judges on the bench in Philadelphia. Uhlman (1979) found that while the sentencing patterns of individual black judges varied considerably, their overall sentencing patterns did not differ from those of white judges, and Spohn (1990b) concluded that there were "remarkable similarities" in the sentencing decisions of black and white judges. One study (Spohn 1990a) found that black female judges imposed longer sentences on offenders convicted of sexual assault, while another (Spears 1999) found that black male judges sentenced offenders to prison at a lower rate but imposed longer sentences on those who were incarcerated. Depending upon the time period, the jurisdiction, and the types of offenses included in the analysis, black judges sentence either no differently, more harshly, or more leniently than do white judges.

The evidence regarding the degree to which black and Hispanic judges impose more racially equitable sentences also is mixed. Two studies found that black judges imposed similar sentences on black and white offenders while white judges gave more lenient sentences to white offenders than to black offenders (Spears 1999; Welch, Coombs, and Gruhl 1988). Another found a similar pattern of results for Hispanic judges and Anglo judges (Holmes et al. 1993). All three studies concluded that white judges discriminate in favor of white offenders. A fourth study, on the other hand, found no race-of-judge differences in the sentences imposed on black and white offenders convicted of violent felonies (Spohn 1990b).

In sum, existing research finds that the gender and race of the judge generally have little or no direct effect on sentencing decisions; when effects are present, they are often inconsistent and indirect. Such findings clearly indicate that judicial decision making is not merely a conversion of physical attributes into sentencing outcomes. This is not surprising, since theoretical frameworks grounded in the physical attributes of the decision maker often ignore individual perception, learning, and experience. In other words, these perspectives are limited to a single sphere of individual level factors when the evidence suggests that multiple individual level spheres come into play during the sentencing process. Such linkage between the individual level spheres is consistent with the *Maximalist* perspective (Steffensmeier and Herbert 1999), where on-the-job decisions and behaviors are the product of beliefs, attitudes, and norms developed and located *within* the individual. Thus, judicial decisions are not a direct product of physical characteristics but rather are derived from psychological and socialization differences — only some of which may stem from physical attributes such as gender, race, or age.

THE EFFECT OF THE JUDGE'S PERSONALITY ATTRIBUTES AND PROFESSIONAL EXPERIENCE

Theories of judicial decision making also highlight the role played by the judge's personality attributes and pre-judicial professional experience. Some researchers focus on judicial self-esteem; they contend that judges with weak self-images seek personal validation through their sentencing decisions. According to Gibson (1981a), judges can accomplish this validation either through decision conformity (they demonstrate that they "belong" on the bench because they conduct themselves in the accepted and expected manner) or nonconformity (they flout convention in order to prove to themselves and others that they are both confident and independent). Other scholars maintain that sentencing outcomes will vary by the religious beliefs of the judge: judges with more fundamentalist religious beliefs are expected to impose more punitive sentences (Nagel 1962; Myers 1988). Additional judicial characteristics predicted to affect sentencing decisions include the judge's background (Ball 1980; Myers 1988), political affiliation (Rowland et al. 1984), and professional experience (Frazier and Bock 1982; Myers 1988).

Research exploring the effect of these background characteristics generally reveals that they either do not affect sentence outcomes at all

(Spohn 1990a; Spears 1999) or have only weak effects (Steffensmeier and Herbert 1999). They also demonstrate that such characteristics do not always affect sentencing decisions as expected. Three studies (Gibson 1978; Myers 1988; Steffensmeier and Herbert 1999), for example, found that judges with prior prosecutorial experience imposed harsher sentences, while one (Welch et al. 1988) found that former prosecutors imposed more lenient sentences. Similarly, two studies found that judges who had been on the bench longer imposed more severe sentences (Gibson 1978; Welch et al. 1988), while two others found that longer tenure on the bench led to more lenient sentences (Spohn 1990a; Steffensmeier and Herbert 1999). Two studies concluded that judges who were members of fundamentalist churches meted out more severe punishment than those who were not (Gibson 1978; Myers 1988). The fact that most of these effects were relatively weak, coupled with the fact that some of them were in the opposite direction of what was predicted, indicates that these background characteristics do not consistently affect the sentences that judges impose. These results also suggest that any judicial variation in sentencing decisions is more the product of other factors — such as case differences — rather than individual attributes.

This position is further bolstered by research exploring the influence of judicial characteristics while simultaneously controlling for case-level attributes. Such findings indicate that judicial characteristics have little direct effect on sentencing outcomes but do condition the weight attached to particular case-level factors. These results demonstrate the importance of considering individual judicial characteristics in conjunction with factors from other levels — such as case attributes — as conditioners of sentencing outcomes (Frazier and Bock 1982; Myers 1988). Such findings clearly indicate that individual level theories alone — even multispherical ones — are inadequate to explain the complexities of judicial decisions and sentencing outcomes.

Returning to the three historical bases for explaining the impact of judicial characteristics on sentencing decisions, the aforementioned concepts of *consensus* and *rationality* suggest an approach for bridging these multilevel factors. *Consensus*-based theories posit that personal characteristics become relevant only when the judge perceives the case as being ambiguous. Conversely, *rationality*-based perspectives argue that the judge uses his or her own personal preferences and attributes to choose between the variety of sentencing alternatives that each case presents (Grossman 1967). In both instances, judicial *perceptions* of characteristics from other levels — most notably case characteristics — dictate the influence of personal characteristics on the sentencing outcome. Similarly, in the *psychometric model* (Schubert 1961), case attributes are stimuli that elicit responses (sentencing decisions) representing individual judicial attitudes toward and perceptions of the case (Goldman 1969). Likewise, *role orientation* links individual attributes to case characteristics at the individual level. There, judicial beliefs about the relevance and rank importance of case criteria dictate the sentencing decision (Gibson 1977, 1978, 1981b). Such concepts linking individual judicial attributes to case characteristics gave rise to a new breed of theories explaining sentencing outcomes. These perspectives, however, are only pseudo-integrated because, while they address factors that stem from multiple levels, these factors are accounted for *only as perceived* by the sentencing judge. As a result, they remain exclusively at the individual level.

JUDICIAL PERCEPTIONS AND JUDICIAL DECISION MAKING

The theoretical perspectives discussed thus far suggest that judges' background characteristics, attitudes, and role orientations have inconsistent and contradictory effects on their sentencing decisions. A second category of theories focuses on the ways in which judges' *perceptions of* and *reactions to* external factors such as the crime, the defendant, other members of the courtroom workgroup, and the environment affect their sentencing decisions. According to these theories, judges' sentencing decisions reflect both their beliefs about the factors that ought to be taken into consideration in determining the appropriate punishment and their perceptions of these factors. If, for example, judges generally believe that more serious crimes and more blameworthy or dangerous offenders deserve harsher punishment, the sentences they impose will depend upon their perceptions of the types of crimes that are most serious and the types of offenders who are most blameworthy and dangerous. As John Hogarth (1971, 279) wrote over thirty years ago, sentencing "is a cognitive process in which information concerning the offender, the offense, and the surrounding circumstances is read, organized in relation to other information and integrated into an overall assessment of the case."

The theories discussed below attempt to explain "how the values and beliefs of individuals and groups are transformed into the policies and practices of controlling organizations" (Bridges and Steen 1998, 568). They attempt to account for how judges develop "an overall assessment of the case." Each of these judge-based theories seeks not simply to identify the relevant predictors of sentencing decisions but also to describe the mechanisms by which characteristics of the crime, the defendant, the organization, and the environment influence the sentences that judges impose. All of the theories assume, explicitly or implicitly, that sentencing is discretionary, that the information available to the judge at sentencing is incomplete, and that judges therefore simplify or routinize the decision-making process by categorizing or classifying crimes, defendants, and cases. As shown below, each of the theories also purports to explain why certain categories of offenders — racial minorities, males, young adults, the unemployed — may be singled out for harsher treatment.

CAUSAL ATTRIBUTION THEORY

A number of scholars argue that judges' sentencing decisions reflect their beliefs about an offender's potential for rehabilitation, which rest, in turn, on their perception of the causes of criminal behavior (cf., Bridges and Steen 1998; J. S. Carroll and Payne 1976; Hawkins 1981). According to this perspective, decision makers attribute causality either to the individual's personal characteristics (i.e., *internal characteristics*, such as antisocial personality, lack of remorse, refusal to admit guilt or cooperate with officials) or to factors within the environment/ *external characteristics* (e.g., delinquent peers, a dysfunctional family, drug or alcohol use, poverty). Individuals whose crimes are attributed to internal factors are viewed as more responsible, and, thus, as more blameworthy, than those whose crimes are viewed as stemming from external forces; more importantly, these attributions affect the sentences that judges impose. As Hawkins (1981, 280) states, "perceptual differences such as this may in turn lead to conclusions regarding the … offender's rehabilitation potential, the threat posed to society, and the type of criminal sanction imposed."

Bridges and Steen (1998, 555), who contend that most studies of racial bias in the courts fail to identify the mechanisms by which race affects court outcomes, suggest that causal attribution theory can be used to explain "the race-punishment relationship." Building on theories of social cognition, which hold that racial and ethnic stereotypes affect officials' perceptions of minority offenders, Bridges and Steen propose that the harsher treatment of racial minorities may be due to the fact that criminal justice officials perceive their crimes as caused by internal forces and crimes committed by whites as caused by external forces. They further argue that these "differential attributions about the causes of crime by minorities and whites may contribute directly to differential assessments of offender dangerousness and risk" and, thus, to "racial differences in perceived risk and recommended punishment" (Bridges and Steen 1998, 557).

Bridges and Steen used juvenile probation officers' narrative reports and sentence recommendations to test these propositions. They found that reports on black youth were more likely to mention negative personality characteristics (internal attributions), while those on white youth were more likely to mention negative environmental factors (external attributions). They also discovered that these causal attributions shaped probation officers' assessments of the risk of reoffending and sentence recommendations. Because the crimes of black youth were more often attributed to negative personality traits or attitudes, black youth were judged to have a higher risk of recidivism than white youth; as a result, probation officers recommended harsher sentences for black youth than for white youth. Thus, Bridges and Steen (1998, 567) note, "attributions about youths and their crimes are a mechanism by which race influences judgments of dangerousness and sentencing recommendations."

Causal attribution theory represents a direct challenge to the legal metaphor. It suggests that sentences result, not from a static process in which "the law" is applied objectively to individual cases, but from a causal sequence that involves subjective perceptions, assessments, and decisions. In fact, subsequent research (Steen et al. 2005) has expanded this framework to incorporate judicial "stereotypes" about crime and offense type — effectively demonstrating that even "the law" and how judges perceive it can change with the characteristics of the defendant before the court.

THE THEORY OF BOUNDED RATIONALITY/ UNCERTAINTY AVOIDANCE

A second theory focusing on the linkages between judges' perceptions of offenders and their crimes and judges' sentencing decisions is the theory of bounded rationality/uncertainty avoidance, which incorporates both organizational theory and causal attribution theory. Albonetti (1991, 248) suggests that "[t]he salience of these two theoretical perspectives to judicial sentencing decisions lies in each perspective's sensitivity to discretionary use of information in decision making." Structural organizational theorists (Simon 1957; Thompson 1967), for example, contend that decision makers rarely have the information needed to make fully rational decisions; because they cannot identify all of the possible alternatives or the costs and benefits of each known alternative, they cannot always select the alternative that will provide the greatest benefit at the lowest cost. Instead, they use a decision-making process characterized by "bounded rationality" to search for a solution that will avoid, or at least, reduce, the uncertainty of obtaining a desirable outcome.

Applied to the sentencing process, the theory of bounded rationality/uncertainty avoidance suggests that judges' sentencing decisions hinge on their assessments of the likelihood of recidivism. Because judges typically do not have the information they need to make accurate predictions regarding the odds of reoffending, they develop perceptual sentencing standards (i.e., "patterned responses") based on case and offender characteristics that they believe will increase or decrease the risk of recidivism. Judges, in other words, attempt to reduce the uncertainty of their predictions by using stereotypes of crime seriousness, offender blameworthiness, and offender dangerousness to classify or categorize offenders and their crimes. Offenders who commit crimes perceived to be more serious are treated more harshly, as are offenders who are deemed more blameworthy and dangerous. According to Albonetti (1991, 250), these perceptions "are themselves the product of an attribution process influenced by causal judgment." Thus, stereotypes linking race, gender, and social class to the risk of recidivism result in harsher sentences for racial minorities, men, and the poor. More to the point, "Discrimination and disparity in sentencing decisions ... may be the product of judicial attempts to achieve a 'bounded rationality' in sentencing by relying on stereotypical images of which defendant is most likely to recidivate" (Albonetti 1991, 250).

Albonetti's (1991) analysis of the sentences imposed on offenders convicted of felonies in a federal district court in 1974 revealed substantial support for her theoretical perspective. She found that sentence severity was affected by the offender's prior record, race, use of a weapon, and bail status; offenders with a prior record of felony convictions received more punitive sentences, as did black offenders, offenders who used a weapon during the commission of the crime, and offenders who were required to post bail as a condition of release. Moreover, being required to post bail had a more aggravating effect on sentence severity for black offenders than for white offenders. These findings, which generally are consistent with the results of other research on sentence outcomes (for reviews, see Blumstein, Martin, and Tonry 1983; Zatz 1987; Spohn 2000), support Albonetti's assertion that judges attempt to reduce uncertainty by imposing harsher sentences on defendants perceived to pose a greater risk of reoffending. They also support assertions regarding the salience of racial stereotypes in judicial decision making.

THE FOCAL CONCERNS THEORY OF SENTENCING

The focal concerns theory of sentencing incorporates and builds on the uncertainty avoidance perspective. As developed by Steffensmeier and his colleagues (Steffensmeier, Ulmer, and Kramer 1998; Steffensmeier and Demuth 2001), this theoretical perspective suggests that judges' sentencing decisions are guided by three "focal concerns": their assessment of the blameworthiness of the offender; their desire to protect the community by incapacitating dangerous offenders or deterring potential offenders; and their concerns about the practical consequences, or social costs, of sentencing decisions.

The first focal concern — offender blameworthiness — reflects judges' assessments of the seriousness of the crime, the offender's prior criminal record, and the offender's motivation and role in the offense. Thus, offenders convicted of more serious crimes or who have more serious criminal histories will be viewed as more blameworthy; consequently, they will be sentenced more harshly. Offenders who suffered prior victimization at the hands of others or who played a minor role in the offense, on the other hand, will be seen as less culpable and will therefore be sentenced more leniently. The second focal concern — protecting the community — rests on judges' perceptions of dangerousness and predictions of the likelihood of recidivism. Like judges' assessments of offender blameworthiness, these perceptions are predicated on the nature of the offense and the offender's criminal history. Thus, judges seek to protect the community by imposing harsher sentences on repeat violent offenders or offenders whose risk of reoffending is high. The third focal concern — the practical consequences or social costs of sentencing decisions — reflects judges' perceptions regarding such things as the offender's "ability to do time," the costs of incarcerating offenders with medical conditions or mental health problems, and the "social costs" of imprisoning offenders responsible for the care of dependent children. It also includes judges' concerns about maintaining relationships with other members of the courtroom workgroup and protecting the reputation of the court.

Like Albonetti's theory of bounded rationality, the focal concerns theory assumes that judges typically do not have the information they need to accurately determine an offender's culpability, dangerousness, or likelihood of recidivism. As a result, they develop a "perceptual shorthand" based on stereotypes and attributions that are themselves linked to offender characteristics such as race, gender, and age. As Steffensmeier, Ulmer, and Kramer (1998, 787) note,

Younger offenders and male defendants appear to be seen as more of a threat to the community or not as reformable, and so also are black offenders, particularly those who also are young and male. Likewise, concerns such as "ability to do time" and the costs of incarceration appear linked to race-, gender-, and age-based perceptions and stereotypes.

Recent studies of sentencing decisions — and particularly studies exploring the effect of race and ethnicity on sentence outcomes — have produced compelling evidence in support of the focal concerns perspective (Steffensmeier, Ulmer, and Kramer 1998; Spohn and Holleran 2000; Steffensmeier and Demuth 2001; Schlesinger 2005; see also Wheeler et al., 1988). These studies reveal that African Americans and Hispanics are sentenced more harshly than whites (Spohn and DeLone 2000; Spohn and Holleran 2000) or that Hispanics are sentenced more harshly than either whites or blacks (Steffensmeier and Demuth 2000; Steffensmeier and Demuth 2001; Schlesinger 2005). They also reveal that men receive more punitive sentences than women (Spohn and Beichner 2000; Steffensmeier, Kramer, and Striefel 1993), that young adults are sentenced more harshly than teenagers or older adults (Steffensmeier, Kramer, and Ulmer 1995), and that the unemployed receive harsher sentences than those who are employed (Chiricos and Bales 1991; Nobiling, Spohn, and DeLone 1998).

These studies also reveal that judges' perceptions of deviance and dangerousness are shaped by a *combination* of offender characteristics. One study (Steffensmeier, Ulmer, and Kramer 1998), for example, used statewide data on sentencing outcomes in Pennsylvania to explore the interrelationships among race, gender, age, and sentence severity. Consistent with the focal concerns perspective, this study revealed that each of the three offender characteristics had a significant direct effect on both the likelihood of incarceration and the length of the sentence: blacks were sentenced more harshly than whites, younger offenders were sentenced more harshly than older offenders, and males more harshly than females. More importantly, the three factors interacted to produce substantially harsher sentences for one category of offenders — young, black males — than for any other age-race-gender combination. According to the authors, their results illustrate the "high cost of being black, young, and male" (Steffensmeier, Ulmer, and Kramer 1998, 789). Spohn and Holleran's (2000) analysis of sentencing outcomes in Chicago, Kansas City, and Miami revealed that offenders with constellations of characteristics other than "young black male" also pay a punishment penalty. They found that young black and Hispanic males faced greater odds of incarceration than middle-aged white males, and unemployed black and Hispanic males were substantially more likely to be sentenced to prison than employed white males.

Each of the theoretical perspectives discussed above — causal attribution, bounded rationality/uncertainty avoidance, focal concerns — posits that judges' sentencing decisions are shaped by their perceptions of the seriousness of the crime and the offender's blameworthiness, dangerousness, and potential for rehabilitation. The fact that the information judges have is typically incomplete and the predictions they are required to make are uncertain helps explain why offender characteristics — including the legally irrelevant characteristics of race, gender, and social class — influence sentencing decisions. Because they lack all the information needed to fashion sentences perfectly fitting both crimes *and* offenders, judges may resort to stereotypes of deviance and dangerousness that rest on considerations of race, ethnicity, gender, age, and unemployment. Thus, men may be perceived as more dangerous than women, younger offenders may be regarded as more crime prone than older offenders, gang members may be viewed as more threatening than nongang members, the unemployed may be seen as more likely to recidivate than the employed, and those who abuse drugs or alcohol may be viewed as less amenable to rehabilitation that those who abstain from using drugs or alcohol. Similarly, racial minorities — particularly those who are also male, young, members of gangs, and unemployed — may be seen as more dangerous and threatening than whites. Judges use these perceptions to simplify and routinize the decision-making process and to reduce the uncertainty inherent in sentencing. As a result, men may be sentenced more harshly than women, African Americans and Hispanics may be sentenced more harshly than whites, the unemployed may be sentenced more harshly than the employed, and gang members may receive more punitive sentences than nongang members.

INTEGRATED THEORIES

In contrast to the perceptual theories discussed above, in which judges' *perceptions* of multilevel factors are incorporated into individual level theories, integrated theories posit that *actual factors* from the different hierarchical levels influence sentencing decisions. Under such perspectives, varied combinations of individual, case, workgroup, organizational, and environmental level factors mutually influence judicial decisions and determine sentencing outcomes. These frameworks improve upon the above perceptual theories in that they account for more than only the individually perceived impact. While, as the saying goes, "perception is reality," the reality represented by individual perception is often conditioned by the attributes of the individual perceiver. Because perception is filtered through the lens of individual experience and biases, it does not necessarily reflect conditions as they actually occur and exist. Thus, two judges within the same jurisdiction, for example, might have very different views of the ways in which local characteristics such as demographics or court resources affect their caseload — both of which might misrepresent reality. Along similar lines, the fact that female defendants are perceived to pose a lower risk of recidivism than are male defendants, or black defendants are seen as more threatening than are white defendants, does not mean that these perceptions are true. As a result, theories and research based solely on judicial perception of these factors may misrepresent or distort their true influence. Thus, multilevel theoretical alternatives intuitively are logical improvements of perceptual frameworks that exemplify Snipes and Maguire's "level of explanation" dimension.

In one respect, such hierarchical frameworks can be visualized as a multilevel funnel into which various hierarchical factors enter and from which the final sentencing decision is extruded. Yet, a more tangible and concrete analogy of the causal mechanisms of these perspectives is the vintage arcade game "*Plinko*" (Cheatwood 2000). There, a ball or token is slid from the top of a steeply angled, nearly vertical board with multiple horizontal rows of pegs. The token passes through each row before reaching the bottom. As it falls, the token strikes pegs at every level — with each collision affecting its downward trajectory. At the bottom of the board, there are a series of labeled cells — any one of which can be the token's final resting place. The object of the game is for the falling token to come to rest in one specific cell (generally that with the highest point value or best prize assigned to it). The *Plinko* board is comparable to the sentencing decision process under multilevel sentencing theories. Here, the cells along the bottom of the board are the possible sentencing decisions. Each horizontal row of pegs represents a different hierarchical level while the individual pegs themselves depict the varied horizontal spheres. Finally, the token is the individual case and its final resting place is the sentencing decision — both of which are affected by various factors (pegs) from different hierarchical levels and spheres. The widely accepted object of the criminal sentencing process is, of course, to reach the most "just" sentence for the given offense.

While *Plinko* boards never represent such simple models, the most basic multilevel perspectives are bilevel theories where two levels of factors are paired to form explanations for sentencing outcomes. There are several examples of these simplified frameworks. For instance, *substantive rationality* bridges the gap between judicial perception theories and integrated theories because it includes components of both perspectives (Ulmer and Kramer 1996). First, like the perceptual theories, it takes into account judicial perceptions of offender danger-ousness, rehabilitation potential, and the practical consequences of sentencing in its explanation of judicial decisions. Yet, at the same time, actual variation between local courts is accounted for and expected to influence sentencing outcomes. Thus this perspective focuses on how both judicial perception and local context — two distinct hierarchical levels — affect judicial decision making. Ulmer and Kramer's findings indicate support for their theoretical linkage between these levels — showing county variation in the effects of plea agreements, trial penal-ties, and defendant characteristics over sentencing outcomes.

Another series of bilevel perspectives pair individual and organiza-tional level factors. Such frameworks attempt to explain how system factors and individual attributes shape judicial decisions and sentencing outcomes. For example, political system variation has been thought to affect judicial decisions through its impact on the judicial selection pro-cess. Such differences can lead to differential patterns of judicial social-ization and recruitment that, in turn, influence the judges' views as well as their decision-making processes. Many studies support this proposi-tion. One early study examined the sentencing behavior of Pittsburgh and Minneapolis judges — finding that differences in sentencing deci-sions are the indirect product of the cities' political systems (Levin 1972). Similarly, *organizational coupling* (Jacob 1997) merges organizational and interpersonal perspectives, describing the organizational impact on the work and activities of trial judges — specifically focusing on how intraorganizational relationships and individual perceptions mutually affect judicial decisions. In other words, this perspective captures how organizational factors affect the degree to which judges will "collaborate with one another or stand in one another's way" (Jacob 1997, 4). Here, judicial sponsoring organizations exert from loose to tight control or "coupling" over their members, which affects the predictability of court interactions and outcomes. The degree of "coupling" has direct impli-cations for the efficiency and effectiveness of the sentencing process as well as the equity of the sentences imposed by individual judges within that particular organization. For example, in organizations with tight coupling, strict authority over judicial case assignment, the caseload volume given to individual judges, and even scheduling of vacations is maintained — resulting in predictable outcomes and consequences. At the same time, tight control can impact judicial perceptions of their organization and, as a result, affect performance and decision making.

Thus, assignments or directives perceived to be undesirable can produce tension and resentment between judges and their organization, which can stifle innovation and slow the process of change. Conversely, loose coupling — while to a large degree alleviating such tension — reduces the predictability of court decisions and therefore increases the chances for disparate decisions. Thus, as Jacob notes "both tight and loose coupling provide benefits and costs to organizations" (1997, 8) as well as to individual defendants.

However, as suggested above, bilevel theories oversimplify the judicial decision-making process in a way that more complex multilevel theories do not. One approach that addresses the bilevel limitation, *structural-contextual theory* (Hagan 1989a, 1989b, 1995), posits that three levels of characteristics (case, organizational, and jurisdictional) interact to determine individual sentencing decisions. In the context of the courts specifically, this theory argues that sentences vary dramatically for common crimes because, for such cases, criminal justice organizations are loosely controlled and judicial discretion is relatively unconstrained; as a result, sentences are based on a variety of individual level factors. However, in extreme cases, such as acts of domestic terrorism, a proactive political jurisdiction (such as one exhibiting strong media pressure) is argued to tighten the organizational constraints on sentencing outcomes through the invocation of proactive techniques (such as mandatory sentencing statutes), which make the sentencing decision more predictable. Thus, this perspective proposes an interactive relationship between factors from different hierarchical levels, suggesting that the predictive value of one level of influences (case level) varies by factors emanating from two other hierarchical levels (organizational and jurisdictional). In other words, legal factors better explain sentence outcomes when the jurisdictional political environment tightens organizational control over sentencing outcomes and when the offense is very severe (Smith and Damphousse 1998). Unfortunately, there is mixed support for this perspective — with some studies supporting it (Spohn and Cederblom 1991; Smith and Damphousse 1998) and others refuting it (Smith and Damphousse 1996).

Using a somewhat different approach, the *court community* framework (Eisenstein and Jacob 1991) also includes explanatory factors from multiple hierarchical levels but focuses primarily on how the courtroom workgroup interactions affect sentencing decisions. Here, while the judge is seen as the formal leader, he or she must still negotiate with the other workgroup members — especially the prosecutor and the defense attorney. Although many strategies are available for reaching a mutually acceptable sentencing outcome, workgroups mainly rely on negotiations in reaching a final sentence. However, the possibility of negotiations depends heavily upon workgroup factors such as familiarity, level of interaction, member stability, and going rates. In addition, factors from other hierarchical levels enter the explanatory equation in terms of how they affect the negotiation process. For example, case factors come into play in terms of the strength of the evidence, while sponsoring organizations (organizational level) affect workgroup negotiations through case assignment practices and through their relationships with the other sponsoring organizations. Likewise, environmental factors influence the negotiation process — and therefore the sentencing decision — through caseload, legislative standards, appellate decisions, political environment, and media influences wield power over the workgroup.

Along these same lines, *rationalized justice* suggests an interaction between factors from multiple hierarchical levels that affects sentencing outcomes (Heydebrand and Seron 1990). Specifically, it posits that environmental, structural, workgroup, and individual forces all influence judicial sentencing decisions. The relevant jurisdictional forces include the range and variability of the cases, the resources available to handle these cases, as well as the overall demographic and economic stability of the jurisdiction. Pertinent organizational aspects include court management techniques, the administrative orientation, the degree of judicial autonomy permitted, as well as the levels of bureaucratization, formalization and centralization. The workgroup characteristics include the degrees of coalition formation, co-optation, and exchange as well as negotiation strategies. Finally, individual level influences mainly stem from the roles and role orientations of the individual workgroup players. According to this perspective, variation in each of these factors across the four hierarchies impacts the ultimate sentencing decision. Thus, judicial activities and decisions vary by organizational, workgroup, environmental, and individual characteristics (Heydebrand and Seron 1990). In much the same vein, other perspectives such as *organizational context* and *tenor of justice* incorporate variations in sentencing processing across these hierarchical levels, holding that individual sentencing decisions are influenced by the political, social, and organizational context of the court in which they occur (Nardulli et al. 1988; Dixon 1995).

Currently, the most complex multilevel framework is the *processual order* or *social worlds* perspective (Ulmer 1997; Ulmer and Kramer 1998). Here, individual, case, workgroup, organizational, and environmental influences each affect sentencing decisions. As opposed to the other multilevel perspectives, however, this framework discourages static depictions of the courts and their decisions by focusing on the activities and interaction strategies of participants. It argues that, as varied court actors — most notably judges — confront sentencing decision situations, they continually engage in various interaction strategies with other court players to reach solutions that further their individual and collective interests. Such strategies or processes become a part of the court environment as social orders. These social orders, in turn, are created, maintained, and changed over time by these same interaction processes. Thus, this perspective views several hierarchical levels as inherently linked because they mutually compose and influence one another through the existing conditions, negotiation activities, and practical consequences — suggesting a nonrecursive relationship between all of these factors (Ulmer and Kramer 1998). For example, individual and workgroup interaction processes and outcomes maintain, develop, and change the local institutional organization. Such organizations, in turn, affect both the individual role and workgroup interactions. Similarly, the boundaries of court communities are not established by formal organizational structures, but by lines of communication, participation, and influence in case processing. As a result, the relative importance of each component varies with location, time, and institution (Ulmer 1997). Simply, "case processing and sentencing practices develop through the ongoing interaction of courtroom workgroup members, which is in turn contextualized by local court interorganizational relationships and state policies" (Ulmer and Kramer 1998, 252). In other words, court actors interpret and use the formal criteria subjectively in a manner that both helps them deal with uncertainty and furthers their political and organizational interests (which are shaped by local context).

While each of the above theorists provides empirical analyses that support their own theoretical perspectives, until recently there has been limited research assessing multilevel theories. Prior to this, the most common approach had been the separate case-level analysis of sentencing data as categorized by factors of another hierarchical level — such as environment or organization. While such research confirms sentencing variation by organizational factors (Kirsch 1995) and workgroup characteristics (Flemming et al. 1992), the bulk of these studies focus on cross-jurisdictional differences — finding significant variation in the effect of case-level factors by environment (Myers and Talarico 1986; Dixon 1995; Crawford et al. 1998; Nobiling, Spohn, and DeLone 1998). Another strategy for investigating multilevel theories, which has become increasingly popular, is the use of multilevel modeling techniques to analyze data from multiple hierarchical levels. Superior to single-level analytical alternatives, such strategies can differentiate between and identify the specific multilevel factors responsible for outcome differences (Kreft and De Leeuw 1998; Heck and Thomas 2000).

In recent years, this latter approach has been widely used to test a variety of macrolevel perspectives. Using case-level data for Pennsylvania sentencing outcomes in conjunction with county-level census data, the first such study (Britt 2000), similar to research using the simpler partitioning approach, found that jurisdictional characteristics impact sentencing decisions even when case characteristics are controlled. However, unlike previous studies, this multilevel analysis further indicates that county attributes condition the influence of most case-level factors — suggesting an interactive effect between the two levels. Yet, at the same time, it also demonstrates minimal direct effect for environmental factors such as urbanization, racial composition, economic conditions, and crime level on sentencing outcomes.

Other multilevel sentencing research yields similar findings. For example, one analysis of federal drug sentences finds that the district in which a case is sentenced significantly affects the influence of case-level factors — such that the effect that both legal and extralegal factors wield over the final outcome significantly varies from one district to another. However, those higher level factors explain only 10 percent of the sentence variation in drug offenses (Kautt 2002). Similarly, research on sentences under the Pennsylvania system demonstrates that while higher level factors such as court caseload, organizational culture, and demographic makeup significantly influence sentences they account for only a small amount of the variance (Ulmer and Johnson 2004). Conversely, other research using sentencing data from multiple U.S. jurisdictions also indicates that county factors wield minimal effects over case-level outcomes (Weidner, Frase, and Schultz 2005). The implications of such results for multilevel theories are unclear. Supporting the propositions of many perspectives, these findings show that contextual variation in sentencing decisions exists. At the same time, they refute elements of these same theories by showing contextual factors are of limited explanatory power when case-level factors are controlled.

Despite the above findings, however, it is important to keep in mind that the utility of these studies in testing the aforementioned multilevel perspectives is limited. To date and despite additional calls for it (Kautt 2002), no studies of judicial sentencing decisions that rely upon this multilevel strategy have incorporated the sentencing judge as a level of analysis. As Britt (2000, 729) himself notes, "by ignoring the individual decision maker, this research assumes that judges will reach decisions in a uniform manner" and goes on to point out that his study also "assumes that judges within the same court jurisdiction will respond in the same way to broader contextual issues." As a result, existing research has yet to fully test the assumptions and propositions of the aforementioned multilevel theories attempting to explain judicial decision making.

CONCLUSION

This chapter has elaborated on various theoretical frameworks that describe the process by which judges reach sentencing decisions — tracing the gradual evolution of such explanations from simple unidimensional perspectives to complex multispherical and multilevel theories. Specifically, we focused on single and multispherical individual level theories as well as those that integrate multiple hierarchical levels. Our examination of the relevant literature revealed only limited support for the unidimensional perspectives and suggests that multilevel and multispherical frameworks most accurately capture the realities of judicial decision making.

Beyond this, we used the characteristics of these theories and their evolution to illustrate and propose an organizational framework for categorizing existing theories of judicial decision making (see Table 7.1). However, this framework's utility is not limited solely to classifying explanations of sentencing outcomes. Rather, it has a wide range of applicability — from categorization of other court-specific theoretical explanations (such as prosecutorial charging decisions or probation officer assessments of offense seriousness and prior record) to that of more broadly based explanations of criminal justice behaviors such as decisions made by police officers (arrest or use of force decisions) or correctional personnel (revocation decisions by probation or parole officers). Simply, the organization framework proposed here can be used to classify any type of theory and serve as a valuable tool for researchers who are new to either using or creating criminal justice theory.

Table 7.1 Classifications of discussed theories

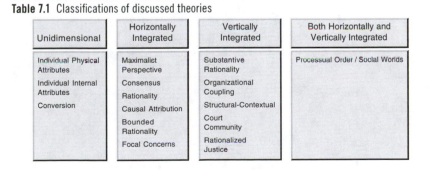

Unidimensional	Horizontally Integrated	Vertically Integrated	Both Horizontally and Vertically Integrated
Individual Physical Attributes	Maximalist Perspective	Substantive Rationality	Processual Order / Social Worlds
Individual Internal Attributes	Consensus	Organizational Coupling	
Conversion	Rationality	Structural-Contextual	
	Causal Attribution	Court Community	
	Bounded Rationality	Rationalized Justice	
	Focal Concerns		

With this structured perspective, we sought to provide an easy framework within which both novice researchers and theorists alike can methodically consider the various spheres and hierarchies they wish to include in their intended research. This formal assessment would, in turn, help them to determine the best theoretical perspective to use or most appropriate form that any new theory they create should take. With thoughtful consideration of the multilevel and multispherical characteristics we identify, both the researcher and the theory framer alike will easily be able to formally examine the pertinent aspects of the area he or she intends to research as well as make concrete choices concerning the theoretical perspectives to be used or created.

We hope such an organizational guide will spark innovative and comprehensive explanations for criminal justice outcomes and processes that incorporate all theoretically relevant influences regardless of sphere or hierarchy. We feel that such a movement would signal the end of "atheoretical criminal justice" as well as result in more comprehensive explanations of the criminal justice process.

8

COURTS AND COMMUNITIES
Toward a Theoretical Synthesis

Alissa Pollitz Worden

INTRODUCTION

The political and historical origins of American criminal courts cast them as distinctly local, community-based institutions. As Americans sorted out the details of postcolonial government, they drew upon a common law heritage of local judicial administration as well as their own distrust of centralized legal authority, and established criminal courts that were more directly accountable to local citizens than to state authorities. Two centuries later, this decentralization of criminal adjudication is still manifested in criminal codes as well as court structures. Criminal statutes define what constitutes crime and punishment in general terms, which are subject to the interpretation of local court actors. In most states, judges and prosecutors are elected by local constituencies. Most defendants are represented by counsel appointed by local judges, or by public defenders authorized and paid by county governments. Linkages to central authorities are limited: few criminal convictions are appealed, and professional associations exercise little control over judges and lawyers. The U.S. Supreme Court regularly reaffirms the role of community values in setting local legal practices (Friedman 1984; Finckenauer 1988).

This tradition of fragmentation and local autonomy is accompanied by institutionalized rules, practices, and structures that reflect unresolved conflicts among social values (Wright 1981, 217; Goodpaster 1987). Courts are expected to apply the law fairly, consistently, rationally, and publicly; but verdicts emerge from the secret, idiosyncratic, and unrecorded deliberations of lay jurors. Verdicts are in theory the result of adversarial challenges of evidence and testimony, but research tells us that defense lawyers and prosecutors face moral and practical incentives to quickly "settle the facts," avoid trials, and instead negotiate the terms of guilty pleas. Judges are supposed to be independent and impartial, yet in most jurisdictions they keep their jobs by winning elections. Court actors must reach equilibrium among these competing values. There is little reason to predict that courts in differing social, political, and economic environments will arrive at the same balances.

In short, the delegation of adjudication and sentencing functions to local courts, the geographic and political isolation of courts from each other, combined with the highly discretionary nature of court actors' work, and the need to reconcile competing values are conditions that favor the evolution of distinctive local legal cultures. While the broad outlines of the criminal process are sketched by state lawmakers, the substantive details are filled in at the local level by court actors themselves, in the form of norms, practices, and customs that prescribe how these actors do their jobs, and what constitutes justice.

This chapter takes as a premise that courthouse culture — court actors' unwritten rules and understandings about local justice — has important political dimensions, and that understanding the relationships among communities and their courts merits social scientists' attention. As two observers of trial courts have noted, "Few government decisions affect citizens more than those made in the criminal process, for courts decide who shall be labeled a criminal and who shall be deprived of liberty or even life. Such decisions shape the context and dynamics of public order" (Eisenstein and Jacob 1977, 4).

The purpose of this essay is to assess the state of theory about the relationships between communities and their criminal courts. This entails cataloging the relevant conceptual domains across which courts and communities vary, and taking stock of social scientists' attempts to theorize about the relationships among these concepts, as a prelude to deciding which lines of thinking are worth pursuing, what linkages have been overlooked but merit exploration, and what obstacles and challenges might stand in the way of theory development.[1]

This is not an easy task, for several reasons. Early attempts to theorize about trial courts were largely derivative; political scientists and sociologists borrowed theories about individual, social, organizational, and political behavior from other contexts, and attempted to fit them, with uneven success, onto courts. Second, court research has emerged from several disciplines, but so far has inspired little integration of theoretical questions or propositions across disciplinary lines. Third, scholars began studying courts' *community* contexts almost as an afterthought, when they happened upon the topic while trying to explain important and troubling discoveries: first, the pervasiveness of guilty pleas and bargaining in urban courts (D. Newman 1956; Sudnow 1965; President's Commission on Law Enforcement and Administration of Justice 1967b; Blumberg 1967); and second, evidence of disparities and discrimination in sentencing (Hagan 1974).

Hence we have come to study the relationships between courts and communities in a roundabout way. In order to sort out the most promising directions for theory development, we must begin with some simple tasks: first, to clarify the meaning of theory as it is applied in this essay; second, to identify key elements and concepts; third, to review theoretical linkages that social scientists have suggested or developed, and critique their efforts to empirically test those theoretical propositions; and then, finally, turn our attention to emerging and unexplored theoretical perspectives among these linkages, in order to identify promising directions for future research.

THE ROLE OF THEORY IN CRIMINAL COURT SCHOLARSHIP

A complete inventory of scholarship on criminal courts and communities would far exceed the scope of this essay, for a good deal of what has been written about the courts falls outside the definition of social science theory adopted here. A full catalog of court scholarship would include normative, doctrinal, and historical works as well as scientific studies, but the boundaries around scientific theory are drawn here around testable propositions about causes of individual, organizational, and community behavior in response to crime (Snipes and Maguire, chapter 2 this volume). This approach sets aside some familiar types of intellectualizing about courts, which are worth noting.

For instance, during the 1960s and 1970s, a lively philosophical argument over the coercive evils and convenient virtues of plea bargaining occupied many journal pages (Vetri 1964; Brunk 1979; T. Church 1979), only occasionally punctuated by empirical tests of authors' assumptions (Feeley 1973; L. Friedman 1979; Mather 1979, 3). Perhaps because legal scholars started writing about courts before social scientists did, treatments of case law and legal reasoning are sometimes described as theoretical studies — but they are typically philosophical and value-based analyses rather than theoretical studies of variation in social or political behavior (e.g., Schulhofer 1984; D. Lynch 1999). Trials make good stories, so most students of the courts are familiar with historical and autobiographical accounts of casework, often involving particularly spectacular, influential, or publicized cases; but these accounts are not generalizable to routine court behavior (A. Lewis, 1964; Dershowitz 1983; Wishman, 1986).

These sorts of work can illustrate theory, and may inspire theorizing, particularly insofar as they prompt reflection on important aspects of decision processes, or sincere concerns about unjust outcomes. Unfortunately, they can also obscure or distract from social scientific thinking about courts. Theory-based work tends to set aside the spectacular trial, the landmark case, the famous attorney, in favor of modeling the routine processes that ordinary actors apply to typical cases. This is hard work, so why do it?

First, theoretical thinking is explanatory, rather than descriptive; so it leads to clearer statements of interesting and important questions, and sometimes improved predictions about the likely success of policy changes. Relatedly, theoretical thinking permits us to formalize conventional wisdom, and test it. What "everyone knows" often turns out to be incorrect, or correct only at the extremes. For instance, marked disparities in the incarceration rates of whites and minorities may be reasonable cause for alarm, but without an understanding of the causes for the disparity, one cannot argue persuasively about the need to address social prejudice, economic inequalities, discriminatory police and court practices, or sentencing statutes.

Second, theory obliges us to discipline our thinking about core concepts, and about cause and effect relationships. Few research tasks prompt more careful reflection than the practical problems of specifying units of analysis, figuring out what aspects of those units should be measured, and diagramming the possible causal connections among variables.

Third, theoretical work is (or ought to be) iterative and cumulative, channeling the opportunities and activities of researchers toward common questions. Over time, the result of this kind of work is greater confidence in social science answers to these questions — and in the study of criminal justice, answers are socially and politically, as well as intellectually, important.

For the purposes of studying courts and communities, theory directs us toward some intriguing questions: Whose "behavior" should we examine, and of what does it consist? What formal and informal structures in courts are related to that behavior, and how? How should we conceptualize communities (an important first step in figuring out what aspects of communities we should model and measure)? How have theorists modeled the relationships among these variables, and how might we add to that work?

DEFINING CONCEPTUAL DOMAINS: COMMUNITY AND COURT CHARACTERISTICS

Figure 8.1 presents six conceptual domains, which can be broadly (but not exclusively) grouped as court characteristics, elite characteristics,

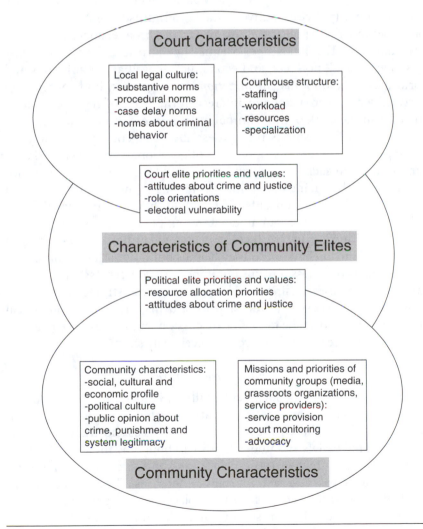

Figure 8.1 Conceptual domains in court-community research

and community characteristics. The diagram directs our attention first to characteristics of courts themselves: *courthouse cultures* comprised of case processing norms and practices, *court organizations' structure*, and *court actors' priorities and attitudes*. Key courthouse actors — judges, prosecutors, and criminal defense lawyers — are specialized members of a *community's political elite*. They share this status with other individuals who occupy positions of political power, control over resources, responsibility for local criminal justice policy, and accountability to constituents. This group might include both elected officials (mayors, county commissioners), as well as directors of criminal justice organizations (police executives, local jail administrators), and local bar associations. These political elites are part of a broader social and political landscape. That landscape is defined by *characteristics of community residents* (social, political, and economic), as well as the missions and priorities of *community organizations and agencies*, both public and private, who claim a stake or interest in the work of the courts (and, usually, in the work of the criminal justice system more generally).

The following sections briefly describe these conceptual domains, with particular attention to four sets of questions. First, what variables are included in each domain, and how should they be differentiated for purposes of theorizing about linkages among them? Second, how (and how much) do these concepts vary, and do they vary in ways that are likely to be relevant to our understanding of court–community relationships? Third, how are these concepts meaningful as variables in models of court behavior (do they help us build hypotheses? have they distracted us from less obvious but important constructs?) and, fourth, are they measurable using social science research strategies? Cataloging these constructs is a first step toward mapping their theoretical relationships; and as the following discussion will suggest, the relationships among these variables are not necessarily simple.

Courthouse Culture

Courthouse culture, or local legal culture, is made up of the norms, customs, practices, and policies that characterize a court's decision processes (T. W. Church 1985). The term serves as shorthand for court actors' shared beliefs and understandings about how their court works, although the content of those beliefs, and the level of agreement on them, varies across several important dimensions. The concept was initially developed to account for the displacement of jury trials by plea bargaining, as social scientists concluded that the very low trial rate in most courts resulted from the widespread belief among court actors that trials were an inefficient and inappropriate means of disposing of most criminal accusations (Eisenstein and Jacob 1977; Heumann 1978). As court observers developed the concept of legal culture, they recognized its value in accounting for variation in plea bargaining norms (as well as rates), its applicability to domains of decision making besides guilty pleas and trials, and its potential value in explaining why courts in otherwise similar communities could generate very different patterns of verdicts and sentences.

Eisenstein and Jacob's (1977) landmark study of Chicago, Baltimore, and Detroit criminal courts explored legal culture as the product of court actors' converging objectives and interests in avoiding time-consuming and unpredictable trials. They hypothesized that structural and organizational features of courts (such as stable workgroups, large volumes of cases) accounted for the development of norms about sentencing, in the form of "going rates" for particular types of offenses or offenders. Later researchers extended and refined this concept, and have measured sentencing norms directly, as collective attitudinal constructs of court actors (Church 1985; Worden 1987; Luskin and Luskin 1987).

Norms encompass procedural as well as substantive dimensions. For example, court actors might agree that the appropriate (or inevitable) outcome of most cases is a guilty plea and a highly predictable sentence, and gear their preparation, time commitment, and conversations with victims and defendants accordingly (Heumann 1978); elsewhere court actors might agree that a plea is inevitable, but routinely plan to negotiate over sentences (McIntyre 1987); and in still other (but probably rare) courts, lawyers may approach each other as adversaries, and may subscribe to traditional advocacy positions (Emmelman 1996). Court cultures, therefore, might be categorized in terms of consensus, negotiation, and adversariness.

Norms about procedural and substantive justice entail more than expectations about whether defendants should (or will) plead guilty, and on what terms, however. They also include expectations about pretrial decisions. Court actors' discretion to withhold formal accusations and sanctions may be more powerful in shaping community standards of crime and justice, as well as more immune to community oversight, than their discretion in setting punishments (Myers and Hagan 1979; Horney and Spohn 1991). Court actors' norms about how to handle many misdemeanor or low-level felony charges can include unwritten rules about the quality of evidence necessary to sustain charges, about the role of the victim in prosecution, and about the use of legal controls other than sentencing, such as pretrial detention and orders of protection. Examples of de facto decriminalization would include the hands-off practices of some courts in drunk driving cases and domestic violence incidents. When court actors agree that certain types of cases do not merit prosecution, or merit it only under unusual conditions, that agreement may have important consequences: it may discourage police from making arrests, and may send signals to complainants and defendants that some offenses are beneath the court's notice.

Local legal culture, adequately conceptualized and measured, is arguably the key construct in any community-level model of court behavior. Researchers have hypothesized, with some empirical support, that courthouse cultures evolve as the products of court structure and elite values, and they have also hypothesized that culture accounts for observable differences in patterns of adjudication and sentencing (Feeley 1973; Nardulli 1978; Alschuler 1979; Ryan 1980; H. Jacob 1983; Glick and Pruet 1985; Scheingold and Gresset 1987; Vance and Stupak 1997; Ulmer 1998). If these hypotheses are correct, then legal culture constitutes the community's unwritten legal code: it defines for a community what protections or burdens are imposed on victims, what costs and risks are faced by defendants, what offenses shall and shall not be sanctioned by the court, and what punishments are faced by convicted offenders.

Court Structure and Organization

Courts are really networks of organizations — the local judiciary and its staff, the prosecutor's office, and the members of the criminal defense bar — who are bound to each other through their formal shared responsibility for adjudicating criminal charges. A comprehensive inventory of the dimensions of court and court organizations' structure is beyond the scope of this discussion; here we simply illustrate three constructs that might influence the character of local legal culture: court caseload; staffing and workload distribution; and indigent defense systems.

Caseload has been conceptualized in two ways: as volume of work processed in a court, and as relative workload or case pressure experienced by court actors. The first measure is of course associated with jurisdictional size and urbanization. Early researchers typically conducted their studies in urban, high volume courts, and often concluded that sheer volume of cases desensitized court workers to individual differences among defendants, fostering routinization and plea bargaining norms (Sudnow 1965; Skolnick 1967). However, few attempted to test this hypothesis by directly comparing low with high volume jurisdictions (but see, e.g., Jacoby 1977; Austin 1981; Myers and Reid 1995); and case studies of moderately sized cities uncovered evidence of routinization as well (Cole 1970; Eisenstein et al. 1988). Another seemingly obvious hypothesis, that heavy case pressure compelled actors to short-circuit adversarial processes, also failed to find much empirical support in comparative studies (Heumann 1975; Church 1985; Worden 1995), or in historical research (Feeley 1978; Friedman 1979).

By the early 1970s, theorists looked more closely at what happened inside courts, recognizing more complex dynamics at the individual and organizational level. One of the most influential among them, Malcolm Feeley, argued that understanding (and reforming) the legal process was "clearly … more than a problem of overcoming workload so that good men can do good work" (1973, 422). The structure and interorganizational relationships among court actors, he suggested, has more to do with courthouse norms than case volume; after all, court actors are largely autonomous, and have considerable discretion in regulating and organizing their work. Eisenstein and Jacob (1977) hypothesized that organizational conditions that favor the formation of stable workgroups tend to produce high rates of guilty pleas, and consensus on sentencing norms for common types of offenses. Although many assume that these conditions obtain primarily in urban courts, contemporary researchers have noted that the economies of scale in urban courts may allow for specialized structures and work assignments that promote more adversarial and individualized adjudication. Examples would include specialized court parts, community courts, and dedicated units in public defender and prosecutors' offices (Weimer 1980; McIntyre 1987; Chaiken and Chaiken 1991).

Finally, court scholars have hypothesized that the organization of criminal defense work shapes the character of courthouse culture. Early studies that simply asserted or assumed the inferiority of publicly paid counsel (e.g., Blumberg 1967; Casper 1972; Lizotte 1978) were soon supplanted by research that models both public and private lawyers' incentives, role definitions, organizational settings, and performance (Mather 1979; Stover and Eckart 1975; Houlden and Balkin 1985; Nardulli 1986; McIntyre 1987), although few such studies utilized comparative data on two important variables, resources and caseload (but see Worden 1995; Priehs 1999).

These examples illustrate the challenges of making sense of empirical findings on court structure and culture. First, some community and structural variables covary (e.g., urbanization, caseload, and use of public defender agencies), which complicates the development of causal models about court behavior. Second, most studies are of highly urbanized courts, and few studies are truly comparative. Third, interesting variables are hard to measure, or to measure reliably at the community and courthouse level; so we tend to measure what we can see, and over-look less visible (but more theoretically important) variables.

Furthermore, court researchers have reasonably focused on formal and structural constructs, giving less attention to more subtle charac-teristics of court cultures such as openness to innovation and nontradi-tional structuring of work. While researchers are quick to evaluate the impact of innovations and reforms, such as community prosecution, alternative sentencing, priority prosecution programs (e.g., Chaiken and Chaiken 1991), and specialized courts, they have devoted less effort to the more challenging task of testing theories about why some courts innovate and others do not.

Finally, the remarkable diversity of court structures frustrates efforts to theorize parsimoniously about them; with so many variants to observe and describe, it is easier to simply continue the work of doc-umenting local idiosyncrasies. However, a more constructive solution might be to inventory structural variables, in order to cull the list for those that hold most promise in explaining court behavior.

Priorities and Attitudes of Courthouse Elites

Because the legal system grants so much discretion to courthouse actors, particularly judges and prosecutors, it is commonsensical to predict that their attitudes, beliefs, and experiences affect their decisions. Early research based on interviews and observations in trial courts provided evidence that court actors indeed hold diverse views about crime, jus-tice, and their roles and functions (Becker 1966; Mather 1979; Carter 1974; Bohne 1978). However, a full accounting of how attitudes and pri-orities vary, and what difference that might make for courts and com-munities, has yet to be conducted.

Such an accounting might begin with a simple categorization of beliefs. Like other people, court actors hold beliefs about the absolute and relative seriousness of offenses; about the virtues and limitations of procedural safeguards; about punishments and punishment ratio-nales; and about their own roles in the court. Unlike other people, however, court actors have daily opportunities to act upon their beliefs. Although judges and prosecutors remain a socially homogeneous group, their views about crime and justice are diverse (T. W. Church 1985; Scheingold and Gressett 1987; Worden 1990, 1995). Defense law-yers vary in their commitment to due process norms, in their beliefs about the integrity of the legal process, and in their feelings of loyalty to clients (Flemming 1986).

Court actors' beliefs about their own roles and functions, independent of their substantive beliefs and values, may shape their use of discretion. Judges who define their job in terms of enforcing community norms may transmit community values more directly into decisions than do judges who rely on their own experience and expertise as trustees of community justice (Gibson 1980). Judges may play an active role in their courts, or they may become referees rather than decision makers, ensuring that prosecutors and defense lawyers play by the rules, but routinely ratifying the results of their contests over verdicts and sentencing (Alpert, Atkins, and Ziller 1979). Role orientation encompasses perspectives on policy as well as case-by-case practice. Some judges may be innovators, willing to experiment with new strategies (such as victim assistance programs, alternative sentencing plans, or specialized courts), while others may limit their job description to traditional particularized adjudication.

Likewise, prosecutors' and defense lawyers' role orientations vary. Like judges, prosecutors are political actors, and must come to terms with their constituents' expectations. Furthermore, some prosecutors adopt an adversarial and combative approach to casework, while others place a premium on finding common ground with their opponents (Nardulli, Flemming, and Eisenstein 1984). Defense lawyers may see their jobs in terms of winning cases, meeting clients' needs, developing good working relationships with others in the courthouse, or defending abstract conceptions of constitutional rights. Few if any lawyers could successfully pursue all these objectives simultaneously.

These attitudinal variables are relevant to understanding courts and communities if we suspect that court actors behave like the elected (or appointed) politicians that they are. Unfortunately, beyond courthouse folklore about hanging judges, relentless prosecutors, and valiant defense lawyers, researchers interested in court actors' political links to their communities have had few opportunities to develop and test hypotheses about constituency preferences and court behavior. First, studies seldom construct replicable measures of actors' beliefs, or even directly measure beliefs, instead relying on proxy measures (such as race, sex, or career background; e.g., Myers 1988; Spohn 1990a, 1990b). Second, researchers have targeted judges to the neglect of prosecutors or defense lawyers, overlooking the fact that case outcomes are more often the products of attorneys' bilateral negotiations than judges' unilateral judgments. Finally, the findings of most theoretically based studies suggest that the attitude–behavior link may hold only under some conditions: when actors define their role in terms of community responsiveness (Gibson 1978, 1980), when information about public preferences is clearly communicated (Kuklinski and Stanga 1979), or when they feel unconstrained by the expectations of other system actors (Spohn and Cederblom 1991; Worden 1995).

Priorities and Values of Community Elites

Community elites are defined as individuals and organizations who possess political power within their communities. This includes criminal justice agents outside the courts (law enforcement agencies, probation departments, jail authorities), local government authorities (mayors, local funding authorities, some criminal justice task forces), and groups with direct access to and influence on the courts (local bar associations). Elite priorities, political motivations, and resources may shape court behavior in several ways.

First, the policies and practices of criminal justice agencies, particularly police departments, generate the raw material of court work. Proactive departments staffed with well-trained officers produce caseloads of differing size and evidentiary quality than understaffed and less professionalized departments. The organizational culture of probation departments can filter the types of information and recommendations that judges receive about defendants (Vance and Stupak 1997).

Second, because courthouse budgets are often highly dependent on city and county funds, funding authorities' capacity and willingness to support key functions affects the structure and capacity of the system. Examples include indigent defense, prosecutors' offices, and courthouse infrastructure, as well as support for treatment programs, victim assistance programs, and jail capacity.

Third, local politicians and political groups exercise influence on who sits on the bench and practices at the bar. Judges' and prosecutors' elections often end in lopsided victories, but important and contested endorsement and nomination decisions are made behind closed doors by local political party chiefs, and often are influenced by the formal or informal endorsements of local bar associations. The crime and justice priorities of local mayors or council members may have more impact on court outputs when those elites hold the political strings of nominations (e.g., Levin 1972).

These variables — agency priorities, policies, and practices; resource allocation; and political power — vary at the community level; and anecdotal evidence suggests that these variables are linked to court behavior. However, community elites, and community groups more generally, have typically been relegated to a position of secondary interest in studies of communities and courts. Researchers acknowledge the role of these groups as part of courts' political environment (e.g., Eisenstein and Jacob 1977; Eisenstein, Flemming, and Nardulli 1988), although seldom at a theoretical and generalizable level. This may be due in part to the difficulty of measuring the behavior of such groups at the community level, and the tendency to assume that these factors are unique to communities.

Community Organizations' Missions and Objectives

Community organizations are defined for our purposes as groups whose self-defined mission includes service provision, advocacy, oversight, or mobilization around crime and justice issues. These organizations have been the least studied elements in research on courts and communities; like political elites, they are sometimes credited with particular changes or outcomes in particular jurisdictions, but seldom researched systematically by court scholars.

A catalog of such groups would include neighborhood associations; reform-oriented political action groups; organizations that provide services to offenders and to victims; political entrepreneurs who import and attempt to implement innovations into local legal systems; and local media. These organizations vary across many dimensions: some are grassroots organizations (shelters for domestic abuse victims) while others are local branches of larger state or national groups (MADD). Some are founded to change or reform court practices (courtwatch organizations), while others operate side-by-side with court actors (offender counseling programs). Some are longstanding features of the local political landscape (newspapers), while others may be mobilized by a controversial case or highly publicized crime (task forces). Some identify with public safety and victim protection, while others work to improve defendants' rights. Some projects are housed in established community institutions (e.g., church-based groups); others may have independent staff, office space, funding, and infrastructure (alternative sentencing programs).

The objectives of these groups may include providing auxiliary or alternative services for courts, lobbying for more or different crime control activities, or challenging the legitimacy of court practices. While theories of community mobilization and change would probably help us conceptualize and theorize about the relationships of these groups to courts and communities, that task has yet to be undertaken. There are glimmerings of interest in these questions, however. For example, researchers who analyze restorative justice initiatives recognize the role of reform advocates in getting such programs underway, and the remarkable diversity of such programs in different community settings (Bazemore 1997; Rose and Clear 1998). Studies of specialized drug courts and domestic violence courts take into account the key roles of service providers as both promoters of and contributors to these innovations (Shepard and Pence 1999).

Community Environment

Researchers often sum up community environments in very simple and general terms: rural, urban, middle-class, crime-ridden, Democratic, conservative, Midwestern, black or white. These words are meant to signal what is (and what is not) relevant for understanding courts' relationships with their social, economic, and political environments. For the purpose of sketching backdrops for community case studies, this level of generality is sufficient. But theorizing about sociopolitical environments and institutional behavior calls for more careful discrimination among social and economic constructs, political culture, and public opinion on crime and justice topics.

COMMUNITIES' SOCIOECONOMIC CHARACTERISTICS

Economic and social conditions, particularly urbanization, crime, and poverty define the demands placed on, and to some extent the resources available to, court organizations. All else being equal, communities with higher crime rates place greater demands on the criminal justice system and require more resources for functions such as indigent defense. Unemployment rates (and their implications for labor markets) might be either a cause or a consequence of high incarceration rates in communities. Community size may influence the level of bureaucratization and routinization in case processing. Furthermore, researchers have scrutinized court behavior in distinctively rural (Hagan 1977; Austin 1981; Eisenstein 1982), predominantly black (Myers and Talarico 1986), and midsized (Eisenstein, Flemming, and Nardulli 1988) communities.

Political Culture

The essence of political culture, as originally described by Elazar (1972, 1988), consists of the public's views about the relationship between government and the governed. Elazar theorized that political culture develops from the shared values and experiences of a region's residents; for example, southern political culture has been described as *traditionalistic,* marked by deference to local political and economic elites, and acceptance of social (and racial) stratification, a consequence of a highly skewed race and class system. The political culture of areas populated by working-class immigrants has been characterized as *individualistic*, implying an opportunistic, self-interested, and pragmatic view of government, giving rise to patronage and machine politics, as well as career politicians. New England and Midwestern political cultures have been described as *moralistic*, molded by the attitudes of affluent northern European settlers whose local political structures reflected a communitarian, reform-minded, "good government" perspective.[2]

The links between political culture and court behavior are largely unexplored, but merit continued development. That political culture may account for court behavior is suggested (although by no means conclusively demonstrated) by intriguing bits of evidence. For example, traditionalistic communities in the South produce unusually high incarceration rates (especially for African-American defendants). Communities that would be classified as moralistic were the first to experiment with comprehensive community-based reforms in the area of domestic violence and victim assistance (Minnesota, Massachusetts). Levin observed that party-dominated machine politics in Pennsylvania tended to select judges with particularistic, individualistic orientations toward defendants, compared with those in Minnesota, where the selection system tended to tap lawyers from private practices, with strong public safety orientations (1972).

Public Opinion about Crime and Justice

Public opinion is multidimensional, and understanding its relationships with court behavior requires that we distinguish at the community level among the objects of opinions, the level of salience, and levels of consensus or heterogeneity.

People's normative opinions about crime can be sorted into at least three dimensions of variation. First, beyond consensus on serious (and relatively rare) crimes of violence and property, people hold different views about what behaviors should and should not be punished as crimes (Glick and Pruet 1985), and about what justifications might excuse criminal acts (P. Robinson and Darley 1995). Examples might include driving while intoxicated, many instances of domestic violence, firearms possession, sexual assaults, possession of controlled substances, and some incidents of child abuse, as well as the legitimacy of the insanity defense and the meaning of self-defense.

Second, people vary even more in their views about appropriate punishments for specific crimes, and more generally in their willingness to see harsh punishments imposed on offenders (Blumstein and Cohen 1980; Durham 1988; Bohm et al. 1990). A third set of normative beliefs involves the perceived legitimacy of the legal system. Researchers have assessed attitudes about procedural justice, as well as opinions about the legitimacy of local criminal justice institutions (Merry 1985; Tyler 1988; Olson and Huth 1998). Finally, in addition to normative beliefs, individuals hold different *empirical* beliefs about crime itself — its prevalence and their own risk of victimization.

Attitudes and beliefs about criminal justice have been examined primarily at the individual level, and from this research we have gleaned a few important observations. First, differences in attitudes about the relative gravity of many common misdemeanors (and minor felonies) are correlated with social background and individual characteristics such as race, sex, and age (Miller, Rossi, and Simpson 1986). Second, views about punishment may be related to deep-seated cultural values, including religious views (Grasmick et al. 1992). Third, views about appropriate punishments may be quite different from (and often harsher than) actual sentencing practice (Durham, Elrod, and Kincade 1996; Blumstein and Cohen 1980). Fourth, views about system legitimacy may be related to personal experiences with the criminal justice system (Casper 1978). Fifth, fear of crime is not closely related to objective risk of victimization across social groups (Glick and Pruet 1985).

These observations offer some guidance in conceptualizing public opinion at the community level. First, because belief dimensions are not correlated in altogether predictable ways, we should be cautious of overgeneralizing about community attitudes, and pay close attention to which dimensions are theoretically and empirically related to court decisions. For example, rural residents may be more punitive than urban counterparts, but also more libertarian in their ideas about what behaviors the criminal justice system should monitor.

Second, an assessment of the relationships between public opinion and court behavior requires attention to the salience of opinion, as well as levels of consensus. One might predict weak associations between opinion and system behavior if opinions, regardless of their content, are casually formed. Most data collection strategies offer no opportunity to measure salience, and may therefore lead to overprediction of the impact of public opinion.

Finally, we should hypothesize not just about *whether* opinion influences court behavior, and *under what conditions*, but also about *whose* opinions are influential, and *how* these opinions are transmitted to court decision makers (a topic to which we shall turn in the next sections). Public opinion varies when measured at the community level, but not all variation is meaningful. For example, two communities whose residents favor tougher DWI sentencing by majorities of 70 and 95 percent respectively may be indistinguishable in terms of their impact on local criminal justice practice, although smaller differences located at a different place on the scale — say, 45 and 60 percent — might prove much more politically interesting. While it is tempting to express public opinion data in terms of interval level variables, more careful thinking suggests it might be better conceived, for some purposes, in categorical or ordinal terms. Furthermore, because attitudes on some crime issues are not distributed in the same way across social groups, and some social groups may have more influence on court behavior than others, community-level soundings of opinion may mask heterogeneity across subpopulations and lead us to underestimate criminal justice agents' responsiveness to constituencies.

SUMMARY

In summary, explorations into community attributes have generated a menu of intriguing variables, but little conceptual clarity or empirical certainty about what is, or theoretically might be expected to be, related to court behavior. Social and economic profiles have sometimes served as shorthand for community values and beliefs, but many conceptual questions remain unsettled, including questions about how best to measure community-level attributes, and what dimensions to measure. Some of the most interesting questions about public opinion may be about criminal acts that are at the edge of unlawful behavior, yet more research has examined public opinion on high-end criminal justice practices (such as capital punishment), where consensus levels are high.

How might communities' political, social, and economic characteristics be associated with court behavior? Crime, and crime's economic correlates of poverty, unemployment, and social disorganization, generates caseloads for the courts through police arrest practices, as well as through the availability of public resources for supporting the courts' work. Political culture may shape the ways in which court elites reach office; attitudes about crime and justice may influence courthouse decision makers who are attuned to public opinion. Controversies among subgroups, or perceived injustices, may materialize in the form of community organizations that lobby for reforms, victim protections, or defendant rights. In short, aggregate characteristics of communities' residents influence court behavior, if at all, through indirect paths.

Theoretical Linkages among Court and Community Variables

These broadly defined conceptual domains — dimensions of court structure, local legal culture, the values and priorities of courthouse elites, community elites, and community-based organizations, and social and political environment — are all seemingly relevant to understanding the relationships among courts and communities, but how does theory direct us toward mapping those relationships? Do community characteristics define the way courts do their work? Does court behavior affect communities, above and beyond individual case outcomes? Or do causal arrows run in both directions?

As it turns out, these three simple questions are illustrated (but by no means exhausted) by three theoretical perspectives that have been adapted to studying courts. Political scientists have adapted theories of constituency representation to account for sentencing patterns, hypothesizing that community values and political elites constrain or guide judges' decisions. Drawing on conflict theory, sociologists have attempted to explain disparate sentencing patterns as consequences of self-interested elite behavior, resulting in court behavior that perpetuates race and class inequalities in communities. Scholars who are trained in organizational theory model local legal culture as the product of local court structure, workgroup relationships, and organizational constraints and incentives shaped indirectly by political environments.

These theoretical perspectives have dominated thinking about how courts work and how they relate to their communities — so much so, in fact, that a casual consumer of court literature might be forgiven for concluding that these perspectives have transcended their status as theories and instead become postulates about court behavior. In fact, however, the discrepancies among these theoretical perspectives have seldom been scrutinized, much less reconciled. These linkages are mapped in Figures 8.2, 8.3, and 8.4, which are discussed briefly below.

Representational Theory

Political scientists have borrowed theories of constituency representation to model the relationships between public opinion and judicial behavior (see Figure 8.2). Implicitly casting judges as local policy makers, and courts' aggregate decisions (usually sentencing decisions) as policy, researchers speculated that as elected officials judges would serve as a conduit for the public opinions about crime and justice. These initial efforts turned out to be overly simplistic, but they have led to theoretical refinements about *the conditions under which* judges might incorporate public opinion into decisions.

Specifically, researchers hypothesized that judges would transmit public opinion if they subscribed to delegate role orientations (defining their job at least partly in terms of public responsiveness; B. Cook 1977;

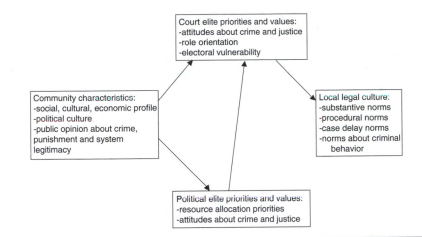

Figure 8.2 Representational theory

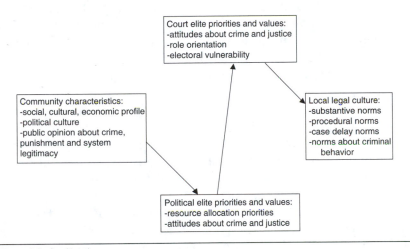

Figure 8.3 Conflict theory

Gibson 1981a); if they believed themselves to be electorally vulnerable (Gibson 1980); or if they shared constituency views (Gibson 1978; Flango, Wenner, and Wenner 1978; Glick and Pruet 1985), or if, as is seldom the case, they were provided with data about their constituents' opinion, particularly on controversial matters (Kuklinski and Stanga 1979).

There is little reason to believe that the electorate is very interested in court electoral politics, and some reason to believe that court actors know this (Sheldon and Lovrich 1982), so court actors' sense of vulnerability may prove to be a weak link between community opinion and court behavior. However, this representational theoretical perspective

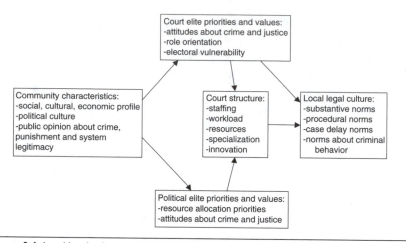

Figure 8.4 Local legal culture and workgroup theory

suggests a second and less direct linkage between public opinion and court behavior: political culture (rather than specific opinions about crime) may define informal elements of judicial and prosecutorial selection processes, as suggested by Levin's comparative study of party-machine careerists and bar-nominated amateurs (Levin 1972; see also Scheingold and Gressett 1987).

Most of the empirical research developed from this theoretical perspective falls short of providing convincing tests of a representational model of court behavior, for several reasons. First, as discussed above, public opinion is a complex set of dimensions, which are difficult to measure. Second, researchers have applied this theory almost exclusively to judges as political decision makers. Yet prosecutors may be more influential in settling case outcomes than judges, and are also more likely to feel politically vulnerable and electorally accountable (Worden 1990). Third, most studies measure court "policy" in terms of felony case sentencing; but court actors exercise more discretion in less serious, more common, and more normatively marginal offenses (Spohn and Cederblom 1991).

Moreover, multijurisdictional studies have yielded contradictory findings about the correlations among community attributes and court behavior: political culture appears to be associated with sentencing outcomes in some studies (e.g., Gibson 1978; Broach, Jackson, and Ascolillo 1978) but not others (Bowers 1997). Studies of community demographic characteristics (Britt 2000; Myers and Talarico 1986 vs. Crawford 2000) and crime rates (Glick and Pruet 1985; Worden 1990 vs. Britt 2000) produce the same sorts of inconsistencies.

If statistics could talk, perhaps these studies' findings would tell us that we should take a more careful look at representational theory, remembering that it is a theory about elite responsiveness to perceived political conditions, and the original question posed by the theory is about how court actors see their responsibilities to their courts, their constituents, and their careers. These questions are interesting, not just because the answers might account for some variation in aggregate outputs, but even more, because the theory, if correct, tells us something important about the roles and functions of these public officials.

Conflict Theory: Courthouse Elites and the Underclass

Since the 1960s, conflict theorists have invoked the notion of elite oppression of an underclass in attempting to account for some patterns of court outcomes, particularly racial and economic disparities (Chambliss and Seidman 1982; see Figure 8.3). Cast as a community-level theory, conflict theory predicts that community elites, including court actors, will use their political power to maintain social and economic stratification, and to reduce threats to their privileged status.

Interpreted as a very general perspective about the creation and behavior of coercive criminal justice institutions and punitive sanctions, this theory might shed some light on cross-cultural comparisons of legal systems (Lynch and Groves 1981; Shelden 2001). However, cast as a theory about American courts, communities, and elites, it has not yet been developed sufficiently to permit a rigorous empirical test of its assumptions and hypotheses.

Instead, many self-described tests of conflict theory are assessments of statistical associations, at the individual level, between defendants' race or social class, and case outcome, usually measured in terms of relative sentencing severity. Absent from these studies are measures of elite intent or motivation. As more critical reviewers point out, even when such correlations are found they might be attributable to unmeasured variables such as court actors' racial prejudice, judgments about the amenability of unemployed defendants to community rather than institutional corrections, or inadvertent structural biases (such as the quality of defense counsel available to the poor) (Hagan 1974; Lizotte 1978). Key elements of conflict theory, such as the incentive and ability to manage underclass populations for economic or other benefits, and the cooptation of working and middle-class citizens into elite strategies, have seldom been discussed. Scholars have not reached agreement on who, exactly, is part of the underclass for purposes of this theory: the poor, the unemployed, the working class, members of racial minorities, immigrants?

This theoretical perspective might offer more insight into court behavior if core assumptions of the theory were substantiated, and if it were more carefully adapted to the question of court-community. This is neither an original nor a recent observation. Chiricos and Waldo (1975), finding no significant relationships among offenders' socioeconomic status and length of prison terms, judiciously concluded that their own empirical model was missing too many links to provide a valid test of conflict theory. Similar research designs continue to produce contradictory findings (e.g., Pruitt and Wilson 1983; Katz and Spohn 1995).

Further, it is not enough to presume that court actors are aligned and behave in concert with social and economic elites at the local level, or that elite priorities are homogeneous; these are variables, not constants. Care should be taken to discern what attributes of communities might prompt more punitive decisions (social heterogeneity? pervasive poverty? economic distress and unemployment? racial tensions?) and whether these characteristics tend to be stable over time, or are instead episodic. Chiricos and Bales argue against settling for generalizations about community conditions, and argue for the importance of attending to local actors' motivations, observing that "The relevance of such macro-analyses [of crime and punishment] are compromised by the fact that both labor markets and punishment policies are highly *localized* and are imperfectly approximated by national or state level measures" (1991, 720).

Hypotheses derived from conflict theory are most plausible (and hence worth the effort of empirical testing) under some simple conditions: first, when they explain changes in the use of criminal court powers over time; second, when the use of court sanctions and power is plausibly related to elite objectives; and third, when they take into account the conditions under which coercive power is likely (or unlikely) to be successfully deployed for strategic purposes.

These conditions are aptly illustrated by Myers's longitudinal study of the use of incarceration and chain gangs in the early twentieth century (1993). Myers hypothesized that fluctuating needs for cheap local labor motivated court elites to strategically deploy misdemeanor-sentencing options in rural Georgia counties. She mapped elites' economic needs in an unstable cotton economy in terms of fluctuating demands for publicly controlled road-building labor (chain gangs) and privately available farm labor. She further observed that courts practiced highly discretionary sentencing practices with both black and white misdemeanants; and she conducted her study in a state characterized by a traditionalistic political culture, in which decisions of local political and economic leaders were seldom questioned by poor whites or blacks. Her key hypothesis, that court elites manipulated sentences (and hence both the free, and the indentured, labor markets) to respond to the needs of economic elites, is a complex but elegant expression of conflict theory.

As this illustration suggests, conflict theory's applicability to courts and communities is more complex than most sentencing severity studies contemplate. Focusing on elites' motivations might suggest dependent variables such as courthouse norms about what merits prosecution (and what does not) — for example, under what conditions is prostitution problematic for community elites (and under what conditions is it tolerable)? Whose victimizations merit prosecutors' time and resources — and whose do not (Myers and Hagan 1979; Paternoster 1983)? Conceiving of elite motivations as a variable (or set of variables) directs our attention toward community organizations and interests, and toward controversies among groups and interests, as well as toward the linkages among those interests and courthouse elites.

A final comment on conflict theory is in order. One might maintain that conflict theory is less useful as a theory about communities and courts and more useful as an historical theory about how courts came to be what they are — formal, adversarial, often unforgiving, and punitive, where decisions about largely poor, minority, and unemployed defendants (and victims) are made by privileged lawyers and career politicians (Snipes and Maguire, chapter 2 this volume). This perspective would imply that variability *across* communities is less interesting or important than apparent commonalities across courts (Lynch and Groves 1981). This is perhaps a defensible position, at least for heuristic purposes. But respect for the intellectual integrity of the theory itself leads us to remember that good theories must be falsifiable, and the tremendous variability in community characteristics (and the lack of strong centralizing or standardizing influences in local courts) may provide that opportunity.

Local Legal Culture and Workgroup Theory

A theoretical perspective on court behavior based on workgroup relationships and courthouse culture directs our attention toward structure, court actors' incentives, common perspectives on court processes, and patterns of decisions. In principle, this theoretical perspective almost stands on its own, independent of community attributes; in fact, the most extensive treatments of workgroup theories fail to develop systematic hypotheses about the effects of community characteristics on workgroup cultures. While we have evidence that courthouse cultures, measured as norms about court work, vary across jurisdictions (T. W. Church 1985; Worden 1987), social scientists rarely have measured cultural and community variables in enough sites to permit systematic hypothesis testing anyway. All the same, given theoretical reasons to draw linkages among community environments, elite priorities, and court structure, and given that social scientists have as yet only incompletely mapped the dimensions of community culture, it makes sense to continue to explore the relationships among community variables and courthouse norms.

This exploration should begin with some simple but important questions. First, which aspects of legal culture are plausibly shaped by community variables? Once again, it may turn out that sentencing norms may be less important than norms about charging practices, pretrial decisions (bail setting, expectations for victim participation and cooperation), and nonincarcerative controls and sanctions (orders of protection, treatment programs).

Second, can we model and assess, at the community level, linkages between variables such as court structure and organization, and informal norms about procedure? For instance, can we determine whether better-funded public defender offices contribute to more advocacy-oriented, adversarial defense practices? Do courts with specialized caseloads (such as drug courts, community courts, domestic violence courts) generate new norms about the use of victim assistance programs, rehabilitation options, or offender accountability?

Finally, an impressive line of case studies has led many experts to believe that most of the time courts successfully resist, deflect, or simply ignore externally imposed attempts to change how they do business (Feeley 1991). Reformers have tried with only limited success to modify court structure (Church and Heumann 1989; Taxman and Elis 1999), substantive and procedural law (Ross and Foley 1987; Horney and Spohn 1991), sentencing codes (Ulmer and Kramer 1996), and sometimes several of these at once (Heumann and Loftin 1979; McCoy 1984). Even when they adopt new ideas, courts adapt them to their own routines, in short order producing a variety of local variants on the original plans (Torres and Deschenes 1997; Harris and Jesilow 2000). Leaving aside the optimism of reform advocates, what do evaluations of these reforms tell us about the power of larger political forces over local courts? Put another way, do these studies reinforce the notion of local legal culture as a durable feature of communities' courts, and prompt us to search more carefully for its distinctive community roots?

Table 8.1 Dimensions of theoretical perspectives. (Adapted from Snipes and Maguire [this volume].)

	Representational theory	Local legal culture	Conflict theory
Level of explanation	Community Individual (judges, prosecutors)	Community Courthouse Workgroup	Society Community Era/ historical period
Socio-political perspective	Consensus	Contingent on authors assumptions about courthouse elites	Conflict
Type(s) of responses	Substantive norms Attitudes Role orientations	Substantive norms Routines Role orientations	Substantive norms Patterns of decisions

EXPLORING NEW LINKAGES

The foregoing discussion suggests that social scientists' sketches of the linkages among courts and communities still need development, testing, and synthesis. We might get some guidance on this challenging undertaking if we briefly review, compare, and contrast these perspectives along some of the dimensions of criminal justice theory proposed by Snipes and Maguire (this volume). Snipes and Maguire propose that theory can be sorted along seven dimensions; Table 8.1 indicates how each of the three perspectives discussed here might be classified on three selected dimensions. First, and most importantly, although these perspectives may be operationalized to apply to different units of analysis, or levels of explanation, they have in common the community. Representational theory ties decision makers to their own perceptions of community values (although as we have seen, they may perceive those values quite differently, and not always accurately); local legal cultures are bounded by the structures, resources, and leadership of communities; conflict theory, at its origins a theory about society generally, nonetheless is most appropriately understood in the context of criminal courts as a theory about how to manage groups in community populations.

Community Mobilization, Symbolic Politics, and Community Impacts

To array these perspectives along a sociopolitical dimension may prove overly simplistic, but attempting to do so reminds us that understanding local legal culture requires that we make assumptions (or get some data) about the motivations of courthouse elites. In principle, this theoretical perspective is compatible with either consensus or conflict theory; but research has not yet told us whether we should expect court actors to organize their working norms around notions of public values, or notions of elites, nor much about the conditions under which we might expect either.

Finally, these perspectives draw our attention to the "what" question: what kinds of behavior does each theory attempt to explain? Representational theory helps us map judges' (and potentially prosecutors') attitudes, beliefs, and role orientations, both as products of community values and as predictors of cumulative decisions — norms about what is or is not criminally culpable, and what shall or shall not be done about it. These substantive norms define legal culture, and that theoretical perspective invites us to measure differences and similarities in those norms across work settings, examining individuals' orientations toward work and the routines that workgroups develop to account for norms. Conflict theory is likewise about norms of justice, measured as patterns of decisions as well as substantive standards about crime and punishment.

This brief review oversimplifies the potential and the complexities of these perspectives, to be sure. However, it provides some evidence of commonalities that might serve the needs of greater theoretical integration as well as parsimony. All three perspectives have been built on the assumption that communities vary in ways that influence how justice is carried out. These perspectives diverge, however, in their assumptions about the motivations of actors.

Figure 8.5 depicts what might happen if these theories were superimposed upon each other, and also suggests theoretical linkages that have seldom captured the attention of social scientists. Of course, any attempt at synthesizing these very complex perspectives is vulnerable to a skeptic's charges of oversimplification, especially when that attempt follows a lengthy discussion of previous studies' failures to capture the complexity of core concepts and to fully specify causal links. Perhaps one should be particularly suspicious of diagrams that approximate symmetry. Figure 8.5 is therefore offered for heuristic purposes only, therefore as a point of departure for continued theorizing about courts and communities. In this speculative spirit, the following observations might be made.

First, this model adds a conceptual domain; community impacts. One might argue that these linkages are out of place in a chapter on court behavior, but there are good reasons to include them in this discussion of theory. Some theoretical perspectives (such as conflict theory) were initially applied to criminal courts precisely because scholars detected social impacts of court behavior at odds with abstract legal norms; moreover, the relationships between courts and communities is probably reciprocal (Figure 8.5 could be redrawn to illustrate this by sketching feedback loops from courthouse culture to community

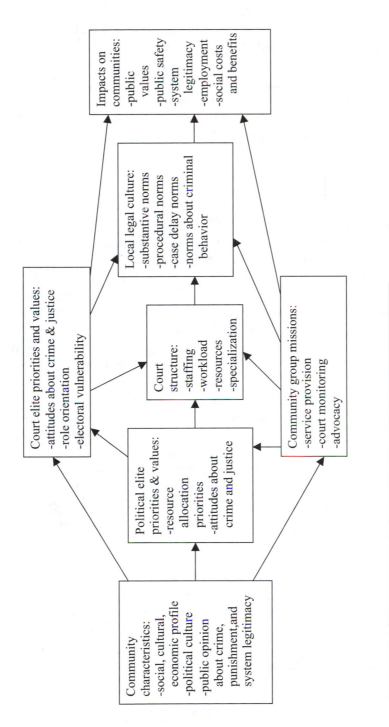

Figure 8.5 Reassessment of theoretical linkages between courts and communities

characteristics). Neglecting one set of arrows could lead to misspecifi-
cation and misestimation of other important linkages.

Second, this diagram suggests that court actors, other political elites
and criminal justice agencies, and groups in communities (including the media) mediate the effects of community characteristics on
court behavior, suggesting that we may have overestimated the direct
significance of public opinion, political culture, and social and economic
profiles as causes of court practices and outcomes. These variables may
shape court decisions and outputs, but they are filtered through the priorities of actors who have more direct interests in the criminal courts
and criminal justice.

Third, court structure, organization, workload, and resources may
influence local legal norms, but these sets of variables may be relatively
independent of community attributes. As noted previously, empirical
research has yielded little evidence that even crime rates and caseloads
have direct consequences for courthouse norms about plea bargaining and about case delay (T. W. Church 1985; Flemming, Nardulli, and
Eisenstein 1987), and these variables have been found to influence plea
bargaining practices only indirectly, through prosecutors' perceptions
of the seriousness of local crime problems (Worden 1990).

Finally, three intriguing paths emerge from this picture, linkages
that have been largely overlooked in court–community studies. The first
is the role of community groups in transmitting and mediating community values and in influencing court structure. The second are the
direct links between community elites' and community organizations'
politically motivated behavior, and community views about crime and
justice — links that bypass the routinized norms of courthouse culture.
The third type of linkages include the relationships between courthouse
norms and communities' expectations about crime and justice, as well
as their social and economic health.

Community Mobilization

The role of community groups is changing court structure and culture.
The activities of community organizations are plausibly related to court
behavior in at least three ways. Some may contribute resources, expertise, or leadership to courthouse innovations, particularly when they
sponsor the adoption of new or experimental programs. For example,
grassroots domestic violence organizations may provide victim advocacy services to courts. Law school internship programs may supply
legal research or other forms of assistance to public defenders. Other

organizations may define their mission in terms of challenging court practices, or holding court actors accountable.

A second path of organization influence is political influence. Groups may mobilize to influence elections, or to endorse candidates or support (or oppose) nominations for court offices. Scheingold and Gressett (1987) document the impacts of this sort of activity in a Midwestern community experiencing a rise in public concern about crime; other case studies have reported similar dynamics (Olson and Batjer 1999).

Third, groups may influence courthouse norms directly, through participation in courtrooms. Victim advocacy programs provide an example: advocates play an active role in encouraging and assisting crime victims to file impact statements and to make appearances (Erez and Tontodonato 1991). Mediation program staff may take up stations in the courtroom itself to invite and encourage complainants and defendants to participate.

Case studies of community groups often acknowledge activity of these actors, but seldom cast their behavior in theoretical terms. However, community organizations may become more salient to studies of courts if notions of community prosecution, community courts, and problem-solving special courts continue to proliferate. We should be cautious in jumping to optimistic conclusions about the success of these wholesome-sounding undertakings, however. Treating communities, and their self-appointed representative groups, as sources of information, problem definitions, and resources is an unfamiliar role for court actors. Partnerships between community groups and court workers have not always proven mutually beneficial or durable. Courts notoriously resist innovations not of their own design. Perhaps the most important questions to pursue on this topic, therefore, are the following: first, under what political or resource conditions are courts most likely to adopt community-sponsored innovations, and of what sort? Second, under what conditions are innovations most likely to be fully implemented and incorporated into routine practices? Third, what organizational and political factors account for organizations' failures to influence how courts work?

Symbolic Politics

Local legal culture has served as a key variable in this chapter, in large part because courthouse norms are thought to define the boundaries of court actors' routine, ordinary decisions and thereby to define justice as communities experience it. However, not all cases are ordinary, and not all court behavior is routine; and it is the extraordinary events or behaviors that are most likely to register with the public. An assessment of the impacts of courts on communities would be incomplete without mention of the potentially powerful role of symbolic acts and statements, especially those made by court actors themselves, and those made by visible community organizations and agents (including the media). Such statements may be isolated and anomalous; they may be sparked by an unusual incident or case; they may involve inaccurate generalizations about court behavior; and they may bear little or no relationship to the ordinary, normal behavior of court actors. However, they may be more likely to register on public consciousness and influence public perceptions about criminal justice than actual routine practices.

Examples would include accounts of a judge's highly visible (but ultimately ineffective) campaign against drunk driving (Ross and Voas 1990), and a Detroit prosecutor's well-publicized (but unsuccessful) attempt to ban plea bargaining by his staff (Heumann and Loftin 1979). Community activists who publicize a new restorative justice program, who successfully lobby for use of victim impact statements at sentencing, or who rally against a prosecutor's attempt to seek the death penalty may have little effect on how cases are handled, but may create strong impressions about how the courts operate among the public. A mayor's campaign promises to crack down on prostitution and drug dealing may leave voters with an image of a tough, intolerant criminal justice system, even as prostitutes and drug dealers continue to ply their trades. A prosecutor's careless racist remark may undermine his office's legitimacy regardless of his staff's behavior. A newspaper's coverage of a sensational trial may be all the education some people ever get on how the legal system works.

It is difficult to place such behavior in the context of a general theory of criminal justice behavior; after all, these sorts of behaviors seem to be idiosyncratic and episodic, and they seldom register in the places social scientists go to gather data. They may not even be legal, or within the legitimate bounds of court actors' authority (Maschke 1995). But social scientists must be very cautious if they choose to disregard evidence of purposive political behavior, particularly when that behavior intentionally (or unintentionally) influences public beliefs about the courts' priorities, punitiveness, or fairness. Exponents of theories about symbolic political behavior have long suggested that social scientists overestimate people's awareness of real political and governmental behavior, and underestimate their appetite for public, eye-catching acts of political elites (Edelman 1964).

Courts' Behavior and Impacts on Community Well-Being

The political behavior of political elites and community groups, although difficult to fit into existing theoretical models of community values, is at least observable (if not easily measurable) and its consequences are often predictable. The impacts of local legal culture on court communities are seldom scrutinized, perhaps because they seem self-evident. If a community's legal culture is very punitive, offenders in that town are punished more; if the culture tolerates long court delays, defendants must bide their time. But the question of how legal culture impacts communities is both more complex, and more interesting, than this. Courthouse practices may influence economic and social conditions, public safety, public opinion and beliefs about crime; and it is only recently that social scientists have begun to argue for more careful attention to these linkages, as illustrated by the examples below.

Conventional applications of conflict theory, for example, predict not only high incarceration rates (at least under some circumstances), but also incarceration rates that disproportionately punish poor, unemployed, and minority defendants. More recently, critics have observed that where such trends exist, they raise equity concerns for defendants, but also for these defendants' communities, whose populations are temporarily depleted and and suffer permanent economic handicaps as a result of incarceration practices (Rose and Clear 1998).

Feminist theorists have argued that the courts' treatment of women as victims of acquaintance assaults can be interpreted as patriarchal protection of men's social autonomy. There is ample historical evidence of this argument in American legal codes (Friedman 1985; Estrich 1987; Horney and Spohn 1991). Statutory and common law that defines assaults on women have been subject to dramatic reforms since the mid-1970s, violence against women has become a federal priority, and these forms of victimization are treated seriously by mainstream media. Yet research tells us that there remains great variability in how courts respond to incidents of domestic violence and sexual assault, so the questions for contemporary theorists and empiricists are these: first, why are such offenses still treated casually in some courts, but taken quite seriously in others? Second, do courts that remain indifferent to these victims inadvertently legitimize this behavior in the eyes of community residents? Third, are victims (and potential victims) at risk, and is their autonomy compromised, where courts treat this behavior as a private matter rather than a public norm violation?

Court norms that prescribe what is (and is not) treated as an offense meriting conviction constitute de facto criminal codes; courts vary in how they handle incidents such as drunk driving and drug possession. These behaviors are quite common so there is reason to believe that many people have formed first- or second-hand beliefs about the legal system's responses to them. Therefore, courthouse norms may tacitly legitimize (or tolerate) these behaviors in the eyes of many, creating an environment that calls for little accountability from or shaming of offenders. Young people may be socialized to believe drug use or impaired driving is not risky behavior.

In short, if we understand local legal cultures as informal and unwritten codes of justice, we should begin to recognize that they may influence community norms about what is, and is not, criminal behavior, fair treatment, and reasonable protection. Community residents are unlikely to think about their courts this formally, of course; laypeople typically do not know exactly what the law stipulates, nor how matters are handled in other communities. They may simply come to know and accept their own courts' definitions of crimes and their going rates of punishment, and their labeling of what constitutes crime and what counts as victimization. At the margins, beliefs about what is and is not legally acceptable may shape behavior. These effects will not materialize around crimes that are universally condemned, to be sure, but rather, around those that occupy the borderlines between socially tolerated and socially condemned behavior.

COURTS AND COMMUNITIES: NOTES TOWARD THEORY DEVELOPMENT

The argument in this chapter can be summed up as follows: Because American communities exhibit wide variation in social, economic, and political characteristics, because their criminal courts are historically defined by links of local rather than state accountability, and because court structure and functions grant actors great discretion but also the imperative to balance competing and sometimes conflicting values about crime and justice, courts develop distinctive norms, practices, and policies. The ways in which these practices are shaped by community environments, elites, and organizations, and their impacts on community values and well being, have been studied from three distinct theoretical perspectives. Although none of these theories has been fully developed in the community context, these theories are not incompatible. But neither do they exhaust the range of plausible and potentially fruitful theoretical perspectives.

Further development and testing of theories about these concepts would benefit from lessons learned through previous research, particularly lessons about theory specification and research design. Ultimately, we may come to understand courts' connections with their communities if we broaden our thinking about how we define communities, and how we define court behavior.

Specifying Theoretical Linkages

Early attempts to model court–community relationships have sometimes settled for oversimplified, inadequately adapted versions of theories that were originally developed to explain something quite different — such as congressional voting behavior, economic disparities — with predictably anemic results. The fault lies not with the theories, though. After all, judges and prosecutors are politicians, and incarceration and unemployment have something in common. The problem is with the adaptation of theory to local settings, and to the special case of court behavior. Sociolegal and institutional theories will tell us the most about courts (as about anything else) if they are crafted with court actors in mind. Studying court behavior is, after all, about studying human decision making (Hogarth 1971). One could argue that court decisions are more peculiarly human than those made by many politicians: court actors share authority for the fates of individuals whom they meet face-to-face, and are obliged to evaluate acts carried out under emotional states of anger, jealousy, greed, and fear. Case by case, they must challenge each other's interpretations of events and of law; and they chalk up their wins and losses to their own professional skills (McIntyre 1987).

Often, however, empirical court research has tended to leave these actors as sketchy shadows, and to leave readers making broad inferences about their motivations and behavior based on associations between community variables and aggregate court outcomes. On the other hand, court research has benefited from some valuable examples of careful theoretical thinking; examples include longitudinal and historical studies that capture and attempt to account for changes in practices at the local level. This sort of research suggests that modeling the nature of linkages, not just their direction, is critical to understanding variations in court behavior. For example, in simple terms, conflict theory may suggest that defendants' race or socioeconomic status is associated with case outcome; a more sophisticated version would suggest that under particular economic, cultural, or political conditions, court actors are motivated to incarcerate unemployed, or minority, defendants at higher rates. Relationships between community attributes and court behavior may be conditional, indirect, spurious, or simply collinear; the one thing that empirical research tells us with certainty is that they are seldom direct, linear, and additive.

Finally, our understanding of courts and communities would be enriched by further specification of relationships among local political groups (elites, community organizations, and the sponsoring organizations within courts themselves), structure, and behavior. Conceiving of communities as pluralistic environments may lead us to more systematic measurement of the dimensions of community variation, and hence to more accurate models of political and social influences on court behavior.

Research Design Challenges

Many of the lessons one might glean from critiquing court–community research apply to most social science research. Research design problems can compromise faithful application of theory and hypotheses to data; when this happens, it is often the theory that is sacrificed. Limited resources and the labor-intensive nature of data collection have led researchers to rely heavily on databases maintained by courts or state criminal justice agencies. Predictably, however, these databases do not always serve the purpose of testing community-level hypotheses. They are often limited to felonies, are most likely found in highly urbanized jurisdictions, and seldom include critical process and outcome variables. Moreover, they tempt the researcher to analyze data at the individual case level, not the community level.

The most basic, but overlooked, lessons one might derive from community–court studies are these: First, we should begin theorizing and data collection at the community or courthouse level of analysis, and measure variables at that level. Second, we should "measure what matters" theoretically, avoiding proxy measures that may be inadequate. Third, we should match research designs to the dynamics of theories. Cross-sectional designs are appropriate for comparing communities, but not for explaining change over time, such as adaptations to legal or structural innovations, or responses to political activity by community groups.

Further, we should match the precision of methodology to the precision of theory. Criminal court research has benefited tremendously from a tradition of exploratory and qualitative case studies, and a student setting out to understand what we know about how courts work, and their connections to communities, would probably be well advised to immerse herself in these studies, and even better advised to carefully compare the findings of scholars across sites.

Rethinking Communities and Courts

It is difficult to liberate recommendations for future theoretical work from critiques of existing efforts. Social scientists tend to rely on what they have done (well or badly) as the point of departure for thinking about what they should do next. This sort of intellectual incrementalism is probably functional, but it can also be limiting, and court research may suffer from some of these limitations. Theorists might do well to set aside conventional ideas about how we define communities and court behavior, reconsider their political and social dynamics, and redirect empirical research efforts toward refining familiar theories and developing overlooked relationships.

While researchers have explored many aspects of communities, they have seldom questioned what a community *is* for the purposes of court research. Communities have been generally and seemingly consensually defined as the political, geographically based jurisdiction of a court, bounded by city, county, or circuit lines. Communities are the populations from which cases are drawn and processed. (Even more specifically, they are the places where crimes take place, since one is tried in the jurisdiction of an alleged offense, not in one's hometown.) For some purposes this definition works: those boundaries constitute judges' and prosecutors' electoral constituencies, for example. We know that communities are not homogeneous (and are certainly less so than when the tradition of community-based courts was institutionalized in this nation); however, we can in principle measure and assess heterogeneity if we believe it affects court behavior.

But that may not be sufficient. If we suspect that community politics and grassroots organizations are elements in understanding court behavior, we may need to reconceptualize communities in pluralistic terms. This is true whether we are interested in local "politics as usual" — understanding decisions about the impact of other criminal justice agencies, public resource allocations, and elections — and also if we are interested in studying grassroots political mobilization around justice issues at the local level, or innovation efforts in court organizations. Community case studies present considerable evidence that court actors think of communities in these terms — as institutions, political forces, dominant social and political groups, rather than as aggregates of citizen characteristics.

We should also revisit longstanding conceptualizations of court behavior. This chapter has argued against relying on variation in final outcomes (such as sentencing), and in favor of closer examination of courthouse norms about what is to be treated as crime, how it is to be processed, and what sorts of outcomes are imposed. Not all courts have consensual norms on these matters; in fact, in some courts it is "normal" for court actors to be adversarial and in perpetual disagreement over cases. Further work on developing typologies of courthouse norms would allow testing of hypotheses about why these procedural and substantive norms of justice are different across communities.[3]

Lastly, rethinking what is important about communities and court behavior might prompt us to rethink how these concepts might be related, and to decide whether it is time to set aside some long-standing hypotheses in order to pursue and prioritize other lines of theory. These judgments can be based on normative or empirical criteria; for example, we might prioritize studying the impacts of incarceration rates on communities because that is an urgent social problem, or we might focus on the relationships between court actors' attitudes and priorities and legal culture, because research tells us that those linkages really exist. Either strategy is likely to contribute to our understanding of court behavior if it is guided by the primary objective of mapping the theoretical relationships that link courts to their communities.

NOTES

1. This chapter focuses almost exclusively on trial courts, because they are uniquely and purposefully local institutions (in ways that federal and appellate courts are not). However, readers should note that federal courts have been the subject of studies of community context as well (Cook 1977; Kritzer 1979; Albonetti 1998).
2. A highly mobile and increasingly diverse population places the permanence of these categories, and their geographical associations, in some doubt, as periodic recalibrations of this concept demonstrate. However, the concept remains valuable for studying state and local government structure and policy.
3. It is worth noting here that almost all studies of court behavior are studies of reactive behavior: responses to the steady supply of criminal charges. There are other dimensions of court actors' behavior that have gone virtually unexamined, or described but not developed theoretically. Judicial leadership (Wice 1995; Jacobs 1997), prosecutorial innovation, and public defense management, are just a few examples of topics that may be shaped by community politics.

Part IV
Testing Correctional Sector Theories: Two Examples

In part IV, we examine the culmination of the theory development process in theory testing and revision. As a number of methodologists point out, no theory (of any complexity) is ever tested directly. Instead, researchers derive empirically testable propositions from the theory and then test those in a series of hypothetically stated expectations about relationships that are compared to empirical relationships. The analyses examine the empirical support for particular hypotheses. Based on these findings, the researchers then must interpret whether and how much empirical support has been gathered for the theory from which the expectations were derived. If findings are not consistent with expectations, what happens next? Perhaps the theory must be revised to accommodate the unexpected findings. Can it be modified to explain the patterns that actually were found? However, the problem may not necessarily be with the theory. Perhaps the measures taken were not the most appropriate to represent the concepts in the theory? Perhaps the hypotheses misinterpret the theory? Data never speak for themselves, they must be interpreted against various standards, conventions, and principles of the scientific process, as the following chapters illustrate.

In part IV, the authors are concerned *primarily* with testing existing theory rather than building new theory or comparing and combining theories. We emphasize *primary* concern, because theory building and critical assessment and revision of theory do play important, albeit secondary roles, relative to the concern for testing. In terms of theory development, for example, it would not be quite accurate to say that these authors are merely testing existing theory. In both chapters 9 and 10, the authors rely heavily on existing theory (and, in chapter 9, on a library of existing research) to guide their data collection, their approach to analysis, and their interpretation of findings. In other words, they state their expectations beforehand and then collect evidence that permits an assessment of those expectations. They then conclude their studies with proposals for theory revision and new investigation.

The reader should note that in both chapters the exact nature of the expectations to be tested is "built" in the study itself, even though the authors are heavily guided by prior theory. Consequently there is some concern for theory building. Additionally, note that the specific theoretical connections that are tested combine approaches and theoretical connections from prior work. In chapter 9, the study looks at both the causes and effects of job satisfaction, rather than just one or the other. In chapter 10, the study combines a concern for the institutionalized environment of public organizations and a concern for social conflict (both of which are, more abstractly, two different aspects of the correctional environment). Consequently, both studies have some concern for conceptual combinations and theoretical integration that helps us assess how theories come together to produce more complicated explanations of more complicated phenomena. For example, the McGarrell and Duffee chapter can be viewed as an attempt to combine (and contrast) the rational-goal and institutional organizational perspectives from chapter 2 with the conflict/consensus views of the sociopolitical perspective from chapter 2.

Both of these theory-testing studies concern corrections in important ways. Equally interesting and valuable, however, is that these correctional theories may also be characterized in noncorrectional terms. Chapter 9 certainly contributes to a general literature on job satisfaction, commitment, and turnover intent. It demonstrates, for example, that the same forces that are most powerful in predicting these outcomes in private firms are also most important in explaining correctional employee attitudes, despite the large differences in characteristics of both employees and organizations. Therefore, the study contributes to our understanding of correctional workers while also assisting with the generalization of job satisfaction or human resources theory.

Chapter 10 focuses directly on correctional outcomes, such as the percent of public dollars that are allocated to corrections rather than other policy sectors such as health and education. Hence, the question raised by the authors is: what characteristics of the state or of the correctional system make corrections more politically powerful or more "valued" by its public? Why do some correctional systems fare better than other correctional systems in the allocation of resources? But the reader should note immediately the deep connections between the concerns of this chapter on correctional systems and the concerns raised in chapters 1 and 4 about entire criminal justice systems. Is dollars devoted to punishment merely a study of corrections? Or is it equally apt to characterize it as a study of the punitiveness of societies? If some states pay more for corrections than other states or pay more for corrections than for other social concerns, are they being more punitive than are their peers? Is this a study of corrections or a study of choices among social policies? To the extent that this conception is acceptable, then this is not a study of corrections theory but a study of criminal justice system theory, or the study of public support (in taxes) for the criminal sanction.

These other important substantive concerns in these chapters would be less visible, and less employable, except for the heavy role of theory that guides both investigations. It is the theoretical guidance visible in these studies that permit the authors and readers to identify how the findings promote knowledge in several of the areas represented by the theoretical elements used in the studies. Thus, these studies become good examples, not only of theory testing, but also of the general knowledge-building process. They illustrate how a study of prison workers can contribute to a general knowledge of human resources in organizations and how a study of corrections tax dollars supports a social conflict approach to societal choice of social controls.

Like the two chapters in part III, chapter 9, by Eric Lambert, and chapter 10, by Edmund McGarrell and David Duffee, can be broadly distinguished by the level of analysis. Lambert is interested in explaining what makes correctional employees satisfied with their work, committed to their organizations, and willing to stay, or the reverse — dissatisfied, uncommitted, and intending to leave. As defined by Kautt and Spohn, Lambert's three dependent variables are micro or individual level variables on the vertical dimension and "attitudinal" variables on the horizontal dimension. Unlike Kautt and Spohn's chapter, however, Lambert's work is not examining a criminal justice decision maker's outcomes for a case, a suspect, or an offender. Instead, he is trying to determine what aspects of the worker or the worker's environment affect the worker's internal reactions to the work. This kind of study is important for any number of reasons. One of the most obvious is that satisfied and committed workers may be more likely to implement organizational goals, such as treating prisoners in ways consistent with policy. Also important is that, if satisfied and committed workers are less likely to leave the organization, then corrections could save significant recruitment and training costs by doing things that led to satisfaction and commitment.

In contrast to Lambert's focus on the individual worker, McGarrell and Duffee are studying entire correctional systems. They are not looking at individual decisions and attitudes. They are examining large structural features of bureaucracies (such as size and complexity) and structural features of society, such as class, wealth, racial composition, and political traditions. This kind of study is also important for quite different reasons. For policy makers, this is one of a growing number of studies that suggest that level of crime is only a minor influence in the level of punishment supported in a system. It would also suggest that a large number of social inequities are built into social control systems, even if individual decision makers are fair and unbiased. (Note that part III was also concerned with the differences in justice outcomes at different units of analysis.)

In terms of the knowledge building process, the two chapters in this section represent the later phases of the theory building-observing-reformulating-expanding cycle. These studies appear to confirm some expectations and disconfirm others. They also "stumble" (in the sense of did not expect) onto findings that suggest new theoretical developments are needed. In addition, they suggest additional research avenues.

One of the avenues implied in both studies is the need to acquire better data with which to test the theories, or data that better fit the theory. Note that both Lambert and McGarrell and Duffee are explicating expectations about processes that unfold over time but they test those expectations with data that is collected at one point in time. This approach is often taken, but it is far weaker (if more feasible) than the alternative of following individual workers or correctional systems over time to see if the variables are actually related temporally the way these theories and analyses assume that they are.

DISCUSSION QUESTIONS

1. Compare the McGarrell and Duffee study in this volume to the study of incarceration rates by McGarrell (1993). In that study, McGarrell examines whether social conflict variables are equally strong in explaining incarceration rates at different points in time. Does such a study of several points in time provide stronger evidence than the study in this chapter about the influence of sociopolitical processes on punishment rates? Compare either of the above studies to McGarrell and Duffee (1995). In that study, the investigators examine prerelease

centers per state and per inmate. Why are there differences in the state level variables that influence the adoption of prerelease centers and the state level variables that influence dollars devoted to corrections? What do these differences say about the importance of the exact nature of the dependent variable?

2. Consider the job satisfaction of other criminal justice system participants. Would you propose that police officers, prosecutors, public defenders, probation officers, or other officials are likely to be influenced by different job and organizational characteristics from those that appear to influence these federal correctional workers? Where would you look to determine if Lambert's theory had been applied elsewhere in criminal justice?

3. Consider either the Lambert or the McGarrell and Duffee theories as calling for examination of processes changing over time. Does either of their tests really examine such processes? Where and how would you gather data that did so? What are the problems with gathering such data?

9

A TEST OF A TURNOVER INTENT MODEL
The Issue of Correctional Staff
Satisfaction and Commitment[1]

Eric G. Lambert

INTRODUCTION

Earlier chapters in this book focused on the development and discussion of theories. While theory development is critical to understand, guide, and reshape the criminal justice system, a theory is only as good as the empirical evidence that supports it. Testing a theory or theories is part of the scientific process. It is through that scientific process that we develop a better, more accurate, and systematic understanding of our world, including the agencies in the criminal justice system. From a theory, testable hypotheses can be developed, and it is these hypotheses which are tested. The empirical evidence generated from hypothesis testing can support a theory or cause it to be discarded or revised. Without hypothesis testing, it is possible that significant policy changes could be made based on political rhetoric or intuition rather than on a sound scientific foundation.

In this book, many theories deal with aggregate groups, such as components of the criminal justice system and agencies — macrotheories. Criminal justice theories are not simply limited to aggregate groups, such as nations, states, agencies, or departments; they can also focus at the individual level, at police officers, judges, probation officers, or correctional workers. The behaviors, perceptions, values, and attitudes of individuals are also examined by criminal justice theories — micro- or individual level theories. In this chapter, the impact of the work environment on correctional staff job satisfaction, organizational commitment, and turnover intent is explored. In other words, an individual theory is tested.

The driving force of organizations is their workers. This is especially true for correctional facilities, where staff are the "heart and soul" of the organization. Nevertheless, correctional organizations are often more concerned with finding the right person for the job instead of making the job right for the person. For example, in a national survey, most top correctional administrators provided reasons for staff turnover that focused on individual characteristics and personalities of employees rather than on organizational reasons (Jurik and Winn 1987). According to Poole and Pogrebin (1991), "We should be asking what the organization means to the worker instead of what the worker means to the organization" (170).

While it is true that correctional staff have significant effects on the operation of correctional organizations, it is also true that correctional organizations have meaningful and real effects on their staff, which can be either positive or negative. In our society, work is viewed as a central, sometimes even the defining factor in a person's life. What takes place at work can have rippling to enormous consequences in a worker's life, even outside of the work environment. Job satisfaction and organizational commitment are the two most important areas by which correctional organizations influence the behaviors, intentions, and attitudes of their employees, such as turnover intent and turnover. Turnover is a significant problem in the field of corrections. By improving the job satisfaction and organizational commitment of correctional employees, both turnover intent and turnover can be significantly reduced.

JOB SATISFACTION

The concept of job satisfaction is a frequently studied concept across a wide and diverse assortment of research fields. In 1976, Locke estimated the number of articles and dissertations dealing in some manner with the subject of job satisfaction to be over 3,300. Twenty years later, Spector (1996) estimated the number of studies incorporating job satisfaction to be over 12,400. No longer is the concept of job satisfaction limited to a particular school of thought or discipline. Job satisfaction is of immense interest to a multitude of researchers from a wide variety of disciplines, including corrections.

Hopkins (1983) defines overall job satisfaction as "the fulfillment or gratification of certain needs that are associated with one's work" (7). Spector (1996) contends job satisfaction is simply "the extent to which people like their jobs" (214). Most other definitions of job satisfaction are very similar. Indeed, in the job satisfaction literature, there is general agreement that job satisfaction is an affective response by an employee concerning his or her particular job in an organization (Cranny, Smith, and Stone 1992).

ORGANIZATIONAL COMMITMENT

Organizational commitment is a newer concept than job satisfaction. It came to prominence in the late 1970s and early 1980s. It has been adopted in many disciplines that focus on worker attitudes and behaviors. It is estimated that over 1,000 studies have incorporated the concept of organizational commitment in some manner. Over the years, various definitions of organizational commitment have been proposed. Early definitions of organizational commitment equated organizational commitment with loyalty to the employing organization (Jauch, Glueck, and Osborn 1978). Organizational commitment has also been described as the level of investments (e.g., pensions) an employee has with the employing organization (H. Becker 1960). The greater the level of investments, the more committed the employee should be to the employing organization. More recent definitions of organizational commitment have expanded the affective bond to include loyalty, identification with the organization (i.e., pride in the organization) and its goals (i.e., internalization of the goals of the organization), and willingness to put forth substantial effort on behalf of the organization and its goals (Mowday, Steers, and Porter 1979).

While there are numerous, differing conceptualizations of organizational commitment, two fundamental points are clear. First, organizational commitment is a bond to the whole organization, and not to the job or position, or belief in the importance of work itself. Second, Mowday, Porter, and Steers (1982) argue that the various definitions can be categorized on a behavioral–attitudinal continuum. At one end of the continuum is the dimension of organizational commitment that is concerned with behavioral indicators or outcomes. This dimension is typically referred to as calculative or continuance commitment. It is referred to as calculative commitment because an employee "calculates" in some manner the costs and benefits of working for a given organization (e.g., monetary, social, physical, psychological, lost opportunities, etc.). These calculations determine the level of commitment to the organization. The synonymous term *continuance commitment* derives its name from the premise that workers highly committed to an organization will want to continue employment with that organization because of the benefits of continued employment as compared to the costs of leaving. In general, definitions at the behavioral end of commitment argue that employees commit to varying degrees based upon the costs and benefits of organizational membership.

At the other end of the continuum are definitions that focus on affective or attitudinal commitment. Attitudinal commitment is primarily concerned with the mental and cognitive bonds an employee feels toward the employing organization. These bonds include loyalty, wanting to belong, attachment, belief in the value system and goals of the organization, and so forth (Mowday et al. 1979).

There is an ongoing debate about which dimensions of organizational commitment, attitudinal or behavioral, are theoretically accurate, especially for the purposes of measuring commitment and its effects (Randall, Fedor, and Longnecker 1990). Measures for the behavioral dimension of organizational commitment are criticized as being underdeveloped, and failing to measure organizational commitment completely (Meyer and Allen 1984). Less criticism is leveled at attitudinal commitment measures, which are the most frequently utilized in research outside of the field of criminal justice (Mathieu and Zajac 1990). Therefore, an affective definition of organizational commitment is used in this study. Specifically, organizational commitment is defined as "the strength of an individual's identification with and involvement in a particular organization" (Mowday, Porter, and Steers 1982, 27).

THE IMPORTANCE OF CORRECTIONAL STAFF JOB SATISFACTION AND ORGANIZATIONAL COMMITMENT

Job satisfaction and organizational commitment have powerful and far reaching consequences for both employers and employees. In many different types of organizations, high levels of job satisfaction or organizational commitment have been linked to positive worker attitudes and behaviors, such as extra work effort, creativeness, innovation, receptivity to change, and openness to innovation (Bateman and Organ 1983; Mathieu and Zajac 1990; Wycoff and Skogan 1994). Even within the field of corrections, there is a small but growing body of correctional research that supports the premise that committed and satisfied correctional workers are linked to positive work outcomes (Culliver, Sigler, and McNeely 1991; Kerce, Magnusson, and Rudolph 1994; Robinson, Porporino, and Simourd 1992).

Low levels of job satisfaction and organizational commitment are theorized to cause negative employee attitudes, intentions, and behaviors. Hulin, Roznowski, and Hachiya (1985) theorize that there are four general categories of employee withdrawal:

1. *Increased Negative Job Outcomes:* theft, misuse of company property, moonlighting on the job, performing personal tasks during work hours (e.g., personal phone calls);
2. *Reduced Job Input:* employee purposely misses meetings, takes long breaks, looks busy, intentionally fails to do quality work;
3. *Change in Work Situation:* transfer, demotion, unionization;
4. *Reduced Work Inclusion:* tardiness, absenteeism, early voluntary retirement, quitting.

While all four withdrawal areas are detrimental, turnover tends to be the most observable, costly, and disruptive to correctional organizations.

Turnover

There are two general categories of employee turnover: voluntary and involuntary. Voluntary turnover is when the employee ends his or her employment with an organization. Involuntary turnover, however, is the end of the employee–organization membership that is not desired or initiated by the worker (Price 1977). In most cases, involuntary turnover is initiated by the employing organization (Mueller, Boyer, Price, and Iverson 1994) but not always (e.g., death; McElroy, Morrow, and Fenton 1995).

Of the two types, voluntary turnover is usually more avoidable, costly, and disruptive to an organization (Price 1977). Involuntary turnover, on the other hand, is usually less controllable, and, in many cases, it is not in the best interest of the organization or the employee that employment continues (Stohr, Self, and Lovrich 1992).

The Extent and Impact of Turnover in the Field of Corrections

Turnover is seen as a significant problem in the field of corrections. Jurik and Winn (1987) state that turnover among correctional staff is a chronic and serious problem. McShane et al. (1991) write, "Turnover rates vary in prisons across the country, from less than 1 percent annually in one state to 45 percent in another. The average of all states' rates is 17 percent" (220). The average annual turnover rate of correctional staff is clearly in the double digits and is probably 15 to 20 percent. Moreover, Locke (1976) contends that it is usually the most competent workers who quit, since it is relatively easy for them to obtain work elsewhere. This outcome is observed in studies of private industry employees (e.g., T. Wright 1991) and correctional staff (T. Wright 1993). Specifically, Wright found that correctional workers who voluntarily left their jobs had, on average, higher performance ratings than the staff who remained.

Voluntary turnover of correctional staff has detrimental, and even devastating effects for most correctional organizations. Recruitment, testing, selection, and training of new correctional staff is expensive, in the region of $10,000 to $20,000 per person (McShane et al. 1991). A reduction of turnover will save correctional organizations substantial expenditures in recruiting and training alone (New Jersey, The Governor's Management Improvement Plan 1983). Furthermore, correctional staff turnover disrupts the social networks and contacts that staff members develop over time with inmates and other employees. Correctional administrators rely on staff to obtain information, directly and indirectly, on what is "happening" in the institution in order to avoid potential problems. It takes time for new staff to learn these subtle but very necessary skills (Stohr et al. 1992). Moreover, should turnover be allowed to reach a critical negative mass, turnover rates may begin to impact on future employee turnover. A chronic, looping turnover pattern may emerge:

> Some effects of turnover are very subtle, and the resulting costs are thus difficult to determine. For example, it can be argued that turnover rates affect morale and that there is a real and significant cost of low morale. If the topic of conversation is not, "How are things going?" but "When are you going to leave?" then turnover begins to generate further turnover. This in turn leads to more recruitment [and other] costs which adds to the problem. (Cawsey and Wedley 1979, 93)

The costs to the employee and his or her family before, during, and after the separation process are also high. Voluntary correctional staff turnover has many negative and costly effects for the correctional staff who have left, the staff who remain, and the correctional organization itself. While job satisfaction and organizational commitment are critical keys to understanding voluntary correctional staff turnover, they do not directly impact turnover. Instead, they influence voluntary turnover indirectly through turnover intent.

The Issue of Turnover Intent

Intentions help shape all types of behavior (Fishbein and Ajzen 1975). In fact, Fishbein and Ajzen argue that "the best single predictor of an individual's behavior will be a measure of his intention to perform that behavior" (369). Intentions "represent a vital link — transitional link — between thought and actual behavior" (Steel and Ovalle 1984, 674). Moreover, withdrawal intentions should have a stronger impact on employee turnover than many other types of behavior (Bagozzi 1981). Leaving employment with an organization is not a decision that is typically made on the spur of the moment. For most individuals, substantial thought goes into the decision to quit before a formal resignation is tendered. The intent to leave a job within a given time period is referred to as turnover intent.

Understanding the causes of turnover intent is very important. Dalessio et al. (1986) argue:

> More attention should be given to the direct and indirect influences of variables on intention to quit as opposed to the actual act of turnover. From the employer's standpoint, intention to quit may be a more important variable then the actual act of turnover. If the precursors to intention to quit are better understood, the employer could possibly institute changes to affect this intention. However, once an employee has quit, there is little the employer can do except assume the expense of hiring and training another employee. (261)

Turnover intent is also important to understand from an employee's standpoint (Martin and Hunt 1980). Many adults accept employment with the intention of remaining with an organization. Voluntary termination of employment with a particular correctional organization is a negative and painful experience for most correctional staff, particularly in terms of economic impact. Therefore, if the antecedents of turnover intent are better understood, it may be possible to avoid the actual act of turnover. This would benefit the correctional employee planning to leave, the employees who remain, and the correctional organization. It is postulated that job satisfaction and organizational commitment help shape turnover intent, and turnover intent, in turn, directly influences actual voluntary turnover behavior.

ANTECEDENTS AND CONSEQUENCES OF JOB SATISFACTION AND ORGANIZATIONAL COMMITMENT

The consequences of job satisfaction and organizational commitment in terms of turnover intent are only part of the equation. It is equally important to explore, confirm, and understand the key antecedents, both direct and indirect, of job satisfaction and organizational commitment. Identifying the factors that influence job satisfaction and organizational commitment provides correctional administrators with meaningful information to make intelligent decisions regarding interventions aimed at increasing organizational commitment and job satisfaction, with the ultimate goal being a decrease in negative withdrawal intentions, such as turnover intent. Therefore, one needs to look at both the potential causes and effects, or as Guion (1992) points out, "Looking independently at antecedents and consequences is a bit like looking at an art museum brochure's detail of a painting: It's intellectually stimulating and informative, but you miss the grandeur of the artist's complete vision" (257).

It is especially important to identify the salient antecedents of job satisfaction and organizational commitment among correctional staff. Correctional work is often hard and dangerous. Working in a prison holds little prestige in society, unlike many other criminal justice professions, such as being a judge. Such a job in itself may help foster negative attitudes. There is no reason for correctional organizations to contribute to or even enhance the development of negative attitudes by employees. However, without knowing the salient antecedents of job satisfaction and organizational commitment, correctional organizations may be unintentionally contributing to unduly negative attitudes and behaviors of staff. Therefore, there is a critical need to identify those factors that positively or negatively influence job satisfaction and organizational commitment among correctional staff.

There are two general viewpoints on the factors that influence workers' attitudes, intentions, and behaviors (Cullen et al. 1993). The first is referred to as the Individual Importation Model. This approach sees workers' reactions mainly as the result of personal characteristics, such as age, tenure, race, gender, personality, or past experiences. These are characteristics that people bring with them into the organization. The second approach, the Work Environment or Organizational Reaction Model, views employees' attitudes and behaviors as predominately shaped by the organizational work environment (e.g., degree of participation, routinization, promotional opportunity, pay, discipline, role ambiguity, type and quality of supervision, etc.).

While both viewpoints have found empirical support, it is generally argued that work environment factors have a far greater impact on job satisfaction (Hepburn and Knepper 1993) and organizational commitment (Lambert 1999). Thus, the work environment ultimately affects employee withdrawal intentions through job satisfaction and organizational commitment. Nevertheless, in the field of corrections, personal characteristics are still given undue focus, while work environment factors fail to receive the attention they warrant. As indicated in the introduction, Jurik and Winn (1987) report that in a national survey, most top correctional administrators provided reasons for staff turnover that focused on individual characteristics and personalities of employees. Rarely were organizational reasons given. Jurik and Winn (1987) strongly criticize such a limited approach:

> Not withstanding its widespread acceptance, practically and academically, the individual-level orientation is problematic. The reasons that turnover rates vary among specific groups of individuals are never adequately identified. This approach ignores organizational level factors that may contribute to the turnover of employees — correctional officers in this instance — who are otherwise qualified for their jobs (6) ... future research endeavors should focus on the role of the organizational environment in the turnover process.... Instead of seeking to develop attribute profiles of officers inclined to remain in status quo prison environments, correctional administrators should direct their attention toward organizational-level problem areas that encourage otherwise qualified officers to leave. (20–21)

Rather than limiting this study to either exclusively personal or work environment measures, both are included to see if and how they impact job satisfaction and organizational commitment, and, in turn, the consequences of job satisfaction and organizational commitment on turnover intent among correctional staff. Before a causal model is proposed, it is necessary to first define and discuss briefly what is meant by the concepts of personal characteristics and work environment.

Personal Characteristics

Personal characteristics are the characteristics that individuals bring with them when they join a particular organization. These characteristics concern an individual's background (e.g., education, place and type of upbringing, etc.), demographic identity (e.g., age, sex, race, ethnicity, etc.), current situation (e.g., married, number of children, tenure, etc.), and other areas (e.g., religion, distance living from work, total family income, etc.; Cammann et al. 1983). It is argued that personal attributes affect how an individual views his or her world. Nonetheless, personal variables tend to be more descriptive than explanatory (Mathieu and Zajac 1990). Since personal characteristics are frequently used in research on correctional employees, several personal characteristics are included in this study as control variables.

Work Environment

The work a person carries out in the course of a job does not take place in a vacuum. It takes place in a setting known as the work environment, which is comprised of much more than just physical elements. It encompasses all the factors that comprise the overall work conditions and situations for a particular employee, including both the tangible and intangible. There are numerous dimensions of the work environment, such as centralization (i.e., employee participation in decision making); financial rewards; integration (i.e., creating group cohesion among the workers and departments in an organization); legitimacy (i.e., fairness in terms of workload, rewards, and punishment); mobility, promotion, supervision, job autonomy, relations with coworkers, job variety, and job stress. Several different areas of the work environment are measured in this study and are discussed in the methods section.

THE PROPOSED COMPREHENSIVE MODEL FOR CORRECTIONAL STAFF TURNOVER

As previously stated, it is important to look at both the antecedents and consequences of job satisfaction and organizational commitment together. This means that a causal or comprehensive model needs to be developed. Comprehensive approaches to complex human processes, such as turnover, provide structure and discipline for researchers. Lee and Mowday (1987) write:

> Without such direction, research on employees leaving organizations would be totally ad hoc. Each researcher would probably focus on a subset of variables he or she found interesting, with little regard for a larger network of variables that could influence the relationships under study. The likelihood that knowledge would accrue from such ad hoc research is minimal. Comprehensive models impose a degree of discipline on researchers and help ensure that evidence from various studies can accumulate in some meaningful fashion. As that process occurs, scholars can refine the theoretical models, which will in turn increase understanding of the process through which employees leave organizations. (738)

Additionally, the comprehensive models provide a framework for correctional administrators to better understand the process of correctional staff voluntary turnover. Many correctional managers feel that they know why employees quit, even though their knowledge is rarely based upon a systematic and complete examination of the problem (Lambert 1999). Lee and Mowday (1987) further argue,

> that comprehensive models have a practical value in helping managers think heuristically about possible cause[s] for employees' leaving. In our experience, managers often feel they know why employees leave, even though their knowledge is seldom based on a systematic diagnosis of the situation. They frequently focus their attention on one plausible cause of employees' leaving without considering a number of alternative explanatory variables. By comprehensively identifying antecedents and suggesting their general relationships, comprehensive models may help managers think more systematically about why employees leave. Variables that managers had not previously considered may become salient, possibly helping to identify potential strategies or interventions for increasing employee retention. (738–39)

Therefore, it is extremely important to investigate the causal processes rather than individual relationships. Most correctional staff turnover studies tend to rely on correlations or other forms of bivariate analysis. A few have utilized multivariate techniques (e.g., regression) for examining the impact of a group of independent variables on turnover. No causal models concerning turnover could be located in the published literature for correctional staff.

Causal models allow for researchers to test for both direct and indirect effects among the variables in the model. Direct effects are the effects of one variable on another that are not moderated by any other variable. Indirect effects represent the impact that a variable has on another variable that is mediated by one or more other variables. Knowing both direct and indirect effects is critical when examining causal processes of complex phenomena. "Considering each type of effect leads to a more complete understanding of the relationship between variables than if these distinctions are not made. In the typical regression analysis the regression coefficient is an estimate of the direct effect of a variable. If we ignore the indirect effects that a variable may have through other variables, we may be grossly off in assessment of its overall effect" (Bollen 1989, 37–38). Hence, a variable that may not have a significant direct effect, may still have a significant indirect effect on the outcome variable of interest. Without taking into account the indirect effects, it is conceivable to reject a variable that is in fact very important in the causal process.

It is postulated that five core areas influence the causal process of voluntary turnover among correctional staff: turnover intent, job

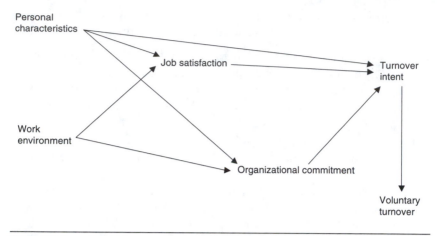

Figure 9.1 Causal model for correctional staff turnover

satisfaction, organizational commitment, work environment forces, and personal characteristics of the employee. The proposed causal model of correctional staff voluntary turnover is presented in Figure 9.1. Testing the proposed causal model can empirically demonstrate that past multivariable correctional research has missed the total effect (i.e., direct and indirect) of salient variables on correctional staff turnover intent, and underestimated the importance of job satisfaction and organizational commitment as mediating variables.

It is postulated that organizational commitment will negatively impact turnover intent. Correctional employees who have low commitment will be less inclined to remain with the organization. Conversely, those with higher commitment have stronger bonds with the organization, and these bonds will generally ensure that they will want to remain members of the organization. People who are highly attached or bonded to something are generally not likely to sever that attachment (Mueller et al. 1994).

Job satisfaction is also predicted to have an inverse effect on turnover intent among correctional staff. Work is a very important part of people's lives. According to Terkel (1974), work provides for most of us "daily meaning as well as daily bread" (xi). However, it is not just financial rewards that are important to people. From a survey of U.S. workers, Naisbitt and Aburdene (1985) report that pay, benefits, and job security were not among the top ten items workers want in a job. The most common responses involved rewarding, enjoyable, and enriching jobs. According to Locke (1976), the reaction to something that is satisfying is to embrace it, while the response to something that is dissatisfying is to withdraw from it. If the person is highly dissatisfied with his or her job, he or she is likely to want to leave the thing that is causing him or her so much pain and discomfort (Roseman 1981). In addition, those employees highly dissatisfied with their jobs will be more likely to voice intentions to leave so as to alleviate the negative feelings (Roseman 1981). Oppositely, those workers who are happy with their overall jobs have far less reason to leave. People do not readily intend to abandon positive experiences that meet their vital needs. Humans seek stimuli that provide them with the pleasure of positive effects while meeting their other needs. While job satisfaction is predicted to have a direct inverse effect on turnover intent, it is also predicted to have an indirect effect on turnover intent through organizational commitment.

Job satisfaction is generally viewed as preceding organizational commitment. Job satisfaction occurs relatively quickly, while organizational commitment takes time to develop (Mowday, Steers, and Porter 1979; Mowday, Porter, and Steers 1982). A person dissatisfied with his or her job has little reason to develop or remain committed to the organization that is causing the dissatisfaction in the first place. Alternately, those workers satisfied with their job are more likely to see the organization in a positive light, and, as such, will probably bond with the organization. Therefore, it is predicted that job satisfaction will directly and significantly impact correctional staff organizational commitment in a positive direction.

Work environment factors are predicted to significantly influence organizational commitment and job satisfaction, with some of the total effects on organizational commitment being through job satisfaction. According to Satir (1972), life in a positive environment is enjoyable, energizing, and uplifting, while life in a negative environment is demoralizing, disheartening, and deenergizing. The specific areas of the work environment measured will dictate the type of predicted relationships (i.e., negative or positive) and, as such, these types of relationships are discussed in the upcoming section on measures. Finally, it is hypothesized that work environment factors are more important than are personal characteristics in shaping the level of job satisfaction and organizational commitment of correctional employees.

METHODS

Data Source

The data used in this study is obtained from the 1994 Prison Social Climate Survey collected by the Federal Bureau of Prisons. The Prison Social Climate Survey was developed by William Saylor (1983), Deputy

Chief of the Office of Research and Evaluation in the Federal Bureau of Prisons. The survey provides a wealth of information, including demographic characteristics and employees' perceptions of the workplace. Not only is the Prison Social Climate Survey an excellent survey instrument, but the survey data has been used in other studies (e.g., Camp 1994; K. Wright and Saylor 1991; K. Wright et al. 1997).

Every year since 1988, the Prison Social Climate Survey has been administered to a representative segment of staff at each federal correctional facility. The employees are selected through a random stratified proportional probability sample design. The sample of employees selected is based upon a set of stratifying characteristics consisting of supervisory status, race, ethnicity, gender, and job category and is representative of an institution's workforce (Saylor 1983). Therefore, this data set is not limited to correctional officers but includes food service, inmate records, unit management, education, custody, medical, maintenance, and industry staff. Staff are assured that their responses are confidential (Camp 1994). With the Prison Social Climate Survey, it is possible to study staff across an entire agency. Most correctional staff studies have collected data limited to only one or a few prisons. Rarely have staff from an entire correctional agency been studied.

The 1994 administration of the Prison Social Climate Survey has a response rate of 88 percent (Camp and Steiger 1995). Out of 1,966 possible respondents, 1,704 are selected for use in this study since they have data on all the measures used in this study (i.e., listwise deletion is used).

Measures

Personal Characteristics

The personal characteristics of race, age, tenure, gender, and educational level are selected in this study and are used more as control than explanatory variables. Race is measured using a dichotomous variable with whites coded as 0 and nonwhites coded as 1. Age is measured in years. Gender is a dichotomous variable with males coded as 0 and females coded as 1. Tenure is measured by the number of months the respondent has worked for the Federal Bureau of Prisons. Finally, education is measured by asking the respondents their highest level of educational attainment. The education measure has five response categories of some high school but no degree, high school degree, some college but no degree or technical training, bachelor's degree, and graduate work or higher. The frequency percentages for the five educational categories respectively are as follows: 0.5, 20, 46, 18, and 16 percent.

Organizational Power

Organizational power refers to the ability to get things done in an organization (Kanter 1977). Workers need sufficient power to get their jobs done. Centralization is a component of organizational power (Heffron 1989). Another part of organizational power is controlling and disseminating information (Downs 1967). Therefore, the measures of organizational power tap into both the areas of centralization and instrumental communication. Organizational power is measured by a summated index of nine items (see appendix A) and has a Cronbach's alpha of 0.90. Cronbach's alpha (Cronbach 1951) is a measure of internal reliability which provides an estimate of how the questions used to form an index are related to one another. It is based on the average intercorrelation of the items that comprise the index (Carmines and Zeller 1979). In reference to Cronbach's alpha, Spector (1992) writes: "Internal consistency reflects the extent to which items intercorrelate with one another. Failure to intercorrelate is an indication that the items do not represent a common underlying construct. Internal consistency among a set of items suggests that they share common variance or that they are indicators of the same underlying construct" (30).

Cronbach's alpha, a widely used reliability measure in the social sciences, ranges from zero to one, and the closer alpha is to one, the stronger the internal consistency of the indicators of the particular index. It is important to remember that an alpha value is not an all or none proposition, but rather a matter of degrees of acceptability. A Cronbach's alpha coefficient higher than 0.70 is generally viewed as a good/high level of internal consistency of an index (Nunnally 1978); but alpha coefficients as low as 0.60 are viewed as being acceptable (Gronlund 1981). Cronbach's alpha values lower than 0.60 are viewed as unacceptable.

It is predicted that the measure for organizational power will have a positive impact on both job satisfaction and organizational commitment. The less power an employee perceives he or she has, the more likely that an employee will be dissatisfied with his or her job and with the organization as a whole. Most adults like to have a degree of input in what they do and how they accomplish their job (Bruce and Blackburn 1992). The greater degree of power that a person perceives that he or she has, the more that individual tends to be satisfied with the job, since the work reflects in part his or her decisions (Kouzes and Posner 1995). As Bruce and Blackburn (1992) write, "People accept what they help to create" (167). Similarly, the more power an employee has, the more likely they will bond with the organization. Workers identify and extend effort toward those organizations that give them greater degree of control.

Promotional Opportunity

Perceived promotional opportunity is another salient dimension of work environment (Price and Mueller 1986). The index for promotional opportunity is designed to measure a respondent's perception of promotional opportunity and practices and is measured by a summated index of three items (see appendix A) and has a Cronbach's alpha of 0.61.

It is predicted that the promotional opportunity index will have direct, positive effects on both organizational commitment and job satisfaction among federal correctional staff. Those employees who perceive themselves as having fair opportunities to move up in the organization are more likely to be committed to the organization (Lowe and Vodanovich 1995). Lincoln and Kalleberg (1990) write, "More than earnings, we think, opportunity for promotion is a key weapon in the corporatist arsenal for winning the compliance and commitment of employees: workers who perceive that they have a career with the company are more likely to be committed to its goals and fortunes over a long period of time" (105). On the other hand, correctional workers are unlikely to attach to an organization that they blame for a system that denies them promotional opportunities.

Moreover, a positive perception of promotional opportunity will influence employees' affective views of their jobs. Most workers have career aspirations and ambitions that they expect to be met by the organization over time (Lincoln and Kalleberg 1990). A perception of little chance for promotion leads many employees to view their job as a dead-end one, one that they are stuck with, and, as such, they are less likely to be satisfied with the job.

Organizational Fairness

The concept of organizational fairness represents an employee's perception of fairness in terms of official organizational recognition. This measure is rooted in the organizational justice theory. This theory is concerned with employees' perceptions of procedural justice (i.e., the perceived fairness of the methods in which important reward and punishment decisions concerning workers are made at the organizational level) and distributive justice (i.e., the fairness in terms of outcomes) (Lind and Tyler 1988). According to Mueller et al. (1994), organizational justice measures are concerned with the "degree to which rewards and punishments are related to performance inputs into the organization. It often is simply referred to as fairness" (186). In this study, organizational fairness is measured by a summated index of four items (see appendix A) and has a Cronbach's alpha of 0.82.

It is hypothesized that the index for organizational fairness will have direct, positive effects on organizational commitment and job satisfaction among correctional employees of the Federal Bureau of Prisons. Those employees who perceive the organizational recognition system as being fair are more likely to be committed to the organization (Lowe and Vodanovich 1995). Human beings desire recognition for hard work. They also want fair outcomes. Organizational fairness demonstrates the administration's respect for employees and produces a bridge of trust that ultimately strengthens the employees' commitment to the organization (Lind and Tyler 1988). Correctional workers are unlikely to attach to an organization that they blame for a system that denies them a chance to be properly and fairly recognized for their work. Similarly, perceptions of lack of recognition and unjust outcomes can lead to resentment on the part of the employee (Lowe and Vodanovich 1995). This resentment will ultimately affect their job satisfaction. When an employee feels betrayed by an unfair organizational process or outcome, it is hard for that employee to feel that his or her job is satisfying. Therefore, positive perceptions of organizational fairness will have a positive influence on correctional staff job satisfaction.

Supervision

A measure concerning supervision is included, since the relationship with supervisors is a significant feature of an employee's work environment (Cammann et al. 1983). This supervision measure is designed to tap a respondent's view of the openness in discussing issues and expectations with his or her supervisor(s) concerning work related matters. Supervision is measured as a single item (see appendix A).

Considerate supervisors are important in the development of positive attitudes among employees. Supervisors are normally seen by workers as providing guidance and support (Locke 1976). Supervisors are intended to give direction and feedback that is necessary for employees to complete their tasks within organizational specifications (Bruce and Blackburn 1992). For most staff, supervisors represent the organization. If supervisors are perceived as failing in their functions, particularly in terms of support and consideration, employees are less likely to be satisfied with their work and committed to the organization (S. Brown and Peterson 1993). On the other hand, employees who perceive positive supervisory consideration are more likely to report positive feelings toward their job and the organization. Therefore, the measure of supervision is predicted to have a positive effect on job satisfaction and organizational commitment among federal correctional staff.

Job Stress

In this study, job stress is defined as feelings of job-related hardness, tension, anxiety, worry, emotional exhaustion, and distress, and is measured by a summated index using six items (see appendix A) and has a Cronbach's alpha of 0.85.

While work is a significant source of stress (Davis and Newstrom 1985), the literature is unclear on the relationship between job stress and job satisfaction. While some scholars argue that job stress negatively impacts on job satisfaction (Ivancevich and Matteson 1980), other scholars contend that job dissatisfaction is a cause of job stress (Sager 1994). In this study, it is hypothesized that job satisfaction will have a negative effect on the stress. Those employees who enjoy their jobs will be less likely to feel stressed. Those correctional staff members who dislike their jobs will report higher levels of job stress because they dread going to a job they dislike.

Furthermore, job stress is hypothesized to have a negative relationship with organizational commitment among correctional staff. Staff members who are highly stressed will generally hold the organization responsible for permitting the stressful situation, particularly if it persists over a significant period of time. On the other hand, workers who perceive little work stress are more likely to be committed to the employing organization since they see the organization to be responsible, at least in part, for creating a peaceful work environment (Parasuraman and Alutto 1984).

Finally, perceived job stress is predicted to have a direct effect on turnover intent. Prolonged and intense stress has been found to have serious physical and mental consequences (Ivancevich and Matteson 1980). These consequences may influence a person to intend to leave the organization permanently (Parasuraman and Alutto 1984).

Job Satisfaction

A global, rather than facet, measure of job satisfaction is used in this study. Global job satisfaction is concerned with the broader domain of an individual's satisfaction with his or her overall job, rather than with specific facets, such as pay, coworkers, benefits, type of work done, and so forth (J. Cook et al. 1981). Global measures are more appropriate for measuring overall job satisfaction and have less methodological concerns than do measures which sum the facets to arrive at an overall measure of job satisfaction (Ironson et al. 1989). A total of five items are used to construct the global job satisfaction scale (see appendix A). The job satisfaction index has a Cronbach's alpha of 0.84.

Organizational Commitment

In line with the definition provided, an attitudinal measure of organizational commitment is used in this study. Unlike many organizations studied in the organizational sciences, there are two levels of commitment that must be accounted for when studying correctional staff: commitment to a particular correctional institution and commitment to the overall correctional agency. The Prison Social Climate Survey measures both institution and agency commitment. The eight items for institution and agency commitment are joined together to form an overall measure of organizational commitment (see appendix A). The organizational commitment index has a Cronbach alpha of 0.88.

Turnover Intent

Turnover intent is measured by a single item (see appendix A). Turnover intent is frequently measured by a single item (Price and Mueller 1986). While it is predicted that turnover intent will directly impact voluntary turnover among correctional staff, this premise can not be tested in this study. It is not possible to measure actual correctional staff turnover in this study using data from the Prison Social Climate Survey. The Prison Social Climate Survey is an anonymous questionnaire, and hence, cannot be linked to actual individuals to see whether they continue or leave employment with the Federal Bureau of Prisons in a given time frame. The next best method is to study turnover intent because it almost always and immediately precedes employee voluntary turnover. Additionally, other studies on noncriminal justice employees have been conducted that examined turnover intent, with no measure of actual turnover (e.g., Sager 1994).

Data Analysis Technique

The proposed causal model will be tested using path analysis. Path analysis is a powerful research method which allows for the examination of complex events in which there is more than one dependent variable and multiple independent variables. A dependent variable is the outcome that is of interest and is said to be dependent on other variables for its cause. Independent variables represent those forces that cause change in dependent variables. For example, a college student's grades are affected, in part, by the amount of time he or she spends studying. In this example, the number of hours spent studying is the independent variable, and course grade is the dependent variable because it depends on the amount of time studying.

A major strength of path analysis is the ability to decompose total effects into direct and indirect effects. Direct effects are the effects between one variable and another that is not moderated by any other variable. Indirect effects represent the impact that a variable has on another variable that is mediated by one or more other variables. For example, it is proposed that the work environment measures will affect correctional staff turnover intent indirectly through job satisfaction and organizational commitment.

There are three main areas of path analysis: path diagram, equations to correlations to estimate the effects of the independent variables on the dependent variable or variables, and decomposition of total effects. Path diagrams are a pictorial or graphical representation of the specified causal effects between variables for a given model (Bollen 1989). The graphical picture presented in Figure 9.1 is a basic path diagram.

The equation part of path analysis refers to estimating the direct effects between the independent variables and the dependent variable. The equations represent the relationships graphically presented in the path diagram. Therefore, path analysis is essentially a series of mathematical equations for each dependent variable in the path model. In this study, four equations need to be estimated, one for each dependent variable. The four dependent variables in this study are job satisfaction, job stress, organizational commitment, and turnover intent.

While there are several estimation techniques that could be used to estimate the direct effects for the four dependent variables of job satisfaction, job stress, organizational commitment, and turnover intent, the estimation technique of Ordinary Least Squares (OLS) regression was selected. OLS regression allows for the effects of a variable on a dependent variable to be estimated while controlling for the shared effects with the other independent variables. Additionally, OLS regression is frequently used in criminal justice research.

RESULTS AND DISCUSSION

Table 9.1 reports the descriptive statistics for the variables. The average age of the respondents is 35.7 years of age. About 26 percent are female correctional staff. Seventy-five percent of the respondents are white. Most respondents (i.e., 46 percent) have some college but no baccalaureate degree. The average tenure with the Federal Bureau of Prisons is 79.1 months (i.e., slightly less than 7 years). The average values for the organizational power, promotional opportunity, organizational fairness, and supervision measures are 3.40, 2.98, 3.33, and 3.92 respectively. The average values for job stress, job satisfaction, and organizational commitment are 2.28, 3.83, and 3.80. About 18 percent agree in some manner (i.e., somewhat agree, agree, or strongly agree) that they desire to leave employment with the Federal Bureau of Prisons. Finally, each of the variables have a significant amount of variation as indicated by the standard deviations, which represent the amount of spread of the cases around the mean value.

Job Satisfaction

An OLS regression equation was computed with job satisfaction as the dependent variable. The coefficient of determination (i.e., R-squared) for the job satisfaction equation is 0.31 and is statistically significant (F = 83.55, df = 9, $p < 0.001$). R-squared can be interpreted as the amount of variance explained in the dependent variable by the independent variables (i.e., the percentage of error reduced by using the independent variables to predict the dependent variable rather than using the mean of the dependent variable) (Draper and Smith 1966). Therefore, the model accounts for about 31 percent of the variance in job satisfaction. Variance is basically the amount of difference observed among the respondents on how they responded to the job satisfaction questions. For example, some staff may indicate that they are very satisfied with their jobs, other staff may respond that they are only somewhat satisfied with their jobs, and still other staff may indicate that they are dissatisfied with their jobs. The different responses are the variance observed in the job satisfaction index. Therefore, the selected independent variables explain about 31 percent of the different responses provided by respondents to the job satisfaction questions.

All the independent variables have a statistically significant impact on job satisfaction at a level of $p \leq 0.05$, except for the gender, race, and organizational fairness measures. Basically, $p < 0.05$ represents the chances of making a type I error. A type I error is when it is concluded that a variable has a real effect on another variable, when in fact there is no such relationship. For example, the chance of wrongly concluding that organizational power has a real impact on job satisfaction based upon the findings is 5 times out of 100. In other words, 95 times out of 100, the conclusion would be right. If there is no real relationship, the findings are probably due to random chance.

It would appear that there is no difference between male and female federal correctional staff in terms of job satisfaction once the effects of the other independent variables are controlled. This finding is consistent

---

Table 9.1 Descriptive Statistics

Variable	Alpha	Mean[a]	Std. Dev.[b]	Median[c]	Min.	Max.
Age		35.71	7.01	35.00	22	69
Gender		0.26	0.44	0.00	0	1
Race		0.25	0.43	0.00	0	1
Tenure		79.10	65.51	60.00	0	399
Education		3.29	0.98	3.00	1	5
Organizational power	0.90	3.40	1.42	3.56	0	6
Promotional opportunity	0.61	2.98	1.37	3.00	0	6
Organizational fairness	0.82	3.33	1.58	3.50	0	6
Supervision		3.92	1.90	5.00	0	6
Job stress	0.85	2.28	1.23	2.33	0	6
Job satisfaction	0.84	3.83	1.38	4.00	0	6
Organizational commitment	0.88	3.80	1.22	4.00	0	6
Turnover intent		1.72	1.88	1.00	0	6

Note: Age was measured in continuous years. Gender was measured with males coded as males=0 and females=1. Race was measured as whites=0 and nonwhites=1. Tenure was measured in months. Education was measured as follows: 1=less than high school, 2=high school diploma, 3=some college but no degree (including technical schooling), 4=bachelor's degree, 5=graduate work (including earning a degree). The specific questions for the remaining variables are presented in the appendix.

[a] The arithmetic mean is reported. To compute the arithmetic mean, the values are summed together and divided by the total number cases.

[b] Std. Dev. stands for standard deviation and is a measure of dispersion that represents how much the values are on average away from the mean. Therefore, the smaller the standard deviation, the tighter the cases are around the mean value, and the larger the value, the more spread out the cases from the mean value.

[c] The median represents the point in which half of cases fall below and half of the cases lie above.

with the results of other correctional staff studies, in which most have found no relationship between gender and job satisfaction (Hepburn and Knepper 1993; Jurik and Winn 1987; K. Wright and Saylor 1991). Additionally, the results indicate that among federal correctional staff there is no significant difference in job satisfaction between whites and nonwhites. The findings of no relationship between race and job satisfaction has been found in other correctional staff studies (Camp and Steiger 1995; Hepburn and Knepper 1993).

The measure of organizational fairness has no significant impact on job satisfaction among federal correctional staff after controlling for the other independent variables in the equation. This is probably because organizational fairness has more to do with how an individual perceives the employing organization than it does with how an individual perceives his or her job. Finally, age, tenure, education, supervision consideration, promotional opportunity, and organizational power all have positive effects on job satisfaction among federal correctional staff. A positive relationship means that an increase in the independent variable is associated with an increase in the dependent variable. Conversely, a decrease in the independent variable results in a decrease in the dependent variable. For example, as Federal Bureau of Prison staff members' age increases, so, too, does job satisfaction. Similar positive effects for these variables have been observed in other correctional staff studies (Camp and Steiger 1995; Hepburn and Knepper 1993; Jurik and Winn 1987).

Looking at the magnitude of effects, organizational power has the largest effect on job satisfaction, followed by promotional opportunity, and supervision. The personal variables have the least impact on job satisfaction. In order to determine the amount of variance accounted for in job satisfaction, the personal variables (i.e., age, tenure, gender, race, and education) and the work environment variables (i.e., supervision, organizational fairness, promotional opportunity, and organizational power) are entered as blocks independent of one another. R-squared for the personal variables is 0.06. R-squared for the work environment variables is 0.27, and R-squared for all the independent variables is 0.31. Therefore, as predicted, work environment factors account for a far greater proportion of job satisfaction of federal correctional staff than do personal characteristics.

Job Stress

Since it is theorized that job satisfaction affects job stress rather than the opposite, job stress is regressed on job satisfaction. Job satisfaction has a significant impact on job stress among federal correctional staff (p = 0.001). In other words, less than 1 time out 10,000 would it be observed that job satisfaction has a impact on job stress due to random chance. Therefore, there is a real negative relationship between job satisfaction and job stress. The negative relationship means that as job satisfaction increases, the level of job stress reported decreases.

Organizational Commitment

An OLS regression equation was estimated with organizational commitment as the dependent variable. R-squared for the organizational commitment equation is 0.53 and is statistically significant (F = 170.50, df = 11, p = 0.001). Therefore, the model accounts for about 53 percent of the variance in organizational commitment. All the independent variables have a statistically significant impact on organizational commitment at a level of $p\_$ 0.05, except for the gender, age, and education measures. As with job satisfaction, there appears to be no statistical difference between male and female federal correctional staff in terms of organizational commitment. This finding is consistent with the results of the few correctional studies that have looked at the antecedents of organizational commitment (Camp and Steiger 1995; K. Wright et al. 1997). Additionally, the results indicate that among federal correctional staff there is no significant relationship between age and organizational commitment. A similar nonsignificant relationship between age and organizational commitment has been found in other correctional staff studies (Camp and Steiger 1995; K. Wright et al. 1997). It is interesting to note that age did have a statistically significant impact on job satisfaction. It would seem that age is a significant antecedent of job satisfaction but not of organizational commitment among federal correctional staff. An insignificant relationship between education level and organizational commitment has also been observed in other correctional staff studies (Camp and Steiger 1995; Wright et al. 1997). As with age, it is interesting to note that education level has a statistically significant effect on job satisfaction. It would appear that education is a significant antecedent of job satisfaction but not of organizational commitment among federal correctional staff.

The measures for tenure, supervision, promotional opportunity, organizational power, organizational fairness, and job satisfaction all have statistically significant positive effects on organizational commitment among federal correctional staff. These findings are in line with what has been found in the few previous studies that looked at organizational commitment of correctional staff (Wright et al. 1997).

As previously indicated, the measure of organizational fairness had no significant impact on job satisfaction among federal correctional staff after controlling for the other independent variables in the equation. It does, however, have a positive impact on organizational commitment. Therefore, it appears that organizational fairness has a greater impact on how an individual perceives the employing organization than it does with how an individual perceives his or her job.

Job stress, as predicted, has a significant negative effect on organizational commitment. Additionally, nonwhite federal correctional staff members are statistically lower than white staff on organizational commitment. As previously mentioned, there is no significant difference between whites and nonwhites in terms of job satisfaction. While both have similar levels of job satisfaction, whites are more likely to have higher organizational commitment as compared to their nonwhite counterparts. These findings are consistent with what has been reported in past correctional staff studies (Robinson et al. 1992).

Looking at the magnitude of effects, promotional opportunity and organizational power have the largest effects on organizational commitment. Job satisfaction has the third largest direct effect on organizational commitment. This is an unexpected finding. Job satisfaction was expected to have the largest direct impact on organizational commitment among federal correctional staff. The reason that job satisfaction does not have the largest magnitude of effect on organizational commitment in this study could be due to how the variables were measured, or that among federal correctional staff, job satisfaction does not have the largest impact on organizational commitment, or a combination of both.

The personal variables, the work environment variables and job stress, and job satisfaction are entered as blocks independent of one another to see the amount of variance explained of organizational commitment among federal correctional staff. R-squared for the personal variables as a block is only 0.01; for the work environment variables and job stress, 0.49; with only job satisfaction is 0.26; and for all the independent variables is 0.53. Therefore, work environment, job stress, and job satisfaction account for a far greater proportion of the variance of organizational commitment for federal correctional staff than do personal characteristics.

Turnover Intent

An OLS regression equation with turnover intent as the dependent variable was estimated. R-squared for the turnover intent model is 0.40 and is statistically significant (F = 137.37, df = 8, p = 0.001). Therefore, the model accounts for about 40 percent of the variance in turnover intent. All the independent variables have a statistically significant impact on organizational commitment at $p = 0.05$. Age and tenure both have a negative impact on turnover intent among federal correctional staff, which is consistent with Becker's (1960) side-bet theory. As employees get older and their tenure increases in an organization, the more sunken costs they have in the organization, and, as such, are less likely to intend to leave. Conversely, education has a positive effect on turnover intent among federal correctional workers. This positive relationship between education and turnover intent was also found by Jurik and Winn (1987) among correctional officers at a Western correctional complex. It could be that educated correctional workers have greater ease in finding alternative employment.

Gender has a negative effect on turnover intent. Specifically, female federal correctional employees are less likely to express turnover intent than are male employees. This is in contradiction to those correctional staff studies that found females were higher in turnover behavior than their male counterparts (Camp 1994) or that there was no significant relationship (Jurik and Winn 1987). There are two explanations for this inconsistency. First, the relationship could vary by the correctional agency that is being studied. This study is looking at federal correctional staff. Based upon personal experience in the Federal Prison System, female employees in the Federal Prison System operate in a friendlier environment than do their female counterparts in many state and local correctional agencies. Second, federal female correctional staff may remain in employment in the field of corrections as a career choice, whereas males may be more likely to accept a job in a correctional setting as temporary employment until something else better comes along.

Race has a positive impact on federal correctional staff turnover intent. Specifically, nonwhite federal staff members are more likely than white staff to express turnover intent. Jurik and Winn (1987) also found that nonwhites are more likely than whites are to leave employment with a correctional agency. It could be that nonwhites perceive the working environment as more hostile than do white workers.

Job stress, as predicted, has a positive effect on turnover intent among federal correctional staff. This finding is consistent with the empirical literature across a wide variety of organizations. However, both job satisfaction and organizational commitment have negative effects on turnover intent. Negative effects by both job satisfaction and organizational commitment on turnover intent have also been observed across a wide variety of organizations (Lambert 1999).

Looking at the magnitude of effects, organizational commitment, as predicted, has the largest effect on turnover intent among federal correctional staff, followed closely by job satisfaction. Job stress has the third largest direct effect on turnover intent, and has only a third to a half of the impact on turnover intent as compared to job satisfaction and organizational commitment. The personal variables have the least impact on turnover intent among federal correctional workers. Personal characteristics only have one-fourth the impact on turnover intent as compared to organizational commitment, and a third of the effect as compared to job satisfaction.

In order to determine the impact of each group of variables on turnover intent, the personal variables, and job stress, job satisfaction, and organizational commitment were entered as blocks independent of one another. Blocks independent of one another means that each set of independent variables was used alone without the variables in the other sets. R-squared for just the personal variables is 0.04; R-squared for the job stress, job satisfaction, and organizational commitment is 0.37; while R-squared for job satisfaction and organizational commitment is 0.36. Finally, R-squared for all the independent variables is 0.40. Therefore, job satisfaction and organizational commitment account for a far greater proportion of turnover intent variance among federal correctional staff than do personal characteristics and job stress.

Direct, Indirect, and Total Effects

Until this point, all the effects discussed have been direct effects. Besides direct effects, path analysis allows for the calculation of indirect and total effects. As previously discussed, indirect effects are the effects between two variables that are mediated by at least one intervening variable (Bollen 1989). Indirect effects are calculated by multiplying the direct standardized coefficients of the direct causal paths leading to the dependent variable of interest. Total effects of an independent variable on a particular dependent variable are calculated by adding the direct and indirect effects together. Table 9.2 reports the direct, indirect, and total effects for turnover intent.

Age, tenure, education, gender, and race have both direct and indirect effects on turnover intent. The indirect effects are through job satisfaction and organizational commitment. Supervision, organizational fairness, promotional opportunity, and organizational power only have indirect effects on turnover intent. The indirect effects are mediated by both job satisfaction and organizational commitment. Of the work environment measures, organizational power has the largest total

Table 9.2 Direct, Indirect, and Total Effects on Turnover Intent

Variable	Direct Effects	Indirect Effects	Total Effects
Age	-0.06	-0.04	-0.09
Education	0.06	-0.04	-0.10
Gender	-0.09	0.00	-0.08
Race	0.06	0.03	0.09
Tenure	-0.06	-0.04	-0.10
Supervision	0.00	-0.07	-0.07
Promotional opportunity	0.00	-0.16	-0.16
Organizational fairness	0.00	-0.05	-0.05
Organizational power	0.00	-0.20	-0.20
Job stress	0.12	0.05	0.17
Job satisfaction	-0.24	-0.13	-0.37
Organizational commitment	-0.38		-0.38

Note: Direct effects are the effects between one variable on another that is not moderated by any other variable. In other words, direct effects are the direct paths between two variables. Indirect effects represent the impact that a variable has on another variable that is mediated by one or more other variables.

impact on turnover intent among federal correctional staff, followed by the promotional opportunity. Supervision and organizational fairness have the smallest total effects. Moreover, the four work environment variables all have larger indirect effects on turnover intent than do the five personal characteristics. In fact, the indirect effects of the work environment variables on turnover intent are either about the same or larger than the direct effects of the personal characteristics. Finally, the total effects of the five personal characteristics on turnover intent are similar to each other in terms of size.

In the correctional literature it is common to test only for the direct effects of work environment measures on turnover intent or turnover of correctional staff. Therefore, turnover intent is regressed on all the variables in the path model. Age, tenure, race, education, job stress, job satisfaction, and organizational commitment all have statistically significant effects on turnover intent, while supervision, organizational fairness, and organizational power all have statistically insignificant effects on turnover intent among federal correctional staff, and promotional opportunity only reaches statistical significance at a $p < 0.05$ level.

If only the direct effects were examined, one would dismiss work environment factors as not having an impact on correctional employee turnover intent, let alone actual turnover, since turnover intent mediates many of the effects on actual turnover. Nevertheless, as evident by the total effects reported in Table 9.2, such a conclusion would be in error. While work environment factors have significant total effects on turnover intent, these effects are mainly indirect, mediated primarily through job satisfaction and organizational commitment. By dismissing work environment factors as not having a significant effect, a researcher would be missing the complex process that actually occurs during the formation of turnover intent by the employee and ultimately voluntary turnover. As predicted, the effects of the work environment on turnover intent are indirect and are mediated by job satisfaction and organizational commitment.

Organizational commitment, as positioned in the path model, has only a direct effect on turnover intent, and, as such, the total effects of organizational commitment are equal to the direct effects. Job stress has both direct and indirect effects on turnover intent among federal correctional staff. The indirect effects of job stress are mediated by organizational commitment. Job satisfaction also has both direct and indirect effects on turnover intent, and the indirect effects are mediated by job stress and organizational commitment. Organizational commitment has the largest total effect on turnover intent among federal correctional staff, followed very closely by job satisfaction. While all the total effects for organizational commitment are direct, over a third of the total effects for job satisfaction are indirect. The total effects of job stress on turnover intent are largely direct and positive. Finally, the total effects of job stress on turnover intent are less than half the size as the total effects for job satisfaction and organizational commitment among federal correctional staff. As predicted, job satisfaction and organizational commitment have the greatest impact on turnover intent of federal correctional staff.

CONCLUSION

The results support the process presented in Figure 9.1 and the core hypotheses made in this study. The work environment is very important in shaping job satisfaction of federal correctional staff. Furthermore, work environment and job satisfaction are key antecedents for shaping organizational commitment. Both job satisfaction and organizational commitment are important antecedents in shaping turnover intent among federal staff, and account for a much larger variance of turnover intent than do personal characteristics. In addition, the work environment has significant effects on turnover intent, and these effects are mainly indirect. By failing to take into account indirect effects, one risks dismissing factors that are in fact critical in the complex process of turnover intent.

In the introduction, it was stated that in the field of corrections, personal characteristics are still given undue focus, while work environment factors fail to receive the attention they warrant. The results of this study suggest that this view is in error. If correctional administrators are truly interested in reducing turnover intent of their staff, it is recommended that they invest resources in improving employee job satisfaction and organizational commitment. In order to build job satisfaction and organizational commitment, effort should be focused on improving the work environment. Key areas of the work environment identified in this study are organizational power, promotional opportunity, supervision, and organizational fairness. Of these, organizational power appears to be the most important. Therefore, it is recommended that correctional administrators improve the flow of important information (i.e., communication) and allow for greater employee participation in decision making, particularly in the area of job autonomy. Similar recommendations for better essential communication and for allowing greater employee participation, regardless of the type of organization, are abundant in the literature.

Implementation of such broad recommendations may be easier said than done, particularly in the bureaucratic setting of most correctional agencies. Nevertheless, it is still recommended that serious consideration be given to improving job satisfaction and organizational commitment of correctional employees through changes in the work environment. Other than reducing turnover intent and other negative work outcomes, higher levels of staff job satisfaction and organizational commitment are also predicted to have positive outcomes in other areas, such as improved home life for workers, improved staff–inmate interactions, and improved employee performance. The knowledge of and ability to understand the antecedents of correctional employee work attitudes and behaviors are critical for all parties involved.

Aside from specific implications for correctional institutions, this chapter also illustrates that there are multiple layers of criminal justice theories. Some theories focus on the aggregate level, while others attempt to explain variations found at the individual level. Additionally, theories are not constrained by inputs and outputs found across the study of criminal justice. Criminal justice theories can examine what the editors of this book call "throughputs." Throughputs lie between the inputs and outputs, and are elements such as values, beliefs, perceptions, and attitudes. Throughputs are appropriate and salient areas for criminal justice theories to address.

NOTE

1. The author thanks the anonymous reviewers for their comments and suggestions. The author also thanks Janet Lambert, Ferris State University, for her help in editing and proofreading this chapter. I am indebted to William Saylor and Scott Camp, of the Office of Research and Evaluation of the Federal Bureau of Prisons, for the information they provided on the Prison Social Climate Survey. I am grateful to the Federal Bureau of Prisons for granting permission to use the findings from my dissertation in this chapter. Finally, Drs. David Duffee, Robert Hardt, David McDowell, Hans Toch, and Robert Worden are thanked for providing valuable comments while serving as members of my dissertation committee.

APPENDIX

Items Used to Create Indexes Used in Chapter 9

The following items are measured with the response categories of strongly disagree, disagree, somewhat disagree, undecided, somewhat agree, agree, and strongly agree. To form a summated index for those concepts with multiple items, the items were summed together and the resulting value was divided by the number of items.

ORGANIZATIONAL POWER

1. I have authority I need to accomplish my work objectives.
2. My supervisor engages me in the planning process, such as developing work methods and procedures for my job.
3. I have a great deal of say over what has to be done on my job.
4. My supervisor asks my opinion when a work-related problem arises.
5. The information I get through formal communication channels helps me perform my job effectively.
6. I am told promptly when there is a change in policy, rules, or regulations that affects me.
7. My supervisor gives me adequate information on how well I am performing.

8. I often receive feedback from my supervisor for good performance.
9. Information I receive about my performance usually comes too late for it to be any use to me (reverse coded).

PROMOTIONAL OPPORTUNITY

1. Under the present system, promotions are seldom related to employee performance (reverse coded).
2. There are job advancement opportunities in the BOP [Bureau of Prisons] for me.
3. There are job advancement opportunities in this facility for me.

ORGANIZATIONAL FAIRNESS

1. The standards used to evaluate my performance have been fair and objective.
2. My last annual performance rating presented a fair and accurate picture of my actual job performance.
3. My own hard work will lead to recognition as a good performer.
4. I will get a cash award or unscheduled pay increase if I perform especially well.

SUPERVISION

My supervisor demonstrates sensitivity to such personal needs as shift and leave requests by fairly balancing them with the needs of the facility.

JOB SATISFACTION

1. I would be more satisfied with some other job at this facility than I am with my present job (reverse coded).
2. My BOP [Bureau of Prisons] job is usually worthwhile.
3. My BOP job is usually interesting to me.
4. My BOP job suits me very well
5. If I have a chance, I will change to some other job at the same rate of pay at this facility (reverse coded).

ORGANIZATIONAL COMMITMENT

Agency level

1. The BOP is better than any of the other correctional agencies (e.g., state).
2. I have a good opinion of the BOP most of the time.
3. Most of the time the BOP [Bureau of Prisons] is run very well.
4. I am usually satisfied with the BOP.
5. If I remain in corrections, I would prefer to remain with the BOP.

Institutional level

1. This facility is the best in the whole BOP.
2. I would rather be stationed at this facility than any other I know about.
3. I would like to continue to work at this facility.

TURNOVER INTENT

I am currently looking for or considering another job outside the BOP [Bureau of Prisons].

The following items are measured with the response categories of never, very rarely, rarely, now and then, often, very often, and all the time.

JOB STRESS

During the past six months, how often have you experienced ...

1. A feeling that you have become harsh toward people since you took this job.
2. A feeling of worry that this job is hardening you emotionally.
3. A feeling of being emotionally drained at the end of the workday.
4. A feeling that you treat some inmates as if they were impersonal objects.
5. A feeling that working with people all day is really a strain for you.
6. A feeling of being fatigued when you get up in the morning and have to face another day on the job.

10

EXAMINING CORRECTIONAL RESOURCES
A Cross-Sectional Study of the States

Edmund F. McGarrell and David E. Duffee

INTRODUCTION

This chapter examines the causes of correctional spending. We will compare the dominant, mainstream political account of why spending on corrections varies with two less popular explanations for state spending on punishment. The dominant view, the one that is usually taken for granted in political speeches, media accounts, and neighborly conversations, is that more crime produces more punishment, which costs more money. In other words, the popular account is that more spending is an inevitable reaction to the behavior of criminals. This view has also been called the "functionalist explanation" (Barlow, Barlow, and Johnson 1996) or the "consensus" explanation (Bernard and Engel 2001).

To this account, we will compare two other accounts of correctional spending. In developing these other accounts, we will draw on three different theoretical traditions. One of these is the sociology of social control most notably associated with the late Allen Liska and his colleagues, who describe their approach as drawing on the "conflict perspective" (Liska 1992a; Liska and Chamlin 1984).

Within this general conflict approach to social control, there are both "structural accounts" and "elite" accounts (Liska 1992a) for the nature and level of social control. In the former, social structure and culture create pressures that permeate society for control of some groups of people, over and above the contribution of those groups to crime, and independent of the decisions of particular people. In the latter, elite theories, particular groups such as economic elites or administrative elites seek control over other groups, such as the poor or minorities. One form of elite theory proposes that a "managerial elite," such as correctional professionals, argue for social policies that are in their interest (Inverarity 1992; Lipsky 1980).

The second tradition that we will rely upon for our theory is the "genealogical" theory associated with Foucault (1979) and his followers, such as David Garland (2001) and Jonathan Simon (1993). These scholars seek to explain the evolution of current social discourses and practice, such as beliefs about and practices of crime control, from a combination of past practices and changes in social structure and culture. We will provide a detailed example of Garland's and Simon's arguments below.

The third and final literature on which we draw is "neoinstitutionalism" (Kraatz and Zajac 1996). There are several branches of institutional theory concerned with culture, politics, and organizations (March and Olsen 1984; Meyer and Rowan 1977; Scott 1995). The branch of most concern to us here is the institutional theory of organizations. As described by Renauer in chapter 6, organizational institutionalism looks at the interplay among political, social, and cultural forces in society and public organizations, which administer major social institutions, such as education and corrections. In chapter 6, Renauer asked what elements in the local and national environments of police departments would pressure departments toward more or less engagement of neighborhoods in social control. In this chapter, we ask almost the opposite question: what elements in the "correctional sector" or correctional environment would push for greater or lesser investment in state control (particularly incarceration)? We will go into greater depth about the institutionalized environment of corrections below.

Correctional genealogy is primarily, but not only, a European development. The sociology of social control and institutional theory are primarily, but by no means exclusively, developments in the United States. There is so much overlap among these theoretical approaches that it is hard at times to tell them apart, and we shall feel free to blend them. Indeed, Garland (2001) says that his most recent study is both a genealogical history and a sociology of social control. While Garland does not explicitly mention institutional theory, much of his argument, as we shall see below, comports well with that tradition as well. Despite this intellectual overlap in research questions and theoretical approaches, these three theoretical traditions are currently more separate than integrated. To some extent, this chapter is concerned with theory integration, as discussed by Snipes and Maguire in chapter 2.

One difference in method between this chapter and typical genealogical study is that the latter is, as the name implies, historical and longitudinal. It tries to identify the confluence of forces over time that produces current practice. While that approach is highly valuable, for reasons that Snipes and Maguire describe in chapter 2 (see the discussion of the historical dimension), it can be, as both Garland (2001) and Simon (1993) admit, difficult to test. There are, after all, only so many histories to come by, so quantitative examination is limited and expensive, although by no means impossible. What the reader will see us doing here is converting the longitudinal, genealogical argument into a cross-sectional, over place argument. That is, if Garland is right about some of the forces that have affected British and U.S. policy over time, is it possible to look for differences in those forces across different states?

PUNISHMENT EXPENDITURES

Before we get more specific about building a theory from these diverse traditions, a word about our research question is appropriate. As prison populations expanded at unprecedented rates since 1974, costs of building and maintaining correctional facilities also exploded. From 1975 to 1985, costs of operating correctional facilities in the United States increased by 240 percent. Indeed, the increase in the costs of corrections was 50 percent greater than the increase in total state and local governmental expenditures for the period from 1971 to 1985 (McDonald 1989). In per capita terms, corrections spending by state and local governments increased 218 percent from 1960 to 1985, the fastest growing policy area in that period (Yondorf and Warnock 1989; see also Taggart and Winn 1991). State aid to local governments for corrections was the fastest growing category of state aid to local governments from 1970 to 1987, increasing 400 percent in that period, easily outstripping aid for education, for example.

This chapter focuses on correctional expenditures in the mid-1980s, toward the end of the period described above. We chose mid-1980 data because that period provided some good institutional data that were not readily available at other periods (Taggart and Winn [1991] examined similar data for similar reasons). We are trying to demonstrate the value of a theoretic approach, and therefore are not too concerned, immediately, about the currency of the data. However, it is relevant to indicate that public spending on corrections increased steadily through the 1990s for reasons that, according to Garland (2001), are the same as the ones we will examine for the 1980s.

The trend data sketched above certainly indicate the importance of asking why punishment cost varies over time. This question becomes even more intriguing when we realize that crime was stable or dropping for much of that time period, at least suggesting the need for factors other than crime to explain the increase (Barlow et al. 1996; Garland 2001). However, does it make equal sense to ask why correctional expenditures vary from place to place? Using juvenile corrections data from 1979, the National Council on Crime and Delinquency (NCCD) answered in the affirmative (Krisberg, Litsky, and Schwartz 1984). The NCCD study noted large differences from state to state in admissions to detention, length of stay, youth confinement in adult facilities, confinement conditions, and expenditures. The Council could not explain away the differences on the basis of crime or arrest data. Looking at Western European countries in the 1980s, Leslie Wilkins (1991) noted that incarceration rates differed more than crime rates. While he did not look directly at expenditures, the correlation between use of imprisonment and correctional expenses would be very high. Using 1984 data, Taggart and Winn (1991) found large per capita expenditure differences across the forty-eight contiguous states in the United States. One motivation for explaining these differences across place would be the potential for finding some causal factors that are controllable and can then be the focus of interventions to control increasing costs over time (Garland 2001; Taggart and Winn 1991; Wilkins 1991). But what are these causes and can they be manipulated?

In this chapter, we consider the role of technical, political, and cultural factors in determining the level of resources available for corrections in the fifty states. We are interested in how variation in the task and institutional environments of corrections systems affect levels of correctional resources. Are variations in the state level structures for mobilizing and distributing correctional resources differentially effective in securing funds for the accomplishment of correctional objectives? Do these characteristics of the correctional bureaucracies affect the level of correctional resources beyond the effect of technical demands for resources? Do social structure and demographic character of states make correctional claims for resources more compelling in some states than others?

THE CHARACTERISTICS OF
INSTITUTIONALIZED ENVIRONMENTS

Our application of institutional theory to the study of corrections follows what Scott (1987) has referred to as the institutionalized environments approach. This approach observes that some societal sectors, or functional areas, are more governed by symbols of form and means than by assessments of outcome. Some environments are more richly endowed with deeply held and often taken-for-granted beliefs about the organization and practice of certain social endeavors (Meyer and Rowan 1977). For example, particular divisions of labor, employee qualifications, and programs may be imposed on organizations if they are to be granted legitimacy (Feeley 1989; Garland 2001; Warren et al. 1974). These forces, according to institutional theory, are embedded in organizational environments and are adopted by organizations in good-faith demonstrations of adherence to modern practice, without much attempt (or capacity) to link such elements to desired outcomes (such as recidivism rates or improved reading ability). Organizational survival depends on conformity more than performance (Crank and Langworthy 1992). Institutional theory assumes that other societal sectors, particularly the profit sector, may be more heavily controlled by tangible outcomes, such as return on investment and market share, so that organizational behaviors are better predicted by competitive advantage and resource dependencies than by conformity to public myths about appropriate organizational conduct. While these technical and economic forces may also be important in the public sector, institutional theory alerts us to the importance of political and cultural influences as well (Garland 2001).

The institutional perspective, therefore, suggests that various characteristics of institutionalized environments may have economic as well as structural consequences for organizations, particularly, as in the case of corrections, when measures of technical proficiency are ambiguous and politically controversial (J. W. Meyer, Scott, and Deal 1983). In terms of the present study of allocation of resources to corrections, this suggests that conformance to widely held beliefs about good organizational practices might be an important factor in securing funding. Actual allocation of funds for corrections will be influenced by a number of elements of the task and institutional environment of the correctional sector (McGarrell and Duffee 1995).

Certainly, the dominant political message that more deviance produces more government control expenditure has some level of credence. Treating crime as the engine for a technically rational demand for punishment has some merit: more criminals may mean more inmates and more resources for punishing. The warden has more mouths to feed. But these are marginal differences and may be offset by economies of scale (the marginal increase for punishing two inmates is not twice the cost of punishing one). Moreover the technical–rational story propounded by our official policy makers sounds circular and suspicious. More crime leads to more punishment. But less crime also leads to more punishment (usually under the argument that punishment works). Additionally, there are no inevitable connections between levels and seriousness of crime and levels of punishment, even under the notion that retribution must take place. Commensurate punishment, and its costs, are set through some political and social process and vary from place to place (see Wilkins [1991] for an elaboration of these arguments).

THE CORRECTIONAL SECTOR

Our theoretical approach to variation in punishment expenditures follows Scott and Meyer, who use the term societal sector to refer to "all organizations within a society supplying a given type of product or service together with their associated organizational sets: suppliers, financiers, regulators, and the like" (1983, 129). But, in addition to the organizations in a sector, a sector would include the values and beliefs about their practices, a phenomenon that Warren called an "institutionalized thought structure." Garland's (2001) and Warren's term (Warren, Rose, and Bergunder 1974) is field rather than sector; however, we think these terms are synonymous.

The correctional sector is comprised of focal organizations, such as state correctional departments, in interaction with their task and institutional environments. The task environment consists of those forces affecting economic/technical processes of organization. In subsequent sections we refer to these forces as the rational–technical base of correctional structures and outcomes. In terms of this study, key elements of the task environment include factors such as the crime-related demand for correctional resources and the resource munificence of the state (i.e., state wealth). States with higher levels of crime should produce more clients for the corrections system and wealthier states should be able to provide higher levels of resources for all state functions including corrections.

The institutional environment comprises the cultural and political forces affecting the organization. It consists of values, norms, and rationalized beliefs about both the efficacy of the correctional function and the organizational structure of "good" correctional practice. In terms of norms and values, we are primarily concerned with variation among the states in the relative use of incarceration as a response to crime. We refer to this as the value base of the corrections function.

In addition, previous work on institutionalized environments suggests two related sets of characteristics that might describe the level and nature of the institutional environment in the correctional sector. One set of variables has to do with the relative strength of the formally organized forces in a society and hence their varying capacity to exert control on societal activity. In particular, we are interested in the role of the professions and similar organized interests of a given sector. The other set has to do with the formal structural arrangements of these institutionalizing forces, such as whether they are unified or fragmented, centralized or decentralized (Carroll, Goodstein, and Gyenes 1988; Scott and Meyer 1983). In subsequent sections, we devote attention to dominant trends in the institutional environment of corrections as a way of deriving hypotheses as to how these characteristics, referred to as the organizing capacity of the correctional sector, might affect levels of resources for corrections.

THE SYSTEMATIZATION OF CORRECTIONS

In 1932, the Wickersham Commission decried the feudalism of corrections in the states and, in 1939, President Roosevelt's First National Parole Conference proclaimed it an outrageously corrupt system, bereft of either bureaucratic or professional standards (National Parole Conference 1939). Administrative reforms in corrections followed shortly but did not really take off until after World War II, when the systems concepts promoted by Secretary of Defense McNamara were applied to domestic problems (Duffee 1990). About twenty-five states reorganized their correctional bureaucracies from 1950 to 1980, with the most potent reforms being the creation of centralized departments of correction and the state takeover or regulation of local correctional services (Council of State Governments 1977).

The most commonly spoken rationale for the structural changes in correctional services was provision of better services. Proponents of unification, state takeover, and state regulation promised improved coordination among units, better quality and enhanced continuity of services to offenders, and heightened administrative accountability (National Advisory Commission on Criminal Justice Standards and Goals 1973; Nelson, Cushman, and Harlow 1980; President's Commission on Law Enforcement and Administration of Justice, 1967a; Skoler

1976). The formal rationale was one of increased technical proficiency in the conduct of correctional tasks.

While increased technical proficiency is a possible result of such reorganizations, improved outcomes by public institutions, including corrections, are quite difficult to demonstrate (Nokes 1960). We can view the major swing to the right in correctional policy since the 1970s as an example of the public collapse of an institutionalized myth (Meyer and Rowan 1977). In the corrections case, the rehabilitation myth emerged in the 1930s, as the new social science based professions gained power (Dession 1938). Since the mid-1970s, we have witnessed the substitution of a new set of beliefs about good correctional practice — retribution, deterrence, incapacitation, and the management of risk (Feeley and Simon 1992; Garland 2001; Simon 1993). The technical proficiency of the new beliefs is just as difficult to demonstrate as was the technical proficiency of rehabilitation. However, demonstrations of technical accomplishment will be infrequently demanded and studiously avoided, so long as the forms used satisfy public notions of what works. These beliefs will have considerable impact on the administration of corrections.

Thus, while centralization and unification may or may not have affected technical proficiency, institutional theory suggests that to the extent that such structures are associated with institutionalized beliefs regarding sound or enlightened practice, centralized and unified departments may fare better in the struggle for resources. Similarly, to the extent that centralization and unification lead to more organized and powerful correctional bureaucracies, such structures may be associated with higher levels of resources (Taggart and Winn 1991).

The main argument that we have pulled from our disparate theoretical sources is generally as follows. There has been a major shift in the economy and in social structure in the United States, although this shift has been differentially felt in the states. It has had particularly marked effects in economically developed states that have urban concentrations of poverty and ethnic and racial difference. Where these changes have occurred, the threat to the political elite will be higher and the middle class who have escaped urban setting will be more mean spirited. In such places a "culture of penal welfarism" has given way to a "culture of control" (Garland 2001).

However, in these states, structures associated with the older penology, which sought to overcome the social disadvantage of correctional clients, are still very active and help to shape current policy and practice (Garland 2001; Feeley and Simon 1992). These more developed bureaucracies and correctional work forces developed and deployed tools of prediction and classification in the allocation of correctional treatment resources. Those resources have now been retracted or diminished, but the agents are still responsible for offender outcomes. They have taken to applying their people technologies to "managing risk" (Feeley and Simon 1992) rather than changing offender behavior.

The coupling of the new value system that values punishment highly and the professional capacity to marshal resources for people control has led to boomerang effects in the social control process. For example, Simon (1993) argues that the California parole system was the best endowed for provision of treatment and reintegration services, but that the supervision practices that were designed for reintegration are now used for rapid revocation. In the more professionalized systems, the new punitive policies are more successful because the more advanced social control agents are best able to make the case for the technical inevitability of greater social control responding to greater crime.

In summary, the new economy and demographic changes do cause more crime and more opportunities for punishment. But it is changes in political culture, the politics of threat, which makes punishment more severe (such as more use of incarceration). It is the professional and highly organized correctional work force that can connect criminogenic forces (such as unemployment and drug use) with punishment (such as by revocation) and can best make the political demand for punishment appear most legitimate (Feeley 1989; Simon 1993).

Our principal interest is in the last part of this three-legged stool: the nature of the "organizing capacity" of the correctional sector itself. Are some correctional structures and some correctional work forces better able to secure funding than others, controlling for the crime effects and controlling for the relative threat in the political environment?

CHARACTERISTICS AFFECTING ORGANIZING CAPACITY OF THE CORRECTIONAL SECTOR

On the basis of these trends in corrections, and following the lead of Scott and Meyer (1983), we have selected five sector variables for initial study. An institutional explanation of societal functions, such as fiscal support for corrections, would propose that these characteristics can have an impact on such functions independent of (but not instead of) economic/technical explanations, such as the number of persons to be processed (McGarrell and Duffee 1995).

Professionalization

One possible measure of the degree of institutionalization in a sector is the extent to which professional bodies are organized and exert influence over how societal functions should be achieved. We would expect states with greater professionalization to spend relatively more on corrections, because the professions should increase the legitimacy of a societal function with which they are associated and impose hiring qualifications and practices that are more expensive.

Unionization

The institutional literature relies more heavily on professionalization than unionization as an institutionalizing force. Since there are many quasi-professions in corrections, and since the state dominates practice more than in other sectors (and perhaps thereby reducing professional influence), we thought unionization was another institutionalizing force to be examined. Correctional officer unions, in particular, have become increasingly concerned with the conditions of work and with the ratio of workers to offenders. While professionalism and unionism can often conflict, we think both forces should work together for the increase of resources for corrections (Lipsky 1980).

In addition to these two characteristics of the correctional staff, states vary considerably in the structures of their corrections bureaucracies. While some overall trends have been cited in the introduction, there are still remarkable differences in the ways in which corrections is structured from state to state. Among the variables that we thought could be important were fragmentation/unification, federalization/concentration, and size.

Fragmented Structure

States vary in the number of separate agencies that have correctional responsibilities. We expect greater fragmentation to increase the level of correctional spending, on the presumption that multiple voices speaking for corrections will increase legitimacy as well as increase the administrative costs associated with provision of correctional services. There is a competing hypothesis, however, that fragmentation would reduce costs by introducing competition among agencies and introduce greater concern for efficiency in the evaluation of correctional sector activities. In this second hypothesis, a single, unified correctional bureaucracy that combined community and institutional punishments would speak louder than separate agencies about correctional needs.

Federalization

States vary on the degree to which correctional functions are concentrated at the state level or shared with local authorities (federalized). The movement toward state takeover of probation may be seen as a trend toward concentration, while the diffusion of community corrections acts (Musheno et al. 1989) may be seen as a countertrend toward federalization. We expect that federalization should increase the level of resources for corrections, again by increasing the number of organizational constituents favoring correctional expenditure. However, again there is a counterhypothesis about this structural characteristic. Garland (2001, 202–203) appears to conclude that the state-concentrated structure is significantly different from the federalized structure. In his view, the federalized, deconcentrated forms of social control may be an emergent countertrend to state-centered social control. Lyons (1999) may be making the same argument about policing. In his study of Seattle community policing, Lyons claims that reciprocal relationships between neighborhood and police department are decentered forms of social control. His analysis of the Seattle police department (SPD) claims that the SPD successfully co-opted neighborhood forces, making them adjuncts to state control, and diminishing reciprocity, or federalization. Garland and Lyons's arguments would say that federalization spreads not just the responsibility for corrections but also the form of control (from state centered to a combination of state and community controls). If they are correct, then federalization may reduce correctional cost.

Size of Bureaucracy

The final structural variable is the size of the state corrections bureaucracy, measured as the number of employees in state correctional agencies. Size is perhaps the most frequently examined structural variable in organizational analysis. We would expect size to generate internal complexity in organizations, which in turn may lead to fragmentation of the bureaucracy itself. Second, we would expect larger correctional work forces, independent of their unionization or professionalization, to be more potent political advocates of correctional expenditure.

ADDITIONAL CHARACTERISTICS OF TASK AND INSTITUTIONAL ENVIRONMENTS

The sector characteristics described above comprise key aspects of the institutional environment of the correctional sector. Structural factors appear important because to the extent these factors conform with institutionalized beliefs about good practice they may lead to greater legitimacy and resources for the organizations that display them. Additionally, sector characteristics such as professionalization, unionization, and size may indicate the greater organizing capacity of correctional interests and lead to greater effectiveness in obtaining resources. Clearly, however, these are not the only characteristics influencing levels of correctional resources. Correctional spending is also likely to be affected by other aspects of the institutional environment such as dominant norms and values, and by elements of the task environment such as the number of persons to be supervised. Consequently, additional variables of the institutional and task environments should be included in the explanation of correctional resources. The other variables in this analysis include the following:

Size

Size was previously described as a bureaucratic trait of the correctional sector that is predicted to relate to increased spending due to specialization and increased political advocacy. Size, however, is also a measure of the "technical" or economic demand for correctional resources within the state. States with larger correctional systems will likely have to spend more on corrections (see M. C. Brown and Warner [1992] for a similar argument about the size of police departments). Thus, a positive relationship between size and correctional resources will be consistent with an interpretation attributing effects to both the institutional and task environment. Size is likely to be affected by the following two variables.

Crime Rate

Crime rate refers to the index crime rate of the state for 1985. On its face, crime rate would appear to be a relatively unambiguous element of the task environment. States with higher crime rates should have greater demand for correctional resources. As a measure of demand for services, it should operate through conviction or incarceration rates. While the violent crime rate might arguably be a better gauge of demand for incarcerative punishments, Arvanites and Asher (1995) report that either violent crime or general crime rates perform about the same, across the states. Clearly, not all states reserve prison space for the violent. Indeed, this is less the purpose of prison use in the new punishment culture (Garland 2001). Crime rate may not be only a measure of "technical demand for punishment." It may also act as a symbolic force, independent of the conversion of crimes into punishments — as when political leaders demand that the criminal justice system, including corrections, must be better endowed to deal with the crime problem (Garland 2001, 8–20; Scheingold 1984).

Level of Development
Population size along with levels of industrialization and urbanization should have a direct effect on the size of the correctional system through the larger population base. The Level of Development is an index of state development based on state population, industrialization, and urbanization. More populous, industrialized, and urbanized states are rated higher on the Level of Development index.

Racial Heterogeneity
States with greater racial and ethnic heterogeneity and economic inequality are hypothesized to be more punitive than are states with more homogeneous populations (Barlow, Barlow, and Johnson 1996; M. C. Brown and Warner 1992; Garland 2001; Liska 1992b; Liska and Chamlin 1984; McGarrell and Castellano 1991). A number of different indicators were considered, including an index of income inequality, poverty level, percent black, and a composite indicator of heterogeneity based on these three dimensions. Percent black emerged as having the strongest and most consistent relationships in the analysis that follows. Percent black is predicted to affect correctional resources through incarceration rate based on the hypothesis that racial heterogeneity leads to more punitive responses to offenders. This is a principal proposition of the conflict sociology on social control, where it would be recognized as the "threat hypothesis." It is a primary proposition of correctional genealogists, who argue that new economic structures produce marginalized groups who are both at high risk for crime and for social control. In Wilkins's terms, blame allocation and punishment protects the economic and political system by explaining system consequences as individual characteristics of the morally undeserving (1991; and see Garland [2001] for an identical but apparently independent argument).

Incarceration Rate
States vary widely on their relative use of incarceration. The sources of this variation have been a matter of debate, with disagreement as to the extent to which the incarceration rate is a product of crescive forces, such as age structure and crime rate, or whether it is the product of policy decisions (Barlow, Barlow, and Johnson 1996; Garland 2001; Sherman and Hawkins 1981). To the extent that incarceration rate affects the size of the correctional system and correctional resources, beyond the effect of the crime rate, it seems to be indicative of institutionalized

norms and values supportive of punishment. Controlling for crime rate, incarceration rate becomes a central measure of punitive values in both the genealogical and social control studies.[1]

Traditionalistic Political Culture

An additional potential source of variation on institutional beliefs toward punishment is the political culture of the state. In particular, states tending toward traditionalistic political culture, characterized as elite-dominated with minimal levels of popular participation and little concern for public welfare (Elazar 1972; Johnson 1976), are likely to have higher rates of incarceration once crime rate has been controlled. Further, because political culture relates to public spending, we would expect traditionalistic culture to affect correctional resources. For example, because of the lack of commitment to social welfare and education in traditionalistic political cultures, corrections may fare well as a proportion of state spending.

The impact of traditionalistic political culture, as measured by Elazar, would appear on its face to be consistent with higher investments in punishment relative to other social sectors; however, Garland (2001) and Feeley and Simon (1992) would argue that this is no longer true. The genealogical analysis concludes that the traditionalistic (particularly southern) style of punishment has become outmoded (Feeley 1989). The new punitive culture appears in highly urban, diverse states, where the postindustrial service economy has done the most to marginalize the poor. Moreover, the southern traditions did not produce the professional correctional institutions that have recently been turned on their head to increase rather than reduce return to prison. Consequently, these theoreticians would argue that the predictive value of traditionalistic political culture has been superseded.

Wealth

A final characteristic of the states that may influence resources for corrections is the general level of wealth in the state. Public organizations are expensive. The wealth in the state (measured as per capita income) permits, but does not guarantee, greater investments in corrections and in other correctional services (Taggart and Winn 1991).

RESOURCES FOR CORRECTIONS

The level of resources for corrections can be measured in a number of ways. In this study, we have explored the use of two different measures, which capture different aspects of investment in punishment.

Correctional Spending Per Total State Spending

Correctional Spending Per Total State Spending refers to the percent of the state budget that is devoted to correctional spending. It is thus a measure of how corrections fares vis-à-vis other categories of state expenditures. We see this as a measure of strategic position of corrections, because the greater its share of state financial support, presumably the relatively more value accorded to corrections compared to education, welfare, transportation, mental health, and so on.

For Garland (2001) this is probably the most theoretically relevant dependent measure. It would arguably stand for the overall punitiveness or control orientation of the state, relative to other ways in which state resources could be used. Garland makes the point that welfare spending has gone down at precisely the same juncture for the same reasons: the disadvantaged are now portrayed as making choices to commit crimes and to be poor.

Correctional Spending Per Citizen

Correctional Spending Per Citizen stands for correctional spending per capita. It is thus an indicator of total correctional spending normed by the population base of the state. We expect some positive relationship between the share of state dollars devoted to corrections and corrections dollars per capita. However, Correctional Spending Per Citizen should be less dependent on the demands, size, and structure of other societal sectors. For example, one state could support corrections at higher levels than another state, without the relative fiscal position of the various societal sectors being affected. If professionalization in corrections is related to professionalization of other sectors, then correctional dollars per citizen should rise in professionalized states, even if the correctional professions do not achieve a greater share of state dollars than professions in other sectors. This is the measure that Taggert and Winn used in their analysis of the impact of environmental and internal factors on correctional spending (1991). It is a measure of punishment dollars per citizen-client rather than punishment dollars per all state expenses.

The appendix to this chapter includes the correlation matrix for the two spending measures. The correlation coefficients indicate the extent to which the variables are related to one another. As anticipated, Correctional Spending Per Total State Spending and Correctional Spending Per Citizen are strongly related. States that spend relatively high amounts per capita on corrections also devote a greater share of the overall state budget to corrections.[2]

HYPOTHESIZED RELATIONSHIPS AND FINDINGS

We shall now describe the specific hypotheses and findings for two models; the first using total state spending as the dependent variable and the second using spending per capita.

Correctional Spending Per Total State Spending

The first outcome measure of interest is Correctional Spending Per Total State Spending, the proportion of total state expenditures devoted to corrections. As noted earlier, Correctional Spending Per Total State Spending is a measure of the correctional share of the state budget and thus indicates how the correctional system fares in relation to other state functions.

Figure 10.1 presents our hypothesized theoretical model. States with a greater demand for correctional resources in terms of both size of the system and values supportive of incarceration and those with greater organizing capacity should be able to command a greater proportion of the state budget. Thus, Correctional Spending Per Total State Spending is viewed as having a rational–technical base, a value base, and an organizing capacity base. These predicted relationships are represented by the arrows indicating direct effects on Correctional Spending Per Total State Spending.

The rational–technical base of Correctional Spending Per Total State Spending is represented by the path from Size of Bureaucracy to Correctional Spending Per Total State Spending. States with larger correctional systems are likely to need greater relative correctional resources. The rational–technical component of size of the system is driven by the population base of the state and the crime rate. That is, larger states are going to have larger correctional systems because of their greater population base. Consequently, the Level of Development, based on population, real gross state product, industrialization, and urbanization, is predicted to have a direct effect on Size of Bureaucracy.

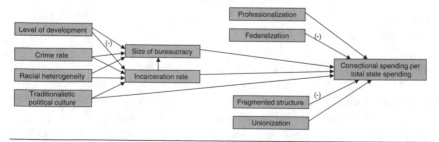

Figure 10.1 Theoretical model of correctional spending per total state spending

Correctional Spending Per Total State Spending will also be influenced by the values and attitudes toward the use of imprisonment in a state. In this analysis, punitive values are measured indirectly by the incarceration rate of the state (Incarceration Rate). Incarceration Rate is predicted to have both a direct and indirect effect on Correctional Spending Per Total State Spending. The direct effect indicates that states committed to the use of incarceration are likely to commit a greater relative share of state resources to corrections. In addition, Incarceration Rate is predicted to have an indirect effect through its relationship to Size of Bureaucracy.

Incarceration Rate, in turn, is seen as driven by Crime Rate, percent black in the state, the Level of Development, and political culture. States with a higher crime rate are likely to have a greater demand for punishment. This can be seen as the rational–technical base of the incarceration rate, at least to the extent that American culture ascribes to incarceration as an efficacious response to crime (Currie 1985; Scheingold 1984). However, incarceration rate is also determined by racial and economic heterogeneity. As noted earlier, we considered a number of indicators of heterogeneity. The percent of the state's population that is black consistently had the strongest zero order relationships to Incarceration Rate and the spending measures and the highest standardized regression coefficients in the multivariate analysis. Therefore, we included percent black as the sole indicator of heterogeneity.

Contradictory predictions can be made for the effect of the Level of Development on Incarceration Rate. Industrialization and urbanization are consistent predictors of the crime rate. Thus, the Level of Development may have a spurious positive effect on incarceration rate due to its relationship to crime rate (r=.4101, see the appendix). However, Joubert et al.'s (1981) study found that having controlled for crime rate, more urbanized and industrialized states actually had lower incarceration rates. They suggested that this might reflect the inability of these states to process a larger number of offenders, or alternatively, the greater availability of alternatives in such states. Consequently, we predicted a negative effect of Level of Development on Incarceration Rate. Finally, we hypothesized that political culture would relate to Correctional Spending Per Total State Spending indirectly through Incarceration Rate as well as having a direct effect. Traditionalistic Political Culture is reflective of states with a tradition of elite dominance, and minimal popular participation, innovation, and concern for public welfare. It is hypothesized that in such a context, correctional spending should be prioritized over other forms of state expenditure and that such a political culture will tend to favor greater relative use of incarceration.

The third set of factors predicted to influence Correctional Spending Per Total State Spending relates to characteristics of the correctional sector reflecting the system's capacity to organize and capture state resources. States with a more professional work force should be able to gain a larger share of state resources. Similarly, although often considered at odds with professionalism, we predict that states in which the correctional officer workforce is unionized will spend proportionately more on corrections.

Additional sector characteristics relate to two aspects of correctional system structure. First, states differ on the extent to which correctional policy and programming are concentrated at the state level or federated between state and local levels. Federalization is an index of federated structure based on whether a state makes intergovernmental transfer payments for correctional activities and the relative proportion of correctional spending and employment at the local versus state level. Competing hypotheses can be drawn on the effects of federated structure. First, Federalization may be related to Correctional Spending Per Total State Spending because the federated structure means more levels of government are lobbying for correctional expenditures. On the other hand, a system where policy and resources are concentrated at the state level may be more powerful and more influential over state resources.

Structure refers to the number of organizations responsible for correctional activities in the state. In some states correctional activities (juvenile and adult institutions, probation, parole, etc.) are consolidated in a single organization. In other states, there are autonomous organizations for two or more of these functions. Fragmented structure is predicted to relate to Correctional Spending Per Total State Spending because in such a context there are more organizations available to lobby for correctional resources. Again, however, a competing hypothesis can be advanced. The trend in corrections has been to unify correctional activities. To the extent unified structures conform with rational myths about good practice, unified sectors may be rewarded with greater resources.

A final sector characteristic is system size. Larger correctional agencies should be more effective at acquiring state resources than smaller agencies. This, of course, is also seen as reflecting the influence of rational–technical demand for a large correctional system. Further, to the extent that Size of Bureaucracy is the product of percent black and Incarceration Rate, independent of Level of Development and Crime Rate, Size of Bureaucracy also reflects values supporting incarceration. Thus, a relationship between Size of Bureaucracy and Correctional Spending Per Total State Spending is consistent with the three hypothesized sources of correctional spending — rational–technical demand, values, and organizing capacity of sector. Of course, this is consistent with institutional theory that posits all three characteristics driving correctional resources.

The models depicted in Figures 10.1 and 10.2 were analyzed using Ordinary Least Squares (OLS). This is a technique that allows us to examine the influence of a set of variables on a dependent variable where the effects of the other variables in the model are taken into account. In addition, indirect effects for the full models were examined using maximum likelihood estimates computed with LISREL VII. The LISREL program allows us to consider both direct and indirect effects of the variables. However, because the key theoretical relationships of the present analysis are based on the hypothesized direct effects on the spending measures and for ease of presentation, Tables 10.1 and 10.2 present the results of the OLS equations.

The results presented in Table 10.1 indicate that the model seemed to provide a reasonable fit to the theoretical expectations. Four variables, Size of Bureaucracy, Incarceration Rate, Professionalization, and Federalization, have significant effects on Correctional Spending Per Total State Spending. Thus, states with larger correctional systems, higher incarceration rates, a more professionalized correctional workforce, and resources concentrated at the state level, tend to devote proportionately more state expenditures to corrections. Three variables, Unionization, Fragmented Structure, and Traditionalistic Political Culture,[3] were not significantly related to Correctional Spending Per Total State Spending in the multivariate analysis.

Three additional variables, the Level of Development, Crime Rate, and Racial Heterogeneity, had indirect effects through their relationships to Size of Bureaucracy and Incarceration Rate.[4] Larger, industrial, and urbanized states have larger correctional systems. Beyond the effects of these characteristics, states with a higher index crime rate and a higher proportion of black population, tend to have larger correctional systems. Similarly, states with higher crime rates and those with larger black populations tend to incarcerate at higher rates. The Level of Development had a negative effect on Incarceration Rate indicating that once the effects of Crime Rate are controlled, larger, industrial and urban states actually incarcerate at a lower rate.[5]

These findings lend support to institutional theory's emphasis on the effects of functional requisites, values, and organizing capacity of the sector. The effect of Size of Bureaucracy on Correctional Spending Per Total State Spending is consistent with explanations pointing to the

Table 10.1 Standardized coefficients and t values of model of correctional spending per total state spending

	Incarceration Rate		Size of Bureaucracy		Correctional Spending per Total State Spending	
	Standardized Coefficient	t value	Standardized Coefficient	t value	Standardized Coefficient	t value
Level of development	−0.262	−2.12*	0.666	9.26**		
Crime rate	0.507	4.36**	0.186	2.32*		
Racial heterogeneity	0.680	3.88**	0.422	5.32**		
Traditionalistic political culture	−0.140	−0.82	−0.111	−1.30	0.126	0.98
Incarceration rate					0.383	3.39**
Size of bureaucracy					0.454	3.48**
Professionalization					0.270	2.59*
Federalization					−0.238	2.02*
Fragmented structure					−0.201	−0.19
Unionization					−0.035	−0.28
Adjusted R-square	0.458		0.820		0.562	

* t value significant < .05
** t value significant < .001

greater rational–technical demands for correctional resources in larger, industrial, urban states with higher crime rates. The finding that percent black contributes to Size of Bureaucracy once the effects of Level of Development and Crime Rate are controlled, however, also suggests the role of values. States characterized by racial heterogeneity appear to be committed to larger correctional systems beyond that expected by these other state characteristics.

The role of values also appears when we consider the role of incarceration rate on Correctional Spending Per Total State Spending.[6] Here again, racial heterogeneity appears to be a prime factor in states' use of incarceration, even after controlling for the effects of crime rate.

Thus, this model is consistent with an explanation that finds the proportion of state funds devoted to corrections to be largely determined by the size of the correctional system and the incarceration rate. These characteristics, in turn, reflect the effect of broader characteristics, of the state including population, urbanization, industrialization, crime rate, and percent black. These traits create sector variation in rational–technical demands for resources and in values supportive of the greater relative use of incarceration as a response to crime. Beyond these factors, two characteristics of the correctional system, professionalism and state-level concentrated structure, seemingly indicative of greater sector capacity to secure resources, affect state spending on corrections.

Correctional Spending Per Citizen

As Figure 10.2 indicates, the hypothesized model for Correctional Spending Per Citizen is quite similar to that for Correctional Spending Per Total State Spending. Size of Bureaucracy and Incarceration Rate is predicted to have positive effects on Correctional Spending Per Citizen. However, the influence of Incarceration Rate may be weaker on Correctional Spending Per Citizen than on Correctional Spending Per Total State Spending. A state in which values supportive of punishment are predominant may also tend to spend less on other forms of government programs such as education and social welfare. In such a setting, Correctional Spending Per Total State Spending may be higher even though spending per citizen may be relatively low. Similarly, Traditionalistic Political Culture was hypothesized, though not found, to relate positively to proportionate spending on corrections. Traditionalistic Political Culture may not, however, have a strong effect on per capita spending because Traditionalistic Political Culture is also characteristic of political values opposing governmental spending. Thus, incarceration rate and traditionalistic culture may lead to greater proportionate

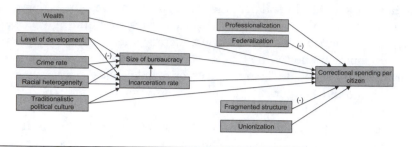

Figure 10.2 Theoretical model of correctional spending per citizen

spending on corrections (Correctional Spending Per Total State Spending) but not to elevated levels of spending per citizen (Correctional Spending Per Citizen).

The characteristics of correctional system structure, Professionalization, Federalization, Unionization, and Fragmented Structure, are all hypothesized to influence Correctional Spending Per Citizen in a similar fashion to Correctional Spending Per Total State Spending. The one additional variable included in the present equation is Wealth. While Wealth was not expected to influence proportionate spending on corrections, it should be positively related to overall levels of spending.

Table 10.2 presents the results of the OLS analysis. It appears that the model is reasonably consistent with the theoretical expectations. Four variables have significant effects on Correctional Spending Per Citizen and the model produces an R^2 of .572. States with high incarceration rates and large correctional bureaucracies tend to devote more resources per citizen to corrections. In addition, states with a more professional work force and in which resources are concentrated at the state level have higher levels of per capita spending.

The findings on federated structure require some mention. Recall that competing hypotheses were discussed in relation to the effects of this sector characteristic. On the one hand, federalization was seen as creating more levels of government and more agencies likely to lobby for increased correctional resources. On the other hand, as noted at the outset, the trend in corrections has been to consolidate correctional programs at the state level. The finding that concentration related to higher per capita correctional spending may indicate that such a structure conforms to institutionalized beliefs about desired practice. In addition, state bureaucracies where correctional resources are concentrated may be more effective advocates for public expenditures than numerous but fragmented voices.

Table 10.2 Standardized coefficients and t values of model of correctional spending per citizen

	Correctional Spending per Citizen	
	Standardized Coefficient	t value
Size of bureaucracy	0.311	2.10*
Incarceration rate	0.520	4.46***
Professionalization	0.228	2.13*
Federalization	−0.330	−2.87**
Unionization	0.151	1.16
Fragmented structure	−0.180	−1.65
Traditionalistic political culture	−0.121	−0.82
Wealth	0.086	0.60
Adjusted R-square	0.572	

*   t value significant < .05
**   t value significant < .01
*** t value significant < .001

Thus, the model is once again consistent with a theoretical explanation that treats technical demand, values, and organizing capacity as three important sets of forces influencing correctional resources.

CONCLUSION

These findings suggest to us the usefulness of institutional theory as a basis for understanding correctional systems. We can see at the moment more implications for research than for practice, although there are some implications for practice that could be exciting.

Future Research

Institutional theory and research are only gradually making their way into the study of criminal justice. Several researchers (notably Hagan 1989b; Hagan, Hewitt et al. 1979) have borrowed the concept of "loose coupling." In Hagan's work, loose coupling has referred to the slippage in the processing of offenders from one criminal justice agency to another, while in most institutional theory, loose coupling has referred to disjointedness between the public consumables of organizations, such as rhetoric and formal structure, and frontline client processing (Meyer and Rowan 1977; Weick 1976). This more typical application of a key institutional concept has only recently been applied in criminal justice, particularly by Crank and colleagues (Crank and Langworthy 1992; McCorkle and Crank 1996).

Certainly the institutional approach to public organizations is far richer and more varied than the idea of loose coupling. It is surprising, given the nature of criminal justice institutions and the success of institutional study in other sectors that more of the theoretical concerns and more of methods associated with the new institutionalism have not been more visible in criminal justice. This does appear to be changing. Crank (1996) has been looking at symbolic communication in community corrections. Feeley (1989) has approached federal courts intervening in state corrections both as an authoritative institutional voice and as an actor borrowing and applying punitive images promoted by other institutional actors, such as national professional groups and the Federal Bureau of Prisons. McGarrell and Duffee (1995) examined the forces leading to reintegration programming adoption. In policing, Hunt and Magenau (1993) have sought to study the power of the police executive from an institutional perspective; and Renauer (chapter 6) has sought to tie several strands of institutional theory together to explain the nature of community policing.

Perhaps one of the reasons that the institutional perspective has not penetrated the study of criminal justice as deeply as education is that many of the traditional institutional research concerns have, in the field of criminal justice, been approached by the social control researchers on the one hand and the genealogists on the other. Both of these scholarly traditions lay claim to much of the same territory as the institutionalists: the interplay of social structure, political systems, and political culture or conventional belief systems and the connection of all three of these to the formal institutions of social control. We hope to have shown that these traditions can be productively combined, although we certainly have done little here but indicate that the boundaries between these intellectual pursuits are quite porous and easily traversed.

We would be remiss not to mention another, perhaps more substantial, barrier to the study of criminal justice as we have practiced it here. As Hagan (1989b) and Sullivan (1994) have noted, research in criminal justice administration more frequently focuses on the behavior of individual decision makers facing case-by-case choices. The dominant research questions since the mid-1960s have been preoccupied with the legality or extralegality of agent decisions and whether agent discretion may be controlled (S. Walker 1993). While this microfocus is decidedly foreign to the sociology or the genealogy of social control, these traditions have not articulated effectively with criminal justice science. Perhaps the dominance of the individual-to-individual research in criminal justice is traceable to the influence of Black's theory of law (1976), which argued that the explanations of the variations in law would be the same at the individual and societal levels. Early research testing of Black's theory (including his own) zeroed in on decisions by victims, police officers, judges, and other individuals (Black 1970; Gottfredson and Hindelang 1979a, 1979b; and see Kautt and Spohn, chapter 7 in this volume). This microapproach was compatible and spurred on by the American Bar Foundation survey and the President's Commission on Law Enforcement and Administration of Justice (Ohlin and Remington 1993; S. Walker 1993).

We are sympathetic with Hagan's desire to explain the behavior of criminal justice systems themselves, rather than concentrating so heavily on the actors in the system. As starting points, we would suggest attention to the following research issues. Clearly, the relationships examined in the present study need to be considered longitudinally. Undoubtedly, some of these relationships are dynamic. For example, while size was shown to relate to spending on corrections, such spending may be hypothesized to lead to future expansion of the system. Similarly, while we emphasized the role of the incarceration rate in driving Correctional Spending Per Total State Spending and Correctional Spending Per Citizen, such spending on corrections could also have feedback effects on the willingness of lawmakers and judicial officials to legislate and impose incarcerative sanctions. Have the changes in crime rates experienced in the 1990s affected levels of funding and the relationships between these factors? Have the stark contrasts between American values of equality and freedom and the American politics of social control begun to cast doubts on the latter? Garland says not yet; but he poses some possible emergent countertrends (2001, 196–204).

The utility of the approach taken in this study could also be examined by a comparative approach such as that undertaken, in limited fashion, by Sherman and Hawkins (1981) and Garland (2001). This type of research could examine not only cultural variation in attitudes toward punishment and incarceration but also comparison of different institutional processes in countries with different governmental forms. Hagan's (1989b) brief comparison of the tightly coupled criminal justice system in the Federal Republic of Germany with the loosely coupled system in the United States suggests the possibility of such comparative analyses. In chapter 3, Howard and Freilich pose the comparative approach to the study of the lower courts; however, they also pose the problems with the comparative method that must be considered in both design issues (e.g., do cultures and national boundaries coincide?) and data sources (are imprisonment counts equivalent across political systems?).

This research also suggests the need for more research on the role of race at the macrolevel — such as the political processes through which race influences the incarceration rate. In a survey of New York State legislators, McGarrell and Flanagan (1987) found race to be a consistent predictor of criminal justice ideology. Further, such ideological stances tend to divide along geographical lines with legislators from urban centers much more likely to endorse liberal and radical crime control positions than their suburban and rural counterparts (see also Castellano and McGarrell 1991). These findings suggest the potential of investigations of political conflict over crime control policy structured by factors such as overall racial heterogeneity, concentration of minorities in urban centers, and racial and party politics. Along similar lines, there is a need for research on the impact of concentrations of other racial/ethnic groups on criminal justice policy and the structure of corrections, as well as on potential outlier states such as Hawaii with its large nonwhite population yet relatively lower incarceration rate.

Most of the extant research on the connection between race and social control is associated with the conflict theorists and their "threat hypothesis" (M. C. Brown and Warner 1992; Liska and Chamlin 1984). As Liska (1992b) indicates, much data showing impacts of racial composition on social control activities, net of crime, are consistent with the threat hypothesis of the conflict theorists. As powerful groups are threatened by changes in size or behavior of less powerful groups, greater social control efforts are exerted. However, as Liska concluded, there are major challenges in converting the threat hypothesis into a real theory. He identified conceptual problems, such as defining threat and defining the powerful, independent of the social control they supposedly exert. He also identified theoretical problems, such as organizing research around different forms of social control rather than around different theoretical propositions and problems in connecting presumed structural threats with specific control processes (1992b).

Liska's general critique of social control research applies to our findings, as well. While diversity, in particular percent black in the general population, appears to exert a powerful influence on the punitiveness of state budgeting, it is necessary to ask for more direct evidence that diversity produces threat, or perceived threat, and that the threat leads directly or indirectly to policy decisions, such as choosing between health, education, and punishment investments of public dollars. There are several avenues for doing this. One is building and executing a design in which the political processes can be shown to mediate the population composition effects on the social control outcomes. This was admirably done by Brown and Warner, for example, at the city level for police arrests (1992). It has not, to our knowledge, been equally successfully pulled off at the state or national levels of comparison. At these levels, we have compelling case studies of single or a few systems, such as Garland (2001) and Simon (1993), which are suggestive of the processes and structures that should be connected but cannot control alternative explanations, and broad cross-jurisdiction comparisons, such as this one, that can control multiple variables but infer the process connections.

While there is much work to be done, we think it is promising that the kinds of forces highlighted in the genealogical case studies also appear influential in this comparative analysis, at least as we have measured those forces. Of particular promise is the possible interplay of administrative or organizational forces, such as the image and structure of the correctional system, and structural and demographic forces such as the economic development, class, and race composition. Taggart and Winn's (1991) finding that "correctional strength" affected per capita correctional spending would appear similar to our findings of the influence of professionalism, concentration, and size.

Garland (2001), Simon (1993), and Feeley and Simon (1992) propose that professional, concentrated, and large correctional bureaucracies, while devised for decidedly different ends, have become the machinery, or the processual connection, that has enabled structural and cultural changes in society and in the political system to drive the type and level of social control. Barlow et al. (1996) argue that the more progressive, modern forms of criminal justice are more effective in implementing threat politics, ironically, because they appear more politically palatable as professional and progressive. In the policing area, both Lyons (1999) and DeLeon-Granados (1999) make a similar argument about the rhetoric or political discourse of community policing. The state, in the form of a well-trained, progressive, and professional police department has successfully translated community-policing messages into support for traditional law enforcement practices. What began as a community building enterprise has been transformed into more traditional sanctioning of marginal groups.

These proposed political functions of the "correctional sector," as we have called it, or the "field," as Garland has called it, are intriguing and should be pursued. More qualitative case studies that couple economic and structural change with bureaucratic, institutional reaction are certainly needed. It would also be fruitful to connect these theories to the studies in political extremism. Both Scheingold (1984) at the national level, and Wilkins (1991) at the international level propose that certain political systems are more given to simplified and extreme social control answers to social problems. They propose that the voices of danger play better in centralized political systems with heavy reliance on mass media campaigns for elections. At the state level, do these happen to be the same states that have professional and concentrated correctional institutions? How does the prior investment in corrections connect to the dynamics of the state political system and the state political economy?

Another interesting set of questions surround the interrelationship among social control forms. Correctional spending as a percent of the state budget provided an initial comparison of correctional expenditure relative to other forms of governmental spending. It is not surprising that we found states supportive of incarceration to spend relatively more on corrections. An additional question of interest is what happens to public spending in states where incarceration is less valued? Do we find increased expenditures on alternative forms of social control such as mental health, social welfare, and education? Or, alternatively, are some states more "control-oriented" with higher levels of expenditures on all of these sources of social control?

Finally, the role of political and cultural forces in the structure of corrections also suggests the need for studying the mobilization and implementation of reform. It is common in corrections to call for adoption in one jurisdiction of an innovation that has apparently worked in another. Such political grafts, however, are often disappointing. They do not take, and policy makers often blame political differences for their failures. It would be useful to study the extent to which policy successes and failures (e.g., Minnesota vs. California sentencing guidelines), succeeded or failed because the political mobilizations fit, or did not fit, the political environment.

Policy Implications

We began this chapter with doubts about the contention that political and cultural variations in the use of incarceration necessarily mean that policy choices are feasible. This study does not allay that doubt. This research indicates that some political and cultural variables are as important as crime rate in predicting correctional expenditures. It is difficult to say that such expenditures will be reduced if they are dependent on the punitiveness of a culture.

However, correctional resources also appear dependent on the extent that the correctional work force is professionalized and whether correctional activity is concentrated at the state level or shared by state and local government. Like cultural beliefs, professional power may also be fairly intractable (DiMaggio and Powell 1983). But professional groups are a more concentrated target than diffuse beliefs about how to punish criminals. Policy makers might have more success negotiating with professionals about the nature of punishment and sentencing than they would seeking to alter the level of punitiveness in society.

Federated correctional structure seems an even more promising variable for manipulation. Planned changes in the distribution of correctional responsibility might be made. Pushing more correctional activity to the local level rather than concentrating corrections in state bureaucracies would seem to reduce expenditures. This finding is consistent with Garland's (2001) and Lyons's (1999) final speculations that restorative justice, community building, and other reciprocal forms of social control may produce less exclusionary and marginalizing results.

More important than attempts to alter any of these variables directly would be the utilization of such information about the states in two types of policy intervention. First, policy makers within a state should be tailoring policy changes to fit their own contexts. We are certain that politicians are well aware of the need for coalition building. However, some evidence (Flanagan, Brennan, and Cohen 1991) suggests that political decision makers could use far more precise information about the nature and strength of forces aligned for and against particular crime control policy choices than they now have available.

Second, the variation among the states should be useful by national organizations that can operate across the states. One of these, of course, is the federal government. Our findings would seem to support Sherman and Hawkins's (1981) contention that no single national policy is likely to be productive across all jurisdictions. Other national organizations with investment in policy change include the NAACP, the ACLU, MADD, and other victim's rights groups, and foundations such as the Burden and Edna McConnell Clark foundations. Policy makers in these groups routinely attempt to concentrate their resources where they might have the most impact. Data on the institutionalized context of corrections in each state could conceivably be used to indicate the vulnerability of a state to change and the nature of the targets in each state that a policy or program must enlist, accommodate, or defeat.

NOTES

1. The use of incarceration rate as an indicator of punitive cultural values within a state receives support from the correlation between incarceration rate and number of death row inmates (normed by state population). For 1985 the correlation was .59 ($p < 0.01$).

2. In a longer, earlier version of this chapter, we also included an analysis of costs per inmate, which have been removed from this version because of limitations on length. However, it is interesting to note that there is no correlation (not shown) between Correctional Spending Per Inmate and either Correctional Spending Per Total State Spending or Correctional Spending Per Citizen. Thus, overall spending for corrections relative to all other state expenses or relative to population may be good measures of state punitiveness but are not useful measures of resources devoted to each offender.

3. One possible explanation for Traditionalistic Political Culture not being related to Correctional Spending Per Total State Spending in the multivariate analysis may be because of Traditionalistic Political Culture's high zero-order correlation with Racial Heterogeneity ($r = -.76$). This may be indicative of conservative, traditionalistic political values and traditions predominating in racially heterogeneous states.

4. As noted, the theoretical models presented in Figures 10.1 and 10.2 were also analyzed using maximum likelihood estimates as a way to examine indirect effects. In the LISREL analysis, Level of Development ($B = -.217$, $t = 2.01$), Crime Rate ($B = .252$, $t = 3.45$), and Racial Heterogeneity ($B = .417$, $t = 4.13$) had significant indirect effects on Correctional Spending Per Total State Spending. For the analysis of Correctional Spending Per Citizen, Crime Rate and Racial Heterogeneity had significant indirect effects ($B = -.312$, $t = -3.28$; $B = -.451$, $t = -3.15$, respectively), but Level of Development did not.

5. The multivariate analysis being employed examines the impact of one variable while controlling or holding constant the effects of the other variables. For example, Level of Development appears to have a negative effect on Incarceration Rate once one holds the effects of Crime Rate constant.

6. It would appear important to extend this analysis through longitudinal research to consider possible two-way effects. For example, while we emphasize the influence of incarceration rate on correctional resources, a plausible rival hypothesis is that resources influence future incarceration rates.

APPENDIX

Descriptive Statistics and Correlation Matrix in Chapter 10

Table A.1 Variable Descriptive Statistics

	Mean	Standardized Deviation	N
Level of Development — Factor Score Based On:			
Population	4762.3	5068.9	50
Real Gross State Product	70909.8	83281.3	50
Industrialization	16463.9	19044.8	50
Urbanization (percent)	63.3	22.3	50
Wealth	13159.8	2058.9	50
Crime Rate	4750.9	1292.3	50
Racial Heterogeneity (percent Black)	9.1	9.2	50
Traditionalistic Political Culture	0.205	0.3	48
Professionalization	2.3	1.0	50
Federalization — Factor Score Based On:			
Correctional Expenditures at State/Local Level (percent)	0.74	0.13	50
Correctional Employment at State/Local Level (percent)	0.71	0.14	50
Correctional Intergovernmental Transfer Payments (0 = no; 1 = yes)	0.52	0.50	50
Unionization (0 = no; 1 = yes)	0.54	0.50	50
Fragmented Structure (range 1-4)	2.0	0.78	50
Size of Bureaucracy	2797.7	3305.9	50
Incarceration Rate	203.2	99.24	50
Correctional Spending Per Total State Spending	0.02	0.01	50
Correctional Spending Per Citizen	35.7	12.35	49

Table A.2 Correlation Matrix of Variables

	Level of Development	Crime Rate	Racial Hetero-geneity	Tradition-alistic Political Culture	Wealth	Size of Bureau-cracy	Incarcer-ation Rate	Profes-sional-ization	Federal-ization	Unioni-zation	Frag-mented Structure	Correc-tional Spending Per Total State Spending	Correc-tional Spending Per Citizen
Level of development	1.0												
Crime rate	.410**	1.0											
Racial heterogeneity	.259*	.033	1.0										
Traditionalistic political culture	.001	−.121	.760***	1.0									
Wealth	.548***	.368**	−.170	−.430***	1.0								
Size of bureaucracy	.838***	.424***	.543***	.314*	.303*	1.0							
Incarceration rate	.122	.439***	.523***	.312*	.163	.273*	1.0						
Professionalization	.313*	.536***	−.046	−.079	.417***	.315*	.163	1.0					
Federalization	.492***	.135	.078	.015	.012	.439***	−.194	.165	1.0				
Unionization	.252*	.143	−.342**	−.539***	.517***	.043	−.226	.218	.040	1.0			
Fragmented structure	.135	−.019	.350**	.385**	−.003	.148	.292*	.026	−.068	−.311*	1.0		
Correctional spending per total state spending	.340**	.479***	.449***	.305*	.298*	.569***	.586***	.413***	−.052	−.039	.060	1.0	
Correctional spending per citizen	.308*	.509***	.241*	−.030	.403**	.403**	.548***	.406**	−.188	.226	−.034	.812***	1.0

* p significant < .05
** p significant < .01
*** p significant < .001

Conclusion

11

DIRECTIONS FOR THEORY AND THEORIZING IN CRIMINAL JUSTICE

David E. Duffee, Alissa Pollitz Worden, and Edward R. Maguire

INTRODUCTION

This volume brings together a broad collection of theory and research in criminal justice. Throughout, the guiding theme is the understanding of criminal justice phenomena in multiple sectors and at multiple levels by using a scientific approach to the study of criminal justice. In other words, the work in this volume pays explicit attention to the development and testing of scientific theory as a means of understanding criminal justice.

THE IMPORTANCE OF CRIMINAL JUSTICE THEORY

Understanding criminal justice behavior is important. Criminal justice is one of the most pervasive and expensive forms of government social control. As commitments to mental health systems and public welfare have been reduced, the governments' relative reliance on criminal justice for social control has increased. Criminal justice is also the primary example of coercive political power. Political decisions about what values to protect, what behavior to criminalize, and how (and how much) to punish criminal behavior are fundamental political decisions that define the nature of society. Understanding criminal justice behavior is just as important, although quite different from, understanding criminal behavior.

If we are to understand criminal justice scientifically, then we need to be guided by theory. Explicit theory is the sine qua non of scientific investigation, far more critical than the precision of measurement or the methods of analysis. Absent theory, there is no science; no way to avoid raw empiricism followed by pure speculation about what the data "might mean." Such speculation inevitably draws upon and is colored by the analyst's personal, cultural, and political values, traditions, and interests, no matter how well intended or carefully crafted such speculations might be (Bernard and Ritti 1990).

Theory is often inappropriately mystified by scientists and denigrated by nonscientists. Theory is often contrasted with real-world pragmatism and objective facts in a misleading way. When one of the authors began his academic career in 1971, it was common to hear both students and many faculty contrast what is "supposed to happen in theory" with "what actually happens in the real world." Students more than thirty years later are still apt to contrast "what the books say" with "what really happens." While theory and facts are not the same, this is not to say the theories are not concerned with facts. Theories that do not help us understand how and why one pattern of facts occurs rather than another are not scientific theories. When students or faculty talk about "what should happen in theory," they most likely mean what ought to happen according to some moral or political theory, not what is likely to happen according to some scientific theory.

Scientific theory is a very practical activity. In Kurt Lewin's popular phrase, there is nothing so practical as a good (accurate) theory. One can think of scientific theory as informed (by prior research) and logical (sensible, plausible, and noncontradictory) "guesses" or explicitly stated expectations about how, why, and under what conditions something happens that is worth knowing about. The human and artistic part of science is in the decision about what is worth knowing. What facts do we attend to? The scientific part lies in establishing and maintaining an approach to answering the what, how, why, when, and where without letting the preinvestigatory human interests that initiated the study get in the way of the facts. While theory is used to control emotional or self-interested biases in scientific investigation, theory does not hold all facts equal. Theory focuses our attention toward some facts and away from others. It helps us sort out from the infinite array of factors that could influence behavior, those that are most worth testing against logical standards and empirical evidence. If we agree that we need to understand scientifically the causes of criminal justice behavior, then a theory is the most important tool in the shed — but no more than a tool. If it works, we proceed. If it does not, we toss it out and find another theory to guide the work.

CHALLENGES OF CRIMINAL JUSTICE THEORY DEVELOPMENT

In many scientific fields, theory is relatively well developed. As a consequence, the work of many contemporary scientists is mostly in testing, refining, replicating, and comparing theories. This is often called the work of "normal science" (Kuhn 1970). This is less the case in the social than in the physical sciences. Indeed, there are arguments that social science is not science but art (DiCristina 1995), or perhaps politics. Certainly the strength of arguments about the applicability of science to social facts varies from one social sector to another. For example, the theories and methods on which Eric Lambert drew for his study of Federal Bureau of Prison employees in chapter 9 are far more developed, refined, and tested than the institutional theory of corrections, which McGarrell and Duffee attempted to test in chapter 10. Scientists examining job satisfaction, job commitment, and turnover rely on vast libraries of theoretical work, measurement advances, and prior empirical studies of causal connections. In contrast, persons seeking to be scientific about how punitive a society is, or how much a people values punishment, are faced with the tasks of expressing theoretical concepts and relationships, developing measures, and conducting tests all at the same time. As we have argued in this volume, criminal justice as a social science is "pretheoretical" or perhaps "prototheoretical" — or whatever term the reader would prefer to connote the infancy of theoretically guided criminal justice research, or the science of criminal justice.

As we seek to develop the science of criminal justice, there are a variety of challenges to be met. A number of these have been documented throughout this volume, perhaps most notably in chapters 1, 2, and 4. A number of these challenges are not scientific ones. Chapter 1 argues that criminological and criminal justice research is often intertwined to the detriment of criminal justice science. Certainly crime and justice are connected and studies of each will inform the other. As Duffee and Allan argue in chapter 1, criminal justice is often treated as an independent variable helping us to understand crime but rarely as a dependent variable to be understood. This is not to say that the effects of criminal justice are unimportant or uninteresting. But even if our long-term concern were reducing crime, we would have to be able to determine if criminal justice policies, programs, and activities can be influenced so that they have more efficacious effects on crime. Hence there is a pressing need to study criminal justice phenomena as the dependent variable.

Independent of, but complementary to, the above argument is the one which Castellano and Gould put forward in chapter 4. In their view, criminal justice scholars should pay more attention to understanding the quality and level of justice in a society rather than focusing so heavily on levels of crime. One of the defining aspects of societies is whether in a given society there are other values beyond order and safety to be pursued in the conduct of social control (also see Moore 2002).

Snipes and Maguire mention another common problem with criminal justice theory in chapter 2. There are many instances of criminal justice theory that are not scientific theory. By its very nature, the field of criminal justice is of concern to philosophers and moralists. What is the rationale for punishment? What kinds of punishments are appropriate, fair, civilized? Many of these statements of moral positions are called "theories" of criminal justice. There is nothing wrong with such work, but it is not scientific theory.

Somewhat different from the above challenges and confusions is overcoming the antiscience, or "everybody knows" approach to criminal justice. Duffee and Allan (chapter 1) and Castellano and Gould (chapter 4) bring up this problem in different ways, most notably, perhaps, in their arguments that scientific criminal justice theory often lags behind because its development is potentially threatening to important political interests, including the elites of the criminal justice system itself. To think of the contrast between the support for science in criminal justice and the support for science in other fields, consider for a moment the likelihood that a politician would claim that he knew how to get to the moon without scientific knowledge. It is quite unlikely. It is perhaps even more unlikely that such a person would actually ride in the vehicle that he designed without scientific know-how. But the same politicians reject the need for scientific knowledge about criminal justice every day. Such people usually begin with a statement that "everyone knows" (or that common sense tells us) what kind of punishment is effective. Recently, this general claim has usually come in the form of politicians claiming that their get-tough crime policies are responsible for the notable drop in crime. While we do not wish to belabor this point, which may be apparent to some of our readers, the belief that criminal justice policies can be made without science is perhaps the most deleterious stumbling block in the path of developing criminal justice science. Since most of the nonscientific beliefs about criminal justice rest on some claim to reducing crime, any criminal justice science that examines other factors affecting such beliefs is potentially threatening to the holder of those beliefs.

Another challenge to criminal justice theory, and a more scientific one, is the reliance on other social science disciplines for the beginnings of criminal justice theory. Many criminal justice concepts and potential relationships emerge from political science, sociology, psychology, economics, management science, and so on, whether we are dealing with individual actors, organizations, or larger systems and contexts. Not only is there nothing wrong with such borrowing, but it is also one of the facets of criminal justice science that can make it so intriguing and interesting. In addition, it is a way to speed development in a new science.

For instance, organizational theorists have relied on institutional theory for many years to explain the behaviors of many kinds of organizations, from corporations to hospitals and schools. In chapter 6, Renauer borrowed propositions from institutional theory to explain variation in urban community policing practices. The multidisciplinary foundations of criminal justice provide numerous avenues for tapping into existing knowledge from other fields.

However, the interdisciplinary and multidisciplinary bases of criminal justice pose a number of potential challenges. The traditional academic employment structure might inhibit orderly progress in theory development. Imagine an economist, a sociologist, and a psychologist all working independently on the same theoretical question. Based on their background, interests, and training, they might approach the same problem from very different angles. While this could be a potential strength, it could also be a liability if they talk past one another and fail to reach any kind of theoretical integration. An example of this state of affairs is organizational studies. Australian sociologist Lex Donaldson (1995) has argued that organizational studies is enmeshed in a series of "paradigm wars" that are inhibiting the growth of the discipline and rendering it irrelevant to those who seek real answers about how organizations work. Donaldson blames the American academic establishment for failing to provide incentives for cooperating and integrating across perspectives. Academics from different disciplines might also publish their work in different journals that do not have wide exposure in criminal justice; they might present their research findings at different professional meetings; and they might rely on very different research methods that are well-accepted within their disciplines but not in others.

Second, researchers who are trained in criminal justice rather than one of the major source disciplines may not be educated in or fully informed about all the traditions, conventions, and findings in the fields from which they borrow concepts and theories. As a result, key elements of a theory may remain unstated or unexamined or underlying assumptions may not be fully appreciated. For example, a doctoral student of one of the authors once sought to devise a theory of criminal justice agency cooperation with citizens using a theory from social welfare organization that had been developed to explain tokenism. As used in this example, tokenism means involving citizens in organizational decision-making processes as a symbolic gesture, with no intention of actually incorporating their input (Arnstein 1969). This student had not been sufficiently versed in the social welfare research tradition that saw interorganizational cooperation as a means of reducing and controlling citizen input rather than increasing it. This research study was eventually reframed successfully, but it got off to a rocky start on the basis of borrowing from another research tradition that pulled one aspect of a relevant but distant theory out of context. Borrowing concepts and theoretical insights from many fields provides constant threat of misuse of the borrowed work (but, of course, also offers the potential benefit of new applications of prior work).

Other related problems involve the confusing plethora of definitions for the same term across disciplines and, vice versa, the not infrequent use of different terms across disciplines to mean the same thing. It can take a very experienced researcher, and often, a well-functioning team of researchers, to recognize and appreciate such distinctions.

One of the best examples of these kinds of problems concerns the term *community*, which has recently become of major importance to both criminal justice theory and practice. To the first author of this chapter, thirty years ago the term *community* simply meant the "public" who might have opinions about corrections or seek to support it at some level (O'Leary and Duffee 1971; Duffee 1974). When Duffee arrived at Pennsylvania State University to teach in a Division of Community Development, his colleagues, who were community development experts, dismissed this work as ignorant of community — and rightly so from their point of view. To them what O'Leary and Duffee had been talking about was something like "the polity" or the "public" but certainly not distinct, geographically defined communities.

Today, we can see the same confusion in relation to community policing, community prosecution, community courts, and more generally community justice. What criminal justice policy makers mean by this term is highly varied and generally not very programmatic in its implications. Instead it is a flag waving, justificatory term with which programs gain approval rather than substance. Indeed, one of the most intriguing (and negative) accounts of community policing focused scientifically on precisely that rhetorical use of the term *community*. Lyons (1999) couches the politics of community policing as a struggle between central government and neighborhoods for the power to define what community will mean and the kind of social control it will entail.

But there is also a great deal of variation in the use of the term as a scientific construct. Community can be and has been defined as cultures, interest groups, enclaves, polities, cities, neighborhoods, and other social entities. This variation is frustrating and potentially useful. But to gain more use and less frustration, criminal justice scientists must have considerable knowledge about other disciplines (or open access to consultants with expertise in these fields) to make good use of concepts, theories, and research from diverse fields.

THE STATE OF CRIMINAL JUSTICE THEORY

What do the preceding chapters say about the state of criminal justice theory? Let us begin with a brief review.

In chapter 1, "Criminal Justice, Criminology, and Criminal Justice Theory," Duffee and Allan propose that criminal justice theory is underdeveloped. They do *not* argue that it is missing. Quite the contrary, they indicate that there are many high quality scientific studies of criminal justice phenomena in the literature and that such work is impossible without theory. But they do argue that explicit attention to criminal justice theory lags behind theory development in other fields. Duffee and Allan propose that both criminology and criminal justice would be strengthened if crime and criminal justice scholars recognized explicitly the need to be scientific about both explaining crime and explaining criminal justice.

In chapter 2, "Foundations of Criminal Justice Theory," Snipes and Maguire begin by discussing the shortcomings of criminal justice theory, tracing the brief history of its foundations, and settling on a loose conception of its domain. Their broad definition states that criminal justice theory *is the study of the official response to behavior that may be labeled criminal.* They criticize current theory by arguing that much of what is labeled criminal justice theory is either not adequate *theory* or does not really belong to *criminal justice.* Most notably, they carve out a distinction between ideologies, criminological theory, and criminal justice theory. They then propose four tests that can be used to determine whether a theory falls within the domain of criminal justice theory. The essential nature of these tests is (1) that the dependent variable must be related to the official response to potentially criminal behavior;

(2) that the deviance could reasonably have been labeled criminal, if it was not; (3) that the response is related in some way to official criminal justice policies, structures, or practices; and (4) that the theory conform to basic standards for constructing social science theories. Students may find it useful to apply these four tests to the theories presented in this volume.

In chapter 3, "Durkheim's Comparative Method and Criminal Justice Theory," Howard and Freilich issue a challenge to criminal justice theorists: to develop, refine, test, and elaborate criminal justice theory using the comparative method. In general terms, the comparative method is a methodological approach in which the analyst compares social collectivities (such as organizations, states, or nations). Howard and Freilich focus specifically on comparing nations, though they suggest that units of analysis in comparative research can vary. As an illustration, they show how Feeley's (1979) organizational theory of the courts can be tested and elaborated using the comparative method. The world is full of interesting and meaningful international variations in criminal justice. Why do courts in some nations sentence offenders to corporal or capital punishment, while others decry such methods? Why are police in some nations more gentle and accommodating, while police in other nations are brutal and corrupt? Why are there such massive international variations in the use of imprisonment? These questions are all within the purview of criminal justice theory, and all can be studied using the comparative method. As globalization continues to increase, the need for theories of criminal justice to account for international variation will grow.

In chapter 4, "Neglect of Justice in Criminal Justice Theory: Causes, Consequences and Alternatives," Thomas Castellano and Jon Gould echo Duffee and Allan's concerns about the overemphasis on explaining crime. They then go on to examine the conceptual footing for criminal justice theories that seek to explain justice rather than other outcomes with a stronger linkage to crime. As they point out, the concerns for justice in society can be as important politically, and for the quality of life that people lead, as concerns for crime. Ignoring complaints about injustice are as perilous to social order as ignoring complaints about crime. Even among those readers who are not convinced by Castellano's and Gould's arguments about the moral need to study the delivery of justice, there exist numerous other reasons. For example, as Mastrofski (2001) writes, police chiefs do not often lose their jobs because there is too much crime. Yet the ceremonial dethroning of the police chief during a scandal involving corruption, brutality, or racism is commonplace. Scientifically, there is no greater difficulty (although certainly no less) in measuring the nature or level of justice adhering in a particular criminal justice system or process as in measuring the level of crime that might ensue. Coming up with scientific theories of justice could send criminal justice researchers off in new and exciting directions.

In chapter 5, "Explaining Police Organizations," Maguire and Uchida survey the landscape of theory and research on police organizations. The chapter begins by demonstrating that police departments are different from one another in many ways: in structures, policies, processes, and outputs. For example, some arrest offenders aggressively while others may rely on different, less formal methods for achieving compliance with the law. A large body of research has developed to explain these variations. Maguire and Uchida review this research, showing how these approaches contribute to a theoretical understanding of variations in police organization. Among the values of such a theoretical review is their discovery, which might otherwise remain hidden, that most theories of police organizations are of the "contingency" variety of organizational theory. While this is not necessarily problematic, it should alert theoreticians interested in policing that a huge variety of other kinds of organizational theory have not been adequately tapped, applied, or developed.

In chapter 6, "Understanding Variety in Urban Community Policing," Brian Renauer provides us with one example of a scholar seeking to build a new theory to explain emergent phenomena in police organization. His starting point is the large and even contradictory variety in the structures and activities that urban police departments adopt as "community policing." Recognizing that police organizations are important legal, political, and cultural institutions, Renauer utilizes the institutional theory of public organizations, initially developed to explain behavior of public utilities (Selznick 1966) and public education (Meyer and Rowan 1977; Weick 1976). He proposes that some of the forces affecting choices of community policing rhetoric, organizational location, and programs are local and some are nonlocal. The nature of community policing could be predicted by knowing the power and trajectory of the relevant forces in the department itself, in the city, and in the city's and the department's transactions with nonlocal powers such as the U.S. Department of Justice.

In chapter 7, "Assessing Blameworthiness and Assigning Punishment: Theoretical Perspectives on Judicial Decision Making," Paula Kautt and Cassia Spohn provide a framework for summarizing, assessing, and integrating theories about individual decision making in criminal justice. They illustrate the promise of this framework with

theory and research about judicial sentencing decisions. Explicit attention to the horizontal or domain characteristics (such as demographic
variables vs. belief and attitude variables at the individual level) and
the vertical or social level characteristics of independent variables (such
as individual vs. organizational forces) allows researchers to determine
what kinds of explanations for decisions have been explored and which
have been ignored. Doing so permits them to design new theory and
new research in a systematic way. It also provides for clues about possible combinations or integration across sectors and levels that could
make our explanations of decision makers more complete. For example, are judges with one set of values and beliefs more or less likely than
others to act on those personal beliefs, and are those tendencies affected
by the community or organization in which the judge is situated?

In "Courts and Communities: Toward a Theoretical Synthesis,"
chapter 8, Alissa Pollitz Worden illustrates yet a different approach to
theoretical review and comparison, and concern for a different unit
of analysis. While Kautt and Spohn were developing a framework for
explaining individual decision outcomes by individual judges, Worden is concerned with the larger (or higher) social levels in the Kautt
and Spohn vertical chain: courts and communities. Worden's review
illustrates the importance of getting concepts properly defined. Some
researchers conceive of the prosecutor, defense attorney, and judge
meeting in the court as itself a community. Since Warren (1978) long
ago argued that communities are largely and increasingly networks
of organizations, this view of courts-as-community is not trivial or
accidental, even if it is not what others might mean by community.
Frameworks for systematically reviewing theory assist in identifying
potential conceptual conflicts and assist in turning them into creative
opportunities. Additionally, Worden seeks to devise a framework that
will work in two directions: enabling us to see the potential effects of
courts on communities, and vice versa, the potential effects of communities on courts. It would be useful to ask whether investigations
in both directions still meet Snipes and Maguire's "official response
test." While community impacts on courts presumably affect official
response to crime and therefore meet this test, do court impacts on
community also meet this test? Can we think of community differences
in criminal justice as connected to the official response to crime? We
will return to this issue below, as we talk about unit of analysis as one
means of developing criminal justice theory.

Eric Lambert's "A Test of a Turnover Intent Model: The Issue of Correctional Staff Satisfaction and Commitment" (chapter 9) provides
the first empirical test of theory presented in this volume. Lambert

examines both the causes and effects of job satisfaction among corrections workers. Working in an area of management and human resources research that is rich in theory development, measurement, and research, Lambert borrows available theory to examine whether it holds in the arguably odd or unusual case of corrections. The patterns that have been often substantiated in private industry also appear to apply in work such as corrections. Worker job satisfaction is more affected by management practice than by worker characteristics. Similar in unit of analysis to the Kautt and Spohn work, Lambert examines individual worker attitudes and decisions. As Worden suggests in chapter 8, these individual level attitudes are, in this case like many others, strongly influenced by levels of explanation above the individual level (in this case, characteristics of the correctional organization).

In chapter 10, "Examining Correctional Resources," Edmund McGarrell and David Duffee seek to explain variations in financial support for corrections. Like Renauer, they draw on institutional theory. While institutional theory has often been more concerned with legitimacy of public organizations than with fiscal resources, the authors reason that greater legitimacy should result in a greater share of tax dollars and greater level of tax dollars per citizen. While the test of institutional theory conducted here is generally supportive of institutional theory, the test is a weak one in the sense that the authors have to assume, rather than directly measure, the underlying processes that would lead to the results that they achieve. The findings also suggest that some facets of the institutional environment are more powerful than are others. In this instance, racial or cultural heterogeneity appears more powerful than professions, unions, or bureaucracy in determining the relative strength of corrections as a public sector investment.

THE DIMENSIONS OF THEORY

In chapter 2, Snipes and Maguire proposed several theoretical themes as potentially useful in thinking about and developing criminal justice theory. We review these themes briefly here, in the order in which they appeared in chapter 2.

Historical vs. Nonhistorical Perspective

Theories vary in their attention to history, or developments over time. One can think such changes both with individuals (such as changing attitudes while at work, as in chapter 9) and with larger constructs such as polities (such as changing the value placed on punishment as the composition of society changes, as in chapter 10). Renauer's theory of community policing probably implies development over time within a city, as a police department reacts incrementally to a mix of local and nonlocal forces. Some of the theories that Kautt and Spohn review (chapter 7) imply changes in judicial decisions as judges age, gain experience, change their attitudes, and so on. In general, however, one should note that while some of the theories discussed in this work are clearly historical or developmental, most of the studies reviewed and the two empirical tests provided are not historical, but are single-point-in-time, cross-sectional studies.

Clearly, stronger science will emerge when historical data are available with which to test longitudinal theories. This need, however, is difficult to fulfill. As criminal justice systems have become more technologically advanced, data about them have become more plentiful and sometimes more accurate. This means that longitudinal data series on criminal justice phenomena may not collect the same data, or may collect data measured in different (even if improved) ways, over time. One problem with historical theories, then, is that there is often disparate quality to the data that would allow us to test them over time for aggregates (like cities, states, or nations). For instance, Maguire and Schulte-Murray (2001) found that many of the nations submitting data to the United Nations on the number of police employees used erratic definitions of what constitutes a "police officer" over time. Maguire and Schulte-Murray's graphs of the number of police officers in several nations showed large peaks and valleys from year to year, when in fact police employment changed only gradually. Testing historical theories of police employment using such data would paint a wholly inaccurate picture.

If one is concerned with changes in individuals, it may be easier to design a study to track individuals over time. Longitudinal studies of delinquents and offenders are commonplace in criminology. Similar studies of criminal justice officials lag behind.

Organizational Perspective

Snipes and Maguire suggest that three main organizational perspectives are most relevant (or at least most prevalent) in relation to criminal justice theory: the rational-goal perspective, the functional systems perspective, and the institutional perspective. It is likely that many other versions of organizational theory will eventually creep into the mix of explanations for criminal justice behavior. Of the three perspectives discussed in chapter 2, arguably this volume has provided greater coverage of and more examples of the latter two than the first. Does this mean rational-goal perspectives are less common? We doubt it. In fact, the opposite is likely to be the case, and one of the main complaints of authors of this volume. The rational-goal perspective often focuses on effectiveness and assumes that reduction in crime is the principal criterion of effectiveness. There are severe limits to the logic of such theories, as discussed by both Snipes and Maguire and Castellano and Gould, including some questions about their status as scientific theories. Nevertheless, they have probably generated the most research in criminal justice. Functional systems perspectives and institutional perspectives need much more attention before we begin to reap real benefits from their potential guidance.

Sociopolitical Perspective

Snipes and Maguire pose the fundamental differences in sociopolitical perspective as the difference between consensus and conflict approaches to criminal justice. Hagan (1989b) and more recently Bernard and Engel (2001) have suggested that this dichotomy in political perspective is overly simplistic and limited in its explanatory value. We suspect these authors are correct. Thinking of criminal justice as resting on only a conflict among groups or consensus among groups seems less than accurate about most complex societies. While the chapters in this volume do not focus only, or often, on the sociopolitical dimension, they do appear to suggest that consensus and conflict may be operating at different levels in the same place and time. For example, there may be more political consensus about how individual criminal justice officials should behave in a system than there is consensus across groups or political interests about basic criminal justice policies.

Objective vs. Subjective Perspective

Recall from chapter 2 that objective theories view social artifacts (such as crime rates) as reflecting reality, while subjective theories treat such artifacts as socially constructed. For subjectivists, reality is in the eye of the beholder. Sullivan (1994) argued that the subjective perspective was limiting the growth of criminal justice theory because it relied more heavily on distinguishing different individual beliefs and attitudes than on examining objective differences among larger units of analysis such as organizations and criminal justice systems. While this volume finds many roadblocks in the path of theory development, it does not portray overreliance on individual subjective experience as one of them. Indeed, most of the works reviewed and presented here would seem to fall on the objective side of the objective/subjective dimension (with the possible exception of Lambert's study and some of the individual attitudinal studies reviewed by Kautt and Spohn). Both the objective and subjective perspectives might be meaningfully integrated to expand our understanding of criminal justice phenomena. We will provide two hypothetical examples to show how this might be done, one from the world of policing, and the other from corrections.

First, when police chiefs think about their departments' performance, they often rely on a series of "objective" indicators such as crime rates, use of force incidents, and citizen complaints. These indicators all have their place within a comprehensive performance evaluation scheme. However, police agencies are much less likely to rely on multiple sources of subjective data about their performance. They sometimes survey citizens, though they often do not ask the right questions. They rarely survey arrestees, crime victims, or officers about the department's performance. Combining official data and subjective survey data from multiple populations is one way of collecting multidimensional data on police performance (Maguire 2003).

Second, students of organizational theory and public administration often wrestle with the term *bureaucratization*. The term is intellectually empty because it combines multiple dimensions of organizational life in a fuzzy way (Langworthy 1986; Maguire 2003). At the same time, it has mass appeal because we can all recall with some degree of misery the problems and hassles we have experienced in dealing with government agencies, whether local, state, or federal. Therefore, though we have intellectual concerns about the validity of the concept, it still makes for a good example to illustrate the difference between objective and subjective approaches. Bureaucratization has been measured in many ways over the years, but some of the most popular "objective" measures are the number of written rules and policies within the organization, the number of people who must sign off on a particular decision, the number of standard operating procedures, or the number of separate forms that must be filled out to accomplish a particular set of tasks. At the same time, we might also think of bureaucratization as having a strongly subjective component. Even if an organization has mountains of red tape, if the worker and the client do not view it as bureaucratic, is it? If objective and subjective measures of bureaucratization are not closely aligned, then theories of bureaucratization should also account for the subjective experiences of those who must deal with the organization, namely its workers and its clients.

Type of Response or Nature of the Dependent Variable

The nature of the dependent variable is another way of distinguishing between criminal justice theories. It is closely tied with the unit of analysis. Frequently, for instance, when the unit of analysis is the individual, the dependent variable is some measure of attitudes or behaviors that varies across individuals. When the unit of analysis is the organization, the dependent variable is some feature that varies across organizations.

Sometimes the dependent variable will be a traditional criminal justice response that involves overt behavior on the part of criminal justice personnel: examples include the use of force, arrest, citation, charging, sentencing, or releasing. Sometimes it may just be an attitude or a value. Is the police officer cynical? Does the correctional officer have high job satisfaction? Other times the dependent variable will not be an individual attitude or behavior, but rather a context within which these attitudes and behaviors operate. Examples include policies, operating standards, organizational cultures, and organizational structures. For instance, Robert Langworthy (1986) examined the effect of various political and social factors on the organizational structures of police organizations. This dependent variable passes the reasonableness test outlined by Snipes and Maguire in chapter 2 because police organizations presumably structure themselves to deal with crime, as well as other issues.

Another way of thinking about the dependent variable is to identify the unit of analysis. All theories strive to make inferences about some entity — that entity is the unit of analysis. Alternately, it is the level at which the dependent variable is measured. In chapter 9, for instance, Lambert describes a theory of correctional officer job satisfaction. The unit of analysis in this case is correctional officers, or more generally, individuals. In chapter 10, McGarrell and Duffee outline a theory of correctional spending which they then test at the state level; therefore states are the unit of analysis.

Units of analysis can sometimes get complex when units are nested within other units. For instance, suppose we develop a theory to explain police officers' behavior in urban neighborhoods. We then test the theory using data collected by observing officers in multiple neighborhoods. If the theory seeks to explain variation in the behavior of individual officers, then the unit of analysis is individuals. If the theory seeks to explain patterns of police behavior in different neighborhoods, then the unit of analysis is neighborhoods. An example of this nesting occurs in chapter 7, in which Kautt and Spohn seek to explain judicial decision making. Typically, we are not interested in comparing individual judges, but in the decisions they make in criminal cases. Thus the criminal case is the unit of analysis, and to test the theory properly, one would need to observe or collect data from multiple criminal cases across multiple judges in multiple courts.

Level of Explanation or Nature of the Independent Variable

Closely tied with the unit of analysis is the level of explanation, or the level at which the independent variables are measured. In many theories, the unit of analysis and the level of explanation are the same. For instance, if we develop a theory in which we attribute the punitive behavior of judges to their political attitudes, both the independent variable (attitudes) and the dependent variable (behavior) are measured at the individual level. Sometimes, however, the independent variables are measured at multiple levels. For an example, we need to look no further than chapter 7, in which Kautt and Spohn attempt to explain variation in judicial decision making. They claim that a "vertically integrated theory" is one that incorporates "influences from two or more hierarchical levels." Among the explanatory or independent variables they discuss are case characteristics, individual characteristics of the defendant and the judge (and other court actors), and the characteristics of the community in which the court is located.

We might picture level of explanation as an inverted pyramid (while Kautt and Spohn use a pyramid in Figure 7.1, the idea might make even more sense upside down). The level at which the independent variables are measured can always be equal to or larger than the level at which the dependent variable is measured. If the dependent variable is the outcome in a criminal trial, then characteristics of the case can be used as independent variables because they are measured at the same (case) level. Furthermore, since cases are nested within courts and districts (both of which are a higher level than an individual case), perhaps characteristics of these levels could also help explain differences in the outcomes of trials. In this instance, we would be relying on multiple levels of explanation.

While discussions of units of analysis and levels of explanation can quickly get tangled up with the jargon of research methods and statistics, once again, the topic is actually quite simple. Picture a patrol officer who has stopped a drunk driver. Suppose the driver is belligerent and refuses to get out of the car as instructed by the officer. Think for a moment about all the potential forces acting on that individual officer when deciding what course of action to pursue. Certainly the officer's own experiences, attitudes, and values will come into play. It is not difficult to imagine two officers handling the situation very differently if one is more predisposed to violence than is the other, for example. The individual characteristics of the suspect might play a role. For instance, the officer might handle a strapping 240 pound young man differently from how he or she might handle a well-dressed older woman. The officer will also respond to cues present in the situation. Is it dark outside? Are the windows of the car tinted? Is the area populated and busy, or is it a lonely stretch of road? Finally, the officer will also presumably be influenced by organizational factors. What does department policy dictate? How has the department interpreted recent procedural law? What would the officer's supervisor expect? In short, the officer would be influenced by a variety of individual, situational, and organizational factors. Each of these factors represents a level of explanation. A theory that accounts for police behavior in drunk driving situations using all of these factors would be relying on multiple levels of explanation.

Institutional Arena

Finally, the easiest way to distinguish among different theoretical approaches to criminal justice is probably to identify the sector in which the theory is focused. Sometimes the theorist focuses only on one part of the criminal justice system like the police or the courts; other times the focus is on the system as a whole. The chapters in this volume were divided up by sector, with part I containing three chapters that address the criminal justice system as a whole and criminal justice theory generally, and parts II through IV addressing the police, courts, and corrections, respectively.

Both Alan Liska, in his sociology of social control (1992a), and Bernard and Engel (2001), in their proposal for a framework of criminal justice theory, make the case for theories that span institutional arenas. Bernard and Engel argue that if we truly have a theory of "criminal justice" then we should be making theoretical statements that would hold across police, court, and correctional officials or agencies. Similarly, but even more expansive, Liska argues that a sociology of social control should be able to deal with theories of control across control sectors, such as crime, mental health, and poverty.

In most instances, the chapters in this book obviously do not get that far. It would seem to us that cross-institutional theories of criminal justice are indeed important, if quite deficient, as Howard and Freilich point out. But we would also suggest that requiring a theory to span sectors in order to make the grade is overly demanding and perhaps too narrow. While it would be interesting to determine if various criminal justice officials respond in the same way to similar stimuli, it is certainly premature to cast off or denigrate studies of or within one sector as too narrow to be useful. Indeed, careful theoretical reviews will be needed that examine systems, organizations, and individuals for similarities and differences. We would not want to ignore what is unique to policing in the pursuit of what police have in common with correctional officers or to lose what is unique about criminal justice in pursuit of what all formal control systems have in common.

A STRATEGY FOR ASSESSING THE STATE OF CRIMINAL JUSTICE THEORY: SOME ILLUSTRATIONS

Given the breadth, complexity, and relatively recent emergence of criminal justice as a research field (Cullen 1995), if we are to sort out and prioritize promising areas for study, we first need a means of organizing the work. The most useful framework would be one that facilitates thinking about causal theory, not merely prediction; one that does not confine our attention to topics and questions that already have been examined; and, similarly, one that permits us to assess readily both what has been done, and what remains to be explored. There are many ways to categorize criminal justice research (chapter 2 in this volume; Bernard and Engel 2001), but we suggest that one of the most promising ways to organize our assessments of previous research, and our recommendations for future study, is around units of analysis — the entities whose behavior we wish to explain (Snipes and Maguire's fifth theme in chapter 2).

A simple taxonomy of units of analysis would include individuals, organizations, communities, and polities. For each of these, we might construct a schema with the following dimensions: types of behavior worth studying, areas of potentially applicable theory, and extant theoretical and empirical work. By mapping these elements of criminal justice scholarship, we may be better able to answer three interesting questions: What has theory taught us about criminal justice behavior? What has our research on behavior taught us about popular theories? Should we be asking different questions, or asking questions differently, about criminal justice behavior? Development of this schema is beyond the scope of this chapter, but the following sections offer illustrations and some observations based on this strategy.

Individuals

As Walker (1993) and others have documented (e.g., chapters 1, 7, and 9), probably the most commonly studied aspect of criminal justice behavior is the discretionary decision making of practitioners. This emphasis on police officers, prosecutors, judges, and correctional officers may stem from the politics that accompanied the emergence of criminal justice as a field of study in the 1960s and 1970s. When policy makers identified challenges to improving the criminal justice process, few questioned the structure or implied objectives of the existing systems and processes; instead, they equated dysfunction with departures from legal norms of equal treatment and due process, and therefore often directed their research toward individuals' failure to perform as expected, or to treat citizens fairly. In particular, they directed their attention toward discretionary decisions such as arrest, charging, and sentencing, and they sought explanations for disparities in these decisions in the behaviors of individual actors.

The simplest theories about individuals account for variation in behavior with individual-level constructs, such as social background, attitudes and beliefs, and experience. Theories linking these attributes have been developed fairly extensively for some kinds of actors (such as police and correctional officers), but much less so for others (prosecutors). For instance, scholars have hypothesized that variability in police officers' job performance (arrest, use of physical force) is influenced by age, sex, race, and family class status. Others have used these same independent variables to predict not only discretionary decisions, but also actors' role orientations, beliefs about their work and about constituencies, and commitment to occupations (Carter 1984; Gibson 1981a; Muir 1977). Researchers have also predicted attitudes about work, and working styles, from preprofessional as well as on-the-job experiences (such as education, other work experiences, and training; e.g., Lambert, chapter 9).

Much of this work stems from importation theories — theories that stipulate that work behavior is shaped by the characteristics of the individual, at least as much as the character of the work or the workplace (see Lambert, chapter 9; Worden 1993). As commonsensical as this sounds, however, importation theory has found limited support in criminal justice research. There are at least two reasons for this. First, the causal theories have not always been carefully specified, and as a result empirical tests only loosely mirror hypotheses. For example, gender and race often serve as proxies for very general (and often underspecified) constellations of experiences and attitudes; but null findings cannot tell us whether the theory is incorrect, or the sampled subjects simply did not fit gender or race stereotypes.

Second, individual-level theories overlook the effects of some powerful social and organizational processes, processes that may lead individuals to change their attitudes, or to set them aside in the workplace. For example, criminal justice workers self-select into their occupations, so variance on some attitude and experience variables is limited in samples of practitioners. Furthermore, many criminal justice jobs have entrance barriers and strong socializing and training regimens that tend to standardize views about the work, and certainly are intended to standardize behavior (e.g., Heumann 1978).

Measuring key constructs in these kinds of theories — theories about organizational structure, culture, and socialization processes — is more challenging than examining individuals, but potentially more promising. Moreover, these theories introduce a larger range of interesting and important behavioral variables and questions. What do police departments or prisons do well (or poorly) to help workers adapt to their work? Is the blue-collar culture of police departments really just the aggregate result of traditional recruitment among the working class, or is it instead sustained (or undermined) by leadership, training, or departmental philosophy?

Organizations

Criminal justice organizations are agencies that process people and information. Like many other organizations, they provide services, respond to needs and complaints, and spend tax money. They are nearly unique in their prerogative to use physical force and coercion to ensure compliance from citizens (in the form of arrest, contempt citations, subpoenas, probation revocation, or solitary confinement in prison, to name a few examples).

Formally, organizational behavior is bounded by responsibilities (e.g., the obligation to respond to 911 calls), constraints (such as the prohibition on unjustified detention), and accountability (the need to answer to political powers that authorize their work, as well as professional standards). Organizations also are characterized by variables such as culture and style of leadership. Although the basic functions of the various types of criminal justice organizations are well established (and are often reflected in their formal structure), other aspects of their activities vary considerably: some police departments innovate, while others do not; some prisons offer more rehabilitative programming than others; some prosecutors create specialized units. The challenge for social scientists is to catalog the behaviors worthy of study, and identify theories that might help us understand variation in those behaviors.

Most commonly, researchers (and the public) are interested in the relationships among the ways work is organized (including the allocation of resources, people, and expertise) and the way work is performed (including quality, fairness, consistency, and efficiency). As an example, in this volume, Maguire and Uchida offer an exhaustive inventory of police department organizational behaviors, including activities, processes, performance, style, administrative arrangements, processing routines, structures, communication patterns, and corporate personalities or subcultures (see also Maguire and Uchida 2000). Researchers and policy makers have asked similar questions about other sectors: do public defenders provide better representation than do appointed counsel? Do vertical prosecution bureaus achieve higher conviction rates than does the horizontal division of labor? Do drug courts result in fewer jail sentences than traditional criminal courts? A second set of questions involves organizational changes: how, how much, and under what conditions can (and will) policy makers rearrange organizations to induce different behavior? Interestingly, systematic studies that assess organizational capacity to innovate are rare in criminal justice (see Worden, chapter 8).

Some of the most successful recent efforts to account for organizational behavior stem from institutional theory, which stipulates that organizational adaptations to environments serve not only practical, functional reasons (such as garnering sufficient resources or managing caseloads) but also the less obvious but critically important need to retain legitimacy by reflecting basic cultural values and beliefs. While criminal justice organizations have something of a monopoly on their business and are therefore unlikely to be put out of business by competitors (although private alternatives are proliferating), their roles as enforcers and arbiters of social norms generate constant potential challenges to their authority and legitimacy. Furthermore, since criminal justice agency leaders would be politically unwise to argue, as some of this volume's authors do, that criminal justice behavior does not significantly affect the rate or amount of crime, they must sometimes justify their existence or activities in other ways.

It is important to recognize that the institutionalization of practices, beliefs, and norms that are not demonstrably connected to performance takes places in two settings, or for two kinds of constituencies. First, practices become institutionalized because they suit local actors' expectations; they may be defended as inevitable or necessary when in fact they are simply familiar, comfortable, and predictable. For example, Church's early research (1985) on case delay in urban courts revealed that pretrial lapses (which vary greatly across jurisdictions) were unrelated to caseload, resources, or personnel; instead, each jurisdiction's court workers firmly believed that their particular turnaround time was the result of case pressure, rules, or resource limits (and were therefore altogether defensible).

Second, practices become institutionalized for the consumption of external constituents. Renauer (chapter 6, this volume) observes that adoption of community policing may be less the consequence of commitment to a different model of crime control and community responsiveness than the result of national peer pressure from other departments and professional organizations, or community pressure for more accountability. Not surprisingly, the prospects for a fully operational community policing system appear to be related to motivation for innovation.

Institutional theory not only helps us understand how organizations negotiate their environments; it may also help us figure out why and how they can successfully disregard important elements of those environments. For example, a small collection of excellent case studies documents the ways in which court organizations subvert externally (often legislatively) imposed procedural rules and sanctioning mandates (Feeley 1983; Heumann and Loftin 1979; Horney and Spohn 1991). Leaving aside the simple political fact that legislatures have little power to bring judges and prosecutors into compliance, these actors have no incentive to set aside norms and standards that they have spent years practicing and justifying.

In short, our theorizing about criminal justice organizations has focused largely on two kinds of questions: First, how do internal organizational arrangements affect performance? Second, how do organizational relationships with political environments affect organizational behavior? What we have learned from the limited empirical research on these questions suggests that future studies would be well served to look beyond formal organizational goals and legal constraints and focus instead on less readily measurable but powerful influences on behavior such as organizational culture and political legitimacy.

Communities

Communities historically have been the basis for criminal justice in American society. Therefore communities, defined as legally and geographically bounded jurisdictions, are units that shape the work of local criminal justice systems and react to those systems' behavior. But as noted previously in this chapter, the notion of communities encompasses a broader array of social groupings than cities and counties: we would also want to include neighborhoods, political wards, and, perhaps, organized grassroots interest groups that cross community boundaries. These social entities practice a diverse range of activities, which have been more commonly the subject of speculation, and, sometimes theorizing, than of empirical scrutiny. Examples include political behavior such as electioneering, coalition formation, and voting; behavior more specifically directed at the performance of criminal justice agencies such as partnering and coproduction; behavior that legitimates (or calls into question) system practices or decisions, such as protesting, mobilization, or participation (as in civilian review boards). Many would also include as behavior collective opinion formation (example: fear of crime, beliefs about system integrity).

Community attributes often appear as independent variables explaining other things, such as organizational behavior (whether police departments adopt community policing models) and individual behavior (whether judges sentence harshly or leniently, in response to perceived community preferences). These sorts of studies typically model communities as static features of the criminal justice environment, to which agents and agencies react. Future researchers may expand this perspective on communities by exploring the nonrecursive relationships among criminal justice agencies and communities (e.g., Renauer's chapter 6; Sung 2001).

Because the most important (if least remarked) feature of many communities is their lack of communal action, researchers would benefit from learning more about what sorts of communities act collectively, and under what conditions. On this question, very different theoretical propositions might arise: one might hypothesize that economic marginality (neither hopeless poverty, nor comfortable affluence) motivates citizens to work together; a more pluralistic perspective would compare the activity levels of residential, commercial, and other interests (as well as their competition); still another proposition is that charismatic leadership generates some kinds of community action. Once researchers make headway on the important challenge of defining communities (perhaps by devising a more helpful lexicon to sort out the many meanings of this phrase), they would be better prepared to address other important questions about communities: for example, what attributes of communities might account for social equilibrium (rather than conflict) over enforcement priorities? What conditions incubate rather than stifle social protests over crime and criminal justice, regardless of levels of community participation? What factors in communities repress or inhibit coproduction or cooperation with authorities (J. D. Scott 2002)?

Polities

Polities are political units of analysis: states, provinces, nations, and, at the international level, policy-making bodies, including states and provinces as well as nations and even international collectives with self-governing treaties (such as the United Nations). They are comprised of citizens, or members, and their governing bodies. One might distinguish them from communities, certainly in a Western context, insofar as they claim explicit authority to make (not merely interpret or implement) law, including laws about what is and is not crime, and how society will deploy its power against those accused of violating law, and in protection of those who are victimized.

American history and law regard crime and justice as peculiarly local phenomena, as Worden demonstrates (chapter 8, this volume), so why should higher order polities be of interest to researchers who study American criminal justice? First, most criminal justice policy is formally made at this level, including substantive and procedural law, many significant organizational and administrative decisions in the area of corrections, and resource allocations. Second, states' and nations' political cultures — their expectations of their government, including their criminal justice systems — vary significantly. In particular, where *crime* is defined broadly, to include whatever popular culture or powerful elites find unacceptable, inappropriate, or threatening, *criminal justice* will be a highly visible function in society.

Therefore, the criminal justice behavior exhibited by polities will include the rules they promulgate, as well as the structures and institutions they create to enforce them; one might also include public and elite expectations for (and reactions to) the system itself. While theorizing at this level may seem rather abstract, a few familiar examples quickly make the task appear not only practical but pressing: Why do some states adopt the death penalty and others do not? Why are some acts defined as crimes in some nations, but not others? Why do Americans value due process so highly? Taking these questions one step further, one might ask whether some features of criminal justice systems (such as a strong rights orientation, punitiveness, or repressive criminal codes) are related to social features including prevalence of crime, poverty, and education?

Answers to these questions can perhaps be found in theories designed to account, more generally, for societies' distributions of benefits and punishments. Some versions of conflict theory attribute legal definitions of crime, and enforcement priorities, to the interests of entrenched elites, who use the criminal justice system (like other social systems) to manage their investments. Consensus theory suggests that these political decisions are more likely to reflect the collective will of citizens, for whom criminal justice is particularly salient to their notions of collective security and safety, as well as their normative views. Frequently these theories are presented as oppositional (e.g., Hagan 1989a; Lynch and Groves 1981), although a skillful (and agnostic) theoretical synthesis of them is not only conceivable but also tantalizing. Comparative and historical theoretical treatments (Beckett 1997; Garland 2001) suggest that the moral panic around crime issues that has dominated since the mid-1980s is the product of the shared exploitation of crime and victimization by the media and politicians; the unwitting consumers of this preoccupation with crime have been mainstream voters (Scheingold 1984, 1991).

These sorts of theories are powerful, but risky from a scientific perspective: they are easily expropriated for ideological purposes, and ideological debates typically leave little room for science. All too often, the standard of plausibility is substituted for the standard of probability, and we stop short of subjecting these theories to the tedious work of hypothesis development, measurement, and testing. This is understandable, since these units of analysis are big and unwieldy, change only gradually, and over spans of time that exceed the average researcher's professional career. It is almost as if such theories are too grand to be put to practical use. Moreover, social scientists have an uneasy and wary relationship with historical studies, which might provide the kinds of data that would yield some tests of these theories (but see Garland 2001; Myers 1993). Yet studies of polities such as American states reveal considerable variation in criminal justice behavior, and some promise in accounting for that variation with political and social variables (Horney and Spohn 1991; McGarrell and Duffee in this volume; McGarrell and Duffee 1995; Taggart and Winn 1991; Talarico and Swanson 1979).

SUMMARY

We offer a simple strategy for taking stock of criminal justice theory: inventory what we know and what questions we have asked around the entities — the units of analysis — that *behave* in the context of criminal justice. This strategy puts the focus on behavior — actions, activities, decisions, responses — that can be attributed to identifiable social units. But is this strategy helpful, and if so, how?

First, organizing our understanding around social units' behavior directs us to look first at attributes of those units for theoretical causes:

this is efficient and commonsensical. It also paves the way for discovering that the most proximate theoretical causes are not always the most powerful ones, however; an important discovery. For example, individuals' behavior may be more deeply influenced by their organizations, and organizations by their political environments, than by their own internal characteristics. It is always good to explore the simplest explanations first; but if and when they fail, then it is wise to move to more complex levels of explanation.

Second, the focus on social units clarifies the importance of two basic scientific tasks that too often get hasty and inadequate attention from researchers: theorizing and measurement. If one is to theorize that a particular force causes an agent's behavior, one must assume or demonstrate the plausibility of that causal relationship. This simple requirement is overlooked surprisingly often. An example occurs in the sentencing literature, where researchers have sometimes modeled case outcomes (such as conviction) as a function of defendant attributes, even when *those attributes were not typically known or knowable by the decision makers at the time of conviction* (such as drug dependence or parental status). One is unlikely to make such a mistake if one simply remembers that human beings (judges and prosecutors) can only base decisions (including good, bad, biased, or fair ones) on information that they actually have. Similarly, theorizing about social units' behavior raises the stakes for careful conceptualization and measurement of those units' attributes and behavior. Hypothesizing that female police officers make fewer arrests than men is much less interesting than finding out whether women (and men) with traditional gender roles do their jobs differently — but sex and gender role are quite different variables, calling for different measures.

Finally, studying more complex social units, such as communities and polities, presents more challenges but possibly more payoffs than the field's traditional prioritization on individual and organizational studies. Such research might raise our awareness of variables that masquerade as constants in studies of other units of analysis. A simple example, entailing a widely regarded theory, is Lipsky's analysis of street-level bureaucrats. Astute readers note that Lipsky (1980) accounts for what many might see as a set of pathologies (and seemingly universal ones) among those who work directly with social agency clients, including criminal justice clients. His accounting for these problematic but pervasive behaviors is compelling, in part because it seems to apply, at least partly, to nearly every bureaucrat: police, probation officers, teachers, and social workers. More astute readers recognize, however, that Lipsky is doing more than describing a seemingly invariable state of affairs, because he attributes those conditions, ultimately, to American society's unwillingness to take on full responsibility for the complexity and costs of responding to the social problems those bureaucrats face each day. *Social indifference* (or ignorance) of these kinds of problems is, of course, a construct that varies across states and other sorts of polities.

Lingering Questions

We are of course not suggesting that reviewing and formulating theory around the device of the unit of analysis is the only, or even the best way to proceed. A number of other rubrics should also be explored. There is a great deal of such work to be done, in part because criminal justice theory has not often been taken seriously enough for long enough to generate systematic comparisons of theoretical schemas. We do not really know what they hold in common and what is different. It is time for that work to begin. While that task is far too vast for this volume, we hope that this collection will spur on such work.

As we close, we want to take another brief look at other lingering and troublesome questions. While we can provide only tentative and suggestive answers here to some of these, we anticipate that the development of criminal justice theory will enable better and more exacting answers in the future.

Is it possible to find or develop a criminal justice theory that would span different units of analysis? Is it even desirable to look? In chapter 3, Howard and Freilich caution against grand theories. It may be very premature or even misleading and dangerous to search for a theory that "explains all criminal justice responses at all times." This, of course, is precisely what Black thought he had done with *The Behavior of Law* (1976). He proposed that the same variables that would explain individual level behavior would explain behavior by communities or polities. Most of the evidence suggests that this was a false hope. Indeed, there appear often to be very different explanations for individual-level and higher unit-level behaviors. We suspect that Howard and Freilich are correct that grand theories of criminal justice are unlikely and perhaps misleading.

Is it useful to think of schools of criminal justice theory, as is often the case with criminological theory? Our view is that this might occur (actually, it is probably an inevitable by-product of theory development). As criminal justice scholars become more explicitly concerned with the nature of the theories that they espouse and test they will seek means of comparing and contrasting different kinds of criminal justice theories. If kept under control, we think this kind of development is a positive sign; it suggests some vibrancy in theoretical thinking. But the identification of schools of criminal justice theory would also suggest some hazards. Schools of thought are often reified and taught; they are valued as truths rather than as tools for research. We would be wary of intellectual (and emotional) commitments to specific theories, as schools of thought might imply. We are convinced that "conflict" and "consensus" "theories" are usually too global, too grand, or too simplistic to be of much help in describing most criminal justice reality — although both Scheingold (1984), and Wilkins (1991), have made some strides trying to think of when and where there is more or less consensus or conflict, or more or less extremism in reaction to crime. Other kinds of schools of thought about criminal justice that have been bandied about, such as radical, liberal, and conservative seem to describe the political rather than scientific intent of some researchers. In any case, we suspect that criminal justice theory is a long way from being codified into schools of thought. It probably will occur several times over, as it has in other sciences. But criminal justice theory is relatively underdeveloped to allow much categorization of types of theory.

Can criminal justice theory develop separately from the broader study of social control? We suspect that it will and should, within limits. First, academic programs of criminology and criminal justice continue to develop rapidly, and the fastest growth in these programs now is at the doctoral level. The field of crime and criminal justice is maturing as a scientific field. It will not continue to mature unless criminal justice theory is taken seriously. And it seems unlikely to us that the field will continue to be serious about crime theory but permit other fields such as political science and sociology to focus on criminal justice theory. Certainly, criminal justice is one form of state social control and sociologists and political scientists will continue to be interested in criminal justice phenomena. But we also think that criminal justice is sufficiently distinct from other forms of social control and other forms of political power that it can and will benefit from criminal justice specialists developing theory uniquely suited to explaining criminal justice behavior.

Finally, how is criminal justice theory related to criminological theory? Our honest answer at the moment is that we do not know but are eager to find out. One of the authors once mentioned to another colleague that the most basic theoretical problem in criminal justice is explaining what will be called a crime. His colleague responded by saying that it was also the most fundamental criminological problem. We are not sure whether these two scholars are agreeing with each other or talking past each other, but we think it could be very productive to explore systematically the relationship between explaining crime and explaining criminal justice. Leslie Wilkins (1991) wrote that crime and the reaction to crime could not be separated because they depend on each other. A crime is not a fact but a decision to respond to a fact in a certain way. To call something a crime means that it should be punished, or presupposes the criminal justice system (of some sort). Crime does not come before punishment; the availability of punishment leads to labeling acts as crimes and some people as criminal. This observation would lead some people to say that criminal justice "causes" crime. The observation is either trivial or profound, but it is not going to help us very much with the practical task of sorting through the theoretical and empirical connections between crime and criminal justice.

Yes, there must be some concept of "crime" in order for some harmful acts to be labeled as such and such labeling may have its own effects on a variety of behaviors by a variety of people. And it may be very interesting to promote more studies that examine how, when, and why the idea of crime and the apparatus of criminal justice emerge in socio-political systems (see Robinson and Scaglion 1987; Schwartz and Miller 1965). Such studies are an important subset of theoretical and research problems in which one is trying to explain why criminal justice rather than some other social control is selected by a society in response to a problem.

Most of the connections between criminological and criminal justice theory will be more mundane and more frequent than these queries about the origins of crime and punishment. Most will start with a base in which responding to a wide range of social acts as crime is commonplace and a criminal justice system is institutionalized. The questions will not concern which is first or more primordial. Instead, we will be concerned with whether specific forms of criminal justice have specific effects on types of crime and similarly whether specific kinds of crime have specific effects on criminal justice. For practical and political reasons, one of the more common connections between criminal justice theory and criminological theory will probably stem from current interests in promoting crime suppression or prevention programs, including those that involve criminal justice policies, agencies, and actions. This will return us to the conundrum described in chapter 1: the government, which funds most criminal justice research is much more interested in criminal justice effectiveness in reducing crime (e.g., in some form of criminological theory) than in criminal justice theory. But, to the extent that such policy or program effects can be found, that might spur interest in replication. If we can control crime in one place, can we replicate the program in another place? While the question has often been asked, we have rarely been seriously interested in the answer, which would require the development of criminal justice theory. If we can reproduce a program, that means we can, or expect that we can, manipulate the variables that cause some forms of criminal justice behavior. Can we?

REFERENCES

Ajzen, I. 1982. On behaving in accordance with one's attitudes. In *Consistency in social behavior: The Ontario Symposium*, ed. M.P. Zanna, E.T. Higgins, and C.P. Herman, 2:,3–15. Hillsdale, NJ: Erlbaum.

———. 1987. Attitudes, traits, and actions: Dispositional prediction of behavior in personality and social psychology. *Advances in Experimental Social Psychology* 20: 1–63.

Akers, R.L. 1992. Linking sociology and its specialties: The case of criminology. *Social Forces* 71(1): 1–16.

Albanese, J.S. 2002. *Criminal justice.* 2nd ed. Boston: Allyn & Bacon.

Albonetti, C.A. 1991. An integration of theories to explain judicial discretion. *Social Problems* 38: 247–66.

———. 1998. Direct and indirect effects of case complexity, guilty pleas, and offender characteristics on sentencing for offenders convicted of a white-collar offense prior to sentencing guidelines. *Journal of Quantitative Criminology* 14(4): 353–78.

Alexander, J.C., B. Giesen, R. Munch, and N.J. Smelser. 1987. *The micro-macro link.* Berkeley: University of California Press.

Alpert, G., and M.H. Moore. 1993. Measuring police performance in the new paradigm of policing. In *Performance measures for the criminal justice system: Discussion papers from the bjs-Princeton project.* 109–42. Washington, D.C.: Bureau of Justice Statistics.

Alpert, L., B. Atkins, and R. Ziller. 1979. Becoming a judge: The transition from advocate to arbiter. *Judicature* 62: 325.

Alschuler, A. 1979. Plea bargaining and its history. *Law and Society Review* 13: 211–45.

Andrews, A.H. 1985. Structuring the political independence of the police chief. In *Police leadership in America: Crisis and opportunity*, ed. W.A. Geller, 5–19. Chicago: American Bar Foundation; New York: Praeger.

Andrews, D., and J. Bonta. 1998. *The psychology of criminal conduct*, 2nd ed. Cincinnati: Anderson.

Arnstein, S.R. 1969. A ladder of citizen participation. *Journal of American Institute of Planners* 35: 216–24.

Arthur, J.A. 1988. *Social change and crime in Africa*. Ann Arbor, MI: University Microfilms International.

Arvanites, T.M., and M.A. Asher. 1995. The direct and indirect effects of socio-economic variables on state imprisonment rates. *Criminal Justice Policy Review* 7: 27–55.

Aupperle, K.E., W. Acar, and D.E. Booth. 1986. An empirical critique of *In Search of Excellence*: How excellent are the excellent companies? *Journal of Management* 12(4): 499–512.

Austin, J., and J. Irwin. 2001. *It's about time: America's imprisonment binge*, 3rd ed. Belmont, CA: Wadsworth.

Austin, T. 1981. The influence of court location on type of criminal sentences: The rural-urban factors. *Journal of Criminal Justice* 9: 305–16.

Bacharach, S.B. 1989. Organizational theories: Some criteria for evaluation. *Academy of Management Review* 14(4): 496–515.

Bagozzi, R. 1981. Attitudes, intentions, and behavior: A test of some key hypotheses. *Journal of Personality and Social Psychology* 41: 607–27.

Baldus, D.C., G. Woodworth, and C.A. Pulaski, Jr. 1990. *Equal justice and the death penalty: A legal and empirical analysis*. Boston: Northeastern University Press.

Ball, H. 1980. *Courts and politics: The federal judicial system*. Engelwood Cliffs, NJ: Prentice-Hall.

Banks, C. 2001. Women, justice, and custom: The discourse of "good custom" and "bad custom" in Papua New Guinea and Canada. *International Journal of Comparative Sociology* 17(1–2): 101–22.

Barlow, D.E., M.H. Barlow, and W.W. Johnson. 1996. The political economy of criminal justice policy: A time series analysis of economic conditions, crime, and federal criminal justice legislation 1948–1987. *Justice Quarterly* 13: 223–42.

Bateman, T., and D. Organ. 1983. Job satisfaction and the good soldier: The relationship between affect and employee citizenship. *Academy of Management Journal* 26: 587–95.

Bayley, D.H. 1985. *Patterns of policing: A comparative international analysis*. New Brunswick, NJ: Rutgers University Press.

_____. 1992. Comparative organization of the police in English-speaking countries. In *Modern policing*, ed. M. Tonry and N. Morris, 509–46. Chicago: University of Chicago Press.

_____. 1994. *Police for the future*, New York: Oxford University Press.

Bazemore, G. 1997. The "community" in community justice: Issues, themes, and questions for the new neighborhood sanctioning models. *Justice System Journal* 19(2): 193–228.

Becker, H. 1960. Notes on the concept of commitment. *American Journal of Sociology* 66: 32–42.

Becker, T. 1966. Surveys and judiciaries: Or who's afraid of the purple curtain? *Law and Society Review* 1: 133.

Beckett, K. 1997. *Making crime pay: Law and order in contemporary American politics*. New York: Oxford University Press.

Bennett, S.F. 1998. Community organizations and crime. In *Community justice: An emerging field*, ed. D. Karp, 31–46. Lanham, MD: Rowman & Littlefield.

Berger, P., and T. Luckman, 1966. *The social construction of reality: A treatise in the sociology of knowledge*. Garden City, NY: Doubleday.

Berk, R.A., P. Burnstein, and I. Nagel. 1980. Evaluating criminal justice legislation. In *Handbook of criminal justice evaluation*, ed. M. Klein and K. Tielman, 611–28. Beverly Hills, CA: Sage.

Bernard, T.J., and R.S. Engel. 2001. Conceptualizing criminal justice theory. *Justice Quarterly* 18: 1–30.

———. R.R. Ritti. 1990. The role of theory in scientific research. In *Measurement issues in criminology*, ed. K.L. Kempf, 1–20. New York: Springer Verlag.

Berns, S. 1999. *To speak as a judge: Difference, voice, and power*. Aldershot, UK: Ashgate.

Black, D. 1970. The production of crime rates. *American Sociological Review* 35: 733–46.

———. 1976. *The behavior of law*. New York: Academic Press.

Blau, P.M. 1964. *Exchange and power in social life*. New York: John Wiley.

Blau, P.M., W.V. Heydebrand, and R.E. Stauffer. 1966. The structure of small bureaucracies. *American Sociological Review* 31: 179–91.

———. R.A. Schoenherr. 1971. *The structure of organizations*. New York: Basic Books.

Blalock, H.M., Jr. 1969. *Theory construction: From verbal to mathematical formulations*. Englewood Cliffs, NJ: Prentice-Hall.

Blumberg, A.S. 1967. *Criminal justice*. Chicago: Quadrangle Books.

Blumstein, A., and J. Cohen. 1973. A theory of the stability of punishment. *Journal of Criminal Law and Criminology* 64: 198–207.

———. 1980. Sentencing of convicted offenders: An analysis of the public's view. *Law and Society Review* 14(2): 223–60.

———. S.E. Martin, and M.H. Tonry. 1983. *Research on sentencing: The search for reform*, vol. 1. Washington, D.C.: National Academy Press.

Bohm, R., T. Flanagan, and P. Harris. 1990. Current death penalty opinion in New York State. *Albany Law Review* 54: 819–43.

Bohne, B. 1978. The public defender as policy maker. *Judicature* 62: 176.

Bollen, K. 1989. *Structural equations with latent variables*. New York: John Wiley.

Bordua, D.J., and A. Reiss, Jr. 1966. Command, control and charisma: Reflections on police bureaucracy. *American Journal of Sociology* 72: 68–76.

Bouza, A.V. 1985. Police unions: Paper tigers or roaring lions? In *Police leadership in America: Crisis and opportunity*, ed. W.A. Geller, 241–80. Chicago: American Bar Foundation; New York: Praeger.

Bowers, D. 1997. Political culture and felony sentencing: An examination of trial courts in 300 counties. *Criminal Justice Policy Review* 8(4): 343–64.

Boyte, H.C. 1986. Introduction. In *The New Populism: The politics of empowerment,* ed. H.C. Boyte and F. Riessman, 1–10. Philadelphia: Temple University Press.

Braithwaite, J. 1999. Restorative justice: Assessing optimistic and pessimistic accounts. In *Crime and justice: A review of research,* ed. M. Tonry, 25: 1–127. Chicago: University of Chicago Press.

_____. P. Pettit. 1990. *Not just deserts: A republican theory of criminal justice.* New York: Oxford University Press.

Brandstatter, A.F., and L.T. Hoover. 1976. Systemic criminal justice education. *Journal of Criminal Justice* 4(1):47–55.

Bridges, G.S., and S. Steen. 1998. Racial disparities in official assessments of juvenile offenders: Attributional stereotypes as mediating mechanisms. *American Sociological Review.* 63: 554–70.

Bright, S.B., and P.J. Keenan. 1995. Judges and the politics of death: Deciding between the bill of rights and the next election in capital cases. *Boston University Law Review* 75: 759–835.

Britt, C. 2000. Social context and racial disparities in punishment decisions. *Justice Quarterly* 17(4): 707–32.

Broach, G., P. Jackson, and V. Ascolillo. 1978. State political culture and sentence severity in federal district courts. *Criminology* 16(3): 373–82.

Brown, M.C., and B.D. Warner. 1992. Immigrants, urban politics, and policing in 1900. *American Sociological Review* 57: 293–305.

Brown, S., and R. Peterson. 1993. Antecedents and consequences of salesperson job satisfaction: Meta-analysis and assessment of causal effects. *Journal of Marketing Research.* 30: 63–77.

Bruce, W., and J. Blackburn. 1992. *Balancing job satisfaction and performance: A guide for the human resource professional.* Westport, CT: Quorum Books.

Brunk, C. 1979. The problem of voluntariness and coercion in the negotiated plea. *Law and Society Review* 13: 527.

Bryk, A.S., and S.W. Raudenbush. 1992. *Hierarchical linear models: Applications and data analysis methods.* Newbury Park, CA: Sage.

Bureau of Justice Statistics. 1998. *State court sentencing of convicted felons, 1994.* Washington, D.C.: U.S. Department of Justice.

_____. 2002. *Prisoners in 2001.* Washington, D.C.: U.S. Department of Justice.

Burns, T., and G.M. Stalker. 1961. *The management of innovation.* London: Tavistock.

Burrell, G., and G. Morgan. 1979. *Sociological paradigms and organizational analysis.* London: Heinemann.

Butterfield, F. 1998. A newcomer breaks into the liberal arts: Criminal justice. *The New York Times* (December 5), <http://www.lexis-nexis.com>

Cammann, C., M. Fichman, G. Jenkins, and J. Klesh. 1983. Assessing the attitudes and perceptions of organizational members. In *Assessing organizational change: A guide to methods, measures, and practices,* ed. S. Seashore, E. Lawler, P. Mirvis, and C. Cammann, 71–138. New York: John Wiley.

Camp, S. 1994. Assessing the effects of organizational commitment and job satisfaction on turnover: An event history approach. *The Prison Journal* 74: 279–305.

———. T. Steiger. 1995. Gender and racial differences in perceptions of career opportunities and the work environment in a traditionally white, male occupation. In *Contemporary issues in criminal justice: Shaping tomorrow's system,* ed. N. Jackson, 258–90. New York: McGraw-Hill.

Caplow, T., and J. Simon. 1999. Understanding prison policy and population trends. In *Prisons,* ed. M. Tonry and J. Petersilia, 63–120. Chicago: University of Chicago Press.

Cardarelli, A.P., J. McDevitt, and K. Baum. 1998. The rhetoric and reality of community policing in small and medium-sized cities and towns. *Policing: An International Journal of Police Strategies & Management* 21(3): 397–415.

Carmines, E., and R. Zeller. 1979. *Reliability and validity assessment.* Beverly Hills, CA: Sage.

Carroll, G.R., J. Goodstein, and A. Gyenes. 1988. Organizations and the state: Effects of the institutional environment on agricultural cooperatives in Hungary. *Administrative Science Quarterly* 33: 233–56.

Carroll, J.S., and J.W. Payne. 1976. The psychology of the parole decision process: A joint application of attribution theory and information processing psychology. In *Cognition and human behavior,* ed. J.S. Carroll and J.W. Payne, 13–32. Hillsdale, NJ: Erlbaum.

Carson, W. 1974. Symbolic and instrumental dimensions of early factory legislation: A case study in the origins of the criminal law. In *Crime, criminology and public policy: Essays in honor of Sir Leon Radzinowicz,* ed. R. Hood, 107–38. London: Heinemann.

Carter, L.H. 1984. *The limits of order.* Lexington, MA: Lexington Books.

Casper, J.D. 1972. *American criminal justice: The defendant's perspective.* Englewood Cliffs, NJ: Prentice-Hall.

———. 1978. Having their day in court: Defendant evaluations of the fairness of their treatment. *Law and Society Review* 12(1): 237–51.

———. D. Brereton. 1984. Evaluating criminal justice reform. *Law and Society Review* 1: 121–44.

Castellano, T.C., and E.F. McGarrell. 1991. The politics of law and order: Case study evidence for a conflict model of the criminal law formation process. *Journal of Research in Crime and Delinquency* 28: 304–29.

Cawsey, T., and W. Wedley. 1979. Labor turnover costs: Measurement and control. *Personnel Journal* 8: 90–95.

Chaiken, M., and J. Chaiken. 1991. *Priority prosecution of high-rate dangerous offenders.* Washington, D.C.: National Institute of Justice.

Chambliss, W. 1964. A sociological analysis of the law of vagrancy. *Social Problems* 12: 46–67.

———. R. Seidman. 1982. *Law, order, and power,* 2nd ed. Reading, MA: Addison-Wesley.

Cheatwood, D. 2000. Getting rid of cause: Improving the impact of theory on policy. Paper presented at the Academy of Criminal Justice Sciences, New Orleans, LA.

Chin, R., and K.D. Benne. 1969. General strategies for effecting changes in human systems. In *The planning of change,* ed. W. Bennis, K.D. Benne, and R. Chin, 2nd ed., 32–59. New York: Holt, Rinehart, and Winston.

Chiricos, T.G. 1998. The media, moral panics, and the politics of crime control. In *Politics and the administration of justice,* ed. G.F. Cole and M.G. Gertz, 58–76. Belmont, CA: Wadsworth.

———. W.D. Bales. 1991. Unemployment and punishment: An empirical assessment. *Criminology* 29(4): 701–24.

———. G. Waldo. 1975. Socioeconomic status and criminal sentencing: An empirical assessment of a conflict proposition. *American Sociological Review* 40: 753–72.

Christie, N. 1994. *Crime control as industry: Toward gulags.* New York: Routledge.

Church, T. 1979. In defense of "bargain justice." *Law and Society Review* 13: 509.

———. M. Heumann. 1989. The underexamined assumptions of the invisible hand: Monetary incentives as policy instruments. *Journal of Policy Analysis and Management* 8(4): 641–57.

Church, T.W. 1985. Examining local legal culture. *American Bar Foundation Research Journal* 1985: 449–518.

Clark, J.P., R.H. Hall, and B. Hutchinson. 1967. Interorganizational relationships and network properties as contextual variables in the study of police performance. In *Police and society,* ed. D.H. Bayley, 177–93. Beverly Hills, CA: Sage.

Clear, T. E. 1994. *Harm in American penology: Offenders, victims, and their communities.* Albany, NY: State University of New York Press.

———. G. F. Cole. 1999. *American corrections,* 5th ed. Belmont, CA: Wadsworth.

Clinard, M.B., and D.J. Abbott. 1973. *Crime in developing countries: A comparative perspective.* New York: John Wiley.

Clingermayer, J.C., and R.C. Feiock. 1991. The adoption of economic development policies by large cities: A test of economic, interest groups, and institutional explanations. *Policy Studies Journal* 18(3): 539–52.

Cole, G. 1970. The decision to prosecute. *Law and Society Review* 4: 331–45.

Coleman, J.S. 1974. *Power and the structure of society.* New York: W.W. Norton.

Cook, B. 1977. Public opinion and federal judicial policy. *American Journal of Political Science* 21: 567–600.

Cook, B.B. 1973. Sentencing behavior of federal judges: Draft cases — 1972. *University of Cincinnati Law Review* 42: 597.

Cook, J., S. Hepworth, T. Wall, and P. Warr. 1981. *The experience of work: A compendium and review of 249 measures and their use.* New York: Academic Press.

Cordner, G. W. 1989. Police agency size and investigative effectiveness. *Journal of Criminal Justice* 17: 145–55.

Cortes, E. 1993. Reweaving the fabric: The iron rule and the IAF strategy for dealing with poverty through power and politics. Working Paper No. 56, Center for Urban Policy Research, Rutgers University.

Council of State Governments. 1977. *Reorganization of state corrections agencies: A decade of experience.* Lexington, KY: Council of State Governments.

Crank, J.P. 1990. The influence of environmental and organizational factors on police style in urban and rural environments. *Journal of Research in Crime and Delinquency* 27(2): 166–89.

———. 1994. Watchman and community: Myth and institutionalization in policing. *Law and Society Review* 28(2): 325–51.

———. 1996. The construction of meaning during training for probation and parole. *Justice Quarterly* 13: 265–90.

———. R.H. Langworthy. 1992. An institutional perspective of policing. *The Journal of Criminal Law and Criminology* 83: 338–63.

———. R.H. Langworthy. 1996. Fragmented centralization and the organization of the police. *Policing and Society* 6: 213–29.

———. L.E. Wells. 1991. The effects of size and urbanism on structure among Illinois police departments. *Justice Quarterly* 8(2): 170–85.

Cranny, C., P. Smith, and E. Stone. 1992. *Job satisfaction: How people feel about their jobs and how it affects their performance.* New York: Lexington Books.

Crawford, C. 2000. Gender, race, and habitual offender sentencing in Florida. *Criminology* 38(1): 263–80.

———. T. Chiricos, and G. Kleck. 1998. Race, racial threat, and sentencing of habitual offenders. *Criminology* 36: 481–512.

Cronbach, L. 1951. Coefficient alpha and the internal structure of tests. *Psychometrika* 16: 297–334.

Cullen, F. 1995. Assessing the penal harm movement. *Journal of Research of Crime and Delinquency* 32: 338–58.

———. E. Latessa, R. Kopache, L. Lombardo, and V. Burton. 1993. Prison wardens' job satisfaction. *The Prison Journal* 73: 141–61.

Culliver, C., R. Sigler, and B. McNeely. 1991. Examining prosocial organizational behavior among correctional officers. *International Journal of Comparative and Applied Criminal Justice* 15: 77–284.

Currie, E. 1985. *Confronting crime: An American challenge.* New York: Pantheon.

Dahrendorf, R. 1970. The intellectual and society: The social function of the "fool" in the twentieth century. In *On intellectuals: Theoretical studies/ case studies,* ed. P. Rieff, 52–56. Garden City, NY: Anchor Books.

Dalessio, A., W. Silverman, and J. Schuck. 1986. Paths to turnover: A re-analysis and review of existing data on the Mobley, Horner, and Hollingsworth's turnover model. *Human Relations* 39: 245–64.

Daly, K., and M. Tonry. 1997. Gender, race and sentencing. In *Crime and justice: A review of research,* ed. M. Tonry, 201–52. Chicago: University of Chicago Press.

Davenport, D.R. 1996. Public agency performance and structure: Assessing the effects of the organizational environment. PhD diss., Lubbock, TX: Texas Tech University

Davis, K., and J. Newstrom. 1985. *Human behavior at work.* New York: McGraw-Hill.

DeLeon-Granados, W. 1999. *Travels through crime and place.* Boston: Northeastern University Press.

Dershowitz, A. 1983. *The best defense.* New York: Vintage Books.

Dession, G. 1938. Psychiatry and the conditioning of criminal justice. *Yale Law Journal* 47(3): 319–40.

DiCristina, B. 1995. *Method in criminology: A philosophical primer.* New York: Harrow & Heston.

———. 1997. The quantitative emphasis in criminal justice education. *Journal of Criminal Justice Education* 8(2): 181–200.

Dilulio, J.J. 1987. *Governing prisons.* New York: Macmillan.

DiMaggio, P., and W.W. Powell. 1983. The iron cage revisited: Institutionalized isomorphism and collective rationality in organizational fields, *American Sociological Review* 48: 147–60.

Dixon, J. 1995. The organizational context of criminal court sentencing. *American Journal of Sociology* 100: 1157–98.

Donaldson, L. 1995. *American anti-management theories of organization: A critique of paradigm proliferation.* Cambridge: Cambridge University Press.

Donzinger, S.R., ed. 1996. *The real war on crime, the report of the National Criminal Justice Commission.* New York: HarperCollins.

Dostoevsky, F. 1864. *Notes from underground,* trans. Mirra Ginsburg. 1974. New York: Bantam Books.

Downes, D. 1988. *Contrasts in tolerance: Post-war penal policy in the Netherlands and England and Wales.* New York: Oxford University Press.

Downs, A. 1967. *Inside bureaucracy.* Boston: Little, Brown.

Draper, N., and H. Smith. 1966. *Applied regression analysis.* New York: John Wiley.

Dubin, R. 1978. *Theory development.* New York: Free Press.

Duffee, D.E. 1974. *Correctional policy and prison organization*. Beverly Hills, CA: Sage.

_____. 1990. *Explaining criminal justice: Community theory and criminal justice reform*. Prospect Heights, IL: Waveland Press.

_____. 1995. Structuring criminal justice theory. Plenary address, Academy of Criminal Justice Sciences Annual Meeting, Boston.

_____. 1996. Working with communities. In *Community policing in a rural setting*, ed. Q. Thurman and E. McGarrell, 85–96. Cincinnati: Anderson.

_____. R. Fluellen, and B. Renauer. 1999. Community variables in community policing. *Police Quarterly* 2: 5–35.

_____. R. Fluellen, and T. Roscoe. 1999. Constituency building and urban community policing. In *Measuring what matters: Proceedings from the policing research institute meetings*, ed. R.H. Langworthy, 91–119. Washington, D.C.: U.S. Department of Justice, National Institute of Justice.

_____. J.D. Scott, B.C. Renauer, S. Chermak, and E.F. McGarrell. 2002. *Measuring community building involving the police: The final research report of the police–community interaction project*. Washington, D.C.: U.S. Department of Justice, National Institute of Justice.

Duncan, R.B. 1972. Characteristics of organizational environments and perceived environmental uncertainty. *Administrative Science Quarterly* 17: 313–27.

Durham, A., III. 1988. Crime seriousness and punitive severity: An assessment of social attitudes. *Justice Quarterly* 5(1): 131–53.

_____. H. Elrod, and P. Kincade. 1996. Public support for the death penalty: Beyond Gallup. *Justice Quarterly* 13(4): 705–36.

Durkheim, E. 1982. *The rules of sociological method*, trans. W.D. Halls. New York: The Free Press.

Eck, J., and E.R. Maguire. 2000. Have changes in policing reduced violent crime: An assessment of the evidence. *The Crime Drop in America*: ed. A. Blumstein and J. Wallman, 207–65. New York: Cambridge.

Edelman, M. 1964. *The symbolic uses of politics*. Urbana: University of Illinois Press.

Eisenstadt, S.N. 1959. Bureaucracy, bureaucratization, and debureaucratization. *Administrative Science Quarterly* 4(3): 302–20.

Eisenstein, J. 1982. Research on rural criminal justice: A summary. In *Criminal justice in rural America*, ed. S. Cronk. Washington, D.C.: National Institute of Justice.

_____. R.B. Flemming, and P.F. Nardulli. 1988. *The contours of justice: Communities and their courts*. Boston: Little, Brown.

_____. H. Jacob. 1977. *Felony justice: An organizational analysis of criminal courts*. Boston: Little, Brown.

_____. H. Jacob. 1991. *Felony justice: An organizational analysis of criminal courts*. Lanham, MD: University Press of America.

Elazar, D. 1972. *American federalism: A view from the states*, 2nd ed. New York: Crowell.

———. 1988. *The American mosaic*. Boulder, CO: Westview.

Ellis, R.D., and C.S. Ellis. 1989. *Theories of criminal justice*. Wolfeboro, NH: Longwood.

Emery, F., and E.L. Trist. 1965. The causal texture of organizational environments. *Human Relations* 18: 21–32.

Emmelman, D. 1996. Trial by plea bargain: Case settlement as a product of recursive decision-making. *Law and Society Review* 30(2): 335–60.

Engle, C.D. 1971. Criminal justice in the city: A study of sentence severity and variation in the Philadelphia court system. PhD diss., Temple University.

Erez, E., and P. Tontodonato. 1990. The effect of victim participation in sentencing on sentence outcome. *Criminology* 28(3): 451–73.

Ericson, R.B., and K.D. Haggerty. 1997. *Policing the risk society*. Toronto, Ont.: University of Toronto Press.

Erikson, K.T. 1966. *Wayward puritans: A study in the sociology of deviance*. New York: John Wiley.

Estrich, S. 1987. *Real rape*. Cambridge, MA: Harvard University Press.

Etzioni, A. 1960. Two approaches to organizational analysis: A critique and a suggestion. *Administrative Science Quarterly* 5: 257–78.

———. Dubow, F.L., eds. 1970. *Comparative perspectives: Theories and methods*. Boston: Little, Brown.

Fairchild, E. 1993. *Comparative criminal justice systems*. Belmont, CA: Wadsworth.

Feeley, M.M. 1973. Two models of the criminal justice system: An organizational perspective. *Law and Society Review* 7(3): 407–25.

———. 1978.The effects of heavy caseloads. In *American court systems: Readings in judicial process and behavior*, ed. S. Goldman and A. Sara, 125–33. San Francisco: W.H. Freeman.

———. 1979. *The process is the punishment: Handling cases in a lower criminal court*. New York: Russell Sage Foundation.

———. 1983. *Court reform on trial: Why simple solutions fail*. New York: Basic Books.

———. 1989. The significance of prison conditions cases: Budgets and regions. *Law and Society Review* 23: 273–82.

———. 1991. *Court reform on trial: Why simple solutions fail*. New York: Basic Books.

———. A. Sarat. 1980. *The policy dilemma: Federal crime policy and the Law Enforcement Assistance Administration*. Minneapolis: University of Minnesota Press.

———. J. Simon. 1992. The new penology: Notes on the emerging strategy in corrections and its implications. *Criminology* 30: 449–74.

Fields, C.B., and R.H. Moore. 1996. Preface. In *Comparative criminal justice: Traditional and nontraditional systems of law and control*, ed. C.B. Fields and R.H. Moore, xi–xiii. Prospect Heights, IL: Waveland Press.

Finckenauer, J. 1988. Public support for the death penalty: Retribution as just deserts or retribution as revenge? *Justice Quarterly* 5(1): 81–100.

Fishbein, M., and I. Ajzen. 1975. *Belief, attitudes, intention, and behavior.* Reading, MA: Addison-Wesley.

Flanagan, T.J., P. Brennan, and D. Cohen. 1991. Attitudes of New York legislators toward crime and criminal justice: A report of the state legislator survey: 1991. Working Paper. Albany, NY: State University of New York at Albany, School of Criminal Justice.

Flango, V., L. Wenner, and M. Wenner. 1978. The concept of judicial role: A methodological note. *American Journal of Political Science* 19: 277.

Flemming, R. 1986. Client games: Defense attorney perspectives on their relations with criminal clients. *American Bar Foundation Research Journal 1986*: 253–77.

_____. P. Nardulli, and J. Eisenstein. 1987. The timing of justice in felony trial courts. *Law and Policy* 9(2): 179–206.

_____. P. Nardulli, and J. Eisenstein. 1992. *The craft of justice: Politics and work in criminal court communities.* Philadelphia, PA: University of Pennsylvania Press.

Fogelson, R.M. 1977. *Big-city police,* Cambridge, MA: Harvard University Press.

Foucault, M. 1979. *Discipline and punish: The birth of the prison.* New York: Vintage.

Fraser, D.M. 1985. Politics and police leadership: The view from city hall. In *Police leadership in America: Crisis and opportunity*, ed. W.A. Geller, 41–47. Chicago: American Bar Foundation; New York: Praeger.

Frazier, C., and E.W. Bock. 1982. Effects of court officials on sentence severity: Do judges make a difference? *Criminology* 20: 257–72.

French, W.L., and C.H.Bell, Jr. 1995. *Organization development,* 5th ed. Englewood Cliffs, NJ: Prentice-Hall.

Friedman, L. 1979. Plea bargaining in historical perspective. *Law and Society Review* 13: 247.

_____. 1984. *American law: An introduction.* New York: W.W. Norton.

_____. 1985. *A history of American law.* New York: Simon & Schuster.

Friedman, W. 1994. The community role in community policing. In *The challenge of community policing: Testing the promise*, ed. D.P. Rosenbaum, 263–69. Newbury Park, CA: Sage.

Friel, C.M., S. Keilitz, C. Wellford, C. Riveland, and J. Jacobs, eds. 2000. *Boundary changes in criminal justice organizations.* Criminal Justice, vol. 2. Washington, D.C.: National Institute of Justice.

Fuchs, S. 1993. A sociological theory of scientific change. *Social Forces* 71(4): 933–53.

Galliher, J., and J. Cross. 1983. *Morals legislation without morality: The case of Nevada.* New Brunswick, NJ: Rutgers University Press.

Garland, D. 2001.*The culture of control: Crime and social order in contemporary society.* Chicago: University of Chicago Press.

Garofalo, J., and J. Laub. 1978. The fear of crime: Broadening our perspective. *Victimology* 3: 242–53.

Giacomazzi, A.L, E. McGarrell, and Q. Thurman. 1998. *Reducing disorder, fear, and crime in public housing: An evaluation of a drug crime elimination program in Spokane, Washington.* Final Report submitted to the National Institute of Justice.

Gibson, J. 1977. Discriminant functions, role orientations and judicial behavior: Theoretical and methodological linkages. *The Journal of Politics* 39: 984–1007.

———. 1978. Judges' role orientations, attitudes, and decisions: An interactive model. *American Political Science Review* 72: 911–24.

———. 1980. Environmental constraints on the behavior of judges: A representational model of judicial decision making. *Law and Society Review* 14: 343.

———. 1981a. Personality and elite political behavior: The influence of self-esteem on judicial decision-making. *The Journal of Politics* 43: 104–25.

———. 1981b. The role concept in judicial research. *Law and Policy Quarterly* 3: 291.

Giddens, A. 1979. *Central problems in social theory: Action, structure, and contradiction in social analysis.* Berkeley: University of California Press.

Gifford, L.S. 1999. *Justice expenditures and employment in the United States 1995.* Washington, D.C.: U.S. Department of Justice, Bureau of Justice Statistics.

Gilligan, C. 1982. *In a different voice: Psychological theory and women's development.* Cambridge, MA: Harvard University Press.

Glick, H., and G. Pruet, Jr. 1985. Crime, public opinion, and trial courts: An analysis of sentencing policy. *Justice Quarterly* 2(3): 319–43.

Goldman, S. 1969. Backgrounds, attitudes, and the voting behavior of judges: A comment on Joel Grossman's social backgrounds and judicial decisions. *The Journal of Politics* 31: 214–22.

Goldstein, H. 1990. *Problem oriented policing.* New York: McGraw-Hill.

Goldstein, J. 1960. Police discretion not to invoke the criminal process: Low visibility decisions in the administration of justice. *Yale Law Journal* 69: 543–94.

Goodpaster, G. 1987. On the theory of the American adversary criminal trial. *Journal of Criminal Law and Criminology* 78(1): 118–53.

Gottfredson, M.R., and D.M. Gottfredson. 1988. *Decision making in criminal justice: Toward the rational exercise of discretion,* 2nd ed. New York: Plenum.

———. M.J. Hindelang. 1979a. A study of *The Behavior of Law. American Sociological Review* 44: 3–18.

_____. M.J. Hindelang. 1979b. Theory and research in the sociology of law. *American Sociological Review* 44: 27–37.

Gould, J.B. 2002. Shaming. In *Legal systems of the world: A political, social, and cultural encyclopedia*, ed. H. Kritzer, C.N. Tate, and J.J. Toharia, 1440–42. Santa Barbara, CA: ABC-CLIO.

Grasmick, H., E. Davenport, M. Chamlin, and R. Bursik, Jr. 1992. Protestant fundamentalism and the retributive doctrine of punishment. *Criminology* 30(1): 21–45.

Gray, V., and B. Williams. 1980. *The organizational politics of criminal justice: Policy in context*. Lexington, MA: Lexington Books.

Greene, J.A. 1997. Zero tolerance: A case study of police policies and practices in New York City. *Crime and Delinquency* 45: 171–87.

Greene, J.R., W.T. Bergman, and E.J. McLaughlin. 1994. Implementing community policing: Cultural and structural change in police organizations. In *The challenge of community policing: Testing the promise*, ed. D.P. Rosenbaum, 92–109. Newbury Park, CA: Sage.

_____. T.S. Bynum, and V.J. Webb. 1985. Paradigm development in crime-related education: The role of the significant others. *Criminal Justice Review* 10: 7–17.

Grinc, R. 1998. Angels in marble: Problems in stimulating community involvement in community policing. In *Community justice: An emerging field*, ed. D. Karp, 167–202. Lanham, MD: Rowman & Littlefield.

Grondahl, P. 1997. *Mayor Erastus Corning: Albany icon, Albany enigma*. Albany, NY: Washington Park Press.

Gronlund, N. 1981. *Measurement and evaluation in teaching*. New York: Macmillan.

Grossman, J.B. 1967. Social backgrounds and judicial decisions: Notes for a theory. *The Journal of Politics* 29: 334–51.

Gruhl, J., C. Spohn, and S. Welch. 1981. Women as policymakers: The case of trial judges. *American Journal of Political Science* 25: 308–22.

Guion, R. 1992. Agenda for research and action. In *Job satisfaction: How people feel about their jobs and how it affects their performance*, ed. C. Cranny, P. Smith, and E. Stone, 257–281. New York: Lexington Books.

Gusfield, J.R. 1963. *Symbolic crusade: Status politics and the American temperance movement*. Urbana: University of Illinois Press.

_____. 1981. *The culture of public problems: Drinking-driving and the symbolic order*. Chicago: University of Chicago Press.

Guyot, D. 1977. Police departments under social science scrutiny. *Journal of Criminal Justice*, 5: 68–81.

_____. 1991. *Policing as though people matter*. Philadelphia: Temple University Press.

Hagan, J. 1974. Extra-legal attributes and criminal sentencing: An assessment of a sociological viewpoint. *Law and Society Review* 3: 357–83.

_____. 1977. Criminal justice in rural and urban communities: A study of the bureaucratization of justice. *Social Forces* 55: 597.

_____. 1989a. *Structural criminology.* New Brunswick, NJ: Rutgers University Press.

_____. 1989b. Why is there so little criminal justice theory? Neglected macro- and micro-level links between organization and power. *Journal of Research in Crime and Delinquency* 26: 116–35.

_____. 1995. *Crime and disrepute.* Thousand Oaks, CA: Pine Forge Press.

_____. Hewitt, and D.F. Alwin. 1979. Ceremonial justice: Crime and punishment in a loosely coupled system. *Social Forces* 58: 506–27.

Haller, M.H. 1976. Civic reformers and the police. In *Police in urban society,* ed. H. Hahn, 39–56. Beverly Hills, CA: Sage.

Hallman, H.W. 1984. *Neighborhoods: Their place in urban life.* Beverly Hills, CA: Sage.

Haney, C., and P. Zimbardo. 1998. The past and future of U.S. prison policy: Twenty-five years after the Stanford prison experiment. *American Psychologist* 53: 709–27.

Harring, S.L. 1981. Policing a class society: The expansion of the urban police in the late nineteenth and early twentieth centuries. In *From crime and capitalism,* ed. D. Greenberg, 292–313. Palo Alto, CA: Mayfield.

_____. 1983. *Policing a class society: The experience of American cities, 1865–1915.* New Brunswick, NJ: Rutgers University Press.

Harris, J., and P. Jesilow. 2000. It's not the old ballgame: Three strikes and the courtroom workgroup. *Justice Quarterly* 17(1): 185–203.

Hawkins, D. 1981. Causal attribution and punishment for crime. *Deviant Behavior* 1: 191–215.

Heck, R.H., and S.L. Thomas. 2000. *Introduction to multilevel modeling techniques.* Mahwah, NJ: Erlbaum.

Heffron, F. 1989. *Organizational theory and public organizations: The political connection.* Englewood Cliffs, NJ: Prentice-Hall.

Henderson, J.H., and R.L. Boostrom. 1989. Criminal justice theory: Anarchy reigns. *Journal of Contemporary Criminal Justice* 5(1): 29–39.

Henderson, T.A. 1975. The relative effects of community complexity and of sheriffs upon the professionalism of sheriff departments. *American Journal of Political Science* 19(1): 107–32.

Henham, R. 2001. Theory and contextual analysis in sentencing. *International Journal of the Sociology of Law* 29(3): 253–76.

Hepburn, J., and P. Knepper. 1993. Correctional officers as human service workers: The effect of job satisfaction. *Justice Quarterly* 10: 315–35.

Hess, D.R. 1999. Community organizing, building, and developing: Their relationship to comprehensive community initiatives. Paper presented on COMM-ORG: the On-Line Conference on Community Organizing and Development. Available: http://comm-org.utoledo.edu/papers.htm

Heumann, M. 1975. A note on plea bargaining and case pressure. *Law and Society Review* 9: 515–28.

_____. 1978. *Plea bargaining: The experiences of prosecutors, judges, and defense attorneys*. Chicago: University of Chicago Press.

_____. C. Loftin. 1979. Mandatory sentencing and the abolition of plea bargaining: The Michigan Felony Firearm Statute. *Law and Society Review* 13: 393.

Heydebrand, W., and C. Seron. 1990. *Rationalizing justice: The political economy of federal district courts*. Albany, NY: State University of New York Press.

Hickman, M.J., and B.A. Reaves. 1999. *Local police departments 1999*. Washington, D.C.: U.S. Department of Justice, Office of Justice Programs, Bureau of Justice Statistics.

Hogarth, J. 1971. *Sentencing as a human process*. Toronto: University of Toronto Press.

Holmes, M.D., H.M. Hosch, H.C. Daudistel, D.A. Perez, and J.B. Graves. 1993. Judges' ethnicity and minority sentencing: Evidence concerning Hispanics. *Social Science Quarterly* 74: 496–506.

Hopkins, A. 1983. *Work and job satisfaction in the public sectors*. Totowa, NJ: Rowman & Allonheld.

Horney, J., and C. Spohn. 1991. Rape law reform and instrumental change in six jurisdictions. *Law and Society Review* 25(1): 117–53.

Houlden, P., and S. Balkin. 1985. Quality and cost comparisons of private bar indigent defense systems: Contract vs. ordered assigned counsel. *Journal of Criminal Law and Criminology* 76(1): 176–200.

Howard, G.J., G. Newman, and W.A. Pridemore. 2000. Theory, method, and data in comparative criminology. In *Measurement and analysis of crime and justice: Criminal justice 2000*, ed. D. Duffee, 4: 139–211. Washington, D.C.: National Institute of Justice.

Hudnut, W.H. 1985. The police and the polis: A mayor's perspective. In *Police leadership in America: Crisis and opportunity*, ed. W.A. Geller, 20–29. Chicago: American Bar Foundation; New York: Praeger.

Huggins, M.K. 1998. *Political policing: The United States and Latin America*. Durham, NC: Duke University Press.

Hulin, C., M. Roznowski, and D. Hachiya. 1985. Alternative opportunities and withdrawal decisions: Empirical and theoretical discrepancies and an integration. *Psychological Bulletin* 97: 233–50.

Hunt, R.G., and J.M. Magenau. 1993. *Power and the police chief: An institutional and organizational analysis*. Newbury Park, CA: Sage.

Hunter, A. 1985. Private, parochial and public social orders: The problem of crime and incivility in urban communities. In *The challenge of social control*, ed. G. Suttles and M. Zald, 230–42. Norwood, NJ: Ablex.

Inverarity, J. 1992. Extralegal influences on imprisonment: Explaining the direct effects of socioeconomic variables. In *Social threat and social control*, ed. A.E. Liska, 113–28. Albany, NY: State University New York Press.

Ironson, G., P. Smith, M. Brannick, W. Gibson, and K. Paul. 1989. Construction of a job in general scale: A comparison of global composite and specific measures. *Journal of Applied Psychology* 74: 193–200.

Ivancevich, J., and M. Matteson. 1980. *Stress and work: A managerial perspective*. Glenview, IL: Scott Foresman.

Jacob, H. 1983. Courts as organizations. In *Empirical theories about courts*, ed. K. Boyum and L. Mather. New York: Longman.

———. 1997. The governance of trial judges. *Law and Society Review* 31(1): 3–30.

Jacobs, J. 1961. *The death and life of great American cities*. New York: Random House.

Jacobs, J.B. 1985. Police unions: How they look from the academic side. In *Police leadership in America: Crisis and opportunity*, ed. W.A. Geller, 286–90. Chicago: American Bar Foundation; New York: Praeger.

Jacoby, J. 1977. *The prosecutor's charging decision: A policy perspective*. Washington, D.C.: National Institute of Law Enforcement and Criminal Justice.

Jauch, L., W. Glueck, and R. Osborn. 1978. Organizational loyalty, professional commitment and academic research productivity. *Academy of Management Journal* 21: 84–92.

Johnson, C.A. 1976. Political culture in American states: Elazar's formulation examined. *American Journal of Political Science* 20: 491–509.

Joubert, P.E., J.S. Picou, and W.A. McIntosh. 1981. U.S. social structure, crime, and imprisonment. *Criminology* 19: 344–59.

Judd, D.R., and Swanstrom, T. 1998. *City politics: Private power and public policy*, 2nd ed. Reading, MA: Addison-Wesley.

Jurik, N., and R. Winn. 1987. Describing correctional security dropouts and rejects: An individual or organizational profile? *Criminal Justice and Behavior* 24: 5–25.

Kanter, R.M. 1977. *Men and women of the corporation*. New York: Basic Books.

Kapsis, R.E. 1977. Weber, Durkheim, and the comparative method. *Journal of the History of the Behavioral Sciences* 13: 354–68.

Karp, D.R. 2001. Harm and repair: Observing restorative justice in Vermont. *Justice Quarterly* 18: 727–57.

Katz, C., and C. Spohn. 1995. The effect of race and gender on bail outcomes: A test of an interactive model. *American Journal of Criminal Justice* 19(2): 161–84.

———. E.R. Maguire, and D.W. Roncek. 2002. The creation of specialized police gang units: Testing contingency, social threat, and resource dependency expectations. *Policing: An International Journal of Police Strategies and Management* 25(3): 472–506.

Katz, C.M. 1997. Police and gangs: A study of a police gang unit. PhD diss., University of Nebraska at Omaha.

Kaufman, H. 1976. *Are government organizations immortal?* Washington D.C.: Brookings Institution.

Kautt, P. 2002. Location, location, location: Interdistrict and intercircuit variation in sentencing outcomes for federal drug-trafficking offenses. *Justice Quarterly* 19(4): 633–71.

———. Spohn C. 2002. Cracking down on black drug offenders? Testing for interactions between offender race, drug type, and sentencing strategy in federal drug sentences. *Justice Quarterly*, 19(1): 1–35.

Kelling, G., and K. Coles. 1996. *Fixing broken windows: Restoring order and reducing crime in our communities.* New York: Free Press.

Kerce, E., P. Magnusson, and A. Rudolph. 1994. *The attitudes of navy corrections staff members: What they think about confinees and their jobs.* San Diego, CA: Navy Personnel Research and Development Center.

King, R.D. 1998. Prisons. In *The handbook of crime and punishment,* ed. M. Tonry, 589–625. New York: Oxford University Press.

King, W.R. 1998. Innovativeness in American municipal police organizations. PhD diss., University of Cincinnati.

———. 1999. Time, constancy, and change in American municipal police organizations. *Police Quarterly* 2(3): 338–64.

———. L.F. Travis, III, and R.H. Langworthy. 1997. Police organizational death. Paper presented at the annual meeting of the American Society of Criminology, San Diego, CA.

Kirsch, C.P. 1995. Federal criminal justice: The decision process from complaint to trial. Graduate School of Public Service, New York University.

Klinger, D. 1994. Demeanor or crime? An inquiry into why "hostile" citizens are more likely to be arrested. *Criminology* 32: 475–93.

Kouzes, J., and B. Posner. 1995. *The leadership challenge.* San Francisco: Jossey-Bass.

Kraatz, M.S., and E.J. Zajac. 1996. Exploring the limits of the new institutionalism: The causes and consequences of illegitimate organizational change. *American Sociological Review* 61: 812–36.

Kreft, I., and J. De Leeuw. 1998. *Introducing multilevel modeling.* Thousand Oaks, CA: Sage.

Krisberg, B., P. Litsky, and I. Schwartz. 1984. Youth in confinement: Justice by geography. *Journal of Research in Crime and Delinquency* 21: 153–81.

Kritzer, H.M. 1978. Political correlates of the behavior of federal district judges: A "best case" analysis. *Journal of Politics* 40: 25–58.

———. 1979. Federal judges and their political environments: The influence of public opinion. *American Journal of Political Science* 23: 194.

Kuhn, T. 1970. *The structure of scientific revolutions,* 2nd ed. Chicago: University of Chicago Press.

Kuklinski, J., and J. Stanga. 1979. Political participation and government responsiveness: The behavior of California superior courts. *American Political Science Review* 73: 1090.

Lafave, W. 1965. *Arrest: The decision to take a suspect into custody.* Boston: Little, Brown.

Lambert, E. 1999. A path analysis of the antecedents and consequences of job satisfaction and organizational commitment among correctional staff (turnover and absenteeism). PhD diss, State University of New York at Albany.

Langworthy, R.H. 1985. Police department size and agency structure. *Journal of Criminal Justice* 13: 15–27.

______. 1986. *The structure of police organizations.* New York: Praeger.

______. 1989. Do stings control crime? An evaluation of a police fence operation. *Justice Quarterly* 6: 27–45.

______. 1992. Organizational structure. In *What works in policing?* ed. G.W. Cordner and D.C. Hale, 87–105. Cincinnati, OH: Anderson.

______. L.F. Travis. 1998. *Policing in America: A balance of forces*, 2nd ed. Upper Saddle River, NJ: Prentice-Hall.

Larson, J.E. 1993. Women understand so little, they call my good nature "deceit": A feminist rethinking of seduction. *Columbia Law Review* 93: 374–472.

Laster, K., and R. Douglas. 1995. Feminized justice: The impact of women decision makers in the lower courts of Australia. *Justice Quarterly* 12: 177–205.

Lawrence, P.R., and J.W. Lorsch. 1967. Differentiation and integration in complex organizations. *Administrative Science Quarterly* 12(1): 1–47.

Lee, T., and R. Mowday. 1987. Voluntarily leaving an organization: An empirical investigation of Steers and Mowday's model of turnover. *Academy of Management Journal* 30: 721–43.

Lefstein, N., V. Stapleton, and L. Teitelbaum. 1969. In search of juvenile justice. *Law and Society Review* 5: 491–563.

Levin, M.A. 1972. Urban politics and policy outcomes: The criminal court. In *Criminal justice: Law and politics*, ed. G.F. Cole, 330–52. Belmont, CA: Wadsworth.

Lewin, K. 1947. Group decision and social change. In *Readings in social psychology*, ed. T.M. Newcomb and E.L. Hartley, 330–44. New York: Henry Holt.

Lewis, A. 1964. *Gideon's trumpet.* New York: Vintage Books.

Lewis, D.A., and G. Salem. 1996. *Fear of crime: Incivility and the production of a social problem.* New Brunswick, NJ: Transaction Press.

Lincoln, J., and A. Kalleberg. 1990. *Culture, control and commitment: A study of work organization and work attitudes in the United States and Japan.* Cambridge: Cambridge University Press.

Lind, E., and T. Tyler. 1988. *The social psychology of procedural justice.* New York: Plenum.

Lipsky, M. 1980. *Street-level bureaucracy: Dilemmas of the individual in public services.* New York: Russell Sage.

Liska, A.E., ed. 1992a. *Social threat and social control.* Albany, NY: State University of New York Press.

_____. 1992b. Conclusion: Developing theoretical issues. In *Social threat and social control*, ed. A.E. Liska, 165–90. Albany, NY: State University of New York Press.

_____. W. Baccaglini. 1990. Feeling safe by comparison: Crime in the newspapers. *Social Problems* 37: 360–74.

_____. M. Chamlin. 1984. Social structure and crime control among macro-social units. *American Journal of Sociology* 90: 383–95.

_____. A Sanchirico, and M. Reed. 1988. Fear of crime and constrained behavior: Specifying and estimating a reciprocal effects model. *Social Forces* 66: 827–41.

Lizotte, A. 1978. Extra-legal factors in Chicago's criminal courts: Testing the conflict model of criminal justice. *Social Problems* 25: 564.

Locke, E. 1976. The nature and causes of job satisfaction. In *Handbook of industrial and organizational psychology*, ed. M. Dunnell, 1297–1349. Chicago: Rand-McNally.

Logan, J.R., and H. Molotch. 1987. *Urban fortunes: The political economy of place*. Berkeley: University of California Press.

_____. R. Whaley, and K. Crowder. 1997. The character and consequences of growth regimes: An assessment of 20 years of research. *Urban Affairs Review* 32(5): 603–30.

Lowe, R., and S. Vodanovich. 1995. A field study of distributive and procedural justice as predictors of satisfaction and organizational commitment. *Journal of Business and Psychology* 10: 99–114.

Luskin, M., and R. Luskin. 1987. Case processing times in three courts. *Law and Policy* 9(2): 207–32.

Lynch, D. 1999. Perceived judicial hostility to criminal trials. *Criminal Justice and Behavior* 26(2): 217–34.

Lynch, M., and W. Groves. 1981. *A primer in radical criminology*. Albany, NY: Harrow & Heston.

Lyons, W. 1999. *The politics of community policing: Rearranging the power to punish*. Ann Arbor: University of Michigan Press.

Maguire, E.R. 1997. Structural change in large municipal police organizations during the community policing era. *Justice Quarterly* 14(3): 701–30.

_____. 2003. *Context, complexity and control: Organizational structure in American police agencies*. Albany, NY: State University of New York Press.

_____. G.J. Howard, and G. Newman. 1998a. Measuring the performance of national criminal justice systems. *International Journal of Comparative and Applied Criminal Justice* 22: 31–59.

_____. J.B. Kuhns, C.D. Uchida, and S.M. Cox. 1997. Patterns of community policing in nonurban America. *Journal of Research in Crime and Delinquency* 34: 368–94.

_____. S.D. Mastrofski. 2000. Patterns of community policing in the United States. *Police Quarterly* 3(1): 4–45.

_____. R. Schulte-Murray. 2001. Issues and patterns in the comparative international study of police strength. *International Journal of Comparative Sociology.* 17: 75–100.

_____. J.B. Snipes, C.D. Uchida, and M. Townsend. 1998b. Counting cops: Estimating the number of police departments and police officers in the USA. *Policing: An International Journal of Police Strategies & Management* 21(1): 97–120.

_____. C.D. Uchida. 2000. Measurement and explanation in the comparative study of American police organizations. In *Measurement and analysis of crime and justice,* ed. D. Duffee, D. McDowall, B. Ostrom, R.D. Crutchfield, S.D. Mastrofski, and L.G. Mazerolle. Criminal justice 2000, 4: 491–558. Washington, D.C.: National Institute of Justice.

_____. J. Zhao, and N. Lovrich. 1999. Dimensions of community policing. Working paper, George Mason University.

Maguire, K., and A.L. Pastore, eds. 1998. *Sourcebook of criminal justice statistics, 1997.* Washington, D.C.: U.S. Department of Justice, Bureau of Justice Statistics.

Manning P.K. 1988. Community policing as a drama of control. In *Community policing: Rhetoric or reality,* ed. J.R. Greene and S.D. Mastrofski, 27–46. New York: Praeger.

_____. 1992. Information technologies and the police. In. *Modern policing,* ed. M. Tonry and N. Morris, 51–98. Chicago: University of Chicago Press.

March, J.G., and J.P. Olsen. 1984. The new institutionalism: Organizational factors in political life. *American Political Science Review* 78: 734–49.

Marsh, R.M. 1967. *Comparative sociology: A codification of cross-societal analysis.* New York: Harcourt, Brace & World.

Martin, T., and J. Hunt. 1980. Social influence and intent to leave: A path analytic process model. *Personnel Psychology* 33: 505–28.

Martinson, R. 1974. What works? Questions and answers about prison reform. *Public Interest* 35: 22–54.

Maschke, K. 1995. Prosecutors as crime creators: The case of prenatal drug use. *Criminal Justice Review* 20(1): 21–33.

Mastrofski, S.D. 1998. Community policing and police organization structure. In *How to recognize good policing: Problems and issues,* ed. J.P. Brodeur, 161–89. Washington, D.C.: Police Executive Research Forum; Thousand Oaks, CA: Sage.

_____. 2001. The romance of police leadership. In *Theoretical advances in criminology,* ed. E. Waring, D. Weisburd, and L.W. Sherman, 153–96. New Brunswick, NJ: Transaction.

_____. R.R. Ritti. 1996. Police training and the effects of organization on drunk driving enforcement. *Justice Quarterly* 13: 291–320.

_____. R.R. Ritti. 2000. Making sense of community policing: A theoretical perspective. *Police Practice and Research: An International Journal* 1(2): 183–210.

_____. R.R.Ritti, and D. Hoffmaster. 1987. Organizational determinants of police discretion: The case of drinking-driving. *Journal of Criminal Justice* 15: 387–402.

_____. C.D. Uchida. 1993. Transforming the police. *Journal of Research in Crime and Delinquency* 30(3): 330–58.

Mather, L. 1979. *Plea bargaining or trial? The process of criminal case disposition*. Lexington, MA: Lexington Books.

Mathieu, J., and D. Zajac. 1990. A review and meta-analysis of the antecedents, correlates, and consequences of organizational commitment. *Psychological Bulletin* 108: 171–94.

Mattessich, P., and B. Monsey. 1997. *Community building: What makes it work, a review of factors influencing successful community building*. Saint Paul, MN: Amherst H. Wilder Foundation, Fieldstone Alliance.

Mauer, M. 1997. *Americans behind bars: U.S. and international uses of incarceration, 1995*. Washington, D.C.: The Sentencing Project.

McCleary, R., B.C. Nienstedt, and J.M. Erven. 1982. Uniform crime reports as organizational outcomes: Three time series experiments. *Social Problems* 29(4): 361–72.

McCorkle, R., and J.P. Crank. 1996. Meet the new boss: Institutional change and loose coupling in parole and probation. *American Journal of Criminal Justice* 21: 1–25.

McCoy, C. 1984. Determinate sentencing, plea bargaining bans, and hydraulic discretion in California. *Justice System Journal* 9(3): 256–75.

McDonald, D.C. 1989. The cost of corrections: In search of the bottom line. *Research in Corrections* 2(1): 1–25.

_____. K.E. Carlson. 1993. *Sentencing in the federal courts: Does race matter?* Washington, D.C.: U.S. Department of Justice, Bureau of Justice Statistics.

McElroy, J., P. Morrow, and J. Fenton. 1995. Absenteeism and performance as predictors of voluntary turnover. *Journal of Managerial Issues* 12: 91–98.

McGarrell, E. F. 1993. Institutional theory and the stability of a conflict model of the incarceration rate. *Justice Quarterly*: 10: 7–28.

_____. 2001. Restorative justice conferences as an early response to young offenders. *Juvenile Justice Bulletin*. Washington, D.C.: U.S. Department of Justice, Office of Justice Programs, Office of Juvenile Justice and Delinquency Prevention (August), pp. 1–12.

_____. T.C. Castellano. 1991. An integrative conflict model of the criminal law formation process. *Journal of Research in Crime and Delinquency* 28: 174–96.

_____. D.E. Duffee. 1995. The adoption of pre-release centers in the states. *Criminal Justice Review* 20(1): 1–20.

342 • Criminal Justice Theory

_____. T. Flanagan. 1987. Attitudes of New York legislators toward crime and criminal justice: A report of the state legislator survey: 1991. Working Paper. Albany, NY: State University of New York at Albany, School of Criminal Justice.

McIntyre, L. 1987. *The public defender: The practice of law in the shadows of repute.* Chicago: University of Chicago Press.

McMichael, P. 1990. Incorporating comparison within a world-historical perspective: An alternative comparative method. *American Sociological Review* 55(3): 385–97.

McShane, M., F. Williams, D. Schichor, and K. McClain. 1991. Early exits: Examining employee turnover. *Corrections Today* 53: 220–25.

Menninger, K. 1969. *The crime of punishment.* New York: Viking.

Merry, S. 1985. Concepts of law and justice among working-class Americans: Ideology as culture. *Legal Studies Forum* 9(2): 59–69.

Meyer, F.A., Jr., and R. Baker, eds. 1979. *Determinants of law-enforcement policies.* Lexington, MA: Lexington Books.

Meyer, J., and N. Allen. 1984. Testing the side-bet theory of organizational commitment: Some methodological considerations. *Journal of Applied Psychology* 69: 372–78.

Meyer, J.W., and B. Rowan. 1977. Institutionalized organizations: Formal structure as myth and ceremony. *American Journal of Sociology* 83: 340–63.

_____. W.R. Scott, and T.E. Deal. 1983. Institutional and technical sources of organizational structure: Explaining the structure of educational organizations. In *Organizational environments: Ritual and rationality,* ed. J.W. Meyer and W.R. Scott, 45–67. Beverly Hills, CA: Sage.

Meyer, M.W. 1979. Organizational structure as signaling. *Pacific Sociological Review* 22: 481–500.

Miller, A., L.E. Ohlin, and R. Coates. 1977. *A theory of social reform.* Cambridge, MA: Ballinger.

Miller, J., P. Rossi, and J. Simpson. 1986. Perceptions of justice: Race and gender differences in judgments of appropriate prison sentences. *Law and Society Review* 20: 313.

Miller, W. 1973. Ideology and criminal justice policy: Some current issues. *Journal of Criminal Law and Criminology* 64: 142–54.

Monkkonen, E.H. 1981. *Police in urban America: 1860–1920.* Cambridge: Cambridge University Press.

Moore, M. 2002. The limits of social science in guiding policy. *Criminology and Public Policy* 2(1): 33–42.

Moore, R.H., and C.B. Fields. 1996. Comparative criminal justice: Why study? In *Comparative criminal justice: Traditional and nontraditional systems of law and control,* ed. C.B. Fields and R.H. Moore, 1–12. Prospect Heights, IL: Waveland Press.

Morgan, D.R., and C. Swanson. 1976. Analyzing police policies: The impact of environment, politics, and crime. *Urban Affairs Quarterly* 11(4): 489–510.

Morton, A.L. 1938. *A peoples' history of England*. London: Lawrence and Wishart.

Mowday, R., L. Porter, and R. Steers. 1982. *Employee–organization linkages: The psychology of commitment, absenteeism, and turnover*. New York: Academic Press.

_____. R. Steers, and L. Porter. 1979. The measurement of organizational commitment. *Journal of Vocational Behavior* 14: 224–47.

Mueller, C., E. Boyer, J. Price, and R. Iverson. 1994. Employee attachment and noncoercive conditions of work. *Work and Occupations* 21: 179–212.

Mueller, G.O.W., and F. Adler. 1996. Foreword. In *Comparative criminal justice: Traditional and nontraditional systems of law and control*, ed. C.B. Fields and R.H. Moore, vii–x. Prospect Heights, IL: Waveland Press.

Muir, W.K., Jr. 1977. *Police: Streetcorner politicians*. Chicago: University of Chicago Press.

Murphy, P.V., and T. Plate. 1977. *Commissioner: A view from the top of American law enforcement*. New York: Simon & Schuster.

_____. 1985. The prospective chief's negotiation of authority with the mayor. In *Police leadership in America: Crisis and opportunity*, ed. W.A. Geller, 30–40. Chicago: American Bar Foundation; New York: Praeger.

Musheno, M.C., D.J. Palumbo, S. Maynard-Moody, and J. Levine. 1989. Community corrections as an organizational innovation: What works and why. *Journal of Research in Crime and Delinquency* 26: 136–67.

Myers, M.A. 1988. Social background and sentencing behavior of judges. *Criminology* 26(4): 649–75.

_____. 1993. Inequality and the punishment of minor offenders in the early 20th century. *Law and Society Review* 27(2): 313–43.

_____. J. Hagan. 1979. Private and public trouble: Prosecutors and the allocation of court resources. *Social Problems* 26(4): 439–51.

_____. S. Reid. 1995. The importance of county context in the measurement of sentence disparity: The search for routinization. *Journal of Criminal Justice* 23(3): 223–41.

_____. S.M. Talarico. 1986. The social contexts of racial discrimination in sentencing. *Social Problems* 33(3): 236–51.

_____. S.M. Talarico. 1986. Urban justice, rural injustice? Urbanization and its effect on sentencing. *Criminology* 24: 367–91.

Nadelmann, E.A. 1993. *Cops across borders: The internationalization of U.S. criminal law enforcement*. University Park, PA: Pennsylvania State University Press.

Nagel, S. 1962. Ethnic affiliations and judicial propensities. *The Journal of Politics* 24: 92–110.

Naisbitt, J., and P. Aburdene. 1985. *Reinventing the corporation*. New York: Warner Books.

Nardulli, P.F. 1978. *The courtroom elite: An organizational perspective on criminal justice.* Cambridge, MA: Ballinger.

———. 1986. "Insider" justice: Defense attorneys and the handling of criminal cases. *Journal of Criminal Law and Criminology* 77(2): 379–417.

———. J. Eisenstein, and R.B. Flemming. 1988. *The tenor of justice: Criminal courts and the guilty plea process.* Urbana, IL: Univ of Illinois Press.

———. R. Flemming, and J. Eisenstein. 1984. Unraveling the complexities of decision making in face-to-face groups: A contextual analysis of plea bargained sentences. *American Political Science Review* 78: 912.

———. R. Flemming, and J. Eisenstein. 1985. Criminal courts and bureaucratic justice: Concessions and consensus in the guilty plea process. *Journal of Criminal Law and Criminology* 76(4): 1103–31.

National Advisory Commission on Criminal Justice Standards and Goals. 1973. *Corrections.* Washington, D.C.: U.S. Government Printing Office.

National Parole Conference, First. 1939. *Proceedings.* Washington, D.C.: U.S. Government Printing Office.

Nelson, E.K., R. Cushman, and N. Harlow. 1980. *The unification of community corrections.* Washington, D.C.: U.S. Government Printing Office.

New Jersey, the Governor's Management Improvement Plan. 1983. *Department of corrections: The correctional system, strategic issues and alternatives.* Trenton, New Jersey.

New Jersey v. Soto, 734 A.2d 350 (N.J. Super. 1996).

Newman, D. 1956. Pleading guilty for considerations: A study of bargain justice. *Journal of Criminal Law, Criminology, and Police Science* 46: 780.

———. 1978. *The punishment response.* New York: J.B. Lippincott.

———. ed. 1999. *Global report on crime and justice.* New York: Oxford University Press.

———. G.J. Howard. 1999. Data sources and their use. In *Global report on crime and justice*, ed. G. Newman, 1–23. New York: Oxford University Press.

Nobiling, T., C. Spohn, and M. DeLone. 1998. A tale of two counties: Unemployment and sentence severity. *Justice Quarterly* 15: 459–85.

Nohria, N. 1992. Introduction: Is a network perspective a useful way of studying organizations? In *Networks and organizations: Structure, form, and action*, ed. N. Nohria and R.G. Eccles, 1–22. Boston: Harvard Business School Press.

Nokes, P. 1960. Purpose and efficiency in humane social institutions. *Human Relations* 13: 141–55.

Nunnally, J. 1978. *Psychometric theory.* New York: McGraw-Hill.

Office of Community Oriented Policing Services. 2001. *Homepage.* http://www.cops.usdoj.gov/ (accessed January 21, 2001).

Ohlin, L.E., and F.J. Remington, eds. 1993. *Discretion in criminal justice: The tension between individualization and uniformity.* Albany, NY: State University of New York Press.

_____. 1993. Surveying discretion by criminal justice decision makers. In *Discretion in criminal justice*, ed. L.E. Ohlin and F.J. Remington, 1–22. Albany, NY: State University of New York Press.

O'Leary, V., and D. Duffee. 1971. Correctional policy: A classification of goals designed for change. *Crime and Delinquency* 17: 373–86.

Olson, S., and C. Batjer. 1999. Competing narratives in a judicial retention election: Feminism versus judicial independence. *Law and Society Review* 33(1): 123–60.

_____. D. Huth. 1998. Explaining public attitudes toward local courts. *Justice System Journal* 20(1): 41.

Ostrom, E. 1973. On the meaning and measurement of output and efficiency in the provision of urban police services. *Journal of Criminal Justice* 1: 93–112.

_____. R.B. Parks. 1973. Suburban police departments: Too many and too small? In *The organization of the suburbs*, ed. L.H. Masotti and J.K. Hadden, 7: 367–405. Urban Affairs Annual Reviews. Beverly Hills, CA: Sage.

_____. R.B. Parks, and G.P. Whitaker. 1978a. *Patterns of metropolitan policing*. Cambridge, MA: Ballinger.

_____. R.B. Parks, and G.P. Whitaker. 1978b. Police agency size: Some evidence on its effects. *Police Studies* 1(1): 34–46.

Packer, H. 1968. *The limits of the criminal sanction*. Palo Alto, CA: Stanford University of Press.

Parasuraman, S., and J. Alutto. 1984. Sources and outcomes of stress in organizational settings: Toward the development of a structural model. *Academy of Management Journal* 27: 330–50.

Parks, R.B. 1984. Linking objective and subjective measures of performance. *Public Administration Review* March/April: 118–27.

Patch, P.C. 1998. The three strikes law and control of crime in California. *ACJS Today* 17(3): 1, 3–4.

Paternoster, R. 1983. Race of victim and location of crime: The decision to seek the death penalty in South Carolina. *Journal of Criminal Law and Criminology* 74(3): 754–85.

Payne, G. 1973. Comparative sociology: Some problems of theory and method. *British Journal of Sociology* 24: 13–29.

Pelfrey, W.V. 1980. *The evolution of criminology*. Cincinnati: Anderson.

Perez, D.W. 1994. *Common sense about police review*. Philadelphia: Temple University Press.

Perrow, C. 1986. *Complex organizations: A critical essay*, 3rd ed. Glenview, IL: Scott, Foresman.

Pfeffer, J., and and G.R. Salancik. 1978. *The external control of organizations*. New York: Harper & Row.

Platt, A., and the Global Options Staff. 1982. *The iron fist and the velvet glove*. San Francisco: Synthesis Press.

Poole, E., and M. Pogrebin. 1991. Changing jail organization and management: Toward improved employee utilization. In *American jails: Public policy issues*, ed. J. Thompson and G. Mayo, 163–79. Chicago: Nelson-Hall.

President's Commission on Law Enforcement and Administration of Justice. 1967a. *Challenge of crime in a free society*. Washington, D.C.: U.S. Government Printing Office.

_____. 1967b. *Task force reports: The courts*. Washington, D.C.: U.S. Government Printing Office.

Price, J. 1977. *The study of turnover*. Ames: Iowa State University Press.

_____. C. Mueller. 1986. *Absenteeism and turnover among hospital employees*. Greenwich, CT: JAI Press.

Priehs, R. 1999. Appointed counsel for indigent appellants: Does compensation influence effort? *Justice System Journal* 21(1): 57–79.

Prison Fellowship. 2000. *Restorative justice briefing paper*. Washington, D.C.: The Prison Fellowship.

Pruitt, C., and J. Wilson. 1983. A longitudinal study of the effect of race on sentencing. *Law and Society Review* 17: 613.

Rafter, N.H. 1990. The social construction of crime and crime control. *Journal of Research in Crime and Delinquency* 27(4): 376–89.

Ragin, C.C. 1981. Comparative sociology and the comparative method. *International Journal of Comparative Sociology* 22: 102–20.

_____. 1987. *The comparative method: Moving beyond qualitative and quantitative strategies*. Berkeley: University of California Press.

Randall, D., D. Fedor, and C. Longnecker. 1990. The behavioral expression of organizational commitment. *Journal of Vocational Behavior* 36: 210–24.

Rawls, J. 1993. *Political liberalism*, 65–82. New York: Columbia University Press.

Reiman, J.H. 1984. *The rich get richer and the poor get prison: Ideology, class and criminal justice*, 2nd ed. New York: Macmillan.

Reiss, A.J., and D.J. Bordua. 1967. Environment and organization: A perspective on the police. In *The police: Six sociological essays*, ed. D. Bordua, 25–55. New York: John Wiley.

Renauer, B.C. 2000. Why get involved? Examining the motivational, identity, and ideological aspects of resident involvement in place-based organizations. PhD diss., State University of New York at Albany.

_____. D.E. Duffee, and J. Scott. 2003. Measuring police-community co-production: Tradeoffs in two observational approaches. *Policing: An International Journal of Police Strategies and Management* 26: 9–28.

_____. J. Scott. 2001. Exploring the dimensionality of community capacity. Paper presented at the annual meeting of the American Society of Criminology, Atlanta, GA.

Richardson, J.F. 1970. *The New York police: Colonial times to 1901*, New York: Oxford University Press.

Robinson, C.D., and R. Scaglion. 1987. The origin and evolution of the police function in society: Notes toward a theory. *Law and Society Review* 21(1): 109–52.

Robinson, D., F. Porporino, and L. Simourd. 1992. *Staff commitment in the Correctional Service of Canada.* NCJ Document Number: 148402. Ottawa, Canada: Canada Correctional Service.

Robinson, P., and J. Darley. 1995. *Justice, liability, and blame.* Boulder, CO: Westview Press.

Rose, D., and T. Clear. 1998. Incarceration, social capital, and crime: Implications for social disorganization theory. *Criminology* 36(3): 441–80.

Roseman, E. 1981. *Managing employee turnover: A positive approach.* New York: Amacom.

Rosenbaum, D.P. 1988. Community crime prevention: A review and synthesis of the literature. *Justice Quarterly* 5: 323–95.

Rosett, A., and D. Cressey. 1976. *Justice by consent.* New York: J.B. Lippincott.

Ross, E.A. 1914. *Social control: A survey of the foundations of order.* New York: Macmillan.

Ross, H., and J. Foley. 1987. Judicial disobedience of the mandate to imprison drunk drivers. *Law and Society Review* 21: 315.

———. R. Voas. 1990. The new Philadelphia story: The effects of severe punishment for drunk driving. *Law and Policy* 12(1): 51–77.

Roth, J.A., and C.C. Johnson. 1997. COPS context and community policing. Paper presented at the annual meeting of the American Society of Criminology, San Diego, CA, November.

Roundtree, P.W. 1998. A reexamination of the crime-fear linkage. *Journal of Research in Crime and Delinquency* 35: 341–73.

Rowland, C.K., R.A. Carp, and R.A. Stidham. 1984. Judges' policy choices and the value basis of judicial appointments: A comparison of support for criminal defendants among Nixon, Johnson, and Kennedy appointees to the federal district courts. *Journal of Politics*, 46: 886–902.

Rusche, G., and O. Kirchheimer. 1939. *Punishment and social structure.* New York: Columbia University Press.

Rutherford, A. 1985. *Prisons and the process of justice: The reductionist challenge.* London: Heinemann.

Ryan, J.A. 1980. Adjudication and sentencing in a misdemeanor court: The outcome is the punishment. *Law and Society Review* 15(1): 79–108.

Sager, J. 1994. A structural model depicting salespeople's job stress. *Journal of Academy of Marketing Science* 22: 74–84.

Satir, V. 1972. *People making.* Palo Alto, CA: Science & Behavior Books.

Saylor, W. 1983. Surveying prison environments. Unpublished manuscript. Washington, D.C.: Office of Research and Evaluation, Federal Bureau of Prisons.

Scheingold, S.A. 1984. *The politics of law and order: Street crime and public policy.* New York: Longman.

_____. 1991. *The politics of street crime: Criminal process and cultural obsession*. Philadelphia, PA: Temple University Press.

_____. L. Gressett. 1987. Policy, politics, and the criminal courts. *American Bar Foundation Research Journal* 1987: 461–505.

Schlesinger, T. 2005. Racial and ethnic disparity in pretrial criminal processing. *Justice Quarterly* 22(2): 170–92.

Schubert, G. 1961. A psychometric model of the supreme court. *American Behavioral Scientist* 5: 14–18.

Schulhofer, S. 1984. Is plea bargaining inevitable? *Harvard Law Review* 97(5): 1037–1107.

Schuman, H., and M.P. Johnson. 1976. Attitudes and behavior. *Annual Review of Sociology* 2: 161–207.

Schwartz, R., and J. Miller. 1965. Legal evolution and societal complexity. *American Journal of Sociology* 70: 159–69.

Scott, J. D. 2002. Assessing the relationship between police-community coproduction and neighborhood-level social capital. *Journal of Contemporary Criminal Justice* 18(2): 147–66.

_____. D.E. Duffee, and B.C. Renauer. 2003. Measuring police-community co-production: The utility of community policing case studies. *Police Quarterly.*

Scott, W.R. 1987. The adolescence of institutional theory. *Administrative Science Quarterly* 32: 493–511.

_____. 1992. *Organizations: Rational, natural, and open systems*, 3rd ed. Englewood Cliffs, NJ: Prentice-Hall.

_____. 1995. *Institutions and organizations*. Thousand Oaks, CA: Sage.

_____. J.W. Meyer. 1983. The organization of societal sectors. In *Organizational environments: Ritual and rationality*, ed. J. Meyer and W.R. Scott, 129–54. Beverly Hills, CA: Sage.

Selznick, P. 1957. *Leadership in administration*. New York: Harper & Row.

_____. 1966. *T.V.A. and the grassroots*. New York: Harper & Row.

Senna, J., and L. Siegel. 2002. *Introduction to criminal justice*, 9th ed. Belmont, CA: Wadsworth.

Shelden, R. 2001. *Controlling the dangerous classes*. Boston: Allyn & Bacon.

Sheldon, C., and N. Lovrich, Jr. 1982. Judicial accountability vs. responsibility: Balancing the views of voters and judges. *Judicature* 65: 470.

Shepard, M., and E. Pence. 1999. *Coordinating community responses to domestic violence*. Thousand Oaks, CA: Sage.

Sherman, L.W., and the National Advisory Commission on Higher Education for Police Officers. 1978. *The quality of police education*. San Francisco: Jossey-Bass.

Sherman, M., and G. Hawkins. 1981. *Imprisonment in America: Choosing the future*. Chicago: University of Chicago Press.

Simon, H.A. 1957. *Administrative behavior: A study of decision making processes in administrative organizations*. New York: Macmillan.

Simon, J. 1993. *Poor discipline: Parole and the social control of the underclass, 1890–1990*, Chicago: University of Chicago Press.

Skogan, W.G. 1990. *Disorder and decline: Crime and the spiral of decay in American neighborhoods.* Berkeley: University of California Press.

———. 1995. *Evaluating problem solving policing: The Chicago experience.* Project paper of the Chicago Community Policing Evaluation Consortium. Chicago: Illinois Criminal Justice Information Authority.

———. S. Hartnett. 1997. *Community policing Chicago style.* New York: Oxford University Press.

Skoler, D.L. 1976. Correctional unification: Rhetoric, reality and potential. *Federal Probation* 40: 14–20.

———. 1977. *Organizing the non-system.* Lexington, MA: DC Heath.

———. J.M. Hetler. 1970. Governmental restructuring and criminal administration: The challenge of consolidation. *The Georgetown Law Journal* 58: 719–40.

Skolnick, J. 1967. Social control in the adversary system. *Journal of Conflict Resolution* 11: 52–70.

Slovak, J.S. 1986. *Styles of urban policing: Organization, environment, and police styles in selected American cities.* New York: New York University Press.

Smith, B.L., and K.R. Damphousse. 1996. Punishing political offenders: The effect of political motive on federal sentencing decisions. *Criminology* 34: 289–322.

———. 1998. Terrorism, politics, and punishment: A test of structural-contextual theory and the "liberation hypothesis." *Criminology* 36: 67–92.

Smith, C.E. 1991. *Courts and the poor.* Chicago: Nelson-Hall.

Snipes, J.B., and S.D. Mastrofski. 1990. An empirical test of Muir's typology of police officers. *American Journal of Criminal Justice* 14(2): 268–96.

Songer, D.R., and K.A. Crews-Meyer. 2000. Does judge gender matter? Decision making in state supreme courts. *Social Science Quarterly* 81: 750–62.

Spader, D.J. 1988. Criminal justice and distributive justice: Has the wall of separation been reduced to rubble? *Justice Quarterly* 5: 589–614.

Spears, J.W. 1999. Diversity in the courtroom: A comparison of the sentencing decisions of black and white judges and male and female judges in Cook County Circuit Court. PhD. diss., University of Nebraska at Omaha.

Spector, P. 1992. *Summated rating scale construction.* Newbury Park, CA: Sage.

———. 1996. *Industrial and organizational psychology: Research and practice.* New York: John Wiley.

Spelman, W. 2001. The limited importance of prison expansion. In *The crime drop in America*, ed. A. Blumstein and J. Wallman, 97–129. New York: Cambridge University Press.

Spohn, C. 1990a. Decision making in sexual assault cases: Do black and female judges make a difference? *Women and Criminal Justice* 2: 83–105.

_____. 1990b. The sentencing decisions of black and white judges: Expected and unexpected similarities. *Law and Society Review* 24(5): 1197–1216.

_____. 1992. An analysis of the "jury trial penalty" and its effect on black and white offenders. *The Justice Professional* 7: 93–112.

_____. 2000. Thirty years of sentencing reform: The quest for a racially neutral sentencing process. In *Policies, processes, and decisions of the criminal justice system*, ed. Julie Horney, 427–501. Crime and Justice 2000, Vol. 4. Washington DC: National Institute of Justice.

_____. D. Beichner. 2000. Is preferential treatment of female offenders a thing of the past? A multi-site study of gender, race, and imprisonment. *Criminal Justice Policy Review* 11: 149–84.

_____. J. Cederblom. 1991. Race and disparities in sentencing: A test of the liberation hypothesis. *Justice Quarterly* 8(3): 305–27.

_____. M. DeLone. 2000. When does race matter? An analysis of the conditions under which race affects sentence severity. *Sociology of Crime, Law and Deviance.* 2: 3–37, ed. By Ulmer J.J. New York: Elsevier.

_____. D. Holleran. 2000. The imprisonment penalty paid by young, unemployed black and hispanic male offenders. *Criminology* 38: 281–306.

Steel, R., and N. Ovalle. 1984. A review and meta-analysis of research on the relationship between behavioral intentions and employee turnover. *Journal of Applied Psychology* 69: 673–86.

Steen, S., R.L. Engen, and R.R. Gainey. 2005. Images of danger and culpability: Racial stereotyping, case processing, and criminal sentencing. *Criminology* 43(2): 435–67.

Steffensmeir, D., and C.L. Britt. 2001. Judges' race and judicial decision making: Do black judges sentence differently? *Social Science Quarterly* 82 (4): 749–64.

_____. S. Demuth. 2000. Ethnicity and sentencing outcomes in U.S. federal courts: Who is punished more harshly? *American Sociological Review* 65: 705–29.

_____. S. Demuth. 2001. Ethnicity and judges' sentencing decisions: Hispanic-black-white comparisons. *Criminology* 39: 145–78.

_____. C. Herbert. 1999. Women and men policymakers: Does the judge's gender affect the sentencing of criminal defendants? *Social Forces* 77: 1163–96.

_____. J. Kramer, and C. Striefel. 1993. Gender and imprisonment decisions. *Criminology* 31: 411–46.

_____. J. Kramer, and J. Ulmer. 1995. Age differences in sentencing. *Justice Quarterly* 12: 583–601.

_____. J. Ulmer and J. Kramer. 1998. The interaction of race, gender, and age in criminal sentencing: The punishment cost of being young, black, and male. *Criminology* 36: 763–98.

Steiker, C.F. 1998. Forward: The limits of the preventive state. *Journal of Criminal Law and Criminology* 88: 771–810.

Stinchcombe, A.L. 1963. Institutions of privacy in the determination of police administrative practice. *American Journal of Sociology* 69: 150–60.

Stoecker, R. 1994. *Defending community: The struggle for alternative redevelopment in Cedar-Riverside.* Philadelphia: Temple University Press.

Stohr, M., R. Self, and N. Lovrich. 1992. Staff turnover in new generation jails: An investigation of its causes and preventions. *Journal of Criminal Justice* 20: 455–78.

Stover, R., and D. Eckart. 1975. A systematic comparison of public defenders and private attorneys. *American Journal of Criminal Law* 3: 265.

Sudnow, D. 1965. Normal crimes: Sociological features of the penal code in a public defender's office. *Social Problems* 12: 255–76.

Sullivan, R. 1994. The tragedy of academic criminal justice. *Journal of Criminal Justice* 22(6): 549–58.

Sundt, J.L. 1999. Is there room for change? A review of public attitudes toward crime control and alternatives to incarceration. *Southern Illinois University Law Journal* 23: 519–37.

Sung, H. 2001. *The fragmentation of policing in American cities: Toward an ecological theory of police-citizen relations.* Westport, CT: Praeger.

Sutherland, E.H. 1947. *Principles of criminology*, 4th ed. Philadelphia: J.B. Lippencott.

Swanson, C. 1978. The influence of organization and environment on arrest practices in major U.S. cities. *Policy Studies Journal* 7: 390–98.

Swanstrom, T. 1985. *The crisis of growth politics: Cleveland, Kucinich, and the challenge of urban populism.* Philadelphia: Temple University Press.

Szockyj, E. 1999. Imprisoning white collar criminals? *Southern Illinois University Law Journal* 23: 485–504.

Taggart, W.A., and R.G. Winn. 1991. Determinants of corrections expenditures in the American states: An exploratory analysis. *Criminal Justice Policy Review* 5: 157–82.

Talarico, S.M., and C.R. Swanson. 1979. Styles of policing: An exploration of compatibility and conflict. In *Determinants of law-enforcement policies*, ed. F.A. Meyer, Jr. and R. Baker, 35–44. Lexington, MA: Lexington Books.

Taub, R. P., D.G. Taylor, and J. Dunham. 1984. *Paths of neighborhood change: Race and crime in urban America.* Chicago: Chicago University Press.

Taxman, F., and L. Elis. 1999. Expediting court dispositions: Quick results, uncertain outcomes. *Journal of Research in Crime and Delinquency* 36(1): 30–55.

Terkel, S. 1974. *Working.* New York: Pantheon Books.

Thompson, J.D. 1967. *Organizations in action.* New York: McGraw-Hill.

Thornberry, T.P., and M.D. Krohn. 2000. The self-report method for measuring delinquency and crime. In *Measurement and analysis of crime and justice*, ed. D.E. Duffee, D. McDowall, Brian Ostrom, R.D. Crutchfield, S.D. Mastrofski, and L.G. Mazerolle. Criminal Justice 2000, 4: 33–84. Washington, D.C.: National Institute of Justice.

Tifft, L., and D. Sullivan. 1980. *The struggle to be human: Crime, criminology, and anarchism*. Orkney, UK: Cienfuegos Press.

Toch, H., and J.D. Grant. 1982. *Reforming human services: Change through participation*. Newbury Park, CA: Sage.

Tomasson, R.F. 1978. Introduction. *Comparative Studies in Sociology* 1: 1–15.

Tonry, M. 1990. Stated and latent functions of ISP. *Crime and Delinquency* 36: 174–91.

———. 1994. Racial politics, racial disparities, and the war on crime. *Crime and Delinquency* 40: 475–94.

Torres, S., and E. Deschenes. 1997. Changing the system and making it work: The process of implementing drug courts in Los Angeles County. *Justice System Journal* 19(3): 267–90.

Travis, J., and J.E. Brann. 1997. Introduction. In *Measuring what matters, Part Two: Developing measures of what the police do*. Research in Action. Washington, D.C.: U.S. Department of Justice, National Institute of Justice.

Tyler, T. 1988. What is procedural justice? Criteria used by citizens to assess the fairness of legal procedures. *Law and Society Review* 22(1): 103–35.

Tyler, T. R. 1997. Procedural fairness and compliance with the law. *Swiss Journal of Economics and Statistics* 133: 219–40.

———. Y.J. Huo. 2002. *Trust in the law: Encouraging public cooperation with the police and court*. New York: Russell Sage Foundation.

Uhlman, T.M. 1979. *Racial justice: Black judges and black defendants in an urban trial court*. Lexington, MA: Lexington Books.

———. N.D. Walker. 1980. He takes some of my time; I take some of his: An analysis of judicial sentencing patterns in jury cases. *Law and Society Review* 14: 323–39.

Ulmer, J.T. 1997. *Social worlds of sentencing: Court communities under sentencing guidelines*. Albany, NY: State University of New York Press.

———. 1998. The use and transformation of formal decision-making criteria: Sentencing guidelines, organizational contexts and case processing strategies. *Social Problems* 45: 248–67.

———. B. Johnson. 2004. Sentencing in context: A multilevel analysis. *Criminology* 42(1): 137–77.

———. J.H. Kramer. 1996. Court communities under sentencing guidelines: Dilemmas of formal rationality and sentencing disparity. *Criminology* 34(3): 383–408.

———. J.H. Kramer. 1998. The use and transformation of formal decision-making criteria: Sentencing guidelines, organizational contexts and case processing strategies. *Social Problems* 45: 248–67.

Umbreit, M.S., and W. Bradshaw. 1997. Victim experience of meeting adult vs. juvenile offenders: A cross-national comparison. *Federal Probation* 61: 33–39.

University of Maryland. 1997. *Preventing crime: What works, what doesn't, what's promising*. Washington, D.C.: U.S. Government Printing Office.

Vago, S. 1988. *Law and society*, 2nd ed. Englewood Cliffs, NJ: Prentice-Hall.

Vance, N., and R. Stupak. 1997. Organizational culture and the placement of pretrial agencies in the criminal justice system. *Justice System Journal* 19(1): 51–76.

Vetri, D. 1964. Guilty plea bargaining: Compromise by prosecutors to secure guilt pleas. *University of Pennsylvania Law Review* 112: 865.

Vogt, W.P. 1993. *Dictionary of statistics and methodology: A nontechnical guide for the social sciences.* Newbury Park, CA: Sage.

Vold, G.T., T. Bernard, and J. Snipes. 1998. *Theoretical criminology*, 4th ed. New York: Oxford University Press.

Wadman, R.C. 1998. Organizing for the prevention of crime. PhD diss., Idaho State University.

Waegel, W.B. 1981. Case routinization in investigative police work. *Social Problems* 28(3): 263–75.

Walker, S. 1977. *A critical history of police reform: The emergence of professionalization.* Lexington, MA: Lexington Books.

_____. 1985. *Sense and nonsense about crime: A policy guide.* Belmont, CA: Wadsworth.

_____. 1992. Origins of the contemporary criminal justice paradigm: The American Bar Foundation Survey, 1953–1969. *Justice Quarterly* 9(1): 47–76.

_____. 1993. *Taming the system.* New York: Oxford University Press.

_____. 1994. *Sense and nonsense about crime and drugs*, 3rd ed. Belmont, CA: Wadsworth.

_____. 2001. *Sense and nonsense about crime and drugs: A policy guide.* Belmont, CA: Wadsworth/Thomson Learning.

Wambaugh, J. 1981. *The glitter dome.* New York: Bantam Books.

Warren, R. 1967. The inter-organisational field as a focus for investigation. *Administrative Science Quarterly* 12: 396–419.

Warren, R.L. 1971. The sociology of knowledge and the problems of the inner cities. *Social Science Quarterly* 52: 469–91.

_____. 1978. *Community in America*, 3rd ed. Chicago: Rand McNally.

_____. S.M. Rose, and A.F. Bergunder. 1974. *The structure of urban reform.* Cambridge, MA: Lexington.

Washington, L. 1994. *Black judges on justice: Perspectives from the bench.* New York: The New Press.

Weick, K.E. 1969. *The social psychology of organizing.* Reading, MA: Addison-Wesley.

_____. 1976. Educational organizations as loosely coupled systems. *Administrative Science Quarterly* 21: 1–19.

Weidner, R. R., R. S. Frase, and J. Schultz. 2005. The impact of contextual factors on the decision to imprison in large urban jurisdictions. *Crime and Delinquency* 51(3): 400–24.

Weimer, D. 1980. Vertical prosecution and career criminal bureaus: How many and who? *Journal of Criminal Justice* 8: 369–78.

Weingart, S.N., F.X. Hartmann, and D. Osborne. 1994. *Case studies of community anti-drug efforts.* Washington, D.C.: National Institute of Justice.

Weiss, A. 1997. The communication of innovation in American policing. *Policing: An International Journal of Police Strategies and Management* 20(2): 292–310.

Welch, S., M. Combs, and J. Gruhl. 1988. Do black judges make a difference? *American Journal of Political Science* 32: 126–36.

Wheeler, S., K. Mann, and A. Sarat. 1988. *Sitting in judgment: The sentencing of white-collar criminals.* New Haven, CT: Yale University Press.

Whetten, D.A. 1989. What constitutes a theoretical contribution? *Academy of Management Review* 14(4): 490–95.

Whitaker, G.P. 1983. Police department size and the quality and cost of police services. In *The political science of criminal justice*, ed. S. Nagel, E. Fairchild, and A. Champagne, 185–96. Springfield, IL: Charles C. Thomas.

Wice, P. 1995. Court reform and judicial leadership: A theoretical discussion. *Justice System Journal* 17(3): 309.

Wilkins, L.T. 1965. *Social deviance.* Englewood Cliffs, NJ: Prentice-Hall.

———. 1981. *The principles of guidelines for sentencing.* Washington, D.C.: U.S. Department of Justice.

———. 1984. *Consumerist criminology.* Totowa, NJ: Barnes and Noble Books.

———. 1991. *Punishment, crime, and market forces.* Brookfield, VT: Dartmouth Press.

———. 2001. *Unofficial aspects of a life in policy research.* Cambridge, UK: The Family of Leslie T. Wilkins.

Willis, C.L. 1983. Criminal justice theory: A case of trained incapacity? *Journal of Criminal Justice* 11: 447–58.

Wilson, J.Q. 1963. The police and their problems: A theory. *Public Policy* 12: 189–216.

———. 1968a. *City politics and public policy.* New York: John Wiley.

———. 1968b. *Varieties of police behavior: The management of law and order in eight communities.* Cambridge, MA: Harvard University Press.

———. 1983. *Thinking about crime.* New York: Basic Books.

Wishman, S. 1986. *Anatomy of a jury.* New York: Times Books

Worden, A.P. 1987. The structure of local legal culture: Explorations of interorganizational models of courthouse norms. PhD diss., University of North Carolina at Chapel Hill.

———. 1990. Policymaking by prosecutors: The uses of discretion in regulating plea bargaining. *Judicature* 73(6): 335–40.

———. 1993. The attitudes of women and men in policing: Testing conventional and contemporary wisdom. *Criminology* 31: 203–41.

_____. 1995. The judge's role in plea bargaining: An analysis of judges' agreement with prosecutors' sentencing recommendations. *Justice Quarterly* 12(2): 257–78.

Worden, R. 1994. The "causes" of police brutality: Theory and evidence on police use of force, In *And justice for all: A national agenda for understanding and controlling police abuse of force*, ed. W.A. Geller and H. Toch, 33–60. Washington, D.C.: Police Executive Research Forum.

Wright, K. 1981. The desirability of goal conflict within the criminal justice system. *Journal of Criminal Justice* 9: 209–18.

_____. W. Saylor. 1991. Male and female employees' perceptions of prison work: Is there a difference? *Justice Quarterly* 8: 505–24.

_____. W. Saylor, E. Gilman, and S. Camp. 1997. Job control and occupational outcomes among prison workers. *Justice Quarterly* 14: 524–46.

Wright, T. 1991. The level of employee utilization and its effects on subsequent turnover. *Journal of Applied Business Research* 7: 25–29.

_____. 1993. Correctional employee turnover: A longitudinal study. *Journal of Criminal Justice* 21: 131–42.

Wycoff, M.A., and W.G. Skogan. 1994. Community policing in Madison: An analysis of implementation and impact. In *The challenge of community policing: Testing the promise*, ed. D.P. Rosenbaum, 75–91. Newbury Park, CA: Sage.

Yondorf, B., and K.M. Warnock. 1989. *State legislatures and corrections policies: An overview*. Denver, CO: National Conference of State Legislatures.

Zalman, M. 1982. Mandatory sentencing legislation: Myth and reality. In *Implementing criminal justice policies*, ed. M. Morash, 61–69. Beverly Hills, CA: Sage.

Zatz, M.S. 1987. The changing forms of racial/ethnic bias in sentencing. *Journal of Research in Crime and Delinquency* 24: 69–92.

Zhao, J. 1996. *Why police organizations change: A study of community oriented policing*. Washington, D.C.: U.S. Department of Justice, Police Executive Research Forum.

_____. N. Lovrich, and Q. Thurman. 1999. The status of community policing in American cities: Facilitators and impediments revisited. *Policing: An International Journal of Police Strategies & Management* 22(1): 74–92.

_____. Q.Thurman, and N. Lovrich. 1995. Community-oriented policing across the U.S.: Facilitators and impediments to implementation. *American Journal of Police* 14: 11–28.

Zvekic, U. 1996. The international crime (victim) survey: Issues of comparative advantages and disadvantages. *International Criminal Justice Review* 6: 1–21.

ABOUT THE CONTRIBUTORS

Edward L. Allan is an associate professor of criminal justice at Curry College in Milton, Massachusetts. After a career as a police officer, he received his PhD in criminal justice from the University at Albany.

Thomas Castellano is professor of criminal justice in the Department of Criminal Justice at Rochester Institute of Technology. He was previously an associate professor and director of the Center for the Study of Crime, Delinquency, and Corrections at Southern Illinois University, Carbondale. He received his PhD in Criminal Justice from the University at Albany in 1986. While he considers himself a criminal justice generalist, his primary research areas are correctional policy and program evaluation and the politics of law and order. He is currently working on studies relating to supermaximum security prisons, the job experiences of prison workers, and attitudes toward criminal justice education. Recent publications can be found in *Criminal Justice and Behavior*, the *Prison Journal*, and the *Southern Illinois Law Review*.

David E. Duffee is professor of criminal justice at the School of Criminal Justice, University at Albany. He is interested in community change, community building, criminal justice theory, and criminal justice agency performance. He was recently the principal investigator for the Police-Community Interaction Project (PCIP) in the National Institute of Justice Measuring What Matters Program. PCIP developed measures of the ways in which police and neighborhood groups interact in urban neighborhoods. In 2002, he began the Services Outcomes Action Research (SOAR) with two residential treatment institutions for youth. SOAR will assist the two institutions to improve their capacity for continual improvement in the delivery of services to juveniles and their families. He is editor of *Measurement and Analysis of Crime and Justice*, volume 4 in the National Institute of Justice series Criminal Justice 2000.

Joshua D. Freilich is an associate professor in the Sociology Department at the John Jay College of Criminal Justice. He is also a lead investigator for the National Consortium for the Study of Terrorism and Responses to Terrorism, a Center of Excellence of the U.S. Department of Homeland Security housed at the University of Maryland. He received his PhD in January 2001 from the School of Criminal Justice, University at Albany and his JD from Brooklyn Law School in 1993. He is also admitted to the New York and New Jersey State Bars. Currently his research interests include deviance and far-right wing political crime and terrorism, hate crime, and criminological theory.

Jon B. Gould is associate professor and acting director in the Administration of Justice Program at George Mason University. His research interests include judicial implementation, legal and constitutional development, comparative justice systems, court and justice administration, and legal mobilization. Before joining the ADJ program, Dr. Gould practiced law in a Washington, DC law firm, directed human rights programming, served on two presidential campaigns, and was the attorney for a liberal arts college. Dr. Gould's book, *Speak No Evil: The Triumph of Hate Speech Regulation*, was a co-winner of the 2006 Herbert Jacob award for the best book in law and society. In 2006–2007, he will be on leave as a U.S. Supreme Court Fellow.

Gregory J. Howard is associate professor of sociology at Western Michigan University where he teaches courses on comparative sociology and criminal justice. His current research centers on civil comparative methods, evolutionary theory and criminology, and surveillance and society. He received his PhD in criminal justice in 1998 from the University at Albany.

Paula M. Kautt is a lecturer of applied criminology at the University of Cambridge. She is currently engaged in a nationwide project funded by the Home Office to evaluate sentencing outcomes in England and Wales. She has a doctorate in criminal justice as well as extensive practitioner experience. Her research interests include criminal courts and sentencing, advanced quantitative methods, policing, hate crime statute implementation and enforcement in addition to a wide variety of correctional topics. Her research has been published by *Justice Quarterly, Criminal Justice Review, The Federal Sentencing Reporter* and the National Institute of Justice. She has also received research grants from the American Statistical Association and the National Institute of Justice.

Eric G. Lambert is an associate professor in the Department of Criminal Justice at the University of Toledo. He received his PhD from the School of Criminal Justice at the University at Albany. His research interests include criminal justice organizational issues, job and organizational effects on the attitudes, intentions, and behaviors of criminal justice employees, the evaluation of correctional interventions, death penalty attitudes, and the ethical behavior of criminal justice students and employees.

Edward R. Maguire is associate professor of Administration of Justice at George Mason University. He received his PhD in criminal justice from the University at Albany, and he has held previous academic and research positions at the University of Nebraska, the Office of Community Oriented Policing Services, and the United Nations. His primary professional interest is testing organizational theories in police agencies. He is currently leading a project intended to improve the capacity of the criminal justice system in Trinidad and Tobago to address a violent crime epidemic. His book, *Organizational Structure in Large Police Agencies: Context, Complexity, and Control*, was published by SUNY Press in 2003.

Edmund F. McGarrell is director and professor of the School of Criminal Justice at Michigan State University (MSU). McGarrell's research interests are in the area of communities and crime. He currently is the principal investigator of a project sponsored by the National Institute of Justice to conduct research and provide technical assistance related to Project Safe Neighborhoods, a major Department of Justice program intended to reduce firearms violence in the United States. His recent articles have appeared in *International Journal of Comparative and Applied Criminal Justice, Journal of Criminal Justice, Justice Quarterly,* and *Policing.*

Brian C. Renauer is an associate professor at Portland State University in the Division of Administration of Justice, Mark Hatfield School of Government. He received his PhD in 2000 from the University at Albany, School of Criminal Justice. Brian's research interests include community crime prevention and citizen involvement, community building, urban theories of crime, organizational theory, and criminal justice policy implementation.

Jeffrey B. Snipes is assistant professor of criminal justice at San Francisco State University. He received his PhD from the University at

Albany and his JD from Stanford University. His legal interests include nonprofit and public interest law, and his research interests include applied statistical models, policing, and criminological theory. He has coauthored *Theoretical Criminology* (Oxford University Press) and journal articles in *Social Forces, Criminology,* and *Law and Society Review.*

Cassia C. Spohn is a professor in the Arizona State University School of Criminology and Criminal Justice where she is also director of graduate programs. She is the author of *How Do Judges Decide? The Search for Fairness and Justice in Punishment.* She is the coauthor of two books: *The Color of Justice: Race, Ethnicity, and Crime in America* (with Sam Walker and Miriam DeLone) and *Rape Law Reform: A Grassroots Movement and Its Impact* (with Julie Horney). She has published a number of articles examining prosecutors' charging decisions in sexual assault cases and exploring the effect of race/ethnicity on charging and sentencing decisions. Her research interests include the effect of race and gender on court processing decisions, victim characteristics and case outcomes in sexual assault cases, judicial decision making, sentencing of drug offenders, and the deterrent effect of imprisonment. Her current research focuses on charging and sentencing in the U.S. District Courts.

Craig D. Uchida is the president of 21st Century Solutions, Inc., a consulting firm that specializes in issues related to crime and public policy. Dr. Uchida is the former assistant director for Grants Administration and senior policy adviser for the Office of Community Oriented Policing Services (COPS Office), U.S. Department of Justice. From 1990 to 1994, he served as the director for the Office of Criminal Justice Research and as the director of the Evaluation Division at the National Institute of Justice (NIJ), U.S. Department of Justice. Before joining the Department of Justice, Dr. Uchida was a member of the graduate faculty at the Institute of Criminal Justice and Criminology at the University of Maryland. Dr. Uchida received his PhD in criminal justice from the University at Albany and holds two masters' degrees, one in criminal justice and one in American history. Dr. Uchida is currently an adjunct professor at George Mason University. He also teaches police leadership seminars at the University of Massachusetts at Lowell and the Fairfax County, Virginia Police Department.

Alissa Pollitz Worden holds a PhD in political science from the University of North Carolina at Chapel Hill. Her primary research interests include informal processes of adjudication, court reform policy, and the role of community politics in court practices and policy. She has substantive expertise in domestic violence policy and has recently engaged in research, supported by the National Institute of Justice, on the effectiveness of community coordination efforts organized around this social problem. Most recently she has collaborated with Professor Bonnie E. Carlson on reviews of policies and interventions targeted at domestic violence and on a study of public attitudes and values about community responses to domestic violence. She is an associate professor in the School of Criminal Justice at the University at Albany.

AUTHOR INDEX

A

Abbott, D.J. 29
Aburdene, P. 234
Acar, W. 98
Adler, F. 51
Ajzen, I. 42, 228–229
Akers, R.L. 32, 48
Albanese, J.S. 77
Albonetti, C.A. 168–170, 216
Alexander, J.C. 44
Allan, E. 1–22, 23, 71, 72, 74, 293, 294, 297, 298, 357
Allen, N. 226
Alutto, J. 240
Alpert, G. 102
Alpert, L. 191
Alschuler, A. 188
Alwin, D.F. 279
Andrews, A.H. 137, 146
Andrews, D. 81
Arnstein, S.R. 296
Arthur, J.A. 29
Arvanites, T.M. 268
Ascolillo, V. 200
Asher, M.A. 268
Atkins, B. 191
Aupperle, K.E. 98
Austin, J. 80–81, 83
Austin, T. 188, 194

B

Baccaglini, W. 82
Bacharach, S.B. 31
Bagozzi, R. 229
Baker, R. 116

Baldus, D.C. 76
Bales, W.D. 171, 202
Balkin, S. 189
Ball, H. 164
Banks, C. 60
Barlow, D.E. 257, 260, 269, 283
Barlow, M.H. 257, 260, 269, 283
Bateman, T. 226
Batjer, C. 209
Baum, K. 122
Bayley, D.H. 60, 69, 94, 102, 116, 121, 123, 150
Bazemore, G. 194
Becker, H. 225, 248
Becker, T. 190
Beckett, K. 315
Beichner, D. 171
Bell, C.H., Jr. 5
Benne, K.D. 5
Bennett, S.F. 14, 124
Berger, P. 49
Bergman, W.T. 129–130, 146–147
Bergunder, A.F. 18, 134, 143, 261, 262
Berns, S. 161
Black, D. 9, 39, 45, 49, 281, 317
Blackburn, J. 237, 239
Blau, P.M. 30, 37, 95, 98
Blalock, H.M., Jr. 20
Blumberg, A.S. 28, 61, 183, 189
Blumstein, A. 80, 156, 169, 195–196
Bock, E.W. 164–165
Bohm, R. 195
Bohne, B. 190
Bollen, K. 233, 242, 249
Bonta, J. 81
Boostrom, R.L. 2, 68
Booth, D.E. 98

363

SUBJECT INDEX

A

abuse of authority, 29, 52, 113, 298
adaptation, 106
adjudication, 65, 181–216
adoption of innovation, *see* innovation
adversarial system/ adversariness, 61, 65, 67, 182, 187–189, 203, 204, 216
age, individual, 160–164, 167, 168, 170–172, 196, 230, 231, 236, 244–250, 306
age, organizational, 105, 107, 108
American Bar Foundation, 11, 12, 28, 281
American Civil Liberties Union, 113, 285
Amnesty International, 58
anthropology, 27, 30
arrest, 95, 96, 100, 117, 197, 283, 299, 305, 309, 310, 316
attitudes (as variables), 47, 161, 162, 166, 185–187, 190, 191, 196, 200, 205–207, 216–220, 223, 226, 241, 273, 281, 300, 301, 304–306, 309, 310

B

bail, 169, 204
behaviors (as variables), 47, 214, 223, 226, 230, 305–310, 315
beliefs (as variables), 166, 186, 190, 191, 196, 197, 206, 212, 226, 300, 309
biological metaphors, 54, 55, 95
Black, Donald, 39, 45, 281, 317

blame, 6, 8, 17–18, 24, 72, 166, 169–172, 269, 299
blameworthiness, *see* blame
boundary spanning, 48–49
bounded rationality /uncertainty avoidance, 167–172
budgets, *see* funding for agencies
Bureau of Justice Statistics, 113
bureaucracy, bureaucratization, 61–64, 194, 220, 264, 266, 267, 301, 304, 316

C

capital punishment, 26, 76, 156, 197, 210, 285, 298, 314
case characteristics, 163, 165–169, 172, 175, 176, 178
case law, 183
case study research, 14, 204, 209, 214, 215, 283
caseloads, 60–64, 176, 178, 187–189, 192, 200, 204, 207, 311, 312
causal attribution theory, 167, 168, 172
causal modeling, 114, 189, 231–234, 241–251
cause and effect, 67, 114, 184, 198, 218, 241, 242, 293, 308, 309, 316
centralization, 63, 105, 140, 176, 181, 232, 237, 252, 263, 264, 267, 284
chain gangs, 202
charging decisions/practices, 204, 305, 309
citizen satisfaction, 15, 304
city managers, 101, 130, 137, 146
civil law, 67
clearances/clearance rates, 102